Travel Guide®

SOUTHERN CALIFORNIA & HAWAII

ACKNOWLEDGEMENTS

We gratefully acknowledge the help of our representatives for their efficient and perceptive inspections of the lodging and dining establishments listed, the establishments' proprietors for their cooperation in showing their facilities and providing information about them, and the many users of previous editions who have taken the time to share their experiences. Mobil Travel Guide is also grateful to all the talented writers who contributed entries to this book.

Front cover photos:

ISBN: 0-8416-0318-9 or 978-0-8416-0318-9
Manufactured in the Canada.

10 9 8 7 6 5 4 3 2 1

CONTENTS

MAPS

SOUTHERN CALIFORNIA AND HAWAII

CELEBRATING 50 YEARS

Because time is precious and the travel industry is ever-changing, having accurate, reliable travel information at your has fingertips is essential. Mobil Travel Guide provided invaluable insight to travelers for 50 years, and we are committed to continuing this service into the future.

The Mobil Corporation (known as Exxon Mobil Corporation since a 1999 merger) began producing the Mobil Travel Guide books in 1958 following the introduction of the U.S.-interstate highway system in 1956. The first edition covered only five Southwestern states. Since then, our books have become the premier travel guides in North America, covering all 50 states and Canada.

Since its founding, Mobil Travel Guide has served as an advocate for travelers seeking knowledge about hotels, restaurants and places to visit. Based on an objective process, we make recommendations to our customers that we believe will enhance the quality and value of their travel experiences. Our trusted Mobil One- to Five-Star rating system is the oldest and most respected lodging and restaurant inspection and rating program in North America. Most hoteliers, restaurateurs and industry observers favorably regard the rigor of our inspection program and understand the prestige and benefits that come with receiving a Mobil Star rating.

The Mobil Travel Guide process of rating each establishment includes:
- ★ Unannouced facility inspections
- ★ Incognito service evaluations for
- ★ A review of unsolicited comments from the general public
- ★ Senior management oversight

For each property, more than 450 attributes, including cleanliness, physical facilities and employee attitude and courtesy, are measured and evaluated to produce a mathematically derived score, which is then blended with the other elements to form an overall score. These scores form the basis that we use to assign our Mobil One- to Five-Star ratings.

This process focuses on guest expectations, guest experience and consistency of service, not just physical facilities and amenities. It's fundamentally a rating system that rewards those properties that continually strive for and achieve excellence each year. The very best properties are consistently raising the bar for those that wish to compete with them.

Only facilities that meet Mobil Travel Guide's standards earn the privilege of being listed in the guide. Deteriorating, poorly managed establishments are deleted. A Mobil Travel Guide listing constitutes a positive quality recommendation. Every listing is an accolade, a recognition of achievement.

★★★★★The Mobil Five-Star Award indicates that a property is one of the very best in the country and consistently provides gracious and courteous service, superlative quality in its facility and a unique ambience. The lodgings and restaurants at the Mobil Five-Star level consistently continues their commitment to excellence, doing so with grace and perseverance.

★★★★The Mobil Four-Star Award honors properties for outstanding achievement in overall facility and for providing very strong service levels in all areas. These award winners provide a distinctive experience for the ever-demanding and sophisticated consumer.

★★★The Mobil Three-Star Award recognizes an excellent property that provides full services and amenities. This category ranges from exceptional hotels with limited services to elegant restaurants with a less-formal atmosphere.

★★The Mobil Two-Star property is a clean and comfortable establishment that has expanded amenities or a distinctive environment. These properties are an excellent place to stay or dine.

★The Mobil One-Star property is limited in its amenities and services but provides a value experience while meeting travelers' expectations. Expect the properties to be clean, comfortable and convenient.

We do not charge establishments for inclusion in our guides. We have no relationship with any of the businesses and attractions we list and act only as a consumer advocate. We do the investigative legwork so that you won't have to.

Restaurants and hotels—particularly small chains and stand-alone establishments—change management or even go out of business with surprising quickness. Although we make every effort to update continuously information, we recommend that you call ahead to make sure the place you've selected is still open.

We hope that your travels are enjoyable and relaxing and that our books help you get the most out of every trip you take. If any aspect of your accommodation, dining, spa or sightseeing experience motivates you to comment, please contact us. Mobil Travel Guide, 200 W. Madison St., Suite 3950, Chicago, IL 60611, or send an e-mail to info@mobiltravelguide.com.
Happy travels.

HOW TO USE THIS BOOK

The Mobil Travel Guide Regional Travel Planners are designed for convenience. Each state has its own chapter, beginning with a general introduction that provides a geographical and historical orientation to the state and gives basic statewide tourist information. The remainder of each chapter is devoted to travel destinations within the state—mainly cities and towns, but also national parks and tourist areas—which, like the states, are arranged in alphabetical order.

MAPS

We have provided state maps as well as maps of selected larger cities to help you find your way.

DESTINATION INFORMATION

We list addresses, phone number and web sites for travel information resources—usually the local chamber of commerce or office of tourism—and a brief introduction to the area. Information about airports, ground transportation and suburbs is included for large cities.

DRIVING TOURS AND WALKING TOURS

The driving tours that we include for many states are usually day trips that make for interesting side excursions. They offer you a way to get off the beaten path. These trips frequently cover areas of natural beauty or historical significance.

WHAT TO SEE AND DO

Mobil Travel Guide offers information about thousands of museums, art galleries, amusement parks, historic sites, national and state parks, ski areas and many other attractions.

Following an attraction's description, you'll find the months, days and, in some cases, hours of operation, address, telephone number and web site (if there is one).

SPECIAL EVENTS

Special events are either annual events that last only a short time, such as festivals and fairs or longer, seasonal events such as horse racing, theater and summer concerts. Our Special Events listings also include infrequently occurring occasions that mark certain dates or events, such as a centennial or other commemorative celebration.

LISTINGS

Hotels, restaurants and spas are usually listed under the city or town in which they're located. Make sure to check the nearby cities and towns for additional options, especially if you're traveling to a major metropolitan area that includes many suburbs. If a property is located in a town that doesn't have its own heading, the listing appears under the town nearest it. In large cities, hotels located within 5 miles of major commercial airports may be listed under a separate Airport Area heading that follows the city section.

THE STAR RATINGS
MOBIL RATED HOTELS

Travelers have different needs when it comes to accommodations. To help you pinpoint properties that meet your particular needs, Mobil Travel Guide classifies each lodging by type according to the following characteristics.

★★★★★The Mobil Five-Star hotel provides consistently superlative service in an exceptionally distinctive luxury environment, with expanded services. Attention to detail is evident throughout the hotel, resort or inn, from bed linens to staff uniforms.

★★★★The Mobil Four-Star hotel provides a luxury experience with expanded amenities in a distinctive environment. Services may include automatic turndown service, 24-hour room service and valet parking.

★★★The Mobil Three-Star hotel is well appointed, with a full-service restaurant and expanded amenities, such as a fitness center, golf course, tennis courts, 24-hour room service and optional turndown service.

★★The Mobil Two-Star hotel is considered a clean, comfortable and reliable establishment that has expanded amenities, such as a full-service restaurant on the premises.

★The Mobil One-Star lodging is a limited-service hotel, motel or inn that is considered a clean, comfortable and reliable establishment For every property, we also provide pricing information. The pricing categories break down as follows:

★   **$** = Up to $150
★   **$$** = $151-$250
★   **$$$** = $251-$350
★   **$$$$** = $351 and up

All prices quoted are accurate at the time of publication, however prices cannot be guaranteed. In some locations, special events, holidays or seasons can affect prices. Some resorts have complicated rate structures that vary with the time of year, so confirm rates when making your plans.

SPECIALITY LODGINGS

A Speciality Lodging is a unique inn, bed and breakfast or guest ranch with limited service, but appealing, attractive facilities that make the property worth a visit.

MOBIL RATED RESTAURANTS

All Mobil Star-rated dining establishments listed in this book have a full kitchen and most offer table service.

★★★★★The Mobil Five-Star restaurant offers one of few flawless dining experiences in the country. These establishments consistently provide their guests with exceptional food, superlative service, elegant décor and exquisite presentations of each detail surrounding a meal.

★★★★The Mobil Four-Star restaurant provides professional service, distinctive presentations and wonderful food.

★★★The Mobil Three-Star restaurant has good food, warm and skillful service and enjoyable décor.

★★The Mobil Two-Star restaurant serves fresh food in a clean setting with efficient service. Value is considered in this category, as is family friendliness.

★The Mobil One-Star restaurant provides a distinctive experience through culinary specialty, local flair or individual atmosphere.

Each restaurant listing gives the cuisine type, street address, phone and website, meals served, days of operation (if not open daily year-round) and pricing category. Information about appropriate attire is provided, although it's always a good idea to call ahead and ask if you're unsure; the meaning of "casual" or "business casual" varies widely in different parts of the country. We also indicate whether the restaurant has a bar, whether a children's menu is offered and whether outdoor seating is available. If reservations are recommended, we note that fact in the listing. When valet parking is available, it is noted in the description. Because menu prices can fluctuate, we list a pricing category rather than specific prices. The pricing categories are defined as follows, per diner, and assume that you order an appetizer or dessert, an entrée and one drink:

★ **$** = $15 and under
★ **$$** = $16-$35
★ **$$$** = $36-$85
★ **$$$$** = $86 and up

All prices quoted are accurate at the time of publication, but prices cannot be guaranteed.

MOBIL RATED SPAS

Mobil Travel Guide is pleased to announce its newest category, hotel and resort spas. Until now, hotel and resort spas have not been formally rated or inspected by any organization. Every spa selected for inclusion in this book underwent a rigorous inspection process similar to the one Mobil Travel Guide has been applying to lodgings and restaurants for five decades. After researching more than 300 spas and performing exhaustive incognito inspections of more than 200 properties, we narrowed our list to the best spas in the United States and Canada.

Mobil Travel Guide's spa ratings are based on objective evaluations of more than 450 attributes. Approximately half of these criteria assess basic expectations, such as staff courtesy, the technical proficiency and skill of the employees and whether the facility is maintained properly and hygienically. Several standards address issues that impact a guest's physical comfort and convenience, as well as the staff's ability to impart a sense of personalized service and anticipate clients' needs. Additional criteria measure the spa's ability to create a completely calming ambience.

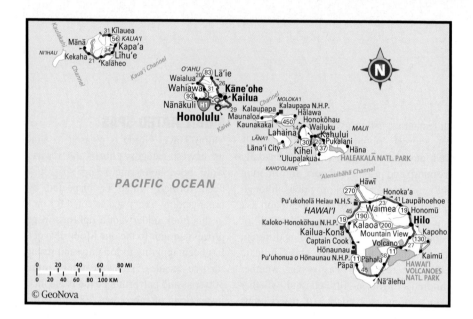

KAUA'I

31 Kīlauea
(56)
Mānā
Kekaha 24 Kapa'a
21 Līhu'e
Kalāheo

NI'IHAU

Kaulakahi Channel

Kaua'i Channel

O'AHU
Waialua 20 (83) Lā'ie
(26)
Wahiawa 31 **Kāne'ohe**
(93) **Kailua**
Nānākuli (H1)
Honolulu 29 Kalaupapa
Maunaloa
Kaunakakai 29

Kaiwi Channel

MOLOKA'I
Kalaupapa N.H.P.
Hālawa
Honokōhau
(450) Wailuku
14 **Kahului**
Lahaina (30) (20) Pukalani
LĀNA'I (37)
Lāna'i City **Kihei**
'Ulupalakua Hāna
MAUI
HALEAKALĀ NATL. PARK
KAHO'OLAWE

'Alenuihāhā Channel

PACIFIC OCEAN

Hāwī
(270)
Honoka'a
Pu'ukoholā Heiau N.H.S. (23) 41 Laupāhoehoe
HAWAI'I (19) Honomū
Kaloko-Honokōhau N.H.P. (19) 45 Waimea
45 (190)
Kalaoa (200) **Hilo**
Kailua-Kona
Captain Cook Mountain View
Hōnaunau Volcano Kapoho
Pu'uhonua o Hōnaunau N.H.P. (11) Pāhala (130)
Pāpa 38 (11) 27 Kaimū
45
Nā'ālehu HAWAI'I VOLCANOES NATL. PARK

0 20 40 60 80 MI
0 20 40 60 80 100 KM

© GeoNova

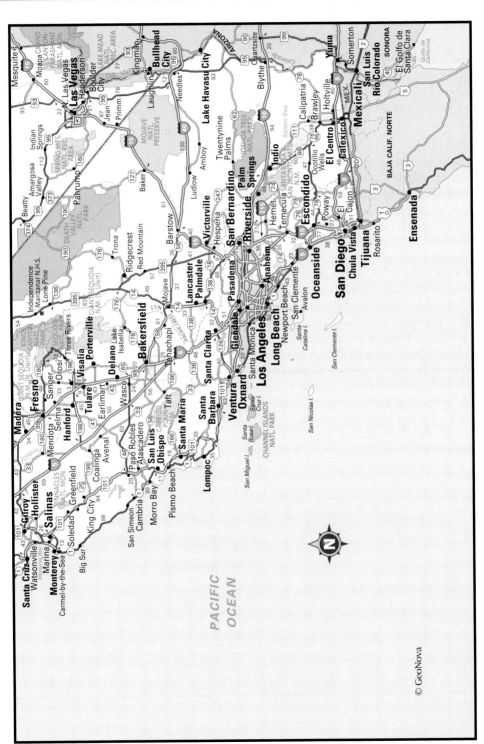

The Mobil Star ratings focus on much more than the facilities available at a spa and the treatments it offers. Each Mobil Star rating is a cumulative score achieved from multiple inspections that reflects the spa management's attention to detail and commitment to consumers' needs.

★★★★★The Mobil Five-Star spa provides consistently superlative service in an exceptionally distinctive luxury environment with extensive amenities. The staff at a Mobil Five-Star spa provides extraordinary service beyond the traditional spa experience, allowing guests to achieve the highest level of relaxation and pampering. A Mobil Five-Star spa offers an extensive array of treatments, often incorporating international themes and products. Attention to detail is evident throughout the spa, from arrival to departure.

★★★★The Mobil Four-Star spa provides a luxurious experience with expanded amenities in an elegant and serene environment. Throughout the spa facility, guests experience personalized service. Amenities might include, but are not limited to, single-sex relaxation rooms where guests wait for their treatments, plunge pools and whirlpools in both men's and women's locker rooms, and an array of treatments, including a selection of massages, body therapies, facials and a variety of salon services.

★★★The Mobil Three-Star spa is physically well appointed and has a full complement of staff.

★ CELEBRATING ★
50 YEARS OF MOBIL TRAVEL GUIDE

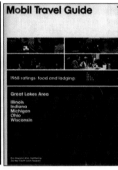

1962 ——— **1964** ——— **1968** ——— **1971** →

← **1973** ——— **1976** ——— **1978** ——— **1979** →

← 1986 ─────── 1988 ─────── 1989 ─────── 1992 →

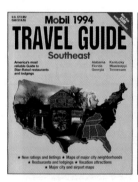

← 1994 ─────── 1997 ─────── 1998 ─────── 2003 →

SOUTHERN CALIFORNIA

THE BEACHES, THE MOVIE STARS, THE ENDLESS SUNNY DAYS. THAT'S LIFE IN SOUTHERN California and it's simply fabulous.

From dining and shopping in Los Angeles to the numerous attractions in San Diego to the lively beach communities, Southern California—or SoCal—is teeming with diversions. Hit the surf, explore the many wilderness areas or get away from it all in the deserts.

Few places offer such a breadth of cultural and natural landscapes. The Pacific Ocean forms the western border, while the arid east is home to the Mojave and Colorado Deserts. The southern border separates California from Mexico, while the Tecahapi Mountains, a range rising about 70 miles north of Los Angeles, separates SoCal from the rest of the nation's most populous state.

Many of the area's towns blossomed around Spanish missions built in the late 18th century after Spain seized colonial rule of the area from its original Portuguese explorers. California changed hands twice more—flying the Mexican flag starting in 1821, after Mexico won independence from Spain. A short-lived California republic followed before Commodore John D. Sloat raised the United States flag over Monterey in July 1846. Two years later, California officially became part of the U.S. That year, 1848, marked another enormous event in California history: the discovery of gold.

The California Gold Rush set off a mass migration that transformed the sleepy, placid countryside into bustling towns. The 49ers who came for gold ultimately found greater riches in the fertile soil of the valleys. Today, almost every crop in the United States is grown in Southern California, including prunes, oranges, avocados, walnuts, grapes, olives and much more. In fact, California leads the nation in the production of 75 crop and livestock commodities. Southern California also produces electronics, aircraft, missiles and of course, movies.

Today, California has the largest population of any state in the Union—24 million people live in Southern California (making it the second most populated region in the country behind the northeast corridor). Spend some time here and you'll see why.
Information: www.gocalif.ca.gov

 SPOTLIGHT

★ More than 300,000 tons of grapes are grown in California annually.

★ More turkeys are raised in California than in any other state in the U.S.

★ The first motion picture theater opened in Los Angeles on April 2, 1902.

BAKERSFIELD

An important trading center surrounded by oil wells and fields of cotton and grain, the Bakersfield founded by Colonel Thomas Baker in 1885 exploded into a wild mining community when gold was discovered in Kern River Canyon. A 1889 fire destroyed most of the old town and resulted in considerable modernization. A decade later, oil was discovered in the area and remains an important part of the city's economy. Nearby vineyards produce 25 percent of California's wine, and surrounding fields provide a colorful flower display in spring.
Information: Greater Bakersfield Chamber of Commerce, 1725 Eye St., 93301, 661-327-4421; www.bakersfieldchamber.org

WHAT TO SEE AND DO
California Living Museum
10500 Alfred Harrell Hwy., Bakersfield, 661-872-2256; www.calmzoo.org
Botanical garden and zoo with plants and animals native to California. Daily 9 a.m.-5 p.m.

Kern County Museum
3801 Chester Ave., Bakersfield, 661-852-5000; www.kcmuseum.org
Outdoor museum on 16 acres with 56 historic exhibits, including an award-winning hands-on oil exhibition. Monday-Saturday 10 a.m.-5 p.m., Sunday noon-5 p.m.

SPECIAL EVENTS
Great Kern County Fair
1142 South P St., Bakersfield, 661-833-4900; www.kerncountyfair.com
This annual fair provides a stage for national country music acts such as Gretchen Wilson and Gary Allan, as well as performance space for local talents like cheering competitions. Late September-early October.

HOTELS
★★Best Western Hill House
700 Truxtun Ave., Bakersfield, 661-327-4064; www.bestwestern.com
97 rooms. Complimentary continental breakfast. Restaurant, bar. $

★★Four Points by Sheraton
5101 California Ave., Bakersfield, 661-325-9700, 800-500-5399; www.fourpoints.com/bakersfield
198 rooms. Complimentary continental breakfast. Restaurant, bar. Airport transportation available. Pool. $

★Holiday Inn Express
4400 Hughes Lane, Bakersfield, 661-833-3000, 800-465-4329; www.hiexpress.com
108 rooms. Complimentary continental breakfast. Pool. Busn. center. $

★Quality Inn
1011 Oak St., Bakersfield, 661-325-0772, 800-228-5050; www.qualityinn.com
89 rooms, Complimentary full breakfast. Pets allowed, fee. Pool. $

SPECIALTY LODGING
Rankin Ranch
23500 Walkers Basin Rd., Caliente, 661-867-2511; www.rankinranch.com
21 rooms. Closed the first week in September through the week before Easter. Restaurant. Children's activity center. Swim. Tennis court. $$

RESTAURANTS
★★Mama Tosca's
9000 Ming Ave., Bakersfield, 661-831-1242
Italian menu. Lunch, dinner. Closed Sunday. Bar. Children's menu. Casual attire. Reservations recommended. Outdoor seating. $$$

★Rosa's
2400 Columbus, Bakersfield, 661-872-1606
Italian menu. Lunch, dinner. Closed holidays. Children's menu. Casual attire. Outdoor seating. $$

SOUTHERN CALIFORNIA

★★Wool Growers
620 E. 19th St.,
Bakersfield,
661-327-9584

French menu. Lunch, dinner. Closed Sunday. Bar. Children's menu. Casual attire. **$$**

BARSTOW

This former frontier town is set in the beautiful high-desert country and has become one of the fastest growing cities in San Bernardino County. Once a desert junction for overland wagon trains and an outfitting station for Death Valley expeditions, Barstow thrives on a $15 million tourist trade. It is the hub of three major highways that carry tourists into the Mojave Desert.

Information: Barstow Area Chamber of Commerce, 681 N. First Ave., Barstow, 760-256-8617; www.barstowchamber.com

WHAT TO SEE AND DO

Calico Early Man Site
18 miles east via I-15,
Minneola Rd. exit, then 2 3/4 miles on graded dirt road

You'll find the oldest evidence of human activity in the Western Hemisphere at these archaeological dig sites. Stone tool artifacts fashioned by man approximately 200,000 years ago are still visible in the walls of the excavations. Small museum. Guided tours. Wednesday 12:30-4:30 p.m., Thursday-Sunday 9 a.m.-4:30 p.m.

Calico Ghost Town Regional Park
36600 Ghost Town Rd.,
Barstow,
760-254-2122;
www.calicotown.com

Restored 1880s mining town with general store, old schoolhouse, railroad and mine tours. Nearby are the Calico Mountains, which yielded $86 million in silver over 15 years. Camping. Daily. East of Calico is Odessa Canyon, a rock-studded landscape created by volcanic action. Erosion has etched striking rock formations. No cars.

Factory Merchants Outlet Mall
2552 Mercantile Way,
Barstow,
760-253-7342;
www.factorymerchantsbarstow.com

More than 90 outlet stores. Daily 10 a.m.-8 p.m.

Mojave River Valley Museum
270 E. Virginia Way, Barstow,
760-256-5452; www.mvm.4t.com

Rock and mineral displays, photographs, archaeology, railroad displays and Native American exhibits. Daily 11 a.m.-4 p.m.

Mule Canyon and Fiery Gulch
Barstow

Cathedral-like rocks, S-shaped formations, crimson walls, natural arches. No cars.

SPECIAL EVENTS

Calico Days
Calico Ghost Town, 36600 Ghost Town Rd., Barstow, 760-254-2122;
www.calicotown.com/calicodays

Country music, Wild West parade, national gunfight stunt championship, burro race, 1880s games. Columbus Day weekend.

Calico Bluegrass in the Spring Festival
Calico Ghost Town, 36600 Ghost Town Rd., Barstow, 760-254-2122;
www.calicotown.com/springfestival

Fiddle and banjo contests, bluegrass music, stunt gunfights, 1880s games, clogging hoedown. Mother's Day weekend.

HOTELS

★★Best Western Desert Villa Inn
1984 E. Main St., Barstow, 760-256-1781;
www.bestwestern.com

95 rooms. Complimentary continental breakfast. Bar. Pool. **$**

3

★
★
★
★
★

BIG BEAR LAKE

This is a growing year-round recreation area in the San Bernardino National Forest. Fishing, canoeing, parasailing, windsurfing, riding, golfing, bicycling, picnicking, hiking and camping are available in summer; skiing and other winter sports are popular in season.
Information: Big Bear Lake Resort Association, 630 Bartlett Rd., Big Bear Lake, 909-866-5671, 800-244-2327; www.bigbearinfo.com

WHAT TO SEE AND DO

Big Bear Queen Tour Boat
Big Bear Marina, 500 Paine Rd.,
Big Bear Lake, 909-866-3218;
www.bigbearmarina.com/queen.html
Board a paddle wheeler for a 90-minute narrated tour of Big Bear Lake. Dinner and Champagne cruises also available. April-October, daily at noon, 2 p.m., and 4 p.m.

Alpine Slide at Magic Mountain
800 Wildnose Lane, Big Bear Lake,
909-866-4626; www.alpineslidebigbear.com
Includes Alpine bobsled ride, water slide and inner tubing. Miniature golf. Daily.

Big Bear Mountain Resorts
880 Summit Blvd., Big Bear Lake,
909-866-5766; www.bearmountain.com
Skiing, golf course and driving range, resort.

Big Bear Mountain Ski Resort
880 Summit Blvd., Big Bear Lake,
909-585-2519, 800-232-7686;
www.bigbearmountainresorts.com
Longest run 2 1/2 miles, vertical drop 1,665 feet. Mid-November-April, Monday-Friday 8:30 a.m.-4 p.m., Saturday-Sunday from 8:30 a.m. Hiking, nine-hole golf course. May-mid-October, daily.

Snow Summit Mountain Resort
880 Summit Blvd., Big Bear Lake,
909-866-5766;
www.snowsummit.com
Longest run 1 1/4 miles; vertical drop 1,200 feet. Mid-November-April, daily. Night skiing, snowboarding. Chairlift also operates in summer May-early September.

SPECIAL EVENTS

Old Miners' Days
Big Bear Lake, 909-866-4607;
www.oldminers.org
Festival celebrating 19th-century frontier heritage with cowboy music, parades, quick-draw contest, children's activities. Three weekends in July.

HOTELS

★★Best Western Big Bear Chateau
42200 Moonridge Rd.,
Big Bear Lake,
909-866-6666, 800-232-7466;
www.bestwestern.com
80 rooms. Restaurant, bar. Pet. Swim. $

★Robin Hood Resort
40797 Lakeview Dr., Big Bear Lake,
909-866-4643, 800-990-9956;
www.robinhoodinn.com
54 rooms. $

★★★Northwoods Resort and Conference Center
40650 Village Dr., Big Bear Lake,
909-866-3121, 800-866-3121;
www.northwoodsresort.com
This rustic mountain resort and conference center offers rooms and suites filled with handcrafted wood furniture. Many rooms feature fireplaces and suites have spa-tubs and wet bars.
147 rooms. Restaurant, bar. Exercise. Swim. $

SPECIALTY LODGINGS

Eagles Nest Bed and Breakfast
41675 Big Bear Blvd.,
Big Bear Lake,
909-866-6465, 888-866-6465;
www.eaglesnestlodgebigbear.com
High in the Bernardino Mountains in Bear Valley, this bed and breakfast is conveniently located close to Snow Summit and Bear Mountain ski resorts.
5 rooms. Complimentary full breakfast. Pets accepted. $

4

SOUTHERN CALIFORNIA

★
★
★
★
★

Switzerland Haus Bed and Breakfast
41829 Switzerland Dr.,
Big Bear Lake,
909-866-3729, 800-335-3729;
www.switzerlandhaus.com

This Swiss chalet at the base of Snow Summit, is close to the lake and village. Recharge with a full breakfast and afternoon snacks in front of the fireplace or on the deck with a great view of the slopes.
5 rooms. Complimentary full breakfast. $$

BLYTHE

Englishman Thomas Blythe came to this area with the idea of turning this portion of the Colorado River valley into another Nile River Valley. The techniques of modern irrigation have made that possible, as a series of dams has converted the desert into rich farmland and a vast recreational area. There is still some mining in the Palo Verde valley, and rockhounding (the hobbyist's term for rock collecting) is good in nearby areas.
Information: Chamber of Commerce, 201 S. Broadway, Blythe, 760-922-8166;
www.blytheareachamberofcommerce.com

WHAT TO SEE AND DO
Desert Canoe Rentals
12400 W. 14th Ave., Blythe, 760-922-8753
One- to five-day self-guided trips on the lower Colorado River. Fishing, boating, water-skiing, camping. Canoe rentals, delivery and pickup.

Palo Verde Lagoon
20 miles south on Hwy. 78, Blythe
Natural lake with fishing, picnicking and camping facilities.

SPECIAL EVENTS
Blythe Bluegrass Festival
Colorado River Fairgrounds,
11995 Olive Lake Blvd., Blythe,
760-922-8166; www.blythebluegrass.com
Blythe's first festival of the year features two stages with live bluegrass music. Third weekend in January.

HOTELS
★Hampton Inn
900 W. Hobson Way, Blythe,
760-922-9000, 800-426-7866;
www.hamptoninn.com
59 rooms. Wireless Internet access. Exercise room. Pool. $

CALEXICO

Once a tent town of the Imperial Land Company, this community at the south end of the Imperial Valley is separated from its much larger sister city Mexicali, Mexico by a fence. The town represents the marriage of two diverse cultures and serves as a port of entry to the United States.
Information: Chamber of Commerce, 1100 Imperial Ave.,
Calexico, 760-357-1166;
www.calexicochamber.org

HOTELS
★★Guesthouse Hotel & Suites
801 Imperial Ave., Calexico, 760-357-3271
57 rooms. Restaurant. Pool. $

5

SOUTHERN CALIFORNIA

CAMBRIA

Centrally located between San Francisco and Los Angeles, this coastal community an artists' colony on California's central coast. There are many art galleries and gift and antique shops throughout town.
Information: Chamber of Commerce, 767 Main St., Cambria, 805-927-3624; www.cambriachamber.org

WHAT TO SEE AND DO
Beach Recreation
Rock and surf fishing at Moonstone Beach. Whale-watching late December-early February. The large rocks at Piedras Blancas are a refuge for sea lions and sea otters.

HOTELS
★Best Western Fireside Inn on Moonstone Beach
6700 Moonstone Beach Dr., Cambria, 805-927-8661, 888-910-7100; www.bestwesternfiresideinn.com
46 rooms. Complimentary continental breakfast. Swim. $

SPECIALTY LODGINGS
Burton Drive Inn
4022 Burton Dr., Cambria, 805-927-5125, 800-572-7442; www.burtoninn.com
Located in the center of town, all the units at this romantic inn are a spacious 600 square feet. Drive to historic Hearst Castle and area wineries or walk to local restaurants and shops.
10 rooms. Complimentary continental breakfast. $

J. Patrick House Bed and Breakfast Inn
2990 Burton Dr., Cambria, 805-927-3812, 800-341-5258; www.jpatrickhouse.com

This charming seven-room carriage house and its accompanying log cabin are minutes from the ocean. A full breakfast is served each morning in the cozy living room.
8 rooms. Complimentary full breakfast. $$

Squibb House
4063 Burton Dr., Cambria, 805-927-9600, 866-927-9600; www.squibbhouse.net
The current owner painstakingly restored this yellow Italianate structure to its original 1877 splendor.
5 rooms. Complimentary continental breakfast. $$

RESTAURANTS
★★Robin's
4095 Burton Dr., Cambria, 805-927-5007; www.robinsrestaurant.com
Asian, vegetarian menu. Lunch, dinner. Outdoor seating. $$

★★The Brambles Dinner House
4005 Burton Dr., Cambria, 805-927-4716; www.bramblesdinnerhouse.com
American menu. Dinner, Sunday brunch. Bar. Children's menu. Outdoor seating. $$

CHULA VISTA

The name Chula Vista is Spanish for "beautiful view." Set between the mountains and the sea, the city lives up to its name.
Information: www.ci.chula-vista.ca.us

WHAT TO SEE AND DO
Olympic Training Center
2800 Olympic Pkwy., Chula Vista, 619-656-1500; www.chulavistaconvis.org/olympic.asp

The nation's first year-round multi-sport Olympic training facility. See Olympic hopefuls training for track and field, tennis, archery, kayaking, rowing, cycling and soccer. Daily.

6

SOUTHERN CALIFORNIA

HOTEL

★Ramada Inn South
91 Bonita Rd., Chula Vista,
619-425-9999, 800-272-6232;
www.ramada.com
198 rooms. Complimentary continental
breakfast. Pool. $

RESTAURANT

★Butcher Shop
556 Broadway, Chula Vista, 619-420-9440
American, steak menu. Lunch, dinner. Bar.
Casual attire. $$$

CLAREMONT

This community located east of Los Angeles is home to the Claremont Colleges, seven institutions of higher learning.
Information: Chamber of Commerce, 205 N. Yale Ave., 909-624-1681;
www.claremontchamber.org

WHAT TO SEE AND DO

The Claremont Colleges
150 E. Eight St., Claremont,
909-621-8000;
www.claremont.edu
A distinguished group of institutions comprised of Pomona College, Claremont Graduate School, Scripps College, Claremont McKenna College, Harvey Mudd College, Pitzer College and Keck Graduate Institute.

Graduate School Art Building
251 E. 10th St., Claremont,
909-621-8071
Exhibits. Daily, weekends by appointment.

Montgomery Art Gallery
333 N. College Ave., Claremont,
909-621-8283
Exhibits Tuesday-Sunday afternoons; closed school holidays, also June-August.

Rancho Santa Ana Botanic Garden
1500 N. College Ave., Claremont,
909-625-8767; www.rsabg.org
More than 6,000 kinds of native plants over 86 acres. Daily.

HOTEL

★Hotel Claremont
840 S. Indian Hill Blvd., Claremont,
909-621-4831; www.magnusonhotels.com/
hotel-claremont
122 rooms. Pets accepted, some restrictions; fee. Complimentary continental breakfast. Outdoor pool, children's pool, whirlpool. Tennis.

RESTAURANT

★★Yiannis
238 Yale Ave., Claremont,
909-621-2413
Greek menu. Lunch, dinner, Sunday brunch. Bar. Outdoor seating. $

CORONA

A Ranger District office of the Cleveland National Forest is located in Corona.
Information: Chamber of Commerce, 904 E. Sixth St., 951-737-3350;
www.coronachamber.org

WHAT TO SEE AND DO

Glen Ivy Hot Springs
25000 Glen Ivy Rd.,
Corona, 951-277-3529;
www.glenivy.com

Natural hot mineral spa. 15 outdoor mineral baths, massage, sauna, clay bath, outdoor poolside dining. Admission limited to guests over 16 years. Daily 9:30 a.m.-6 p.m.

7

SOUTHERN CALIFORNIA

HOTELS

★Ayres Inn Corona East
2260 Griffin Way, Corona,
951-734-2140, 800-451-7463;
www.ayreshotels.com
101 rooms. Complimentary full breakfast.
Pool. **$**

★Dynasty Suites Corona
1805 W. Sixth St., Corona,
951-371-7185, 888-348-4828;
www.dynastysuitescorona.com
56 rooms. Complimentary continental breakfast. Pets accepted. Pool. **$**

DANA POINT

Named in honor of the noted author Richard Henry Dana of *Two Years Before the Mast* fame, this quiet, unhurried town located about halfway between Los Angeles and San Diego, has nearly seven miles of prominent ocean-facing bluffs and an exquisite man-made marina. The harbor has more than 50 specialty shops and restaurants and is a popular spot for boaters from around the world. It's also the main funnel to the 62-acre Doheny State Park, a popular beach for surfing, snorkeling and camping.

HOTELS

★★★Marriott Laguna Cliffs Resort
25135 Park Lantern, Dana Point,
949-661-5000, 800-533-9748;
www.lagunacliffs.com
Located on cliffs above the bay, this hotel sits on 42 acres and has great views of the Pacific Ocean. Rooms have a beachy décor and pop with color.
376 rooms. High-speed Internet access. Restaurant, bar. Spa. No smoking. Pets accepted. Fitness center. Pool. Tennis. Business center. **$$$**

★★★★St. Regis Resort, Monarch Beach
1 Monarch Beach Resort, Dana Point,
949-234-3200, 800-722-1543;
www.stregismb.com
Tucked away on 200 acres high above the Pacific Ocean, even road warriors will swoon over the luscious, secluded setting and the Tuscan-inspired design. Elegant marble floors, plush carpets and massive sofas grace the public areas. The oversized guest rooms have dramatic contemporary décor with wood shutters, marble bathrooms, private balconies, goose down comforters and 300-thread count sheets. The resort has an 18-hole championship golf course, award-winning spa, beach club (with surfing lessons) and nature trails. In between, dine at one of the six ocean-view restaurants.

400 rooms,. High-speed Internet access. Six restaurants, three bars. Spa. Beach. Pets accepted. Fitness center. Pool. Golf. Tennis. Business center. **$$$$**

★★★★The Ritz-Carlton, Laguna Niguel
1 Ritz-Carlton Dr.,
Dana Point,
949-240-2000, 800-241-3333;
www.ritzcarlton.com
Avid golfers come here to play one of the eight spectacular courses surrounding the property, but there are lots of other reasons to love this place. Situated atop a 150-foot bluff overlooking the ocean, this Mediterranean-style villa is a first-class haven. The soft sand and sea colors in the sumptuous rooms are perfect for unwinding, as are the ocean and pool. Surfing lessons are available at the beach, as are sensual escapes at the spa.
393 rooms. High-speed Internet access, wireless Internet access. Two restaurants, bar. Pets accepted. Fitness center. Swim. Tennis. Business center. **$$$$**

SPECIALTY LODGINGS

Blue Lantern Inn
34343 St. of the Blue Lantern,
Dana Point,
949-661-1304, 800-950-1236;
www.bluelanterninn.com

8

SOUTHERN CALIFORNIA

★
★
★
★
★

This inn is located on a bluff overlooking the harbor. Some rooms have views of the coast.

29 rooms. Complimentary full breakfast. High-speed Internet access. Exercise. **$$**

RESTAURANTS

★★★Restaurant 162'
1 Ritz Carlton Dr., Dana Point,
949-240-2000; www.ritzcarlton.com

Named for its location 162 feet above sea level, this restaurant provides a spectacular view from its dazzling blue- and cream-colored dining room. The cuisine focuses on fresh fish, with dishes such as Alaskan king crab with red Thai curry risotto. This *is* California, so there is also the barley edamame burger with avocado and the chef's pizza inspiration.

California menu. Breakfast, lunch, dinner. Bar. Children's menu. Business casual attire. Reservations recommended. Valet parking. **$$$**

★★Savannah Steak & Chop House
32441 Golden Lantern St.,
Laguna Niguel, 949-493-7107;
www.culinaryadventures.com

American, steak menu. Dinner. Bar. Business casual attire. Reservations recommended. Valet parking. Outdoor seating. **$$$**

★★★★Stonehill Tavern
1 Monarch Beach Resort,
Dana Point, 949-234-3318;
www.michaelmina.net/stonehill

Famed San Francisco chef-turned-restaurateur Michael Mina returns with an urban bistro at the site of his first restaurant at the St. Regis Monarch Beach Resort. The space that formerly housed Mina's seafood restaurant, Aqua, has been transformed into a sleek, intimate spot by acclaimed New York-based interior designer Tony Chi with comfortable couches, glass-enclosed booths and a large terrace. The menu includes Mina's signature appetizer trios—three different

preparations of one ingredient, such as tuna, lobster or duck, as well as twists on American classics. Think whole fried chicken with mascarpone polenta and a root beer float for dessert. An impressive wine program focuses on boutique California producers, but also includes a diverse selection from Austria and Burgundy.

American menu. Dinner. Closed Monday-Tuesday. Bar. Business casual attire. Reservations recommended. Valet parking. Outdoor seating. **$$$$**

SPAS

★★★★The Ritz-Carlton Spa, Laguna Niguel
1 Ritz-Carlton Dr.,
Dana Point,
949-240-2000, 800-241-3333;
www.ritzcarlton.com

Eleven treatment rooms, a full service beauty salon, a circular manicure and pedicure station and a modern fitness room are available to guests at the Ritz-Carlton Spa. Choose from holistic treatments grounded in ancient practices as well as the latest skin treatments, massages and exfoliations. Collagen infusion facials and California citrus body polishes stand out among the spa's signature treatments. There are also seasonal treatments such as a summer chocolate sugar scrub pedicure. Treatments are rooted in the sea's purifying elements: rich minerals, sea salt, or nutrient-rich algae and water. **$$**

★★★★Spa Gaucin
1 Monarch Beach Resort, Dana Point,
949-234-3200, 800-722-1543;
www.stregismonarchbeach.com

Spa Gaucin at the St. Regis is the picture of elegance with dark woods, Asian-style accents and three-story waterfalls. The spa menu includes everything from Thai massage to vitamin C facials to the signature pear body polish. There's also an extensive offering of beauty treatments from tanning to microdermabrasion. **$$**

★

★

★

★

★

DEATH VALLEY NATIONAL PARK

Approximately 300 miles northeast of Los Angeles, you'll find more than 5,200 square miles of rugged desert, peaks and depressions. Death Valley was named in 1849 when a party of gold hunters took a shortcut here and were stranded for several weeks awaiting help. The discovery and subsequent mining of borax, hauled out by the famous 20-mule teams, led to development of the valley as a tourist attraction.

The park is one vast geological museum. Millions of years ago, this was part of the Pacific Ocean. Violent uplifts of the earth occurred, creating mountain ranges and draining water to the west. Today, 200 square miles of the valley are at or below sea level. The lowest point on the continent (282 feet below sea level) can be found here. Telescope Peak, at 11,049 feet, towers directly above it. The average rainfall is less than two inches a year. The climate is pleasant from October to May, but it's very hot in summer—a maximum temperature of 134 F has been recorded.

Venturing off paved roads in this area in summer months can be dangerous. Carefully obey all National Park Service signs and regulations. Make sure that your vehicle has plenty of gas and oil. Carry water when you explore this park, especially in hot weather.
Information: 760-786-3200; www.nps.gov/deva

WHAT TO SEE AND DO

20-Mule-Team Canyon
Lone Pine, 760-786-2331
This canyon is viewed from a twisting road on which RVs and trailers are not allowed, this is an unpaved, one-way road.

Artist's Palette
Death Valley National Park
A particularly scenic drive (nine miles one way) with spectacular colors. Because of difficult roads.

Dante's View
Death Valley National Park, 760-786-2331
View of Death Valley with a steep drop to 279 feet below sea level at Badwater.

Devil's Golf Course
Death Valley National Park, 760-786-2331
Vast beds of rugged salt crystals.

Golden Canyon
Death Valley National Park, 760-786-2331
Offers a display of color ranging from deep red to rich gold. A one-mile trail provides access.

Natural Bridge
Death Valley National Park, 760-786-2331

A bridge spanning a rugged canyon in the Black Mountains. One-mile walking trail.

Rhyolite Ghost Town
Death Valley National Park, 760-786-2331;
www.nps.gov/deva/rhyolite.htm
This was the largest mining town in Death Valley in the early 1900s. By 1911, it was a ghost town. One structure still left standing from that era is the "bottle house," constructed of beer and liquor bottles.

Scotty's Castle
Death Valley National Park, 760-786-2392
This desert mansion (circa 1922-1931) was designed to be viewed both as a work of art and as a home. The furnishings are typical of the period and many were specially designed and handcrafted for this house. Costumed interpreters lead living history tours. Daily 8:30 a.m.-6 p.m.

Telescope Peak
Death Valley National Park, 760-786-2331
Highest point in the Panamint Range (11,049 feet). Fourteen-mile round-trip hiking trail (inaccessible in the winter months).

Ubehebe Crater
Death Valley National Park, 760-786-2331

SOUTHERN CALIFORNIA

★
★
★
★
☆

Colorful crater left by a volcanic steam explosion.

Zabriskie Point
Death Valley National Park, 760-786-2331
Scenic view.

HOTELS
★★Carriage Inn
901 N. China Lake Blvd., Ridgecrest,
760-446-7910; www.carriageinn.biz
160 rooms. Pool. **$$**

★★Heritage Inn and Suites
1050 N. Norma St., Ridgecrest,
760-446-6543, 800-843-0693
169 rooms, all suites. Restaurant. **$**

★★Stovepipe Wells Village
Hwy. 190, Death Valley,
760-786-2387;
www.stovepipewells.com
83 rooms. High-speed Internet access. Restaurant, bar. Pets accepted. Pool. **$**

RESTAURANT
★The 19th Hole
Hwy. 190, Furnace Creek,
760-786-2345;
www.furnacecreekresort.com
Located on a site overlooking the world's lowest golf course (214 feet below sea level). American menu. Breakfast, lunch. Closed June-September. **$**

EL CENTRO

This busy marketplace in the center of the Imperial Valley is the largest town in the United States that's entirely below sea level. Water from the All-American Canal and Hoover Dam has turned arid desert into lush farmland that produces bumper crops of sugar beets, melons and lettuce. Mountains east of El Centro are ringed with coral reefs.
Information: Chamber of Commerce, 1095 S. Fourth St., 760-352-3681;
www.elcentrochamber.com

HOTELS
★★Ramada
1455 Ocotillo Dr., El Centro,
760-352-5152, 800-805-4000;
www.ramada.com
147 rooms. Restaurant, bar. Airport transportation available. Pets accepted. Fitness center. Pool. **$**

★★Vacation Inn
2015 Cottonwood Cir., El Centro,
760-352-9523, 800-328-6289
170 rooms. Complimentary continental breakfast. Restaurant, bar. Pets accepted. Fitness center. Pool. **$**

★★Barbara Worth Golf Resort and Convention Center
2050 Country Club Dr., Holtville,
760-356-2806;
www.bwresort.com
104 rooms. Restaurant, bar. Pets accepted. Fitness center. Pool. Golf. Business center. **$**

RESTAURANTS
★Scribbles
2015 Cottonwood Circle, El Centro,
760-352-9523
American menu. Breakfast, lunch, dinner. Children's menu. Casual attire. **$$**

FALLBROOK

Fallbrook is the self-proclaimed avocado capital of the world. Twenty-eight square miles are devoted to growing and packing the fruit. One day each April is set aside to celebrate the crop with a festival that includes crafts, games, contests, entertainment and a tour of the Del Rey Avocado Company. The best reason for coming is to taste the world-class guacamole, avocado sandwiches, grilled avocado halves with lemon and other samples.
Information: 233 E. Mission Rd., Fallbrook, 92028, 760-723-5845; www.fallbrookca.org

11

SOUTHERN CALIFORNIA

SPECIAL EVENTS
Fallbrook Avocado Festival
233 E. Mission Rd., Fallbrook,
760-728-5845;
www.fallbrookca.org/avofest.htm

HOTELS
★Franciscan Rodeway Inn
1635 S. Mission Rd., Fallbrook,
760-728-6174
51 rooms. Complimentary continental breakfast. Pets accepted. Pool. **$**

★★★Pala Mesa Resort
2001 Old Hwy. 395, Fallbrook,
760-728-5881, 800-722-4700;
www.palamesa.com
At one of California's most unique golf settings, guests can enjoy a round of golf, as well as a winery and tours.
133 rooms. Restaurant, bar. Pets accepted. Pool. Golf. Tennis. **$$**

FRESNO
In the geographic center of the state and the heart of the San Joaquin Valley, Fresno is undergoing tremendous growth. The county claims the greatest agricultural production of any in the United States, handling more than $3 billion annually. The world's largest dried fruit packing plant, Sun-Maid, is here.
Information: Convention & Visitors Bureau, 848 M St., 559-445-8300, 800-788-0836; www.fresnocvb.org

WHAT TO SEE AND DO
California State University, Fresno
5241 N. Maple Ave., Fresno,
559-278-4240; www.csufresno.edu
Includes a farm, arboretum and California wildlife habitat exhibits. Tours available.

Discovery Center
1937 N. Winery Ave., Fresno,
559-251-5533;
www.thediscoverycenter.net
Natural and physical science exhibits. Cactus garden; picnicking. Tuesday-Friday 9 a.m.-4 p.m.

Forestiere Underground Gardens
5021 W. Shaw, Fresno, 559-271-0734;
www.undergroundgardens.com
This former home of Italian immigrant Baldasare Forestiere has 10 acres of underground tunnels filled with citrus plants, grape vines, rose bushes and other flora. April-September, Wednesday-Sunday.

Fresno Art Museum
2233 N. First St., Fresno, 559-441-4221;
www.fresnoartmuseum.org
The only modern art museum between Los Angeles and San Francisco, here are works from an international group of contemporary artists as well as an impressive collection of Mexican art dating from the pre-Columbian era to present day. Tuesday-Wednesday, Friday-Sunday 11 a.m.-5 p.m.; Thursday to 8 p.m.

Fresno Metropolitan Museum
933 Van Ness Ave., Fresno, 559-441-1444;
www.fresnomet.org
Learn all about the heritage and culture of the San Joaquin Valley. Hands-on science exhibits; touring exhibits. Tuesday-Wednesday, Friday-Sunday 11 a.m.-5 p.m., Thursday to 8 p.m.

Kearney Mansion Museum
7160 W. Kearney Blvd., Fresno,
559-441-0862; www.valleyhistory.org/kearneymansionmuseum.html
Restored historic mansion with many original furnishings, European wallpapers and Art Nouveau light fixtures. Narrated 45-minute tour of mansion. Friday-Sunday 1 p.m., 2 p.m. and 3 p.m.

Millerton Lake State Recreation Area
5290 Millerton Rd., Fresno,
559-822-2332; www.parks.ca.gov

★
★
★
★

Swimming, water-skiing, fishing, boat launching, hiking and riding trails, picnicking, camping.

Roeding Park
890 W. Belmont Ave., Fresno,
559-621-2900;
www.fresno.gov/parks-rec/roeding
Variety of trees and shrubs, ranging from high mountain to tropical species, on 157 acres. Boating. Tennis. Camellia garden, picnic areas, Daily.

Fresno Chaffee Zoo
894 W. Belmont Ave., Fresno,
559-498-5910;
www.fresnochaffeezoo.com
This 18-acre zoo has more than 650 animals representing 200 species. Includes a reptile house, elephant exhibit, sunda forest. Also includes a tropical rain forest exhibit containing plants and animals found primarily in South American regions. February-October: daily 9 a.m.-4 p.m.; November-January: daily 10 a.m.-3 p.m.

Sierra National Forest
1600 Tollhouse Rd., Clovis,
www.fs.fed.us/r5/sierra
Nearly 1.3 million acres ranging from rolling foothills to rugged, snow-capped mountains. Two groves of giant sequoias, hundreds of natural lakes, 11 major reservoirs and unique geological formations. The topography can be rough and precipitous in higher elevations, with deep canyons and many beautiful meadows along streams and lakes. Five wilderness areas. Rafting, boating, sailing, fishing, hunting, downhill and cross-country skiing, picnicking, camping.

Sierra Summit Ski Area
59265 Hwy. 168, Huntington Lake
559-233-2500;
www.sierrasummit.com
Twenty-five runs. The longest is 2 1/4 miles. Three triple and two double chairlifts, four surface lifts. Vertical drop 1,600 feet. Half-day rates weekends and holidays. Mid-November-mid-April, daily.

Wild Water Adventures
11413 E. Shaw Ave., Clovis,
559-299-9453, 800-564-9453;
www.wildwater.net
This water park with rides, slides and picnicking has one of the west coast's largest wave pools, plus water slides for teens and a water play area for children. June-mid-August, daily.

SPECIAL EVENTS
Big Fresno Fair
1121 S. Chance Ave., Fresno,
559-650-3247; www.fresnofair.com
Carnival, horse racing, livestock exhibits, and arts and crafts. October.

Clovis Rodeo
Clovis Arena, 559-299-5203;
www.clovisrodeo.com
Four-day festival featuring a parade, kids rodeo and competition categories that include bull riding, team roping, barrel racing and bareback riding. Late April.

Fresno County Blossom Trail
2629 S. Clovis Ave., Fresno, 559-262-4271;
www.co.fresno.ca.us/4510/tourism/
agtrails.aspx
Take this 62-mile driving tour of fruit orchards, citrus groves and vineyards during peak season February-mid-March.

Highland Gathering and Games
Roeding Park 890 W. Belmont, Fresno,
559-265-6507; www.scottishsociety.org
Scottish athletics, dancing contests, bagpipe competition. Mid-September.

Swedish Festival
1475 Draper St., Kingsburg, 559-897-1111
After a traditional Swedish pancake breakfast, stick around for a parade, entertainment, arts and crafts, carnival, folk dancing and more food. Third weekend in May.

HOTELS
★★Four Points by Sheraton
3737 N. Blackstone Ave., Fresno,
559-226-2200, 888-627-7141;
www.fourpoints.com

SOUTHERN CALIFORNIA

204 rooms. High-speed Internet access. Restaurant, bar. Airport transportation available. Fitness center. Pool. Business center. **$$**

★**Piccadilly Inn-University**
4961 N. Cedar Ave., Fresno,
559-224-4200, 800-468-3587;
www.piccadillyinn.com
90 rooms. Complimentary continental breakfast. Airport transportation available. Fitness center. Pool. **$$**

★★**Radisson Hotel & Conference Center Fresno**
2233 Ventura St., Fresno,
559-268-1000, 800-201-1718;
www.radisson.com

321 rooms. Restaurant, bar. Airport transportation available. Fitness center. Pool. Business center. **$**

RESTAURANT
★★**Ripe Tomato**
5064 N. Palm Ave., Fresno,
559-225-1850
French menu. Lunch, dinner. Closed Sunday-Monday. Business casual attire. Reservations recommended. Outdoor seating. **$$$**

HEMET

Located in the beautiful San Jacinto Valley, Hemet was once the largest producer of alfalfa and herbs in the country. Today, it's proximity to Corona, Riverside and San Berardino has made it an attractive destination for families.
Information: www.ci.hemet.ca.us

WHAT TO SEE AND DO
San Jacinto Valley Museum
695 Ash St., San Jacinto, 951-654-4952
Permanent and temporary exhibits of genealogy, Native American archaeology and a variety of historical items of San Jacinto Valley. Daily, mornings.

SPECIAL EVENTS
The Ramona Outdoor Play
27400 Ramona Bowl Rd., Hemet,
800-645-4465; www.ramonabowl.com
This is the world's largest outdoor play, based on Helen Hunt Jackson's novel *Ramona*. More than 350 people participate in this romance of early California, presented annually since 1923. Shown in the Ramona Bowl, a 5,959-seat outdoor amphitheater built into the side of a mountain. Three weekends in late April-early May.

HOTELS
★★**Best Western Inn of Hemet**
2625 W. Florida Ave., Hemet,
951-925-6605; www.bestwestern.com
70 rooms. Complimentary full breakfast. Pets accepted. Pool. **$**

RESTAURANT
★★**Dattilo**
2288 E. Florida Ave., Hemet,
951-658-4248
Lunch, dinner. Bar. **$$$**

HUNTINGTON BEACH

This quirky city features more than eight miles of beaches, all of them great for swimming and many favorable to surfers. Locals call Huntington Cliffs "Dog Beach" because pooches are welcome. It's also the site of Huntington Pier, a structure that has seen damage from heavy surf, earthquake and fire. This version, the locals say, is built to last. Take a hike out to the very end and have a meal at Ruby's Restaurant.

Named after Henry E. Huntington, a fabled entrepreneur from California's freewheeling past, Huntington Beach was a vital rail terminus, an oil boom town and a posh resort. The Newland House evokes the feel and architecture of the first decade of the 20th century in California. The City Gym and Pool on Palm Avenue dates to the early 1930s, and has survived numerous earthquakes.
Information: www.hbvisit.com

HOTELS

★Comfort Suites
16301 Beach Blvd., Huntington Beach,
714-841-1812; www.comfortsuites.com
102 rooms. Complimentary continental breakfast. Fitness center. Pool. $

★★Hotel Huntington Beach
7667 Center Ave., Huntington Beach,
714-891-0123, 877-891-0123;
www.hotelhb.com
224 rooms. Complimentary continental breakfast. Restaurant, bar. Airport transportation available. Fitness center. Pool. Business center. $

★★★Hilton Waterfront Beach Resort
21100 Pacific Coast Hwy.,
Huntington Beach,
714-845-8000, 800-822-7873;
www.waterfrontbeachresort.hilton.com
This hotel was recently updated with touches such as flat screen TVs, sleek furniture and vanities with more space for stashing stuff. Beach views and an indoor waterfall add to the charm.

290 rooms. Restaurant, bar. Airport transportation available. Pets accepted. Fitness center. Pool. Tennis. Business center. $$

IDYLLWILD

Located in the San Jacinto Mountains, Idyllwild is a small alpine village at the gateway to thousands of acres of national forest and state and county parks. This popular resort and vacation area provides fishing in backcountry streams and lakes, hiking, rock climbing and riding.
Information: Chamber of Commerce, 54295 Village Center Dr., 951-659-3259,
888-659-3259; www.idyllwildchamber.com

WHAT TO SEE AND DO

Mount San Jacinto State Park
Hwy. 243, Idyllwild, 951-659-2607;
www.sanjac.statepark.org
On 14,000 acres. Nature and hiking trails; picnicking; camping (reservations required).

Hurkey Creek
56375 Hwy. 74, Mountain Center,
951-659-2050
Camping, picnicking, play area, hiking. Pets on leash.

Idyllwild Park
54000 County Park Rd., Idyllwild,
951-659-2656
Camping, picnicking, play area, hiking. Pets on leash only. Visitor center with museum.

HOTELS

★★★Strawberry Creek Inn
26370 Scenic Hwy. 243, Idyllwild,
951-659-3202, 800-262-8969;
www.strawberrycreekinn.com
Each room at this cozy inn has a different style. Four are in the cedar-shingled main

★

★

★

★

inn and four in a courtyard wing. Read in the library, laze around in a hammock or walk along Strawberry Creek. Hundreds of miles of hiking trails surround the inn.

9 rooms. Complimentary full breakfast. $

RESTAURANTS
★★Gastrognome
54381 Ridgeview Dr., Idyllwild,
951-659-5055; www.gastrognome.com
Seafood menu. Lunch, dinner. Closed Monday. Bar. Outdoor seating. **$$$**

INDIAN WELLS

This city, which hosts the Indian Wells Masters golf tournament, is in the Palm Springs area and boasts the highest proportion of millionaires of any city in the United States. Information: www.indianwells.org

HOTELS
★★★Hyatt Grand Champions Resort and Spa
44-600 Indian Wells Lane, Indian Wells,
760-341-1000, 800-554-9288;
www.grandchampions.hyatt.com
This classic California Palm Desert resort has luxury accommodations with furnished balconies and marble baths with separate tubs and showers. Golfers will enjoy the 36 holes of the Golf Resort at Indian Wells, which surrounds the hotel. There's a 30,000-square-foot spa, an espresso bar, cocktail lounge, outdoor grill and a cafe offering light fare.

479 rooms. Restaurant, bar. Children's activity center. Pets accepted. Pool. Golf. Tennis. Business center. **$$$**

★★★Indian Wells Resort Hotel
76661 Hwy. 111, Indian Wells,
760-345-6466, 800-248-3220;
www.indianwellsresort.com
This European boutique-style hotel features spacious accommodations and personalized service and is close to top shopping and recreation.

155 rooms. Complimentary continental breakfast. Restaurant, two bars. Airport transportation available. Fitness center. Pool. Tennis. **$$**

★★★Renaissance Esmeralda Resort
44-400 Indian Wells Lane, Indian Wells,
760-773-4444;
www.renaissanceesmeralda.com
This resort has a full-service spa, championship golf, tennis, plus a camp for kids

with arts-and-crafts activities, swimming and poolside play. Each of the cheerful and contemporary rooms has a private balcony, with a view of the surrounding mountains, golf courses and desert.

560 rooms. Restaurant, bar. Children's activity center. Beach. Airport transportation available. Fitness center. Pool. Golf. Tennis. Business center. **$$**

★★★Miramonte Resort and Spa
45-000 Indian Wells Lane, Indian Wells,
760-341-2200, 800-237-2926;
www.miramonteresort.com
Just 15 minutes from Palm Springs, this charming resort is nestled at the base of the Santa Rosa Mountains. The lovely grounds are dotted with courtyards and manicured rose gardens. Order lunch from the restaurant and someone will hop on a bike and deliver it to your room or wherever you are. Three golf courses surround the property.

222 rooms. Restaurant. Fitness center. Pool. Tennis. Business center. **$$$**

RESTAURANTS
★★★Le Saint Germain
74-985 Hwy. 111, Indian Wells,
760-773-6511;
www.lestgermain.com
This is a charming and elegant restaurant where classic French and California flavors are fused together to create an eclectic dining experience. Dine on Maine lobster with avocado, papaya, tomato and mango vinaigrette, or grilled Black Angus beef with a Roquefort crust. There's also an extensive wine list.

French, Mediterranean menu. Dinner. Closed Sunday in summer. Bar. Casual attire. Valet parking. Outdoor seating. **$$$**

SPAS

★★★The Well Spa at Miramonte Resort
45000 Indian Wells Lane, Indian Wells, 760- 341-2200; www.miramonteresort.com
This Tuscan-inspired jewel will awaken your senses with a setting that is distinctive and tranquil. Outdoor and indoor treatment rooms are available to ensure the ultimate spa experience. Services incorporate thera-peutic muds, wine extracts, pure essential oils and refreshing waters. There's a com-plete fitness center with an array of classes, a full service salon, a spa boutique and a smoothie bar. **$$**

INDIO

Founded as a railroad construction camp, the town took its name from the large population of Native Americans nearby. The All-American Canal turned the area into fertile ground that now produces 59 types of crops, including 95 percent of all American dates.
Information: Chamber of Commerce, 82-921 Indio Blvd., 760-347-0676, 800-775-8440; www.indiochamber.org

WHAT TO SEE AND DO

Fantasy Springs Casino
84-245 Indio Springs Pkwy., Indio, 760-342-5000, 800-827-2946; www.fantasyspringsresort.com/index.html
Offers off-track betting, video gaming machines, 1,200-seat bingo room and more than 35 card tables. Entertainment and din-ing. Daily, open 24 hours.

General George S. Patton Memorial Museum
2 Chiriaco Rd., Indio, 760-227-3483; www.generalpattonmuseum.com
General Patton selected this site to pre-pare his soldiers for combat in North Africa. Patton memorabilia, artifacts. Daily 9:30 a.m.-4:30 p.m.

Salton Sea State Recreation Area
100-225 State Rd., North Shore, 760-393-3052, 760-393-3059; www.saltonsea.statepark.org
The Colorado River flooded through a bro-ken canal gate into the Salton Basin, creat-ing a vast new lake which is now a popular inland boating and fishing area. The recre-ation area covers 17,913 acres and has areas for swimming and water-skiing. Daily.

SPECIAL EVENTS

Indio Desert Circuit Horse Show
81-500 Ave., 52, Indio, 760-775-7731
The largest hunter/jumper horse show west of the Mississippi River. Six weeks from January-March.

Indio International Tamale Festival
100 Civic Center Mall, Indio, 760-391-4175; www.tamalefestival.net
Celebration of traditional Latin American fare. Dance, music, entertainment. Carnival, petting zoo, arts and crafts, holiday parade. First weekend in December.

Riverside County Fair and National Date Festival
Riverside County Fairgrounds
82-503 Hwy. 111, Indio, 800-811-3247; www.datefest.org
Fair and pageant done in Arabian Nights-style. Mid-late February.

HOTELS

★★Best Western Date Tree Hotel
81-909 Indio Blvd., Indio, 760-347-3421; www.datetree.com
119 rooms, 2 story. Complimentary con-tinental breakfast. Pets accepted. Fitness center. Pool. **$**

★Quality Inn
43505 Monroe St., Indio, 760-347-4044, 877-424-6423; www.qualityinn.com
62 rooms. Complimentary continental breakfast. Pets accepted. Pool. **$**

17

SOUTHERN CALIFORNIA

★
★
★
★

JOSHUA TREE NATIONAL PARK

Information: www.nps.gov/jotr

WHAT TO SEE AND DO

Hidden Valley Nature Trail
74485 National Park Dr.,
Joshua Tree National Park, 760-367-5500
One-mile loop. Access from picnic area across Hidden Valley Campground. Valley enclosed by wall of rocks.

Joshua Tree National Park
74485 National Parks Dr.,
Twentynine Palms, 760-367-5500;
www.nps.gov/jotr
Covering more than 1,236 square miles, this park preserves a section of the Mojave and Colorado desserts that is rich in vegetation. The park shelters many species of desert plants. The Joshua tree, which gives the park its name, was named by the Mormons for its upstretched "arms" reaching for heaven. A member of the Lily family, this giant yucca attains heights of more than 40 feet. The area consists of a series of block mountains ranging in altitude from 1,000 to 5,800 feet and separated by desert flats. The summer gets very hot and the temperature drops below freezing in the winter. Water is available only at the Black Rock Canyon Visitor Center/Campground, Cottonwood Campground, the Indian Cove Ranger Station and the Twentynine Palms Visitor Center. Pets are permitted on leash only and not on trails. Guided tours and campfire programs. February-May and October-December. Picnicking is permitted in designated areas and campgrounds, but no fires may be built outside the campgrounds.

Keys View
74485 National Park Dr., Joshua Tree National Park, 760-367-5500
Sweeping view of Coachella valley, desert and mountain. A paved path leads off the main road.

Lost Palms Canyon
74485 National Park Dr.,
Joshua Tree National Park,
760-367-5500

Eight-mile round-trip hike reached by four-mile trail from Cottonwood Spring. Shelters the largest group of palms (120) in the park. Day use only.

Oasis Visitor Center
74485 National Park Dr.,
Joshua Tree National Park,
760-367-5500
Exhibits, self-guided nature trail through the Oasis of Mara, discovered by a government survey party in 1855. Daily.

SPECIAL EVENTS

Pioneer Days
Twentynine Palms Chamber of Commerce, 760-367-3445;
www.29chamber.com/pioneer_days.83.o.html
Children's carnival, parade, rodeo, concerts, outhouse races and more. Third weekend in October.

HOTELS

★Best Western Garden Inn & Suites
71487 Twentynine Palms Hwy.,
Twentynine Palms,
760-367-9141, 800-780-7234;
www.bestwestern.com
84 rooms. Complimentary continental breakfast. Pets accepted. Fitness center. Pool. $

★Oasis of Eden Inn & Suites
56377 Twentynine Palms Hwy.,
Yucca Valley,
760-365-6321, 800-606-6686;
www.oasisofeden.com
39 rooms. Complimentary continental breakfast. Pets accepted. Pool. $

SPECIALTY LODGINGS

Joshua Tree Inn
61259 Twentynine Palms Hwy.,
Joshua Tree,
760-366-1188;
www.jtinn.com
10 rooms. Complimentary continental breakfast. Pool. $

KERNVILLE

Kernville offers a variety of outdoor recreation, including camping and trout fishing in Kern River.

Information: Chamber of Commerce, 11447 Kernville Rd., 760-376-2629; www.kernvillechamber.org

WHAT TO SEE AND DO

Greenhorn Mountain Park
12 miles W. via Hwy. 155 in Sequoia National Forest, 559-565-3341
Ninety campsites with barbecue pits, 115 picnic tables, camping supplies. Camping limited to 14 days, no reservations; pets on leash only.

Isabella Lake
4875 Ponderosa Dr., Kernville, 760-379-5646
Swimming, water-skiing, fishing, boating and more than 700 improved campsites.

Kern River Tours
2712 Mayfair Rd., Lake Isabella, 760-379-4616, 800-844-7238; www.kernrivertours.com
Rafting trips down the upper and lower Kern River, a Class II-V river. April-September.

SPECIAL EVENTS

Kernville Rod Run
Features more than 350 vintage hot rods and classic cars on display. October.

Whiskey Flat Days
Hwy. 178, Kernville, 760-376-2629

Celebrate the Gold Rush days when Kernville was known as "Whiskey Flat." Carnival rides, activities for kids, games, pet parade and costume contests. Early January.

SPECIALTY LODGINGS

Kern River Inn Bed and Breakfast
119 Kern River Dr., Kernville, 760-376-6750, 800-986-4382; www.kernriverinn.com
5 rooms. Complimentary full breakfast. **$**

Whispering Pines Lodge
13745 Sierra Way, Kernville, 760-376-3733, 877-241-4100; www.kernvalley.com/whisperingpines
17 rooms. Complimentary full breakfast. Pool. **$**

RESTAURANT

★Johnny McNally's Fairview Lodge
Star Rte. 1, Kernville, 760-376-2430; www.mcnallysfairviewlodge.com
Seafood, steak menu. Dinner. Closed December-February. Bar. Children's menu. **$$**

LAKE ARROWHEAD

People are drawn to this mountainous lake region in the San Bernadino National Forest for the outdoor recreation. Although the lake itself is private (visitors can tour it on the *Arrowhead Queen*, take water-skiing lessons or use the beach as guests of the Lake Arrowhead Resort), everyone can enjoy hiking, biking, horseback riding and camping. There are also plenty of shops, restaurants and other attractions, including the ice skating rink where Michelle Kwan trained. In winter, skiers and snowboarders take to the powdery slopes.

Information: Chamber of Commerce, 909-337-3715; www.lakearrowhead.net

WHAT TO SEE AND DO

Arrowhead Queen & Leroy's Sports
28200 Hwy. 189, Lake Arrowhead, 909-336-6992

Enjoy a 50-minute narrated boat cruise on Lake Arrowhead, past architectural points of interest and historical sites.

HOTELS

★Lake Arrowhead Tree Top Lodge
27992 Rainbow Dr., Lake Arrowhead,
909-337-2311, 800-358-8733;
www.arrowheadtreetop.com
20 rooms. Pets accepted. Pool. $

★★★Lake Arrowhead Resort and Spa
27984 Hwy. 189, Lake Arrowhead,
909-336-1511, 800-800-6792;
www.lakearrowheadresort.com
There's much to do around Lake Arrowhead but this lakefront resort nestled in the
San Bernardino forest is so warm and luxurious, visitors may never want to leave.
Guest rooms feature plush with goose
down comforters, granite bathrooms and
private balconies or patios. Guests have
access to the private beach as well as golf
and tennis privileges at Lake Arrowhead
Country Club. The resort's fine dining restaurant Bin 189 offers a menu of contemporary American fare for breakfast, lunch
and dinner. Weekly movies featuring films
made in Arrowhead are also shown.
173 rooms. High-speed wireless Internet
access. Restaurant, bar. Spa. Beach. Pool.
Tennis. $$

SPECIALTY LODGINGS

Chateau Du Lac
911 Hospital Rd., Lake Arrowhead,
909-337-6488
5 rooms. Complimentary full breakfast. $$

★★Romantique Lakeview Lodge
28051 Hwy. 189, Lake Arrowhead,
909-337-6633, 800-358-5253;
www.lakeviewlodge.com
This quaint Victorian-style bed and breakfast is within distance of shops and restaurants and close to activities such as fishing,
hiking, boating and skiing.
9 rooms. Complimentary continental
breakfast. Wireless Internet access. $

LANCASTER
This Los Angeles suburb is located 70 miles north of the city in the Antelope Valley.
Information: Chamber of Commerce, 554 W. Lancaster Blvd., 661-948-4518;
www.lancasterchamber.org

SPECIAL EVENTS

Antelope Valley Fair and Alfalfa Festival
Antelope Valley Fairgrounds,
2551 W. Ave. H, Lancaster, 661-948-6060;
www.avfair.com
Rural Olympics including events like hay
baling and tractor races, as well as concerts
featuring star country singers. Eleven days
in late August-early September.

Wildflower Season
Antelope Valley California Poppy Reserve,
15101 Lancaster Rd., Lancaster,
661-724-1180; www.parks.ca.gov
Seven miles of walking trails with poppies,
lupines and other flowers that bloom each
spring. Mid-March-mid-May.

HOTELS

★★Best Western Antelope Valley Inn
44055 N. Sierra Hwy.,
Lancaster,
661-948-4651, 800-780-7234;
www.bestwestern.com
148 rooms. Complimentary full breakfast.
Restaurant, bar. Pets accepted. Pool. $

LOMPOC

More than two dozen murals around this community showcase the works of internationally acclaimed artists such as Roberto Delgado and Dan Sawatsky. Lompoc is also the flower seed capital of the world, and most of the world's flower seeds come from here. From May through September, the city is bordered by more than 1,000 acres of vivid zinnias, marigolds, sweet peas, petunias and other blossoms. Vandenberg Air Force Base is 10 miles west of here.

Information: Chamber of Commerce, 111 South I St., 805-736-4567; www.lompoc.com

WHAT TO SEE AND DO

La Purisima Mission State Historic Park
2295 Purisima Rd., Lompoc, 805-733-3713; www.lapurisimamission.org
Founded in 1787, this is the 11th of the 21 Spanish missions established in what became California. The mission was moved in 1812 and restored in its current setting. Daily 9 a.m.-5 p.m.

Mural Walk
More than 24 giant murals painted by world-class artists adorn the exterior walls of buildings in old downtown.

SPECIAL EVENTS

Greenhouse Tour
805-736-5118
Spectacular display of flowers by Bodger Seed Company. April.

Lompoc Valley Flower Festival
Ryon Park, 800 W. Ocean Ave., Lompoc, 805-735-8511; www.flowerfestival.org
Floral parade, flower exhibits, arts and craft show, entertainment plus bus tours of 1,200 acres of flower fields. June.

HOTELS

★★Embassy Suites
1117 N. H St., Lompoc, 805-735-8311, 800-362-2779; www.embassysuites.com
155 rooms. Complimentary full breakfast. Fitness center. Pool. **$**

★Quality Inn
1621 N. H St., Lompoc, 805-735-8555, 800-638-7949; www.qualityinn.com
218 rooms. Complimentary full breakfast. Pets accepted. Pool. **$**

21

SOUTHERN CALIFORNIA

LOS ANGELES

On September 4, 1781, the governor of California, Don Felipe de Neve, marched to the city and founded "the town of our lady the queen of the angels of Porciuncula," later thankfully shortened to "Los Angeles."

The little city slumbered until 1846, when the seizure of California by the United States converted it into a vigorous frontier community. The gold rush of 1849 fanned its growth to a breaking point: lawlessness became so prevalent that the city was referred to as "Los Diablos."

The railroads brought a tidal wave of new settlers in 1886. By 1890, a land boom developed and the population reached 50,000, with oil derricks appearing everywhere. The piping in of water from the Owens Valley in 1913 paved the way for expansion. Between 1890 and 1940, the city grew from 50,395 to 1,504,277 residents—a gain of more than 2,000 percent. The war years added new industries and brought new waves of population that continued throughout the 1980s. Currently, the city's economic assets are invested in growth industries such as electronics, machinery, chemicals, oil, printing, publishing, tourism and of course, entertainment.

Today, Los Angeles occupies 463 square miles and has spilled over into the canyons and foothills. The city limits are twisting and confusing, as the city is spread around the communities of Beverly Hills, Santa Monica, Culver City, Universal City and Inglewood. The geographic scope makes it almost essential that visitors drive their own car for sightseeing in areas other than the downtown section and Westwood.

The city is also very diverse and eclectic. It's glamorous and exciting but also laid-back, thanks to the Mediterranean climate, which encourages a general informality. (The dress code is very casual.) There's a mix of sun and smog, big mansions and tiny cottages, small windy roads and superhighways clogged with traffic. There are also numerous libraries, museums and art galleries.

Information: Convention and Visitors Bureau, 685 S. Figueroa St., 213-624-7300; www.lacvb.com

*THE FIRST MOTION PICTURE THEATER OPENED IN LOS ANGELES ON APRIL 2, 1902.

*IF THE LOS ANGELES AREA WERE A STATE, IT WOULD BE THE FOURTH MOST POPULOUS IN THE COUNTRY.

Los Angeles Dodgers (MLB)
Dodger Stadium, 1000 Elysian Park Ave.,
Los Angeles, 323-224-1500;
www.dodgers.com
Professional baseball team.

Los Angeles Farmers' Market
6333 W. Third St., Los Angeles,
323-933-9211;
www.farmersmarketla.com
A much-loved part of the city since 1934, the market includes 70 shops, most of which are owner-operated. Monday-Friday 9 a.m.-9 p.m., Saturday 9 a.m.-8 p.m., Sunday 10 a.m.-7 p.m.

Los Angeles Fashion District
Fifth and San Pedro Streets,
Los Angeles, 213-488-1153;
www.fashiondistrict.org
Stylists and costume designers shop here for deals. Every Saturday, half of the nearly 2,000 wholesalers in this 82-block district sell their samples and extras to the public at prices 40 to 70 percent off retail. More than 200 wholesalers are always open to the public. Also be sure to check out the buys in Santee Alley, an open-air bazaar where items like prom dresses are priced as low as $20.

Los Angeles Galaxy (MLS)
Home Depot Center, 18400 Avalon Blvd.,
Carson, 877-342-5299;
www.lagalaxy.com
Calling all David Beckham fans. See the English soccer star play with the L.A. Galaxy at the Home Depot center.

Los Angeles Kings (NHL)
Staples Center, 1111 S. Figueroa St.,
Los Angeles, 888-546-4752;
www.lakings.com
Professional hockey team.

Los Angeles Lakers (NBA)
Staples Center, 1111 S. Figueroa St.,
Los Angeles, 213-742-7333;
www.nba.com/lakers
Professional basketball team.

Los Angeles Sparks (WNBA)
Staples Center, 1111 S. Figueroa St.,
Los Angeles, 310-426-6031;
www.wnba.com/sparks
Women's professional basketball team.

Lummis Home and Garden State Historical Monument
200 E. Ave. 43, Los Angeles,
323-222-0546
Charles Lummis, the noted writer, photographer, historian and archaeologist, spent 14 years (1896-1910) building this L-shaped house of concrete and granite boulders. One look at this residential piece of art, now the headquarters for the Historical Society of Southern California, conjures thoughts of this eccentric man's keen interest in pueblos and missions (he founded the Southwest Museum). Lummis named the house El Elisal, the Spanish word for sycamore, after the large tree that once grew beside it. Many drought-tolerant plants native to Southern California flourish in the gardens, offering a lesson in regional horticulture. Tours, Friday-Sunday noon-4 p.m.

Museum of Contemporary Art (MOCA)
250 S. Grand Ave.,Los Angeles,
213-621-1741; www.moca.org
This gorgeous tribute to current art focuses solely on works from the 1940s to the present. See pieces by John Baldessari, Lee Krasner, Jackson Pollock, Andy Warhol and many other distinguished artists. Monday, Friday 11 a.m.-5 p.m., Thursday to 8 p.m., Saturday-Sunday to 6 p.m. Free admission on Thursday.

Music Center of Los Angeles County
135 N. Grand Ave., Los Angeles,
213-972-7211
The Music Center in downtown Los Angeles include four separate venues: the Dorothy Chandler Pavilion, the Ahmanson Theater, the Mark Taper Forum and the new Frank Gehry-designed Walt Disney Concert Hall. This is home to the Los Angeles Philharmonic, the Los Angeles Opera, the Los Angeles Master Chorale and the Center

23

SOUTHERN CALIFORNIA

Theatre Group. Tours of the Walt Disney Concert Hall are available.

Museum of Tolerance
Simon Wiesenthal Center, 9786 W. Pico Blvd., Los Angeles, 310-553-8403; www.museumoftolerance.com
Opened in 1993, the museum uses interactive exhibits and film to engage visitors' minds. Nibble on controversial topics in the "Point of View" diner, experience human rights violations around the world in the "Millenium Machine" and read original letters written by Anne Frank in the Holocaust section. Monday-Thursday 11:30 a.m.-6:30 p.m.; Friday 11:30 a.m.-5 p.m., until 3 p.m. November-March; Sunday 11 a.m.-7:30 p.m.

Natural History Museum of Los Angeles County
900 Exposition Blvd., Los Angeles, 213-763-3466; www.nhm.org
Permanent science exhibits feature mammal, bird, insect and marine life, as well as dinosaurs and other prehistoric fossils. The minerals and metals display includes an extensive collection of cut gems. Docent tours (one tour every afternoon except first Tuesday of each month, when you can tour by yourself for free). Monday-Friday 9:30 a.m.-5 p.m., Saturday-Sunday from 10 a.m.

Page Museum at the La Brea Tar Pits
5801 Wilshire Blvd., Los Angeles, 323-934-7243; www.tarpits.org
Get a glimpse of the kinds of saber-toothed cats and mammoths that lived in Los Angeles 10,000 to 40,000 years ago. In the past century, more than a million bones have been removed from these tar pits, which still spurt out eight to 12 gallons of hot asphalt each day. Monday-Friday 9:30 a.m.-5 p.m., Saturday-Sunday from 10 a.m. Free admission the first Tuesday of each month.

Petersen Automotive Museum
6060 Wilshire Blvd., Los Angeles, 323-930-2277; www.petersen.org
Dedicated to the history and cultural impact of the automobile, this museum contains more than 150 rare and classic vehicles, from Ford Model Ts and vintage motorcycles to muscle cars and movie wheels, like Fred Flinstone's Rockmobile. - Daily.

Old Plaza Firehouse
134 Paseo de la Plaza, Los Angeles, 231-625-3741
Built as Los Angeles's first firehouse in 1884, it's now a museum with photographs and firefighting equipment from the 19th century. Tuesday-Sunday.

Rancho Park Golf Club
10460 W. Pico Blvd., Los Angeles, 310-839-9812; www.rpgc.org
This challenging course is beautiful in the fall, since its fairways are lined with tall oaks.

Rustic Canyon Golf Course
15100 Happy Camp Canyon Rd., Moorpark, 805-530-0221; www.rusticcanyongolfcourse.com
Interesting features include a natural alley to the 16th green and swales of up to four feet on greens, including numbers six and nine. The greens have a tendency to be shaped uniquely, like a boomerang or with bunkers covering just one side, forcing players to be inventive and courageous to reach them in regulation. All this for less than $50 a round makes it one of the best courses in the Los Angeles area.

San Antonio Winery
737 Lamar St., Los Angeles, 323-223-1401; www.sanantoniowinery.com
Winery, gift shop, wine tasting; restaurant. Self-guided tours. Daily.

Sepulveda House
622 N. Main St., Los Angeles, 213-628-1274
(1887) Partially restored Victorian business block; also houses a visitor center . Monday-Saturday 10 a.m.-3 p.m.

Sony Pictures Studio Tour
10202 W. Washington Blvd., Culver City, 310-520-8687

★
★
★
☆
☆

This storied lot used to be MGM Studios, where Louis B. Mayer, one of Hollywood's most feared bosses, was once head and where movie legends Judy Garland and Clark Gable filmed the *The Wizard of Oz* and *Gone with the Wind* respectively. Sony has owned the lot since 1989 and it's now home to Columbia Pictures and Columbia Tri Star, which produces popular television shows such as *Jeopardy!* and *Wheel of Fortune*. The two-hour tour includes visits to sets. Monday-Friday. Photo ID required for entrance.

South Coast Botanic Garden
26300 Crenshaw Blvd.,
Palos Verdes Peninsula, 310-544-6815
Hillside and coastal plants on 87 acres. Daily 9 a.m.-5 p.m.

Southwest Museum
234 Museum Dr., Los Angeles,
323-221-2164;
www.southwestmuseum.org
Learn all about Native American life at the oldest museum in Los Angeles (1907). See a Cheyenne tepee, prehistoric painted pottery and basketry and more. The museum recently merged with the Autry Museum of Western Heritage, forming the Autry National Center of the American West, which also includes the Institute for the Study of the American West. Tuesday-Sunday 10 a.m.-5 p.m.

Tijeras Creek Golf Club
29082 Tijeras Creek, Rancho Santa Margarita, 949-589-9793;
www.tijerascreek.com
Located in the suburb of Rancho Santa Margarita in northern Orange County. Like many other courses in the area, Tijeras Creek is set in a gradually sloping canyon, which makes for a challenging and fun course. Hole 16, a 172-yard par-three, requires a shot over water to a green guarded by bunkers and deep rough.

UCLA Mildred Mathias Botanical Garden
Hilgard and Le Conte Aves., Los Angeles,
310-825-1260; www.botgard.ucla.edu
Collection of plants, trees and shrubs. Monday-Friday 8 a.m.-5 p.m., Saturday-Sunday to 4 p.m.

University of California, Los Angeles (UCLA)
405 Hilgard Ave., Los Angeles,
310-825-4321; www.ucla.edu
Tours Monday-Friday. Art gallery, botanical garden, Franklin D. Murphy Sculpture Garden.

University of Southern California
Los Angeles, 213-740-2311; www.usc.edu
(1880) The oldest and largest private university in the Western United States.

Walt Disney Concert Hall
111 S. Grand Ave., Los Angeles,
323-850-2000; wdch.laphil.com

This striking 293,000-square-foot facility designed by Frank Gehry is home to the Los Angeles Philharmonic Orchestra and hosts other noted ensembles and orchestras from around the world. The main auditorium seats 2,265 people. Includes two outdoor amphitheaters as well as an inviting urban park with lush public gardens and ornamental landscaping. .

Watts Towers
1765 E. 107th St., Los Angeles,
213-847-4646; www.parks.ca.gov
In 1921, Italian immigrant Simon Rodia began building what are now known as the Watts Towers around his house in Los Angeles. Using steel rods and concrete and decorating the towers (the tallest of which stands at almost 100 feet) with pieces of broken glass and ceramics, it took Rodia 33 years to construct this masterpiece of folk art. Tuesday-Friday 11 a.m.-2:30 p.m., Saturday 10:30 a.m.-2:30 p.m., Sunday 12:30-3 p.m.; closed Monday, rainy days.

Westfield Shoppingtown Century City
10250 Santa Monica Blvd.,
Los Angeles, 310-277-3898;
www.westfield.com/centurycity
This high-end outdoor shopping mall includes 141 shops (Bloomingdale's, Crate and Barrel) and restaurants (Johnny Rocket's). Movie theater. Monday-Saturday 10 a.m.-9 p.m., Sunday 11 a.m.-6 p.m.

Westside Pavilion
10800 W. Pico Blvd., Los Angeles,
310-474-6255; www.westsidepavilion.com
Located in the prestigious Westside community, this three-level, glass-ceiling mall was the hangout for the well-to-do shop-a-holics in the movie *Clueless*. The movie theater usually features a selection of flicks that lean toward the artsy. Monday-Friday 10 a.m.-9 p.m., Saturday 10 a.m.-8 p.m., Sunday 11 a.m.-6 p.m.

SPECIAL EVENTS
Chinese New Year Festival
Los Angeles;
www.lagoldendragonparade.com

Two weeks of festivities, usually in late January or early February, including the annual Golden Dragon Parade, the Miss Los Angeles Chinatown Pageant and the Chinese New Year Banquet.

Cinco de Mayo Celebration
El Pueblo de Los Angeles Historic Monument
Known to attract even more celebrants than Mexico City, Los Angeles hosts numerous public festivals in honor of the Mexican victory at the Battle of Puebla. The party starts the last Sunday in April with the downtown Fiesta Broadway festival and continues on May 2 on historic Olvera Street, with a free three-day celebration that includes traditional music, dance, food and live entertainment.

Fiesta Broadway
Downtown, Los Angeles,
310-914-0015;
www.fiestabroadway.la
Given its large Latino population, Los Angeles observes Cinco de Mayo in a big way, with rousing celebrations throughout the area. The largest of the parties, Fiesta Broadway, kicks off the festivities each year on the Sunday before May 5th. More than 500,000 people crowd into 36 blocks of downtown to celebrate with top-name Latin entertainment and plenty of south-of-the-border food.

Hollywood Christmas Parade
11904 Long Beach Blvd., Lynwood,
310-631-0691
Features floats, marching bands and more than 50 of Hollywood's famous stars. Televised worldwide. Sunday after Thanks-giving.

Los Angeles Opera
Music Center of Los Angeles County, Dorothy Chandler Pavilion, 135 N. Grand Ave.,
Los Angeles, 213-972-8001;
www.losangelesopera.com
Directed by Placido Domingo and conducted by Maestro Kent Nagano, the LosAngeles Opera has hosted several world premiere productions. Early September-June.

SOUTHERN CALIFORNIA

Lotus Festival

Echo Park Lake, 751 Echo Park Ave.,
Los Angeles, www.laparks.org

Celebrates various Asian and Pacific island cultures. Mid-July.

Nisei Week

Little Tokyo, 244 S. San Pedro St.,
Los Angeles,
213-687-7193;
www.niseiweek.org

First held in 1934, Nisei Week is one of the oldest Japanese-American festivals in the country. Commencing with the crowning of the queen at the coronation ball, the festival features a variety of sporting and martial arts events, stage performances, a 5k run and parade. August.

HOTELS

★★Best Western Carlyle Inn

1119 S. Robertson Blvd.,
Los Angeles,
310-275-4445, 800-322-7595;
www.carlyle-inn.com

32 rooms. Complimentary full breakfast. Wireless Internet access. Whirlpool. $

★Best Western Eagle Rock Inn

2911 Colorado Blvd., Los Angeles,
323-256-7711, 888-255-7970;
www.bestwestern.com

49 rooms. Complimentary continental breakfast. High-speed Internet access. Pool. $

★★Courtyard by Marriott

10320 W. Olympic Blvd., Los Angeles,
310-556-2777, 800-321-2211;
www.courtyard.com

135 rooms. High-speed Internet access. Restaurant, bar. Fitness center. $$

★★Courtyard Los Angeles Century City/ Beverly Hills

6161 W. Century Blvd., Los Angeles,
310-649-1400, 800-321-2211;
www.courtyard.com

178 rooms. High-speed Internet access. Restaurant, bar. Airport transportation available. Airport. Fitness center. $$

★★★Hilton Checkers Los Angeles

535 S. Grand Ave., Los Angeles,
213-624-0000, 800-445-8667;
www.hiltoncheckers.com

Restored to its 1920s splendor, this downtown landmark features luxury bedding, flat-screen TVs and marble bathrooms. The rooftop pool is a great place to get away from it all. Located in the financial district, the hotel is within walking distance of restaurants, theaters and the Staples center.

188 rooms. High-speed Internet access. Restaurant, bar. Spa. Pool. $$$

★★★★★Hotel Bel-Air

701 Stone Canyon Rd., Los Angeles,
310-472-1211, 888-897-2804;
www.hotelbelair.com

Amenities are plentiful at this timeless hotel situated close to the action of Los Angeles, yet far enough to transport guests to a romantic world dotted with intimate courtyards, fountains and the Bel-Air's signature Swan Lake. Guest rooms are spread throughout the 12-acre grounds, giving visitors privacy as they enjoy a well-equipped fitness center or the luxurious pool. Gourmands will enjoy the in-kitchen dining experience of Table One as well as the enchanting garden setting of the Terrace.

91 rooms. Pets accepted, some restrictions; fee. Wireless Internet access. Restaurant, bar. Pets accepted. Fitness center. Pool. Business center. $$$$

★★★Hyatt Regency Century Plaza

2025 Ave. of the Stars, Los Angeles,
310-228-1234, 888-591-1234;
www.hyatt.com

Enveloped by lush tropical gardens, the guest rooms at this contemporary hotel have balconies with views of the Los Angeles cityscape and the tree-lined boulevards of Beverly Hills. Rooms are decorated in warm tones with Asian accents, leather headboards and striking light fixtures. Be sure to fit in a treatment at the Spa Mystique, which uses feng shui design principles in its 27 treatment rooms and four outdoor cabanas.

726 rooms. Restaurant, two bars. Fitness classes available. Pets accepted. Pool. $$$

SOUTHERN CALIFORNIA

★
★
★
★
★

★★★InterContinental Los Angeles Century City

2151 Ave. of the Stars, Los Angeles, 310-284-6500, 877-348-2424; www.intercontinental.com

Though largely a business hotel, the Inter-Continental makes a great getaway, too, thanks to an indoor pool, outdoor sun deck, complimentary limo service to nearby Rodeo Drive shops and a concierge who will arrange golf outings at several area courses.

363 rooms. High-speed wireless Internet access. Restaurant, bar. Spa. Pool. Fitness center. $$$

★★★Luxe Hotel Sunset Boulevard

11461 W. Sunset Blvd., Los Angeles, 310-476-6571, 866-589-3411; www.luxehotels.com

A golf cart transports guests between buildings on the beautifully-landscaped grounds, and the contemporary rooms come with many conveniences, including a base station for an iPod next to the bed. Another cool feature: blackout curtains.

164 rooms. Restaurant, bar. Airport transportation available. Pets accepted. Fitness center. Pool. Tennis. $$

★★★Marriott Los Angeles Downtown

333 S. Figueroa St., Los Angeles, 213-617-1133, 800-228-9290; www.marriott.com

Connected to the World Trade Center by skywalk, the spacious rooms and suites at this hotel have floor-to-ceiling windows and are fully wired for business travelers.

469 rooms. Wireless Internet access. Three restaurants, bar. Fitness center. $$

★★★Millennium Biltmore Hotel Los Angeles

506 S. Grand Ave., Los Angeles, 213-624-1011, 800-245-8673; www.millenniumhotels.com

Built in 1923, this bar at this hotel's signature cocktail, the Black Dahlia, pays homage to the mysteriously murdered starlet who was last sighted here. The frescoes, decorative pillars and chandeliers transport guests into the past, as does the Roman-style tiled swimming pool.

682 rooms. High-speed Internet access. Two restaurants, two bars. $$

★★★New Otani Hotel & Garden

120 S. Los Angeles St., Los Angeles, 213-629-1200, 800-639-6826; www.newotanihotels.com

On the edge of Little Tokyo, this high-rise hotel with a tranquil plant-filled two-story lobby and manicured Japanese roof garden offers some traditional Japanese rooms with sunken futons and tatami mats. There are also rooms with traditional beds. Hit the health spa for a shiatsu massage and belt out karaoke in the bar.

434 rooms. High-speed Internet access. Three restaurants, two bars. Fitness center. $

★★★Omni Los Angeles Hotel at California Plaza

251 S. Olive St., Los Angeles, 213-617-3300; www.omnihotels.com

Kids love the Kids' Fantasy Suite, with bunkbeds, a bean bag chair and more toys than they'll know what to do with—parents can relax in the adjoining room. This comfortable hotel sits on Bunker Hill, next to the Museum of Contemporary Art.

453 rooms. Wireless Internet access. Two restaurants, bar. Spa. Pets accepted. Pool. $$

★★★The Orlando

8384 W. Third St., Los Angeles, 323-658-6600, 800-624-6836; www.theorlando.com

This hip, European boutique-style hotel recently underwent a $6 million renovation. All of the rooms feature iPod docking stations, in-room laptop safes, 400 thread-count Egyptian cotton linens, cotton robes, gourmet honor bars, coffeemakers with the hotel's special blend of coffee, 30" plasma screen TVs and gourmet chocolate truffles with turndown service. The new executive garden rooms also sport outdoor private patios, Bulgari bath products and taxi vouchers. iPods and DVD players are available for rent at the front desk. Activities

★
★
★
★
★

include an outdoor saltwater swimming pool and two dry saunas. The hotel's restaurant, LaTerza, provides a complimentary European breakfast buffet.

98 rooms. Pets accepted, some restrictions. Restaurant, bar. **$$**

★★★Renaissance Montura Hotel
9620 Airport Blvd., Los Angeles,
310-337-2800, 800-468-3571;
www.renaissancelosangeles.com

Located one half mile from Los Angeles International Airport and convenient to freeways, the vast art collection here isn't typical of an airport hotel. Neither are the newly remodeled ultra-contemporary rooms, which look more like they belong in Hollywood than near LAX.

499 rooms. High-speed wireless Internet access. Restaurant, bar. Airport shuttle. Pets accepted. Fitness center. Pool. **$$**

★★★Sheraton Gateway Hotel Los Angeles Airport
6101 W. Century Blvd., Los Angeles,
310-642-1111, 800-325-3535;
www.sheratonlosangeles.com

Stylishly redesigned in black, white and gray, those seeking a refuge from the airport won't be disappointed with this contemporary hotel. The spacious rooms are outfitted with custom pillow-top mattresses, fleece blankets and extra-fluffy pillows.

802 rooms. High-speed Internet access. Two restaurants, two bars. Airport transportation available. Pool. **$$$**

★★★Sheraton Los Angeles Downtown Hotel
711 S. Hope St., Los Angeles,
213-488-3500;
www.sheraton.com/losangeles

This contemporary business and convention hotel is adjacent to LA Live, the new sports and entertainment destination. It's also within walking distance of the Los Angeles Convention center. A Metro station is next door, or rent a car on-site. Guest rooms feature Sweet Sleeper beds.

485 rooms. High-speed Internet access. Two restaurants, bar. Pets accepted. **$**

★★★Sofitel Los Angeles
8555 Beverly Blvd., Los Angeles,
310-278-5444, 800-763-4835;
www.sofitel.com

Fresh from a multi-million dollar renovation in 2006, this European-style hotel across from the Beverly Center includes comfy rooms with rain showers and fresh flowers. Two trendy restaurants top off the experience. Free shuttle service to the airport and Union Station is available.

297 rooms, all suites. High-speed Internet access. Restaurants, bar. Pets accepted. Pool. **$$$**

★★★W Los Angeles Westwood
930 Hilgard Ave.,
Los Angeles,
310-208-8765; www.whotel.com

People stay at the W for the cool minimalist boutique-hotel ambience. Locals come to sip cocktails at Whiskey Blue or to savor Latin fusion cuisine at Mojo.

257 rooms. High-speed Internet access. Restaurant, bar. Spa. Pets accepted. **$$**

★★★Westin Los Angeles Airport
5400 W. Century Blvd., Los Angeles,
310-216-5858, 800-937-8461;
www.westin.com/losangelesairport

Located just four blocks from Los Angeles International Airport, all guest rooms feature Westin's signature Heavenly Beds with pillow-top mattresses and down blankets. Many include fax machines, printers and high-speed Internet access. The hotel also offers a heated outdoor pool, a well-equipped weight room and concierge service. A kid's club provides coloring books, bath toys and a phone line dedicated to bedtime stories. Pets are welcomed with their own amenities and bed.

740 rooms. High-speed Internet access. Restaurant, bar. Airport transportation available. Airport. **$$**

RESTAURANTS
★★A.O.C.
8022 W. Third St., Los Angeles,
323-653-6359;
www.aocwinebar.com

★
★
★
★
★

Tapas menu. Dinner. Bar. Business casual attire. Reservations recommended. Valet parking. Outdoor seating. **$$$**

★★ABC Seafood
205 Ord St., Los Angeles,
213-680-2887
Seafood menu. Lunch, dinner. Casual attire. **$**

★Alegria on Sunset
3510 W. Sunset Blvd., Los Angeles,
323-913-1422;
www.alegriaonsunset.com
California, Mexican menu. Breakfast, lunch, dinner. Closed Sunday. Children's menu. Casual attire. Outdoor seating. **$**

★★Angeli Caffe
7274 Melrose Ave., Los Angeles,
323-936-9086; www.angelicaffe.com
Italian menu. Lunch, dinner. Bar. Casual attire. **$$**

★★Angelini Osteria
7313 Beverly Blvd., Los Angeles,
323-297-0070; www.angeliniosteria.com
Italian menu. Lunch, dinner. Casual attire. Reservations recommended. Outdoor seating. **$$$**

★Anna's
10929 W. Pico Blvd., Los Angeles,
310-474-0102; www.annaitalian.com
Italian menu. Lunch, dinner. Bar. Casual attire. Reservations recommended. Valet parking. **$$**

★The Apple Pan
10801 W. Pico Blvd., Los Angeles,
310-475-3585.
American menu. Lunch, dinner. Closed Monday. Casual attire. **$**

★★Ca'Brea
346 S. La Brea Ave., Los Angeles,
323-938-2863; www.cabrearestaurant.com
Italian menu. Lunch, dinner. Bar. Casual attire. Reservations recommended. Valet parking. **$$$**

★Cafe Brazil
10831 Venice Blvd., Los Angeles,
310-837-8957
Latin American, Brazilian menu. Lunch, dinner. Bar. Casual attire. Outdoor seating. **$**

★★★Cafe Pinot
700 W. Fifth St., Los Angeles,
213-239-6500;
www.patinagroup.com/cafepinot
With its garden setting and city views, Cafe Pinot offers a little romance amid the downtown business setting, which is largely void of quality eateries. The California fare showcases seafood and is a popular destination for theatergoers.
California menu. Lunch, dinner. Bar. Business casual attire. Reservations recommended. Valet parking. Outdoor seating. **$$**

★Cafe Stella
3932 W. Sunset Blvd., Los Angeles,
323-666-0265
French menu. Dinner. Closed Sunday-Monday. Casual attire. Reservations recommended. Outdoor seating. **$$**

★★★Campanile
624 S. La Brea Ave., Los Angeles,
323-938-1447;
www.campanilerestaurant.com
Chefs Mark Peel and Nancy Silverton have scaled culinary highs with Campanile, a California-Mediterranean restaurant that has received many awards. Built by Charlie Chaplin in 1929, the building was adapted in 1989 to house both the restaurant and La Brea Bakery. The menu changes frequently, but always relies on seasonal ingredients in dishes such as dandelion salad, battered soft-shell crab, charred baby lamb and seared spot prawns. Red-tile floors, a fountain and a sky-lit atrium in the dining room all add to a setting reminiscent of an old Mediterranean village. The casual dining area faces the open kitchen, and the formal dining area is in the back. Come Monday night for convivial family-style dinners and

SOUTHERN CALIFORNIA

Thursdays for sandwiches on bread from the bakery.

California, Mediterranean menu. Lunch, dinner. Bar. Business casual attire. Reservations recommended. Valet parking. **$$$**

★Canter's Delicatessen
419 N. Fairfax Ave., Los Angeles, 323-651-2030; www.cantersdeli.com
Deli menu. Breakfast, lunch, dinner, late-night. Bar. Children's menu. Casual attire. **$$**

★Casa Bianca Pizza Pie
1650 Colorado Blvd., Los Angeles, 90041, 323-256-9617.
Pizza. Dinner. Closed Sunday-Monday. Bar. Children's menu. Casual attire. **$**

★★Charisma Cafe
5400 W. Century Blvd., Los Angeles, 310-216-5858
American menu. Breakfast, lunch, dinner, brunch. Bar. Children's menu. Casual attire. Reservations recommended. Valet parking. **$$**

★★Ciao Trattoria
815 W. Seventh St., Los Angeles, 213-624-2244; www.ciaotrattoria.com
Italian menu. Lunch, dinner. Closed Sunday. Bar. Casual attire. Reservations recommended. Valet parking. **$$**

★★Cicada
617 S. Olive St., Los Angeles, 213-488-9488; www.cicadarestaurant.com
Italian menu. Lunch, dinner. Closed Sunday. Bar. Business casual attire. Reservations recommended. Valet parking. **$$$**

★★Ciudad
445 S. Figueroa St., Los Angeles, 213-486-5171; www.ciudad-la.com
Latin menu. Lunch, dinner. Bar. Children's menu. Casual attire. Outdoor seating. **$$$**

★★Cobras & Matadors
7615 W. Beverly Blvd., Los Angeles, 323-932-6178

Spanish, tapas menu. Dinner. Casual attire. Reservations recommended. **$$**

★Dan Tana's
9071 Santa Monica Blvd., Los Angeles, 310-275-9444
Italian menu. Dinner. Bar. Casual attire. Reservations recommended. Valet parking. **$$$**

★★Dolce Enoteca e Ristorante
8284 Melrose Ave., Los Angeles, 323-852-7174; www.dolceenoteca.com
Italian menu. Dinner. Bar. Casual attire. Reservations recommended. Valet parking. Outdoor seating. **$$$**

★★El Cholo
1121 S. Western Ave., Los Angeles, 323-734-2773; www.elcholo.com
Mexican menu. Lunch, dinner. Bar. Casual attire. Reservations recommended. Valet parking. **$$**

★El Coyote
7312 Beverly Blvd., Los Angeles, 323-939-2255; www.elcoyotecafe.com
Mexican menu. Lunch, dinner. Bar. Heated patio. Children's menu. Casual attire. Valet parking. **$$**

★★Engine Co. No. 28
644 S. Figueroa St., Los Angeles, 213-624-6996; www.engineco.com
American menu. Lunch, dinner. Bar. Casual attire. Reservations recommended. Valet parking (dinner). **$$**

★Fred 62
1850 N. Vermont Ave., Los Angeles, 323-667-0062; www.fred62.com
American menu. Breakfast, lunch, dinner, late-night. **$$**

★★★Grace
7360 Beverly Blvd., Los Angeles, 323-934-4400; www.gracerestaurant.net
Neal Fraser is the new darling of Los Angeles' dining scene with his original take on contemporary American cuisine. The

sexy dining room is appointed with orchids floating in vases, massive fish-eyed mirrors and chandeliers that seem to drip with seashells. The kitchen delivers excellent cuisine like pumpkin and sea urchin risotto and skate in a raisin-caper emulsion. Entrées such as bacon-wrapped saddle of rabbit and wild boar with violet mustard sauce impress even the toughest food critics. Come on a Wednesday to enjoy pastry chef Mariah Swan's doughnuts filled with butterscotch. Sundays are burger nights.

American menu. Dinner. Closed Monday. Bar. Business casual attire. Reservations recommended. Valet parking. **$$$**

★★Guelaguetza
3337 1/2 W. Eighth St., Inolo,
213-427-0601
Mexican menu. Breakfast, lunch, dinner. Bar. Casual attire. **$**

★★HamaSaku
11043 Santa Monica Blvd., Los Angeles,
310-479-7636; www.hamasakula.com
Japanese menu. Lunch, dinner. Closed Sunday. Casual attire. Reservations recommended. Valet parking. Outdoor seating. **$$$**

★Hide Sushi
2040 Sawtelle Blvd., Los Angeles,
310-477-7242
Japanese, sushi menu. Lunch, dinner. Closed Monday. Casual attire. No credit cards accepted. Valet parking. **$$**

★★Il Fornaio
301 N. Beverly Dr., Los Angeles,
310-550-8330; www.ilfornaio.com
Italian menu. Breakfast, lunch, dinner. Bar. Children's menu. Casual attire. Valet parking. Outdoor seating. **$$$**

★★The Ivy
113 N. Robertson Blvd.,
Los Angeles, 310-274-8303
California menu. Lunch, dinner. Casual attire. Reservations recommended. Valet parking. Outdoor seating. **$$$**

★★★Jar
8225 Beverly Blvd., Los Angeles,
323-655-6566; www.thejar.com
Chef Susan Tracht (formerly of Campanile) serves up retro dishes like pot roast, Kansas City Steak and deviled eggs at this modern version of a 1940s Supper Club near the Beverly center.

Steak menu. Dinner. Bar. Business casual attire. Reservations recommended. Valet parking. **$$$**

★★★Katana
8439 W. Sunset Blvd., Los Angeles,
323-650-8585; www.sushiroku.com
In the middle of the Sunset Strip, this modern Japanese eatery is lavishly adorned with hammered metal, roughly hewn stone and flickering, floating candles. The open kitchen seems to employ an army of chefs carving up flawless sashimi and grilling robata-yaki skewered meats like soy garlic lamb chops and king crab legs over a charcoal grill.

Japanese menu. Dinner. Bar. Business casual attire. Reservations recommended. Valet parking. Outdoor seating. **$$$**

★The Kitchen
4348 Fountain Ave.,
Los Angeles, 90029,
323-664-3663.
American menu. Lunch, dinner, late-night. Casual attire. Outdoor seating. **$$**

★★★Koi
730 N. La Cienega Blvd., Los Angeles,
310-659-9449; www.koirestaurant.com
This famous launching spot for Hollywood club-goers is renowned for unusual dishes, such as a baked crab roll in soy paper and spicy tuna on crispy fried rice. Bamboo terraces are reminiscent of an exotic resort, while the inner dining room's low lights, red walls and fireplaces flatter the stunning crowd.

Japanese menu. Dinner. Bar. Business casual attire. Reservations recommended. Valet parking. Outdoor seating. **$$$$**

★★Koutoubia
2116 Westwood Blvd.,
Los Angeles, 310-475-0729;
www.koutoubiarestaurant.com
Moroccan menu. Dinner. Closed Monday.
Bar. Children's menu. Casual attire. Out-
door seating. **$$$**

★La Brea Bakery
624 S. La Brea Ave., Los Angeles,
323-939-6813; www.labreabakery.com
Sandwiches, bakery. Breakfast, lunch, din-
ner. Casual attire. Outdoor seating. **$**

★★La Cachette
10506 Santa Monica Blvd.,
Los Angeles, 310-470-4992;
www.lacachetterestaurant.com
French menu. Lunch, dinner. Bar. Casual
attire. **$$$**

★★La Paella
476 S. San Vicente Blvd.,
Los Angeles, 323-951-0745
Spanish, tapas menu. Lunch, dinner. Closed
Sunday. Bar. Casual attire. **$$**

★La Serenata de Garibaldi
1842 E. First St., Los Angeles,
323-265-2887;
www.laserenataonline.com
Mexican menu. Lunch, dinner. **$$**

★★La Serenata Gourmet
10924 W. Pico Blvd.,
Los Angeles, 310-441-9667
Mexican menu. Lunch, dinner. Bar. Casual
attire. Reservations recommended. Outdoor
seating. **$$**

★★Locanda Veneta
8638 W. Third St., Los Angeles,
310-274-1893;
www.locandaveneta.com
Italian menu. Lunch, dinner. Casual attire.
Reservations recommended. Valet parking.
Outdoor seating. **$$$**

★Loteria Grill
6333 W. Third St., Los Angeles,
323-930-2211; www.loteriagrill.com

This Mexican menu. Breakfast, lunch,
dinner. Casual attire. Outdoor seating. No
credit cards accepted. **$**

★Luna Park
672 S. La Brea Ave.,
Los Angeles, 323-934-2110;
www.lunaparkla.com
American menu. Lunch, dinner, brunch.
Closed holidays. Bar. Casual attire. **$$**

★Mexico City
2121 Hillhurst Ave., Los Angeles,
323-661-7227
Mexican menu. Lunch, dinner. Children's
menu. Casual attire. **$$**

★★Mimosa
8009 Beverly Blvd., Los Angeles,
323-655-8895;
www.mimosarestaurant.com
French bistro menu. Dinner. Closed Sunday-
Monday. Casual attire. Reservations recom-
mended. Valet parking. Outdoor seating. **$$**

★★Mori Sushi
11500 W. Pico Blvd., Los Angeles,
310-479-3939
Japanese menu. Lunch, dinner. Casual
attire. **$$**

★★Musso & Frank Grill
6667 Hollywood Blvd., Los Angeles,
323-467-5123
American menu. Lunch, dinner. Closed
Sunday-Monday. Bar. **$$$**

★★Nick & Stef's
330 S. Hope St., Los Angeles,
213-680-0330;
www.patinagroup.com/nickstef
Steak menu. Lunch, dinner. Bar. Children's
menu. Casual attire. Reservations recom-
mended. Valet parking. Outdoor seating.
$$$

★★Nyala
1076 S. Fairfax Ave., Los Angeles,
323-936-5918; www.nyala-la.com
Middle Eastern menu. Lunch, dinner. Bar.
Casual attire. **$$**

★**The Original Pantry**

877 S. Figueroa St., Los Angeles,
213-972-9279

American menu. Breakfast, lunch, dinner, brunch. Casual attire. No credit cards accepted. **$**

★★★★**Ortolan**

8338 W. Third St., Los Angeles,
323-653-3300;
www.ortolanrestaurant.com

French chef Christophe Eme, formerly of L'Orangerie, has ventured out on his own with Ortolan (named for a small song-bird) and created an exquisite menu that blends classic French style with contemporary elements. Signature dishes include crispy langoustines with basil, chickpeas and minestrone, and roasted squab breast and leg with a gratin of macaroni and tapenade salad. The modernized provincial atmosphere, with cream-colored booth and banquettes, floor-to-ceiling velvet drapes, crystal chandeliers and antique mirrors, is equally dazzling.

French menu. Dinner. Closed Sunday. Bar. Business casual attire. Valet parking. **$$$**

★★**Pacific Dining Car**

1310 W. Sixth St.,
Los Angeles, 213-483-6000;
www.pacificdiningcar.com

Steak menu. Breakfast, lunch, dinner, late-night. Bar. Children's menu. Casual attire. Reservations recommended. Valet parking. **$$$**

★**Pampas Grill**

6333 W. Third St., Los Angeles,
323-931-1928

Latin American menu. Lunch, dinner. Casual attire. Outdoor seating. No credit cards accepted. **$**

★★★★**Patina**

141 S. Grand Ave., Los Angeles,
213-972-3331;
www.patinagroup.com/patina/

Celebrity chef Joachim Splichal's French-California cooking, interpreted here by executive chef Theo Schoenegger, celebrates local and regionally sourced foods in dishes such as foie gras with Ranier cherry jam, salmon with heirloom tomatoes, and olive-oil poached squab with truffles from Umbria. The polished dining room, with walnut-paneled walls and curved ceilings, echoes the hall itself, prepping concertgoers for events. Make a night of it by reserving the kitchen table and indulging in a six-course market tasting menu. The bar serves nibbles and drinks after performances, and a lunch menu caters to tourists visiting the hall, as well as the downtown business crowd.

California menu. Lunch, dinner. Bar. Business casual attire. Reservations recommended. Valet parking. Outdoor seating. **$$$**

★★**Pecorino**

11604 San Vicente Blvd., Brentwood,
310-571-3800;
www.pecorinorestaurant.com

Italian menu. Lunch, dinner. Bar. Casual attire. Reservations recommended. Valet parking. **$$**

★**Philippe the Original**

1001 N. Alameda St., Los Angeles,
213-628-3781;
www.philippes.com

Since American menu. Breakfast, lunch, dinner. Casual attire. No credit cards accepted. **$**

★★**Prado**

244 N. Larchmont Blvd., Los Angeles,
323-467-3871

Caribbean menu. Lunch, dinner. Casual attire. Outdoor seating. **$$**

★★**R-23**

923 E. Second St., Los Angeles,
213-687-7178; www.r23.com

Japanese, sushi menu. Lunch, dinner. Closed Sunday. Casual attire. Reservations recommended. **$$$**

★★★★**The Restaurant at Hotel Bel-Air**

701 Stone Canyon Rd.,
Los Angeles, 310-472-1211;
www.hotelbelair.com

The constantly changing menu at this restaurant in the Hotel Bel-Air continues to be a superior draw for diners looking for a fresh, innovative meal, whether its breakfast, lunch, afternoon tea, dinner or Sunday brunch. Those who want a close look at the pure brilliance of the restaurant's cooking staff can reserve Table One, an exclusive dining room adjacent to the kitchen where chef Douglas Dodd personally leads guests through a seven-course meal. The main Mediterranean-style dining room is decorated in butter cream tones with a Venetian chandelier, and the Tuscan-inspired terrace has a heated terra cotta floor and outdoor fireplace to keep diners warm on cool nights.

California menu, French menu. Breakfast, lunch, dinner, brunch. Bar. Children's menu. Business casual attire. Reservations recommended. Valet parking. Outdoor seating. $$$$

★★The Restaurant Getty Center
1200 Getty Center Dr., Los Angeles, 310-440-7300;
www.getty.edu
California menu. Lunch. Closed Monday. Reservations recommended. $$$

★Seoul Garden
1833 W. Olympic Blvd., Los Angeles, 213-386-8477
Korean menu. Lunch, dinner. Bar. Casual attire. $

★★Seoul Jung
930 Wilshire Blvd., Los Angeles, 213-688-7880
Korean menu. Lunch, dinner. Bar. Casual attire. Reservations recommended. Valet parking. $$

★★★★Sona
401 N. La Cienega Blvd., Los Angeles, 310-659-7708;
www.sonarestaurant.com
Since it opened in 2002, Sona has received numerous accolades. Chefs David and Michelle Myers (executive chef and pastry chef, respectively) turn out refined plates,

and the seasonally-inspired menu incorporates organic and free-range artisanal products. Signature dishes include Maine lobster risotto, Elysian Fields lamb and any one of the adventurous desserts. This restaurant is perfection down to the little details, including Izabel Lam china and Riedel stemware. French menu. Dinner. Closed Sunday-Monday. Bar. Business casual attire. Reservations recommended. Valet parking. $$$

★★Sonora Cafe
180 S. La Brea Ave., Los Angeles, 323-857-1800;
www.sonoracafe.com
Southwestern menu. Lunch, dinner. Bar. Casual attire. Reservations recommended. Valet parking. $$

★★★Table 8
7661 Melrose Ave., Los Angeles, 323-782-8258; www.table8la.com
Unexpectedly tucked under a Melrose tattoo parlor is this honey-colored oasis with dark leather booths, curvy bars and tropical plants. Market-fresh ingredients are creatively paired to form dishes like green bean salad with truffles, sweetbreads in torn pasta and morsels of lamb done three ways. The polished clientele celebrates special occasions at linen-draped tables, while those at the bar enjoy fondue, duck skewers and pomegranate martinis.

California menu. Dinner. Closed Sunday. Bar. Business casual attire. Reservations recommended. $$$

★★Takao
11656 San Vicente Blvd., Los Angeles, 310-207-8636
Japanese menu. Lunch, dinner. Casual attire. Reservations recommended. Valet parking. $$

★★Tanino Ristorante Bar
1043 Westwood Blvd.,
Los Angeles, 310-208-0444;
www.tanino.com
Italian menu. Lunch, dinner. Bar. Children's menu. Casual attire. Reservations recommended. Valet parking. $$$

★

★

★

★

★

★★Tantra
3705 W. Sunset Blvd.,
Silver Lake, 323-663-9090;
www.tantrasunset.com
Indian menu. Dinner. Closed Monday. Bar. Casual attire. Reservations recommended (six or more people). Valet parking. $$

★★Tengu
10853 Lindbrook Dr.,
Los Angeles, 310-209-0071;
www.tengu.com
Pan-Asian menu. Lunch, dinner. Bar. Casual attire. Reservations recommended. Valet parking. $$$

★Toast Café
8221 W. Third St., Los Angeles,
323-655-5018
American menu. Breakfast, lunch. Casual attire. Outdoor seating. $

★★Toscana
11633 San Vicente Blvd.,
Los Angeles, 310-820-2448
This clubby Italian restaurant oozes with style, from the glossy wooden shades to the warm glow of the copper pizza oven. Effusive waiters with thick accents will steer you through the superb menu, which includes fresh pastas, creamy risottos and big cuts of meat.
    Italian menu. Dinner. $$$

★★Traxx
800 N. Alameda, Los Angeles,
213-625-1999;
www.traxxrestaurant.com
American menu. Lunch, dinner. Closed Sunday. Bar. Casual attire. Reservations recommended. Outdoor seating. $$$

★★Vermont
1714 N. Vermont Ave.,
Los Angeles, 323-661-6163;
www.vermontrestaurantonline.com
American menu. Lunch, dinner. Bar. Casual attire. Reservations recommended. Valet parking. Outdoor seating. $$$

★Versailles
1415 S. La Cienega Blvd.,
Los Angeles, 310-289-0392
Seafood menu. Lunch, dinner. Casual attire. $$

★Villa Sombrero
6101 York Blvd., Los Angeles,
323-256-9014
Mexican menu. Lunch, dinner. Bar. Casual attire. $

★★Vincenti
11930 San Vicente Blvd., Los Angeles,
310-207-0127;
www.vincentiristorante.com
Italian menu. Dinner. Closed Sunday. Bar. Casual attire. Reservations recommended. Valet parking. $$$

★★★Water Grill
544 S. Grand Ave., Los Angeles,
213-891-0900; www.watergrill.com
This long-standing favorite, which serves flawlessly prepared seafood, is the place to take a business colleague or romantic partner. The downtown location makes it a good pre-theater option.
    Seafood menu. Lunch, dinner. Bar. Business casual attire. Reservations recommended. Valet parking. $$$

★Yang Chow
819 N. Broadway, Los Angeles,
213-625-0811; www.yangchow.com
Chinese menu. Lunch, dinner. Casual attire. Valet parking. $

★★Yongsusan
950 S. Vermont Ave., Los Angeles,
213-388-3042
Korean menu. Lunch, dinner. Bar. Casual attire. $$

★★Zucca
801 S. Figueroa St.,
Los Angeles, 213-614-7800;
www.patinagroup.com/zuccaristorante
Italian menu. Lunch, dinner. Bar. Casual attire. Reservations recommended. $$$

★

★

★

★

★

SPAS

★★★Equinox Spa and Fitness Center

10220 Constellation Blvd., Los Angeles, 310-286-2900; www.equinox.com

Designed with feng shui in mind, this Asian-influenced spa is the ultimate urban retreat. The 35,000-square foot space has 27 indoor treatment rooms, four outdoor treatment cabanas, two Japanese furo baths, Vichy and Swiss showers, saunas and a meditation garden. From an Asian-inspired treatment menu and pampering at the salon to a full-service fitness center and a café, this spa offers a well-rounded experience. For a unique experience, book a manicure or pedicure—in varieties such as hayaku, centering or tea. **$$**

LOS ANGELES AREA TOWNS AND CITIES

ANAHEIM

Once part of a Spanish land grant, Anaheim was bought and settled by German colonists as a place to tend vineyards and make wine. The town's name reflects its dual heritage: "Ana" is derived from the nearby Santa Ana River, while "heim" is from the German word for "home." The area's best-known settlers are all-American—Mickey, Minnie, Donald and Goofy, residents of Anaheim's Disneyland.

Information: Anaheim/Orange County Convention and Visitors Bureau, 714-765-8888; www.anaheimoc.org

WHAT TO SEE AND DO

Anaheim Angels (MLB)

Edison Field, 2000 Gene Autry Way, Anaheim, 714-940-2000; www.angels.mlb.com

Professional baseball team.

Anaheim Ducks (NHL)

Arrowhead Pond, 2695 Katella Ave., Anaheim, 714-704-2500; www.ducks.nhl.com

Professional hockey team.

Disney's California Adventure

1313 S. Harbor Blvd., Anaheim, 714-781-4565; www.disneyland.com

Located adjacent to Disneyland, Disney's California Adventure celebrates the history, culture, landscape and industry of California in each of its themed areas. Events that draw crowds include a parade and a light show daily. The Hollywood Pictures Backlot lets visitors explore Hollywood Boulevard during the Golden Age of filmmaking. It includes Jim Henson's Muppet Vision 3-D, Disney Animation, Hyperion Theater and Superstar Limo, as well as a musical theater, rides, and films. Daily.

Disneyland

1313 S. Harbor Blvd., Anaheim, 714-781-4565; www.disneyland.com

This theme park was the first Walt Disney opened in 1955.

SPECIAL EVENTS

Obon Festival

909 S. Dale Ave., Anaheim, 714-827-9590; www.bca-ocbc.org

Japanese-American outdoor celebration with hundreds of costumed dancers and Taiko drummers; games, food, crafts. Mid-July.

HOTELS

★Ayres Hotel

2550 E. Katella Ave., Anaheim, 714-634-2106, 800-448-7162; www.ayreshotel.com

133 rooms, all suites. Complimentary full breakfast. Pool. **$**

★Ayres-Country Suites Yorba Linda

22677 Oakcrest Circle, Yorba Linda, 714-921-8688, 800-706-4891; www.ayreshotel.com

SOUTHERN CALIFORNIA

112 rooms, all suites. Complimentary full breakfast. Fitness center. Pool. **$**

★★Crowne Plaza
1500 S. Raymond Ave.,
Fullerton,
714-635-9000;
www.crowneplaza.com/fullertonca
256 rooms. Restaurant, bar. Fitness center. Pool. Business center. **$**

★★★Disney's Grand Californian
1600 S. Disneyland Dr., Anaheim,
714-956-6425, 800-207-6900;
www.disneyland.com
Conveniently situated between Disney's California Adventure theme park and the vibrant Downtown Disney entertainment complex, this giant alpine lodge is designed in an early 20th century Arts and Crafts style. The Napa Rose, a gourmet restaurant with an extensive list of California wines, offers enough sensory pleasure to compete with the nearby rides and shows.
751 rooms. High-speed Internet access. Two restaurants, two bars. Fitness center. Pool. Business center. **$$**

★★Disneyland Hotel
1150 W. Magic Way,
Anaheim,
714-778-6600;
www.disneyland.com
990 rooms. Three restaurants, bar. Children's activity center. Fitness center. Pool. Business center. **$$**

★★Disney's Paradise Pier Hotel
1717 S. Disneyland Dr., Anaheim,
714-999-0990;
www.disneyland.com
489 rooms. Two restaurants, bar. Children's activity center. Fitness center. Pool. Business center. **$$**

★Fairfield Inn Anaheim Disneyland Resort
1460 S. Harbor Blvd., Anaheim, ,
714-772-6777, 800-403-3818;
www.fairfieldinn.com
467 rooms. Pool. **$$**

★★★Fullerton Marriott at California State University
2701 E. Nutwood Ave., Fullerton,
714-738-7800, 800-228-9290;
www.marriott.com
This newly renovated hotel is adjacent to California State University and a short drive to Disneyland. Rooms have Marriott's new elegant beds with down comforters.
224 rooms. Restaurant, bar. Pets accepted. Fitness center. Pool. Business center. **$**

★★★Hyatt Regency Orange County
11999 Harbor Blvd.,
Garden Grove, 92840,
714-750-1234, 800-233-1234;
www.hyatt.com
Business and leisure clientele mingle at this gleaming hotel, brushing up their golf swings on the adjacent driving range, dipping in the rooftop pool, or sipping drinks beneath the soaring 17-story atrium. One- and two-bedrooms suites offer convenience and comfort. Knotts Berry Farm, Crystal Cathedral, and the Discovery Science Center are among the top attractions within a 10-mile radius; popular Southern California beaches are a short drive away. Complimentary shuttle to the Anaheim Convention Center and Disneyland Resort.
654 rooms. High-speed Internet access. Two restaurants, bar. Airport transportation available. Fitness center. Pool.Tennis. Business center. **$**

★Ramada Main Gate
1650 S. Harbor Blvd., Anaheim,
714-772-0440;
www.ramada.com
185 rooms. Complimentary continental breakfast. Pool. **$**

★★★Sheraton Anaheim Hotel
900 S. Disneyland Dr., Anaheim,
714-778-1700, 325-3535;
www.sheratonanaheim.com
This English manor-style lodge may seem misplaced so close to Disneyland, but its grand rotunda, stone fireplace and koi pond, which runs through the lobby to the outside rose garden, makes it the perfect post-theme park refuge.

SOUTHERN CALIFORNIA

489 rooms. High-speed wireless Internet access. Two restaurants, bar. Game and billiards room. Pets accepted. **$**

★★★Sheraton Hotel at Towne Center
12725 Center Court Dr., Cerritos,
562-809-1500, 800-598-1753;
www.sheraton.com

This hotel is located among the Towne Center shops and is adjacent to the Cerritos Center for Performing Arts. Many corporate offices (Siemens, Yamaha) are nearby, making this hotel a convenient choice for business travelers. The elegant, contemporary guest rooms and suites have large windows (some with park views), dark wood furniture, comfortable chairs and ottomans, large work desks and ergonomic chairs. The on-site restaurant, Grille 91, serves breakfast, lunch and dinner and offers a delicious California menu in a casual, bistro-style setting.

203 rooms. Restaurant, bar. Fitness room. Pool. Business center. **$**

★★Wyndham Anaheim Park
222 W. Houston Ave., Fullerton,
714-992-1700

287 rooms. Restaurant, bar. Fitness center. Pool. **$$**

RESTAURANTS

★★★Anaheim White House
887 S. Anaheim Blvd., Anaheim,
714-772-1381;
www.anaheimwhitehouse.com

Many celebrities have visited this converted 1909 Victorian-style mansion. Eight intimate dining rooms bring back Hollywood glamour with fabric-draped ceilings. A roaring fireplace warms the Reagan Room, while those who prefer a porch setting can reserve a table in the Nixon Room. The wine list includes more than 200 selections. Free shuttle service is offered to and from area hotels.

French, Italian menu. Lunch, dinner. Business casual attire. Reservations recommended. Outdoor seating. **$$$**

★★Mr. Stox
1105 E. Katella Ave., Anaheim,
714-634-2994; www.mrstox.com

The bread is baked fresh and the herbs are grown on the premises at this family-run restaurant that specializes in fresh seafood, top-quality meats, and pasta dishes. Extensive wine list.

American menu. Lunch, dinner. Bar. Business casual attire. Reservations recommended. Valet parking. Outdoor seating. **$$$**

★Mulberry Street Ristorante
114 W. Wilshire Ave., Fullerton,
714-525-1056; www.mulberry-st.com
Italian menu. Lunch, dinner. Bar. Casual attire. **$$**

★★★Summit House Restaurant
2000 E. Bastanchury Rd., Fullerton,
714-671-4111; www.summithouse.net
This cozy, friendly inn is situated on the hilltop of Vista Park, offering one of the best views in Orange County while diners dig into filet mignon or Colorado lamb.

American menu. Lunch, dinner. Bar. Valet parking. Outdoor seating. **$$$**

★★★The Cellar
305 N. Harbor Blvd., Fullerton,
714-525-5682; www.cellardining.com
The path to this restaurant—literally a cellar underneath Villa del Sol (the old California Hotel)—is down a set of dimly lit stairs. Once there, visitors are transported to what feels like an old European restaurant. The cave-like walls are decorated with wine casks and lanterns. The French cuisine includes roasted pheasant and filet of ostrich.

French menu. Dinner. Closed Sunday-Monday. Bar. Valet parking. **$$$**

★★Yamabuki
1717 S. Disneyland Dr., Anaheim,
714-956-6755; www.disneyland.com
An appealing option for parents who are tired of kid food but still need to find a family-friendly place to eat, the restaurant features a full sushi bar, teriyaki and tempura entrees, as well as Japanese beers and sake.

Japanese menu. Lunch, dinner. Bar. Children's menu. Casual attire. Reservations recommended. Valet parking. **$$**

39

SOUTHERN CALIFORNIA

★
★
★
★
★

ARCADIA

Arcadia is home to the Santa Anita Park Racetrack, a world-class thoroughbred racing facility.

Information: Chamber of Commerce, 388 W. Huntington Dr., Arcadia, 626-447-2159, 626-445-1400; www.arcadiachamber.com

WHAT TO SEE AND DO

Irwindale Speedway
500 Speedway Dr., Irwindale, 626-358-1100; www.irwindalespeedway.com
Located less than 25 minutes from downtown Los Angeles in California's San Gabriel Valley, Irwindale hosts NASCAR events from mid-March through November. The award-winning NASCAR Toyota All-Star Showdown, first run in 2003, brings together the top regional touring drivers from across the country in a one-of-a-kind, head-to-head event.

Los Angeles County Arboretum & Botanic Garden
301 N. Baldwin Ave., Arcadia, 626-821-3222; www.arboretum.org
This 127-acre public garden has been a Los Angeles area oasis since 1948. Featured are beautiful plants from around the world and wildlife such as fish, turtles and migrating birds, which roam the arboretum's lakes and grounds. Classes, lectures, workshops and resources abound. Take advantage of everything from the Botanical Watercolor Workshop to the Plant Science Library, a reference collection for the general public that contains information on garden design, flower gardening and vegetable and fruit growing. Daily 9 a.m.-4:30 p.m.; extended summer hours.

Santa Anita Park
285 W. Huntington Dr., Arcadia, 626-574-7223; www.santaanita.com
Located on 320 acres at the base of the San Gabriel Mountains, Santa Anita has been a favorite of Southern California horseracing fans since it opened in 1934. In his last race in 1940, the legendary Seabiscuit won the Santa Anita Handicap. Wednesday-Sunday, some Mondays; closed late April-late December.

HOTELS

★★Embassy Suites
211 E. Huntington Dr., Arcadia, 626-445-8525; www.embassy-suites.com
192 rooms, all suites. Complimentary full breakfast. Restaurant, bar. Airport transportation available. Pool. $

★Hampton Inn
311 E. Huntington Dr., Arcadia, 626-574-5600, 800-426-7866; www.hampton-inn.com
131 rooms. Complimentary continental breakfast. Pool. $

★★Holiday Inn
924 W. Huntington Dr., Monrovia, 626-357-1900; www.holiday-inn.com
174 rooms. Complimentary continental breakfast. Restaurant, bar. Pool. $

RESTAURANT

★★The Derby
233 E. Huntington Dr., Arcadia, 626-447-2430; www.thederbyarcadia.com
Seafood, steak menu. Dinner. Valet parking. $$$

40

SOUTHERN CALIFORNIA

★
★
★
★
★

AVALON (CATALINA ISLAND)

Chewing gum magnate William Wrigley, Jr., bought controlling interest in the Santa Catalina Island Company in 1919 and established a program of conservation on the island that still applies today. Located 26 miles off the coast near Los Angeles, tourism is the island's only industry. Scuba diving, kayaking, golf, tennis, horseback riding, swimming and hiking are popular. Avalon, Catalina's quaint harbor town, offers sport fishing and is dotted with resorts. Daily air or boat service to the island is available year-round from Long Beach and San Pedro; boat service available from Newport Beach.

Information: Catalina Island Chamber of Commerce and Visitors Bureau, P.O. Box 217, 310-510-1520; www.catalina.com

WHAT TO SEE AND DO

Catalina Island Museum

Casino Building, 1 Casino Way, Avalon, 310-510-2414; www.catalina.com/museum.html

Permanent exhibits on the history of the island, natural history and archaeology displays. Daily 10 a.m.-4 p.m.; January-March, closed Thursday.

Catalina Tours and Trips

150 Metropole Ave., Avalon, 310-510-2500

Santa Catalina Island Company Discovery Tours (www.scico.com) and Catalina Adventure Tours (www.catalinaadventuretours.com) offer boat and bus tours to several points of interest.

Wrigley Memorial and Botanical Garden

1400 Avalon Canyon Rd., Avalon, 310-510-2595

Native trees, cacti, succulent plants and flowering shrubs on 38 acres surround a memorial to the man who contributed much to Catalina Island. Daily.

HOTELS

★Hotel Catlina

129 Whittley Ave., Avalon, 310-510-0027, 800-540-0184; www.hotelcatlina.com

28 rooms. **$$**

★Hotel St. Lauren

231 Beacon St., Avalon, 310-510-2299; www.stlauren.com

42 rooms. Complimentary continental breakfast. **$**

★★Hotel Villa Portofino

111 Crescent Ave., Avalon, 310-510-0555, 888-510-0555; www.hotelvillaportofino.com

44 rooms. Complimentary continental breakfast. Restaurant, bar. **$$**

★Hotel Vista Del Mar

417 Crescent Ave., Avalon, 310-510-1452, 800-601-3836; www.hotel-vistadelmar.com

15 rooms. Complimentary continental breakfast. Beach. **$**

★★★Hotel Metropole

205 Crescent Ave., Avalon, 310-510-1884, 800-300-8528; www.hotel-metropole.com

Only steps from the beach, this charming hotel features cottage-style guest rooms with a choice of ocean, mountain or courtyard views.

48 rooms. Complimentary continental breakfast. **$**

RESTAURANTS

★★Armstrong's Fish Market and Seafood

306 Crescent Ave., Avalon, 310-510-0113; www.armstrongseafood.com

Seafood menu. Lunch, dinner. Closed the first three weeks in December. Bar. Outdoor seating. **$$**

SOUTHERN CALIFORNIA

BEVERLY HILLS

Surrounded by Bel-Air, Westwood, Century City and West Los Angeles, Beverly Hills might just be the most famous six square miles in the United States. It's a neighborhood of mansions, shops and restaurants that has come to symbolize the high fashion and thick wallets of Los Angeles.

Start a visit on a pair of famous streets: Big Santa Monica Boulveard, which offers access to the glitzy homes of the Hills, and Little Santa Monica which holds shops, quirky restaurants and hip clothing boutiques. Driving through the residential streets on either side of Sunset Boulevard (hint: the bigger houses are north of this east-west street), drivers are bound to intersect one of the three great canyons that add to Beverly Hills' character: Coldwater, Benedict and Franklin. These canyons point to the physical heart of the city, where Sunset and Beverly Boulevards converge.

Between Wilshire and Sunset Boulevards, you'll find what's referred to as the Golden Triangle. Within is a grid of seven small streets filled with shops and restaurants, and at the center is glitzy, glamorous Rodeo Drive.
Information: Visitors Bureau, 239 S. Beverly Dr., 310-248-1015, 800-345-2210; www.beverlyhills.org

WHAT TO SEE AND DO

Beverly Hills Public Art Walking Tour
450 N. Crescent Dr., Beverly Hills, 310-285-2455; www.beverlyhills.org
This hour-long guided tour ambles past outdoor artworks in the vicinity of the Civic Center, a gorgeous mission-style landmark. First Saturday of the month, May-August, 1 p.m.

The Paley Center for Media
465 N. Beverly Dr., Beverly Hills, 310-786-1000; www.mtr.org
Founded in New York in 1975 by William Paley, a former head of CBS, the Los Angeles branch of this museum opened in 1996. With an archive of more than 100,000 television and radio programs to choose from, vistors can watch scheduled screenings or sit back in one of the library's private consoles to view that lost episode of a favorite show or watch famed broadcasts, from Walter Cronkite reporting JFK's assassination to footage of the Beatles arriving in America. Wednesday-Sunday noon-5 p.m.

HOTELS

★★★Luxe Hotel Rodeo Drive
360 N. Rodeo Dr., Beverly Hills, 310-273-0300, 800-805-8210; www.luxehotels.com
The only boutique hotel on Rodeo Drive, the Luxe has gorgeous artwork and mahogany accents throughout its sleek interior. The Luxe is also big on personal amenities, including complimentary fruit baskets, Frette linens, private sundecks and Swiss truffles at turndown. Café Rodeo features inspired California cuisine, while Bar 360 serves a namesake $3.60 martini during cocktail hour Monday through Friday. Concierge, business and babysitting services are available.
88 rooms. High-speed wireless Internet access. Restaurant, bar. Pets accepted. Fitness center Business center. $$

★★★Avalon Hotel Beverly Hills
9400 W. Olympic Blvd., Beverly Hills, 310-277-5221, 800-511-5743; www.avalonbeverlyhills.com
With its mid-century modernist spirit—Marilyn Monroe once bunked here—the Avalon remains one of the coolest scenes in Beverly Hills. The boutique hotel is set around a dramatic hourglass-shaped swimming pool with private cabanas. Guest rooms include custom-designed furnishings and beds with Italian linens, Molton Brown amenities and in-room spa treatments. The highly acclaimed Blue on Blue restaurant is a great spot for dining.
82 rooms. Complimentary continental breakfast. High-speed Internet access. Restaurant, bar. $$

★

★

★

★

★

★★★★Beverly Wilshire, A Four Seasons Hotel

9500 Wilshire Blvd., Beverly Hills,
310-275-5200, 800-819-5053;
www.fourseasons.com

It doesn't get any better than this prestigious address at the intersection of Rodeo Drive and Wilshire Boulevard. Bridging old and new, this Italian Renaissance-style hotel is a happy marriage of two distinctive sensibilities. The guest rooms of the Beverly Wing have contemporary décor, while the Wilshire Wing's rooms appeal to guests with an eye for classic design. As with any Four Seasons hotel, the service is exemplary. A very British afternoon tea is served at the Lobby Lounge, and the convivial bar is a perfect place to sit back and watch the glamorous parade of this star-studded city.

399 rooms. Pets accepted, some restrictions. Complimentary continental breakfast. High-speed Internet access. Two restaurants, two bars. Spa. Pets accepted. Exercise. Swim. Business center. **$$$**

★★★★Four Seasons Hotel Los Angeles at Beverly Hills

300 S. Doheny Dr., Beverly Hills,
310-273-2222, 800-819-5053;
www.fourseasons.com

Located on a quiet, palm-lined street just a mile from the exclusive boutiques of Rodeo Drive and Robertson Boulevard, this hotel is a wonderful retreat. Guest rooms include Frette linens and oversized marble bathrooms with Bulgari toiletries. The rooftop pool is surrounded by lush gardens and dotted with private cabanas. Don't miss the marvelous sunset massage from a candlelit cabana. Gardens restaurant features California-style cuisine with Latin American and Asian influences. Complimentary limousine rides to shopping and restaurants are available.

285 rooms. Pets accepted, some restrictions. High-speed wireless Internet access. Three restaurants, bar. Spa. Pets accepted. Fitness center. Pool. Business center. **$$$$**

★★★The Tower Beverly Hills

1224 S. Beverwil Dr., Los Angeles,
800-916-8592; www.thetowerbeverlyhills.com

Perched on a knoll adjacent to Beverly Hills and affording city, mountain and ocean views, this boutique hotel delivers luxurious yet playful European-style sophistication to a discriminating leisure and business clientele. Private balconies, pricy lithographs and pastel hues fill the guest rooms. Concierge service is available, and the continental on-site restaurant, Lot 1224, makes for a cozy social hub. Close to Rodeo Drive, Hillcrest Country Club and Twentieth Century Fox studios, the Tower offers complimentary sedan service to downtown Beverly Hills.

137 rooms. Pets accepted. High-speed Internet access. Restaurant, bar. Fitness room. Outdoor pool. **$$**

★★Maison 140

140 S. Lasky Dr., Beverly Hills,
310-281-4000, 800-670-6182;
www.maison140.com

Designer Kelly Wearstler's trendy Hollywood Regency décor includes deep colors and bold designs, and guests can choose between Mandarin- or Parisian-style rooms.

43 rooms. High-speed Internet access. Restaurant, bar. Fitness center. **$$**

★★★★★Raffles L'Ermitage Beverly Hills

9291 Burton Way, Beverly Hills,
310-278-3344, 800-768-9009;
www.raffles-lermitagehotel.com

This hotel maintains a sanctuary-like ambience in the heart of Beverly Hills with its stylish and serene Asian-inspired contemporary décor. The spacious rooms are equipped with state-of-the-art technology including 40-inch flat-screen TVs, Bose stereos and computer-controlled lighting and climate. Crowds flock to JAAN's for sumptuous French dishes infused with Indochine flavors. The Writer's Bar (named for the scripts that adorn the walls) is a nice spot to sip cocktails. The rooftop pool provides guests with a view of the prestigious neighborhood and the Amrita spa offers Ayuverdic techniques. Pets are not only welcome here, they get their own beds, snacks and toys and private dog walkers are available.

43

SOUTHERN CALIFORNIA

119 rooms. Wireless Internet access. Restaurant, bar. Spa. Outdoor pool, whirlpool. $$$$

★★★★★The Beverly Hills Hotel
9641 Sunset Blvd., Beverly Hills,
310-276-2251, 888-897-2804;
www.beverlyhillshotel.com

Deliciously pink, this iconic hotel oozes Hollywood glamour. It has long been a hideaway for stars, who like to stay in the bungalows tucked away along the lush garden paths. The hotel maintains the allure of 1940s Hollywood in both its public and private rooms. The guest rooms and suites are decorated in soothing sage, yellow and beige and are furnished with canopied beds. Fireplaces add a romantic touch and terraces and balconies focus attention on the gardens. A variety of dining venues, such as the classic Polo Lounge and the recently opened Sunset Bar, still attract producers and stars, but visitors in the know head for the pool where the scene is best viewed from a fantastic private cabana.

204 rooms. Pets accepted; restrictions; fee. Wireless Internet access. Restaurant, bar. $$$$

★★★★The Beverly Hilton
9876 Wilshire Blvd.,
310-274-7777;
www.beverlyhilton.com

This celebrated hotel at the corner of Wilshire and Santa Monica Boulevards has been completely renovated. After a long day of shopping, make an appointment at the new Aqua Star Spa or take a dip in the Olympic-sized pool. Even with the sparkling new interiors and amenities, there's still a touch of Old Hollywood. Black and white photos of celebrities can be found throughout the hotel and the carpeting in the lobby is, of course, red. Stop by the lounge for a cocktail and to spy on celebrities. There's also the famous Polynesian-themed Trader Vic's Lounge, now located poolside. The hotel's Circa 55 restaurant offers a California twist on breakfast, lunch and dinner.

570 rooms. Pets accepted, some restrictions; fee. Wireless Internet access. Two restaurants, two bars. $$$

★★★The Crescent Hotel
403 N. Crescent Dr.,
Beverly Hills,
310-247-0505;
www.crescentbh.com

Originally built in 1926, this modern hotel, located in Beverly Hills, takes a minimalist approach in its crisp white rooms with down duvet-topped beds and dark wood furniture, but stuffs in must-haves including flat-screen TVs, DVD/CD players, cordless phones and printers. The indoor/outdoor bar has a cozy fireplace, while the restaurant Boe offers eclectic American cuisine in an elegant setting.

35 rooms. Wireless Internet access. Restaurant, bar. Pets accepted. $$

★★★★★The Peninsula Beverly Hills
9882 S. Santa Monica Blvd.,
Beverly Hills, 310-551-2888;
www.beverlyhills.peninsula.com

This French Renaissance-style hotel is designed to resemble a luxurious private residence (one you'll never want to leave). The antique-filled guest rooms feature oversized marble tubs and state-of-the-art electronic systems that allow visitors to control the environment with the touch of a button. The meticulous gardens, rooftop pool and relaxing spa make the space feel like home. Even pets are pampered, with doggie beds (including turndown) and a pet-friendly room service menu. The dining here is exceptional, from the delicious West Coast cuisine of the Belvedere to the wonderful afternoon tea of the Living Room. Particularly convenient is the flexible check-in/check-out policy: whenever a guest checks in, they have 24 hours before check-out.

194 rooms. Pets accepted for a fee. some restrictions. Wireless Internet access. Two restaurants, bar. $$$$

RESTAURANTS

★Barney Greengrass
9570 Wilshire Blvd., Beverly Hills,
310-777-5877

American, Deli menu. Breakfast, lunch, dinner. Bar. Casual attire. Reservations recommended. Valet parking. Outdoor seating. $$$

★★Chin Chin

206 S. Beverly Dr., Beverly Hills,
310-248-5252;
www.chinchin.com
Chinese menu. Lunch, dinner. Casual attire.
Outdoor seating. $$

★★★Crustacean

9646 Little Santa Monica Blvd., Beverly
Hills, 310-205-8990;
www.anfamily.com
The rich and famous—Annette Bening and
Warren Beatty have been spotted here—dine
on the French-Vietnamese fare whipped up
by three generations of women.
    Vietnamese menu. Lunch, dinner. Bar.
Children's menu. Business casual attire.
Reservations recommended. Valet parking.
Outdoor seating. $$$

★★Da Pasquale

9749 Little Santa Monica Blvd.,
 Beverly Hills, 310-859-3884;
www.dapasqualecaffe.com
Italian menu. Lunch, dinner. Closed Sunday.
Children's menu. Casual attire. Reservations
recommended. Outdoor seating. $$

★★Frida Restaurant

236 S. Beverly Dr., Beverly Hills,
310-278-7666;
www.fridarestaurant.com
Mexican menu. Lunch, dinner. Closed
holidays. Bar. Casual attire. Valet parking.
Outdoor seating. $$$

★★★Gardens

300 S. Doheny Dr., Beverly Hills,
310-273-2222;
www.fourseasons.com
Celebrities and movie moguls come here to
dine on contemporary regional and seasonal
fare with Asian accents. Some samples from
the ever-evolving menu include Pacific halibut with butternut squash risotto and grilled
ahi tuna with saffron aioli. The elegant dining
room is adorned with gold-framed oil paintings of the European countryside, elaborate
flower arrangements and posh banquettes.
    California menu. Breakfast, lunch, dinner,
Sunday brunch. Bar. Children's menu. Business

casual attire. Reservations recommended.
Valet parking. Outdoor seating. $$$$

★★★Grill on the Alley

9560 Dayton Way, Beverly Hills,
310-276-0615;
www.thegrill.com
Although the Grill is located in an alley near
Wilshire Boulevard, you can simply follow
the streams of fans filing in to find it. Modeled after the great grills of New York and
San Francisco, the focus is on classic American food, including steaks and comfort foods
like chicken pot pie, meat loaf and pasta
dishes. The décor is also classic American,
with mirrored walls, large chandeliers, dark
wood flooring and semi-private booths.
    Steak menu. Lunch, dinner. Bar. Busi-
ness casual attire. Reservations recom-
mended. Valet parking. $$$

★★★Il Cielo

9018 Burton Way, Beverly Hills,
310-276-9990;
www.ilcielo.com
Often called the most romantic restaurant
in Los Angeles, this cozy Tuscan restaurant
serves up warming dishes like pumpkin
risotto and Florentine steak. Dine indoors
under hand-painted ceilings or outdoors
under the twinkling lights of the garden
patio.
    Italian menu. Lunch, dinner. Closed
Sunday. Bar. Business casual attire. Reser-
vations recommended. Valet parking. Out-
door seating. $$$

★★Il Pastaio

400 N. Canon Dr., Beverly Hills,
310-205-5444;
www.giacominodrago.com
Italian menu. Lunch, dinner. Bar. Casual
attire. Valet parking. Outdoor seating. $$

★★Kate Mantilini

9101 Wilshire Blvd., Beverly Hills,
310-278-3699
American menu. Breakfast, lunch, dinner,
brunch. Bar. Children's menu. Casual attire.
Reservations recommended. Valet parking.
Outdoor seating. $$$

SOUTHERN CALIFORNIA

★★Mako
225 S. Beverly Dr., Beverly Hills,
310-288-8338;
www.makorestaurant.com
Japanese menu. Lunch, dinner. Closed
Sunday. Bar. Business casual attire. Reservations recommended. Valet parking. Outdoor seating. **$$$**

★★★Mastro's Steakhouse
246 N. Canon Dr., Beverly Hills,
310-888-8782;
www.mastrossteakhouse.com
Everything is big at this swanky steakhouse—
the massive cutlery, the towering seafood
appetizers chilling on dry ice and the huge
slabs of world-class aged beef. Big names
show up, too: Bill Clinton often dines in the
private back room. The Wine Room offers
privacy for intimate parties and upstairs a
one-man band plays standards to a sophisticated crowd sipping Champagne in the sleek
and modern surroundings.

Steak menu. Dinner. Bar. Business casual
attire. Reservations recommended. Valet
parking. **$$$**

★★★Matsuhisa
129 N. La Cienega Blvd., Beverly Hills,
310-659-9639; www.nobumatsuhisa.com
This sushi bar broke culinary ground when
it opened in 1987 and began serving lobster
ceviche and sashimi with cilantro or garlic,
influences acclaimed chef Nobu Matsuhisa
picked up cooking in Peru. Given the vast
menu, regulars recommend putting yourself
in the chef's hands with the omakase tasting
menu. Though Matsuhisa later opened the
more stylish Nobu chain with partners that
include Robert De Niro, the original restaurant remains casual.

Japanese menu. Lunch, dinner. Bar.
Business casual attire. Reservations recommended. Valet parking. **$$$**

★★Mr. Chow
344 N. Camden Dr., Beverly Hills,
310-278-9911; www.mrchow.com
Chinese menu. Lunch, dinner. Bar. Business casual attire. Reservations recommended. Valet parking. **$$$**

★Nate 'n Al's Delicatessen
414 N. Beverly Dr., Beverly Hills,
310-274-0101; www.natenal.com
Deli menu. Breakfast, lunch, dinner. Children's menu. Casual attire. **$$**

★★★Polo Lounge
9641 Sunset Blvd., Beverly Hills,
310-276-2251; www.beverlyhillshotel.com
Still a hot spot for celebrities and power
brokers, the Polo Lounge is synonymous
with Hollywood. Stars and starmakers
wheel and deal in the large velvet booths
or on the dramatic patio, where blooming
vines and striking pink archways accent a
lone, knotted oak tree. The California cuisine includes the grilled Kobe-style burger
(a house favorite) and the grilled veal chop
with Oregon morel mushrooms, parsley
gnocchi and a laurel-scented veal sauce.

California menu. Breakfast, lunch, dinner, brunch. Bar. Business casual attire.
Reservations recommended. Valet parking.
Outdoor seating. **$$$**

★★★Ruth's Chris Steak House
224 S. Beverly Dr., Beverly Hills,
310-859-8744; www.ruthschris.com
Born from a single New Orleans restaurant
that Ruth Fertel bought in 1965 for $22,000,
the chain is a favorite among steak lovers.
Aged prime midwestern beef is broiled and
served on a heated plate sizzling with butter
and with sides like creamed spinach and au
gratin potatoes.

Steak menu. Dinner. Bar. Business casual
attire. Reservations recommended. Valet
parking. **$$$**

★★★Spago Beverly Hills
176 N. Canon Dr., Beverly Hills,
310-385-0880; www.wolfgangpuck.com
The first restaurant from the Wolfgang Puck-
Barbara Lazar culinary dynasty, Spago is
as famous for the late-night Oscar bashes it
caters as it is for its innovative, sophisticated
American cuisine prepared with European
and Asian influences. The restaurant is still
packed with celebrities, studio executives and
models munching on gourmet pizzas. The stylish room is awash in rich wood and accented

SOUTHERN CALIFORNIA

★
★
★
★
★

with tones of amethyst, jade and amber. The open-air garden with a sculpted fountain and a pair of 100-year-old olive trees balances the restaurant's high-energy atmosphere.

American menu. Lunch, dinner. Bar. Business casual attire. Reservations recommended. Valet parking. Outdoor seating. $$$$

★★★★The Belvedere
9882 S. Santa Monica Blvd.,
Beverly Hills, 310-788-2306;
www.beverlyhills.peninsula.com

The Belvedere may be the best hotel restaurant in the country. The spacious dining room, located in the Peninsula hotel, is dressed in cream tones, with tables topped with Villeroy & Boch china and pewter vases filled with fresh seasonal flowers. A pianist performa nightly and completes the elegant setting. Guests can also dine on the stunning sun-soaked patio, which is landscaped with beautiful greenery and flowers. The cuisine is a lively combination of heartland staples and global-accented fare. Diners are encouraged to create their own tasting menu with small bites including the famed macaroni and cheese.

Modern American menu. Lunch, dinner, brunch. Bar. Children's menu. Business casual attire. Reservations recommended. Valet parking. Outdoor seating. $$$$

★★Xi'an
362 N. Canon Dr., Beverly Hills,
310-275-3345; www.xian90210.com

Chinese menu. Lunch, dinner. Bar. Casual attire. Reservations recommended. Valet parking. Outdoor seating. $$

SPAS

★★★Aqua Star Spa
9876 Wilshire Blvd., Beverly Hills,
310-274-7777; www.beverlyhilton.com

The décor at this new spa inside the Beverly Hilton takes its design cues from the 1950s, when the hotel was built. But the treatments here are thoroughly modern. Massages come in hot stone, Swedish or deep tissue versions, while body treatments include everything from a warm aromatic scrub to a spray-on tan. The onsite fitness center offers yoga and Pilates classes as well as state-of-the-art equipment. $$

★★★★The Beverly Hills Hotel Spa by La Prairie
9641 Sunset Blvd., Beverly Hills,
310-887-2505; www.beverlyhills.com

The Clinic La Prairie in Montreux, Switzerland is among the world's leading spas, and its anti-aging treatments are considered revolutionary. The staff at this spa uses the same treatments while providing guests with white-glove treatment in its plush surroundings. La Prairie's commitment to anti-aging is perhaps best experienced through one of the spa's many decadent facials. The Caviar Firming Facial is an extravagant treat, using a concentration of caviar extracts and alpha hydroxy acids to lift and polish skin. The Intensive De-Aging facial uses a cellular complex and glycolic acid blend to reduce the appearance of fine lines. Massages and nail services are available at the spa, in a poolside cabana or in the privacy of a guest room.

★★★★The Four Seasons Spa, Los Angeles at Beverly Hills
300 S. Doheny Dr., Los Angeles,
310-786-2222, 800-819-5053;
www.fourseasons.com

Book the spa's private poolside cabana for the California Sunset massage. The Punta Mita massage is another signature treatment, combining tequila and sage. Body scrubs use an array of products, including chamomile and Turkish salt, to exfoliate and polish skin. The Thermal Mineral Kur begins with a moor mud wrap, followed by a bath filled with mineral crystals from Hungary's renowned Sarvar Springs, before finishing with a soothing massage. The spa's divine facials cleanse, refresh and revive with a variety of options, including a fruit and pumpkin enzyme peel.

★★★★The Spa at Beverly Wilshire
9500 Wilshire Blvd., Beverly Hills,
310-275-5200, 800-545-4000;
www.fourseasons.com

This spa is instantly inviting. The entrance features subtle lighting and rich mahogany walls accented with pictures of the spa's

★
★
★
★
★

signature Gerber daisy, while a curving sauna anchors the entire facility. Choose from a cart overflowing with fruits and snacks as you lounge on long beds in the tranquility lounge. In addition to the nine treatment rooms, you can enjoy an aromatherapy crystal steam room and showers that automatically adjust to certain temperatures and fragrances. A variety of facials and body wraps tout the healing benefits of volcanic mud or warm marine algae.

★★★★The Peninsula Spa, Beverly Hills
9882 S. Santa Monica Blvd., Beverly Hills, 310-712-5288, 800-462-7899; www.beverlyhills.peninsula.com
The staff at the Peninsula knows how to help guests relax, and the technicians manning the hotel spa are no exception. Try the exclusive Shiffa precious gem treatment, which uses massage oils containing ruby, emeralds, sapphires and diamonds. The signature pedicure includes foot reflexology, a flowering herbal foot bath, a massage with Jasmine oil and a warming mask and paraffin treatment. The red carpet facial involves a crystalline gemstone mask to help remove fine lines and a cactus extract to lift and tighten skin. It also includes a hand microdermabrasion treatment with glycolic peppermint cream. There are several treatments for men, and the facility includes a well-equipped fitness center as well as a 60-foot rooftop lap pool lined with private cabanas.

BUENA PARK
Information: Convention & Visitors Office, 6601 Beach Blvd., 714-521-0261; www.buenapark.com

WHAT TO SEE AND DO

Knott's Berry Farm
8039 Beach Blvd., Buena Park, 714-220-5200; www.knotts.com
At this amusement park, the official home of Snoopy and the other beloved Peanuts characters, riders can test their moxie on GhostRider. At 4,533 feet, it's the longest wooden roller coaster in the Western United States. It's just one of the more than 165 rides, shows, attractions, restaurants and shops that make this 160-acre park a favorite with families. Opens at 10 a.m. daily; closing times vary by season.

Ripley's Believe It or Not Museum
7850 Beach Blvd., Buena Park, 714-522-7045; www.ripleyssbp.com
A collection of oddities and anthropological artifacts allow visitors to experience firsthand that truth is indeed stranger than fiction. Monday-Friday 11 a.m.-5 p.m., Saturday-Sunday 10 a.m.-6 p.m.

HOTELS

★Best Western Inn Hotel & Suites
7555 Beach Blvd., Buena Park, 714-522-7360, 888-522-5885; www.bestwestern.com
172 rooms, all suites. Complimentary continental breakfast. Pool. **$**

★★Courtyard Anaheim Buena Park
7621 Beach Blvd., Buena Park, 714-670-6600, 800-321-2211; www.marriott.com
145 rooms. High-speed Internet access. Restaurant, bar. Fitness center. Pool. Business center. **$**

★Goodnight Inn
7032 Orangethorpe Ave., Buena Park, 714-523-1488
134 rooms. Complimentary continental breakfast. Pool. **$**

★★Holiday Inn
7000 Beach Blvd., Buena Park, 714-522-7000; www.hibuenapark.com
248 rooms. High-speed Internet access. Restaurant, bar. Fitness room. Pool. Business center. **$**

SOUTHERN CALIFORNIA

★
★
★
★
★

★★Radisson Suites Hotel
7762 Beach Blvd., Buena Park,
714-739-5600; www.radisson.com
201 rooms, all suites. Complimentary full breakfast. Restaurant, bar. Fitness room. Pool. Business center. **$$**

★★★Marriott Norwalk
13111 Sycamore Dr., Norwalk,
562-863-5555; www.marriott.com

This hotel is easily accessible from major highways and is close to many Southern California attractions and activities, including Disneyland, Knotts Berry Farm, golf courses and horseback riding. Contemporary guest rooms feature down pillows and comforters, marble bathrooms and wet bars. The hotel's restaurant, Cabrio's, serves up California cuisine in a casual setting.
173 rooms. Restaurant, bar. **$**

BURBANK

Founded by noted botanist Luther Burbank, this beautiful area is thriving with television and movie studios, as well as first-rate lodging, dining and shopping.

Long a favorite with Los Angelenos, the Burbank airport has direct and convenient connecting flights to major California and U.S. cities. By taking the venerable Cahuenga Pass heading east off the 101 in Hollywood, drivers can arrive in downtown Burbank in minutes, ready to see mountainous corridors to the north and west, a variety of local parks and several neighborhoods off Burbank Boulevard with excellent samples of classic California/ Spanish/Mediterranean architecture. Burbank is convenient to Glendale and downtown Los Angeles to the southeast, the Simi Valley and Thousand Oaks to the west.
Information: www.ci.burbank.ca.us

WHAT TO SEE AND DO

NBC Studios Tour
3000 W. Alameda Ave., Burbank,
818-840-4444; www.nbc.com
Get a behind-the-scenes look at NBC's television operations. The tour shows where sets are designed and gives visitors a peek at wardrobe and makeup. A limited tour, but the appealing price tag—and the fact that the other networks don't offer studio tours—makesthisanappealingdestination.Monday-Friday 9 a.m.-3 p.m.

Warner Brothers Studios VIP Tour
4000 Warner Blvd., Burbank,
818-846-1403; www.studio-tour.com
Because it's a working studio, every instance of this two-hour tour is different. Some potential sights include a New York Street set that has been used in the filming of *ER*, French Street, where the Paris scenes from *Casablanca* were filmed or even the sets of shows like *Two and a Half Men*. Lucky tourists may also spot celebrities walking around the lots. No children under 8 years allowed. October-April: Monday-Friday 9 a.m.-3 p.m.; May-September: Monday-Friday 9 a.m.-4 p.m.; closed Saturday-Sunday.

HOTELS

★★★Graciela
322 N. Pass Ave.,
Burbank,
818-842-8887;
www.thegraciela.com
Located in the heart of Burbank, this cheery hotel is a luxurious place from which to access the area's many attractions. Guest rooms are modern with simple, clean lines and decorated with white bed linens and blond wood furniture. Though the hotel doesn't have a pool, you can soak in the Jacuzzi or lounge on the rooftop deck.
101 rooms. High-speed Internet access. Restaurant, bar. Airport transportation available. **$$**

RESTAURANT

★Bob's Big Boy
4211 Riverside Dr.,
Burbank,
818-843-9334;
www.bobs.net
American menu. Breakfast, lunch, dinner, late-night. Children's menu. Casual attire. Outdoor seating. **$**

COSTA MESA

Information: Chamber of Commerce, 1700 Adams Ave., 714-885-9090;
www.ci.costa-mesa.ca.us

WHAT TO SEE AND DO

Noguchi Garden

South Coast Plaza Town Center,
Costa Mesa, 714-384-5500

World-renowned sculptor Isamu Noguchi's tribute to California's environment, this 1 1/2-acre sculpture garden features tranquil walks, fountains, flowers and native grasses and trees. Noguchi's *The Spirit of the Lima Bean* is the centerpiece. Daily.

SPECIAL EVENTS

Highland Gathering and Games

Fairplex, 1101 W. McKinley Ave.,
Pomona, 909-623-3111;
www.unitedscottishsociety.com

Scottish games, dancing, soccer, rugby, piping, drumming competition. Memorial Day weekend.

Orange County Fair

Orange County Fairgrounds, 88 Fair Dr.,
Costa Mesa, 714-708-1500; www.ocfair.com

Rodeo, livestock, exhibits, home arts, contests, photography, nightly entertainment, floriculture display, wine show, carnival, motorcycle races. July.

HOTELS

★★★Ayres Hotel & Suites Costa Mesa-Newport Beach

325 S. Bristol St., Costa Mesa,
714-549-0300, 800-454-1692;
www.countrysuites.com

This European boutique-style hotel has hand-painted frescoes, tapestries and antique furnishings. The cobblestone courtyard is reminiscent of a French village square with outdoor dining and beautiful gardens.

171 rooms. Complimentary full breakfast. Restaurant, bar. Airport transportation available. $$

★Best Western Newport Mesa Inn

2642 Newport Blvd., Costa Mesa,
949-650-3020, 800-554-2378;
www.bestwestern.com

97 rooms. Complimentary continental breakfast. Pool. $

★Cozy Inn

325 W. Bay St., Costa Mesa,
949-650-2055, fax 949-650-6281;
www.cozyinn.com

28 rooms. Pool. $

★★★Hilton Costa Mesa

3050 Bristol St., Costa Mesa,
714-540-7000, 800-774-1500;
www.hilton.com

An airy seven-story atrium with towering palm trees greets guests at this contemporary hotel in Orange County. Most of the recently renovated oversized guest rooms have balconies. Families can opt for a suite, which includes a separate guest room, sitting area and whirlpool tub. The Bristol Palms California Bistro, located in the middle of the hotel's atrium, serves light California cuisine, while pizza-lovers can head over to the Bristol Palms Pizza Bar for authentic brick-oven pies. The Bristol Palms Bar, with its exotic martini menu, is a popular nightcap destination.

484 rooms. Restaurant, bar. Airport transportation available. Pets accepted. Pool. $

★★Holiday Inn

3131 S. Bristol St., Costa Mesa,
714-557-3000, 800-221-7220;
www.holiday-inn.com

230 rooms. Restaurant, bar. Airport transportation available. Pets accepted. Pool. $

★Ramada

1680 Superior Ave., Costa Mesa,
949-645-2221, 800-272-6232;
www.ramada.com

140 rooms. Complimentary continental breakfast. Airport transportation available. Pets accepted. Pool. $

SOUTHERN CALIFORNIA

★Vagabond Inn
3205 Harbor Blvd., Costa Mesa,
714-557-8360, 800-522-1555;
www.vagabondinn.com
133 rooms. Complimentary continental breakfast. Pets accepted. Pool. $

★★Wyndham Orange County Airport
3350 Ave. of the Arts, Costa Mesa,
714-751-5100; www.wyndham.com
238 rooms. High-speed Internet access. Restaurant, bar. Airport transportation available. $

★★★Marriott Suites Costa Mesa
500 Anton Blvd., Costa Mesa,
714-957-1100; www.marriott.com
The suites at this business district hotel offer separate living and sleeping areas, two TVs and two phones lines. John Wayne Airport (Orange County), golf, beaches and more are just minutes away.
253 rooms, all suites. Restaurant, bar. Airport transportation available. Pets accepted. Pool. $$

★★★Westin South Coast Plaza
686 Anton Blvd., Costa Mesa,
714-540-2500; www.westin.com
This hotel is connected to the South Coast Plaza Mall and is near the Anaheim Convention Center, Disneyland and the Orange County Performing Arts Center.
400 rooms. Restaurant, bar. Airport transportation available. Pets accepted. Pool. Tennis. Business center. $$

RESTAURANTS

★★★Golden Truffle
1767 Newport Blvd., Costa Mesa,
949-645-9858; www.goldentruffle.com
Alan Greeley's trendy restaurant features unforgettable food including a truffle ground chuck cheeseburger and fries with homemade ketchup and prime beef bourguignon with horseradish egg noodles. Starters include duck tacos and fried chicken livers.
Caribbean, French menu. Lunch Tuesday-Friday, dinner. Closed Sunday-Monday. Outdoor seating. $$$

★★Habana
2930 Bristol St., Costa Mesa,
714-556-0176;
www.restauranthabana.com
Latin American menu. Lunch, dinner. Bar. Casual attire. Outdoor seating. $$

★Memphis Cafe
2920 Bristol St., Costa Mesa,
714-432-7685;
www.memphiscafe.com
American, Cajun/Creole menu. Lunch, dinner, brunch. Bar. Casual attire. Outdoor seating. $$

★Nello Cucina
3333 S. Bear St., Costa Mesa,
714-540-3365;
www.nellocucina.com
Italian menu. Lunch, dinner. Bar. Outdoor seating. $$

★★★Pinot Provence
686 Anton Blvd., Costa Mesa,
714-444-5900;
www.patinagroup.com
Housed in the Westin South Coast Plaza, a sun-drenched patio and rustic French-country décor set the scene for this upscale bistro's hearty, full-flavored French plates. The menu changes seasonally but expect to find offerings like ahi tuna tartare with crispy sweetbreads and truffle vinaigrette to start, and bone-in New York with Portobello fries as a main course. Fresh seafood and bountiful produce round out the menu.
French menu. Breakfast, lunch, dinner, brunch. Casual attire. $$$

★★Scott's Restaurant
3300 Bristol St., Costa Mesa,
714-979-2400; www.scottsseafood.com
Seafood menu. Lunch, dinner, brunch. Bar. Valet parking. Outdoor seating. $$$

★Tea and Sympathy
369 E. 17th St., Costa Mesa,
949-645-4860;
www.englishtearooms.com
Traditional English tea room. Continental menu. Lunch and afternoon tea. $

SOUTHERN CALIFORNIA

DISNEYLAND

It's the happiest place on earth. Disneyland opened in 1955 with 18 major attractions. The park is divided into eight themed lands, each packed with exciting rides and upbeat entertainment. Disneyland attractions are open daily, with extended hours during holidays. Passports to Disneyland are good for unlimited use of rides and attractions (except arcades). Guided tours are available.

Information: www.disneyland.com

GLENDALE

Set at the foot of the Verdugo Mountains and bordered on the west by Burbank and on the east by Pasadena, Glendale is the third largest city in Los Angeles County. More than half of the city's 200,000 residents are foreign-born, giving Glendale a rich diversity.

Information: www.ci.glendale.ca.us

WHAT TO SEE AND DO

Glendale Galleria
2148 Glendale Galleria,
Glendale,
818-240-9481;
www.glendalegalleria.com
This mega mall houses more than 250 stores, including Nordstrom, Macy's, Aveda, Bath & Body Works, Brookstone, Coach, Eddie Bauer and Williams-Sonoma.

Monday-Friday 10 a.m.-9 p.m., Saturday to 8 p.m., Sunday 11 a.m.-7 p.m.

HOTELS

★Best Western Eagle Rock Inn
2911 Colorado Blvd., Los Angeles,
323-256-7711, 888-255-7970;
www.bestwestern.com
49 rooms. Complimentary continental breakfast. High-speed Internet access. Pool. **$**

SOUTHERN CALIFORNIA

HEARST-SAN SIMEON STATE HISTORICAL MONUMENT

750 Hearst Castle Rd., San Simeon, 805-927-2020; www.hearstcastle.com
Crowning La Cuesta Encantada—the Enchanted Hill—is the former home of William Randolph Hearst. After his death in 1951, the estate was given to California as a memorial to the late publisher's mother, Phoebe Adderson Hearst. For years, Hearst Castle could only be glimpsed through a telescope at the nearby village of San Simeon, but today it's open to the public. Construction began in 1919 under the direction of noted architect Julia Morgan and took 28 years to finish.

The estate includes 115 rooms and three guest houses. Features of the castle include the Refectory, a long room with a hand-carved ceiling and life-size statues of saints, silk banners from Siena and 15th-century choir stalls from a Spanish cathedral; the Assembly Room, with priceless tapestries; and the lavish theater where the latest motion pictures were shown.

The grounds include the Neptune Pool, with a colonnade leading to an ancient Roman temple facade and an array of marble statuary, an indoor pool and magnificent gardens with fountains and walkways.

Access to the castle and grounds is by guided tour only. Day tours take approximately one hour and 45 minutes; evening tours take approximately two hours and 15 minutes. Reservations are recommended and are available up to eight weeks in advance by phoning 800-444-4445. Tickets are also available at the ticket office in the visitor center. Daily.

★Best Western Golden Key Motor Hotel
123 W. Colorado St.,
Glendale,
818-247-0111, 800-651-1155;
www.bestwestern.com
55 rooms. Complimentary continental breakfast. Pool. **$**

RESTAURANTS
★★Far Niente
204 1/2 N. Brand Blvd., Glendale,
818-242-3835, 818-242-2956;
www.farnienteristorante.net
Italian menu. Lunch, dinner. Bar. Casual attire. Reservations recommended. Valet parking. Outdoor seating. **$$**

HOLLYWOOD

To most tourists, Hollywood is synonymous with Los Angeles. It symbolizes the glitz of the movie industry, but you'll probably find more grit than glamour here. In Hollywood, thousands of workers in production houses edit miles of footage, mix and edit sound, color-correct and physically compose the movies themselves. These neighborhoods appear more industrial than swanky, as this is the underbelly of filmmaking. Several major motion picture studios are centered in Hollywood and they are like cities unto themselves. The studios have a campus-like feel, with their own transit, restaurants, shops and stores. A smattering of trendy dining spots for power lunches and not much else,surround these gated complexes.

Still, Hollywood Boulevard is the ultimate tourist destination. Tour groups from around the globe gather here to snap photos of the stars embedded in the sidewalk, gawk at the outlandish Grauman's Chinese Theatre and take their pictures with celebrity impersonators. There's also shopping at the Hollywood and Highland Center, which houses upscale chain stores and restaurants, as well as the Kodak Theatre, home of the Academy Awards.

From the rotunda of the mall, you can spot the famed Hollywood sign in the Hollywood Hills. The Hollywood Bowl is an iconic alfresco concert venue, with its white shell-shaped stage. During summer, it's the home of the Los Angeles Philharmonic. A drive on historic Mulholland Drive offers great views of the city below.
Information: Chamber of Commerce, 7018 Hollywood Blvd., 323-469-8311; www.hollywoodchamber.net or Hollywood Convention & Visitors Information Center, 685 S. Figueroa St., 213-689-8822; www.seemyla.com

WHAT TO SEE AND DO
Barnsdall Art Park
4808 Hollywood Blvd., Hollywood,
www.barnsdallartpark.com
Named after socialite Aline Barnsdall who commissioned Frank Lloyd Wright to build her home and later gave the property to the city of Los Angeles. Daily.

CBS Television City
7800 Beverly Blvd., Hollywood,
323-575-2458
West Coast studios of CBS Television and the source of many of its network telecasts. Write for free tickets well in advance (specify dates and shows preferred) and enclose a self-addressed, stamped envelope. Tickets may also be picked up at the information window (daily) on a first-come, first-served basis. Age limits for admittance vary and are specified on tickets; children under 16 not admitted to any broadcast. Monday-Friday.

Farmers' Market
6333 W. Third St., Hollywood,
323-933-9211; www.farmersmarketla.com
This historic landmark features outdoor food stalls, restaurants and shops. Monday-Friday 9 a.m.-9 p.m., Saturday 9 a.m.-8 p.m., Sunday 10 a.m.-7 p.m.

Grauman's Chinese Theatre
6925 Hollywood Blvd., Hollywood,
323-464-8111;
www.manntheatres.com/chinese
Grauman's Chinese Theatre opened in 1927 and has been an operating cinema ever since. What makes this pagoda-shaped

53

SOUTHERN CALIFORNIA

★
★
★
★

HOORAY FOR HOLLYWOOD

In the first half of the 20th century, Hollywood Boulevard was a legendary place, where all the stars went out to restaurants and nightclubs. But in the latter part of the century, as film studios deserted Hollywood for other parts of greater Los Angeles, it fell into decline. Today, the boulevard is making a comeback. Walking is the best way to see its sights, which include renowned theaters, old-time restaurants and hotels and much of the Hollywood Walk of Fame. Start at Hollywood and Vine. The Walk of Fame heads north on Vine Street up to Sunset Boulevard. Nearby, visitors can also view the famous circular Capitol Records Building (1750 N. Vine St.), designed to resemble a stack of records. Return to Hollywood Boulevard and walk west, following the Walk of Fame. There are several gaudy vintage theaters along this stretch, including the Pantages (6233 Hollywood Blvd.), the Egyptian (6712) and El Capitan (6838). Topping them all is Grauman's Chinese (6925), where stars ranging from Shirley Temple to Harrison Ford have left their handprints and footprints in the cement in the theater courtyard. Next to Mann's is the Academy of Motion Pictures Arts and Sciences Complex and just across the street is the Hollywood Roosevelt Hotel (7000 Hollywood Blvd.), where Hollywood's golden years are chronicled in a photo exhibit on the Mezzanine level. Grab a bite at Musso & Frank Grill (6667 Hollywood Blvd.), an old time Hollywood hangout that retains its vintage flavor.

★
★
★
★
★

theater so famous is the forecourt, home to the thousands of stars of the Hollywood Walk of Fame. Daily guided tours of the theater are available.

Griffith Park
4730 Crystal Springs Dr., Los Angeles, 323-913-4688; www.laparks.org/dos/parks/griffithPK/index.htm
With more than 4,100 acres, this is one of the country's largest municipal parks and is an urban wilderness eight miles from downtown Los Angeles. Camping, golfing, hiking, horseback riding, jogging, swimming, soccer and tennis are available. Daily 6 a.m.-10 p.m.; bridle trails, hiking paths, and mountain roads close at sunset,

Greek Theatre
2700 N. Vermont Ave., Los Angeles, 323-665-5857; www.greektheatrela.com
An outdoor theater set in a tree-enveloped canyon, the Greek Theatre has been host to some of the music world's biggest stars, including James Taylor, Elton John, Tina Turner, Santana and Pearl Jam. Have a world-famous Pinks hot dog, available at the concession stand, during the show.

Griffith Park Golf Course
4730 Crystal Springs Dr., Los Angeles, 323-664-2255
The park, which has four golf courses, has been in operation since the 1930s and hosts the city's junior golf championship every year. The Barber Shop, one of the best golf shops in the country, is located in the clubhouse and offers club fitting, junior instruction and demo days to try out new equipment.

Los Angeles Zoo
5333 Zoo Dr., Los Angeles, 90027 (In the center of Griffith Park.), 323-644-4200; www.lazoo.org
Komodo dragons, snow leopards and other unique creatures prowl, fly and swim about this 80-acre animal kingdom. The zoo displays more than 1,200 amphibians, birds, mammals and reptiles representing more

than 370 different species. Two notable exhibits feature animals in replicas of their natural habitats: the Red Ape Rain Forest, home to lovable orangutans, and the Chimpanzees of Mahale Mountain in Tanzania. (September-June: daily 10 a.m.-5 p.m., July-early September: daily 10 a.m.-6 p.m.)

Museum of the American West
4700 Western Heritage Way,
Los Angeles, 90027,
323-667-2000.
Founded in 1988 by the singing cowboy himself, Gene Autry, the museum is a treasure trove of more than 70,000 objects relating to the American West, including everything from paintings by Bierstadt, Moran and Remington to Western furniture and clothing. There is also an excellent collection of radio, TV and film memorabilia, such as Gene Autry's guitar and artifacts from legendary filmmaker Cecil B. DeMille. (Tuesday-Wednesday, Friday-Sunday 10 a.m.-5 p.m., Thursday to 8 p.m.) Free admission on Thursday after 4 p.m.

Municipal Art Gallery
4804 Hollywood Blvd., Hollywood,
323-644-6269
Features works by regional and local artists. Thursday-Sunday noon-5 p.m.

Travel Town
5200 W. Zoo Dr., Los Angeles,
323-662-5874
Outdoor transportation museum, including 15 locomotives (the oldest dating to 1864), 11 freight cars and cabooses, nine passenger cars and four inter-urbans and motorcars. Take a ride on the miniature train that runs around the park's perimeter. Monday-Friday 10 a.m.-5 p.m., Saturday-Sunday 10 a.m.-6 p.m.

Hollywood Sign
Grffith Park, Mount Lee, Los Angeles,
Originally constructed in 1923 to advertise the Hollywoodland housing development, the letters spelling LAND on this larger-than-life sign somehow disappeared and the world-famous landmark was born. Though it can be seen from all over Los Angeles, head

to Beachwood Drive off Franklin Avenue in Hollywood near the 101 Freeway for a great snapshot. Follow Beachwood all the way to its end point, park your car and hike up the Hollyridge Trail to the sign itself. A fence surrounds the sign, but visitors will get a great view of Los Angeles and (on a clear day) the Pacific Ocean.

Hollywood Boulevard
Hollywood
From the storefront murals to the world-renowned Walk of Fame, the legends of Hollywood are immortalized here. Take the walk to Hollywood and Highland, the hotel-retail complex that houses the Kodak Theatre, permanent home to the Academy Awards, and continue past Grauman's Chinese Theatre to the Guinness World of Records Museum and famous restaurants and clubs such as the Pig N Whistle.

Hollywood Bowl
2301 N. Highland Ave., Hollywood,
323-850-2000; www.hollywoodbowl.org
This huge outdoor amphitheater has been a Los Angeles landmark for more than 80 years, with performances ranging from symphony orchestras to rock concerts. Over the years, everyone from Frank Sinatra to Luciano Pavarotti to the Beatles has played here. Even those without a ticket can stop by the Hollywood Bowl Museum, open daily throughout the year and two hours before every performance, to find out more about this landmark venue.

Hollywood Entertainment Museum
3200 Wilshire Blvd., Los Angeles,
323-465-7900;
www.hollywoodmuseum.com
This interactive museum let's you assume command of the *Starship Enterprise*, take a seat in Norm's chair from *Cheers* or tour one of the actual sets from *The X-Files*. These exhibits and many others celebrate the entertainment industry and offer an exciting behind-the-scenes look at show-biz magic. Memorial Day-Labor Day: daily 10 a.m.-6 p.m.; rest of the year: Thursday-Tuesday 11 a.m.-6 p.m.

SOUTHERN CALIFORNIA

Hollywood Heritage Museum
2100 N. Highland Ave.,
Hollywood,
323-874-2276;
www.hollywoodheritage.org/museum/
museum.html
Across the street from the Hollywood Bowl in a restored barn that served as the site of Hollywood's first feature-length Western *The Squaw Man*, this treasure trove is packed with the largest public display of memorabilia from Hollywood's heyday: rare photos of silent film sets and casts, original props and weapons from director Cecil B. DeMille's films including *Cleopatra* and *Samson and Delilah*, and historic postcards of Hollywood streets and buildings. Saturday-Sunday 11 a.m.-4 p.m.

Hollywood Walk of Fame
Hollywood Blvd. and La Brea Ave.,
Hollywood,
323-469-8311;
www.hollywoodchamber.net
Begun in 1960, the Walk of Fame honors celebrities from film, television, theater and music. There are more than 2,000 stars on the Walk, with roughly one or two new ones added every month.

Hollywood Wax Museum
6767 Hollywood Blvd., Hollywood,
323-462-8860;
www.hollywoodwax.com
The Hollywood Wax Museum immortalizes more than 350 Hollywood legends with lifelike wax sculptures. Expertly designed and created by the Masters FX studio and curator Ken Horn, sculptures of film and TV stars such as Clark Gable, Elvis Presley and Tom Cruise are part of elaborate movie sets designed to entertain and inform visitors about films and their actors. Daily 10 a.m.-midnight.

Melrose Avenue
Melrose and Highland Avenues,
Los Angeles,
323-469-8311

On this street synonymous with bohemian style, shops offer great buys on vintage clothing. There are also chic boutiques such as Betsey Johnson, Liza Bruce and Miu Miu.

Mulholland Drive
Hollywood
The best way to view Los Angeles' beautiful Santa Monica Mountains is to go for a spin on Mulholland Drive. This 21-mile road runs along the top of the range from Hollywood to Ventura, dipping through the peaks and canyons of the Hollywood Hills. The views of the San Fernando Valley and the Los Angeles Basin are breathtaking—as are the celebrity homes you'll spot along the way.

Pantages Theater
6233 Hollywood Blvd.,
Hollywood,
213-480-3232
Since its opening in 1930, the Pantages has hosted A-list movie premieres, the Academy Awards, performances by some of the world's greatest musicians and more recently national touring productions of Broadway's biggest hits. Just seeing the 2,691-seat theater with its Art Deco statues, gilded columns and hand-painted murals is worth the price of a ticket.

Sunset Ranch/Hollyridge Trail
3400 Beachwood Dr.,
Hollywood,
323-469-5450;
www.sunsetranchhollywood.com
Rent a horse and a guide to ride the trails that weave through the hills of Griffith Park, or walk partway up the driveway to reach the trailhead of the Hollyridge Trail. A relatively easy hike on a wide dirt-fire road, it circles around the east side of Mount Lee, where there's a great view of the San Fernando Valley. Continue around the mountain for the Hollywood sign and a scenic view that overlooks Los Angeles. Daily 9 a.m.-5 p.m.

SOUTHERN CALIFORNIA

★
★
★
★
★

SPECIAL EVENTS

Easter Sunrise Services
Hollywood Bowl, 2301 N. Highland Ave.,
Hollywood,
323-850-2000
An interdenominational service with music from select choral groups.

Hollywood Christmas Parade
6925 Hollywood Blvd.,
Los Angeles
Star-studded parade with floats and marching bands. Televised worldwide. Sunday after Thanksgiving.

HOTELS

★★Best Western Carlyle Inn
1119 S. Robertson Blvd., Los Angeles,
310-275-4445, 800-322-7595;
www.carlyle-inn.com
32 rooms. Complimentary full breakfast. Wireless Internet access. $

★★★Renaissance Hollywood Hotel
1755 N. Highland Ave.,
Hollywood,
323-856-1200, 888-897-2806;
www.renaissancehollywood.com
This hotel anchors the Hollywood and Highland Center, Los Angeles' shopping and entertainment hub, as well as the Kodak Theatre, the Hollywood Walk of Fame and numerous restaurants. Inside, the mid-century modern design, retro art and chic furnishings are reminiscent of 1950s Hollywood. The Hollywood Bowl, Universal Studios and other attractions are within a short drive.
637 rooms. High-speed Internet access. Restaurant, bar. $$$

RESTAURANTS

★★★Vert
6801 Hollywood Blvd.,
Hollywood,
323-491-1300;
www.wolfgangpuck.com
Located in the Hollywood and Highlands Center, Wolfgang Puck's chic brasserie is a welcome respite for shoppers, hungry tourists and dressed-up locals on their way to the Hollywood Bowl or the theater. The room is large and cheerful, with green walls, blue booths, funky lighting and an open kitchen. European classics like steamed mussels, fritto misto and pork chops dominate the bistro-style menu, which also features Puck's signature gourmet pizzas.
French menu. Lunch, dinner. Bar. Children's menu. Casual attire. Reservations recommended. Valet parking. $$$

★★★Cafe des Artistes
1534 N. McCadden Pl.,
Hollywood, 90028,
323-469-7300;
www.cafedesartistes.info
This intimate French restaurant, located in a converted house on a Sunset Boulevard side street, is Parisian in design. The parquet-floored room is dim and flatteringly lit, and the outdoor patio is tented, creating a romantic setting. Classics like escargot and duck leg confit are offered, but the place is famous for its mac 'n' cheese.
French menu. Lunch, dinner. Bar. Casual attire. Reservations recommended. $$$

★★★Falcon
7213 Sunset Blvd., Hollywood,
323-850-5350;
www.falconslair.com
This sleek spot with a sexy 1970s aura is evocative of a Case Study house, with clean lines, shag carpets and cozy booths. The ultra-hip crowd nibbles on organic salads and crisp pizzas made with farmers' market-fresh ingredients before spilling into the fire-lit back patio for cocktails and the late night DJ's spins.
American menu. Dinner. Closed Sunday. Bar. Casual attire. Outdoor seating. $$

★★Uzbekistan
7077 Sunset Blvd., Hollywood,
323-464-3663
Eastern European menu. Lunch, dinner. Bar. Casual attire. Reservations recommended. $$

57

SOUTHERN CALIFORNIA

★
★
★
★
★

IRVINE

In the heart of Orange County, Irvine is one of the nation's largest planned communities.
Information: Chamber of Commerce, 2485 McCabe Way, 949-660-9112;
www.irvinechamber.com

WHAT TO SEE AND DO

University of California, Irvine
Campus and University Drives,
Irvine, 949-824-5011; www.uci.edu
Undergraduate, graduate and medical schools on a 1,489-acre campus. Tours of campus. Daily.

Wild Rivers Waterpark
8770 Irvine Center Dr., Irvine,
949-788-0808; www.wildrivers.com
One of Southern California's biggest water parks (20 acres), with rides designed for children, teens and adults. Mid-May-late September: days and times vary.

HOTELS

★★Atrium Hotel at Orange County Airport
18700 MacArthur Blvd., Irvine,
949-833-2770, 800-854-3012;
www.atriumhotel.com
215 rooms. Restaurant, bar. Airport transportation available. Pool. $

★★★Crowne Plaza
17941 Von Karman Ave., Irvine,
949-863-1999, 877-348-2424;
www.crowneplaza.com
Ideal for business travelers because of its location near company headquarters such as Washington Mutual and Taco Bell. The executive floor was renovated in summer of 2007.

335 rooms. Complimentary continental breakfast. Restaurant, bar. High-speed wireless Internet. Airport transportation available. $$

★★★Hyatt Regency
17900 Jamboree Rd., Irvine,
949-975-1234, 800-233-1234;
www.irvine.hyatt.com
Centrally located to the business districts of Irvine and Newport, all rooms at this hotel feature luxury bedding and pillow-top mattresses. Opting for the business plan rooms offers free breakfast and local calls and 24-hours access to copying, printing and business supplies, plus city mountain views and marble baths.

536 rooms. Restaurant, bar. Airport transportation available. Fitness center. Pool. $$

RESTAURANT

★★★Ruth's Chris Steak House
2961 Michelson Dr., Irvine, 949-252-8848;
www.ruthschris.com
Born from a single New Orleans restaurant that Ruth Fertel bought in 1965 for $22,000, the chain is a favorite among steak lovers. Aged prime midwestern beef is broiled and served on a heated plate sizzling with butter and with sides like creamed spinach and au gratin potatoes.

Steak menu. Dinner. Bar. Children's menu. Casual attire. $$$

LAGUNA BEACH

The beaches are beautiful and artists have contributed to the quaint charm of this seaside town. Lots of art and antique shops make leisurely strolling a pleasure.
Information: Chamber of Commerce, 357 Glenneyre St., 949-494-1018;
www.lagunabeachchamber.org

58

SOUTHERN CALIFORNIA

WHAT TO SEE AND DO

Laguna Playhouse
606 Laguna Canyon Rd., Laguna Beach,
949-497-2787; www.lagunaplayhouse.com
Theater company presents dramas, comedies, musicals, children's theater. Main stage mid-July-June, Tuesday-Sunday.

SPECIAL EVENTS

Festival of Arts and Pageant of the Masters
650 Laguna Canyon Rd., Laguna Beach,
949-494-1145, 800-487-3378;
www.foapom.com
Exhibits by 160 artists. Entertainment. Daily. Mid-July-August.

Sawdust Fine Arts and Crafts Festival
935 Laguna Canyon Rd., Laguna Beach,
949-494-3030;
www.sawdustfestival.org/index.htm
More than 175 Laguna Beach artists create paintings, photographs, sculptures, jewelry, ceramics, hand-blown glass and other works of art. Daily, July-early September.

HOTELS

★★Aliso Creek Inn
31106 S. Pacific Coast Hwy.,
Laguna Beach,
949-499-2271, 800-223-3309;
www.alisocreekinn.com
In a secluded area of Aliso Canyon near the beach.
60 rooms, all suites. High-speed Internet access. Restaurant. Pets accepted. Golf. Business center. $$

★Best Western Laguna Reef Inn
30806 Pacific Coast Hwy.,
Laguna Beach,
949-499-2227, 800-423-7846;
www.bestwestern.com
43 rooms. Complimentary continental breakfast. High-speed Internet access. Pool. $$

★★Holiday Inn
25205 La Paz Rd., Laguna Hills,
949-586-5000, 800-972-2576;
www.holidayinn.com

147 rooms. Complimentary continental breakfast. Restaurant, bar. Pool. $

★★★Marriott Laguna Cliffs Resort
25135 Park Lantern, Dana Point,
949-661-5000, 888-236-2427;
www.lagunacliffs.com
This elegant and comfortable hotel with very California coastal décor occupies 42 acres and overlooks the Pacific. On-site croquet and tennis, a new spa and fitness center and two ocean-view pools provide plenty of recreation. Other perks include a gourmet coffee bar and free snacks in the lobby.
376 rooms. High-speed Internet access. Restaurant, bar. Pets accepted. Pool. Tennis. Business center. $$$

★★★★Montage Resort & Spa
30801 S. Coast Hwy., Laguna Beach, 92651,
949-715-6000, 877-782-9821;
www.montagelagunabeach.com
Reigning over Laguna Beach from its rugged clifftop location, this stylish getaway blends arts and crafts style with the luxury of a full-service resort. Rooms, suites and bungalows feature 400-thread-count linens and five-fixture marble bathrooms with a large shower and tub and private balconies or patios with ocean views. The full-range spa has more than 20 treatment rooms and the poolside cabanas are decked out with flat-screen TVs and DVD/CD players.
262 rooms. High-speed wireless Internet access. Three restaurants, four bars. Fitness classes available. Beach. Pets accepted. $$$$

★★★Surf & Sand Resort
1555 S. Coast Hwy., Laguna Beach,
949-497-4477, 877-786-6835;
www.surfandsandresort.com
This resort blends coastal elegance with West Coast cool. Guest rooms feature marble tiled entryways and private balconies with ocean views. The Aquaterra Spa offers a wide variety of treatments and the fitness center and yoga studio will get guests in shape. The restaurant and lounge serve up signature southern California views with a Mediterranean-inspired menu.

59

SOUTHERN CALIFORNIA

★
★
★
★
★

165 rooms. High-speed Internet access. Restaurant, bar. Fitness center. Pool. **$$$$**

SPECIALTY LODGINGS
Blue Lantern Inn
34343 Blue Lantern St., Dana Point, 949-661-1304, 800-950-1236; www.bluelanterninn.com
This inn is located on a bluff overlooking yacht harbor; some rooms have views of the coast.
29 rooms. Complimentary full breakfast. High-speed Internet access. **$$**

Casa Laguna Inn
2510 S. Coast Hwy., Laguna Beach, 949-494-2996, 800-233-0449; www.casalaguna.com
22 rooms. Pets accepted; fee. Complimentary full breakfast. High-speed Internet access. Pets accepted. **$$**

Eiler's Inn
741 S. Coast Hwy., Laguna Beach, 949-494-3004, 866-617-2696; www.eilersinn.com
12 rooms. No children allowed. Complimentary full breakfast. **$$**

Inn at Laguna Beach
211 N. Coast Hwy., Laguna Beach, 949-497-9722, 800-544-4479; www.innatlagunabeach.com
Village shops, restaurants and art galleries all within walking distance.
70 rooms. Complimentary continental breakfast. Wireless Internet access. **$$**

RESTAURANTS
★A La Carte Gourmet
1915 S. Coast Hwy., Laguna Beach, 949-497-4927; www.alacartelagunabeach.com
American menu. Lunch, dinner. Casual attire. **$**

★★Beach House Inn
619 Sleepy Hollow Lane, Laguna Beach, 949-494-9707; www.thebeachhouse.com
Seafood, steak menu. Breakfast, lunch, dinner. Bar. Children's menu. Casual attire.

Reservations recommended. Valet parking. Outdoor seating. **$$$**

★★Cedar Creek Inn
384 Forest Ave., Laguna Beach, 949-497-8696; www.cedarcreekinn.com
California menu. Lunch, dinner. Bar. Children's menu. Casual attire. Reservations recommended. Outdoor seating. **$$**

★The Cottage
308 N. Coast Hwy., Laguna Beach, 949-494-3023; www.thecottagerestaurant.com
American menu. Breakfast, lunch, dinner. Children's menu. Casual attire. Reservations recommended. Outdoor seating. **$$**

★★Five Feet Restaurant
328 Glenneyre St., Laguna Beach, 949-497-4955; www.fivefeetrestaurants.com
Chinese menu. Dinner. Casual attire. Reservations recommended. **$$$**

★Laguna Thai by the Sea
31715 S. Coast Hwy., Laguna Beach, 949-415-0924; www.lagunathai.com
Thai menu. Lunch, dinner. Casual attire. Outdoor seating. No credit cards accepted. **$$**

★★Las Brisas de Laguna
361 Cliff Dr., Laguna Beach, 949-497-5434; www.lasbrisaslagunabeach.com
Continental menu. Breakfast, lunch, dinner, Sunday brunch. Bar. Casual attire. Reservations recommended. Valet parking. Outdoor seating. **$$$**

★San Shi Go
1100 S. Coast Hwy., Laguna Beach, 949-494-1551
Japanese, sushi menu. Lunch Tuesday-Friday, dinner. Casual attire. **$$**

★★★★Studio
30801 S. Coast Hwy., Laguna Beach, 949-715-6000; www.studiolagunabeach.com

Housed in a cozy arts and crafts cottage overlooking the ocean, this restaurant at Montage Resort is a study in understated elegance. The menu is the creation of award-winning chef James Boyce, and features contemporary California cuisine, made with the freshest local ingredients. Settle in for a supper made up of dishes like pan-seared John Dory with baby fennel, cipollini onions and caramelized cauliflower and madras curry, or vinegar-braised short ribs with butter-roasted asparagus. The wine cellar features more than 1,800 bottles with plenty of California selections and wines available by the glass. **$$$**

★★**Ti Amo Ristorante**
31727 South Coast Hwy.,
Laguna Beach,
949-499-5350;
www.tiamolagunabeach.com
Italian, Mediterranean menu. Dinner. Bar. Casual attire. **$$$**

SPAS

★★★★★**Spa Montage at Montage Resort**
30801 S. Coast Hwy., Laguna Beach,
949-715-6000, 866-271-6953;
www.spamontage.com
Spa Montage is a stunning facility that takes advantage of its superior beachfront setting. An indoor-outdoor structure and floor-to-ceiling windows framing 160-degree views alleviate any guilt guests may feel for opting to stay in for a bit of pampering on a sunny day. The spa's holistic, get-back-to-nature approach is evident in its design, as well as in the products it uses. Custom-mixed lotions and oils blend natural ingredients, including eucalyptus, lavender, orange blossoms and citrus. Wrap up in one of the spa's cashmere robes and try any number of therapies, from a California citrus polish to an algae cellulite massage. Hungry spa-goers can find a cozy spot by the lap pool, where healthy snacks and meals are available from the Mosaic Grille. **$$**

LONG BEACH

A multi-billion dollar redevelopment program helped Long Beach become one of Southern California's most diverse waterfront destinations, recapturing the charm it first attained as a premier seaside resort in the early 1900s. Today, the state's largest beach city (the beach is indeed long at 5 1/2 miles) derives its economic security from aerospace (McDonnell Douglas is its largest employer), harbor, oil and tourism industries. A 21 1/2-mile light rail system, the Metro Blue Line, connects Long Beach and Los Angeles.
Information: Long Beach Area Convention & Visitors Bureau, 562-436-3645, 800-452-7829; www.visitlongbeach.com

WHAT TO SEE AND DO

Queen Mary Seaport
1126 Queens Hwy.,
Long Beach, 562-435-3511;
www.queenmary.com
For 25 years, the rich and famous boarded this 12-deck luxury ocean liner to cross the Atlantic in grand style. Since 1967, the ship has been docked in Long Beach and people board it for tours, special events, shipboard dining or an overnight hotel stay in one of its 365 staterooms. The price of admission includes a ghosts and legends tour (some say the vessel is haunted) but for $5 extra, a World War II tour is offered, giving insight into the role the ship played in transporting American military personnel from 1940 to 1946. Visitors can also board a Foxtrot submarine Russians used to track enemy forces in the Pacific during the Cold War. Monday-Thursday 10 a.m.-5 p.m., Friday-Sunday 10 a.m.-6 p.m.

Alamitos Bay
205 Marina Dr.,
Long Beach,
www.alamitosbay.com
Seven miles of inland waterways for swimming, sunning, windsurfing and boating (includes more than 2,000 slips). Guest docks. Surrounding Seaport Village includes restaurants and shops. Daily.

SOUTHERN CALIFORNIA

Aquarium of the Pacific

100 Aquarium Way, Long Beach,
562-590-3100;
www.aquariumofpacific.org

This enormous aquarium houses more than 12,000 animals in 50 exhibits including a hands-on shark lagoon where visitors can actually touch the sharks. Check out the museum's Animal Vision 3-D exhibit and get a behind-the-scenes tour. Daily 9 a.m.-6 p.m.; closed during Toyota Grand Prix.

California State University, Long Beach

1250 Bellflower Blvd., Long Beach,
562-985-4111; www.csulb.edu

The 320-acre campus includes sculptures created by artists who participated in the first International Sculpture Symposium, held in the United States in 1965. Also see an art museum with displays and exhibits and the Earl Burns Miller Japanese Garden. Campus tours Monday-Friday, by appointment.

Catalina Express

Berth 95, San Pedro, 800-481-3470;
www.catalinaexpress.com

Board one of eight state-of-the-art catamarans and whip over to Catalina Island in about an hour. The boats include airline-style seating, panoramic viewing windows and on-deck seating.

El Dorado Regional Park East and Nature Center

7550 E. Spring St., Long Beach,
562-570-1745

This 450-acre park includes four lakes, boat rentals, an archery range and nature and hiking trails. Picnicking. Museum and visitor center. Daily 7 a.m.-dusk.

Long Beach Convention & Entertainment Center

300 E. Ocean Blvd., Long Beach,
562-436-3636; www.longbeachcc.com

Houses a major sporting arena, convention/exhibition center and two performing theaters. Resident companies include the Long Beach Symphony, Long Beach Opera, Civic Light Opera and Classical Ballet.

Long Beach Museum of Art

2300 E. Ocean Blvd., Long Beach,
562-439-2119; www.lbma.org

Permanent collection featuring American art, German expressionists and video art. Also includes a contemporary sculpture garden and an education gallery. The cafe and gift shop are housed in a 1912 mansion overlooking the Pacific Ocean. Tuesday, Saturday-Sunday 11 a.m.-5 p.m., Wednesday-Friday 11 a.m.-9 p.m.

Long Beach Sport Fishing

555 Pico Ave., Long Beach, 562-432-8993

Entertainment/fishing complex with full range of sport fishing vessels for half-day, three-quarter-day, full-day and night fishing excursions. Restaurants, fish market, bar. Whale-watching November-February.

Los Alamitos Race Course

4961 Katella Ave., Los Alamitos,
714-820-2800; www.losalamitos.com

Quarter Horse, Arabian, Thoroughbred, Paint and Appaloosa racing. Thursday-Sunday.

Municipal Beach

Cherry and Ocean Streets, Long Beach,
562-436-3645

Lifeguards at many areas in summer. Daily.

Rancho Los Alamitos Historic Ranch and Gardens

6400 Bixby Hill Rd., Long Beach,
562-431-3541;
www.rancholosalamitos.com

Take a guided tour of an adobe ranch house (circa 1800) with antique furnishings, six barns and outbuildings including a blacksmith shop, plus five acres of gardens. 30 minutes. Wednesday-Sunday 1-5 p.m.

Shoreline Village

419 Shoreline Village Dr., Long Beach,
562-435-2668; www.shorelinevillage.com

This seven-acre shopping, dining and entertainment complex recaptures the look and charm of a turn-of-the-century California seacoast village. Includes a collection of unique shops and galleries. There's also an historic carousel and a

SOUTHERN CALIFORNIA

complete marine center with daily harbor cruises and seasonal whale-watching excursions. Alternative transportation to Shoreline Village is available via the free Promenade Tram from downtown Long Beach, the Runabout Shuttle (also from downtown Long Beach) and the water taxi that transports passengers between Shoreline Village and the downtown marina. Daily.

SPECIAL EVENTS

Naples Christmas Boat Parade
562-570-5333; www.longbeach.gov
Festively decorated boats wind through the canals of Naples Island and along the water by Shoreline Village each year. December.

Long Beach Jazz Festival
www.longbeachjazzfestival.com
Held every year on a grassy knoll, this annual event features top artists, delicious food and fabulous art. Mid-August.

Toyota Grand Prix
3000 Pacific Ave., Long Beach,
562-981-2600; www.longbeachgp.com
International race held on downtown streets. Usually three days in April.

HOTELS

★★Best Western Golden Sails Hotel
6285 E. Pacific Coast Hwy., Long Beach,
562-596-1631, 800-762-5333;
www.bestwestern.com
173 rooms. Restaurant, bar. Airport transportation available. **$**

★★The Coast Hotel
700 Queensway Dr., Long Beach,
562-435-7676, 800-716-6199;
www.coasthotels.com
195 rooms. Restaurant, bar. Airport transportation available. Pets accepted. Pool. Tennis. **$**

★★Guesthouse International Hotel
5325 E. Pacific Coast Hwy., Long Beach,
562-597-1341;
www.guesthouse.net

143 rooms. Restaurant, bar. Airport transportation available. Pets accepted. Pool. **$**

★★★Hilton Long Beach
701 W. Ocean Blvd., Long Beach,
310-983-3400, 800-345-6565;
www.longbeach.hilton.com
Conveniently located in downtown Long Beach, this hotel is close to Long Beach and LAX airports, within walking distance of theaters and shopping and within four blocks of the convention center and beach. The comfortable guest rooms feature luxury mattresses, interesting artwork of historic Long Beach, large showers and Crabtree & Evelyn bath amenities.
393 rooms. High-speed wireless Internet access. Two restaurants, bar. Pets accepted. Fitness center. Swim. Business center. **$$$**

★★★Hyatt Regency Long Beach
200 S. Pine Ave., Long Beach,
562-491-1234; www.longbeach.hyatt.com
Located next to the convention center and within walking distance of the Pier and the downtown area, this California-style Hyatt is a good choice for both business and leisure travelers. The spacious guest rooms provide plush bedding, work areas and views of the harbor.
528 rooms. High-speed wireless Internet access. Restaurant, bar. Airport transportation available. **$$**

★★★The Pacific Inn Seal Beach
600 Marina Dr.,
562-493-2416, 800-443-3292;
www.sealbeachinn.com
This quirky, newly renovated inn is filled with antiques and historical pieces, and all the rooms are non-smoking and have balconies.
23 rooms. Complimentary full breakfast. Restaurant, bar. Pool. **$$**

★★★Renaissance Long Beach Hotel
111 E. Ocean. Blvd., Long Beach,
562-437-5900, 888-236-2427;
www.renaissancehotels.com
This downtown Long Beach property recently underwent a renovation of the lobby, banquet halls and guest rooms,

which were given white-on-white plush bedding and marble bathrooms. The new restaurant, Tracht's, serves steaks and seafood in a sleek dining space.

374 rooms. Pets accepted; fee. High-speed wireless Internet access. Restaurant, two bars. Airport transportation available. No smoking. **$$$**

SPECIALTY LODGING
The Turret House Victorian Bed and Breakfast
556 Chestnut Ave., Long Beach, 562-624-1991, 888-488-7738; www.turrethouse.com
5 rooms. Complimentary full breakfast. **$**

RESTAURANTS
★★King's Fish House
100 W. Broadway Ave., Long Beach, 562-432-7463; www.kingsfishhouse.com
Seafood menu. Lunch, dinner, brunch. Bar. Children's menu. Outdoor seating. **$$**

★★★L'Opera Ristorante
101 Pine Ave., Long Beach, 562-491-0066; www.lopera.com

This local favorite serves up modern northern Italian cuisine. Sample dishes include ravioli stuffed with duck, and mint pasta filled with fava beans and ricotta cheese. Massive marble columns grace the lovely dining room and the service is warm and attentive.

Italian menu. Lunch, dinner, late-night. Bar. Children's menu. Business casual attire. Reservations recommended. **$$$**

★★Parker's Lighthouse
435 Shoreline Village Dr., Long Beach, 562-432-6500; www.parkerslighthouse.com
Seafood menu. Lunch, dinner. Bar. Children's menu. Casual attire. Outdoor seating. **$$**

★★The Yard House
401 Shoreline Village Dr., Long Beach, 562-628-0455; www.yardhouse.com
California menu. Lunch, dinner, late-night. Bar. Children's menu. Casual attire. Outdoor seating. **$$$**

64

MALIBU
This coastal community, which stretches along Pacific Coast Highway, is the home of countless movie stars. It's also known for its sandy beaches. Every local seems to have his or her own secret spot, but Zuma and Will Rogers are always popular. Fresh seafood can also be enjoyed seaside, from funky fish shack the Reel Inn to the classy Chart House.
Information: www.ci.malibu.ca.us

WHAT TO SEE AND DO
Pepperdine University
24255 Pacific Coast Hwy., Malibu, 310-506-4000; www.pepperdine.edu
Spanning 830 acres, the campus includes the School of Law as well as colleges of arts, sciences and letters; cultural arts center and Weisman Museum of Art. Tuesday-Sunday.

HOTELS
★Malibu Beach Inn
22878 Pacific Coast Hwy., Malibu, 310-456-6444, 800-462-5428; www.malibubeachinn.com

47 rooms. Complimentary continental breakfast. **$$$**

★★★Malibu Country Inn
6506 Westward Beach Rd., Malibu, 310-457-9622, 800-386-6787; www.malibucountryinn.com
This cozy, Cape Cod-style inn built in 1943 is set on three well-tended acres atop a bluff overlooking spectacular Zuma Beach. The uniquely decorated guest rooms have private patios overlooking magnificent gardens, and several have ocean views and Jacuzzis. Most accommodations feature fireplaces, refrigerators and coffeemakers.

Room service is available for breakfast, lunch and dinner.

16 rooms. Complimentary continental breakfast. Restaurant, bar. **$$**

RESTAURANTS

★★Allegria
22821 Pacific Coast Hwy., Malibu,
310-456-3132; www.allegriamalibu.com
Italian menu. Lunch, dinner. Bar. Casual attire. Reservations recommended. Valet parking. **$$$**

★★Geoffrey's
27400 Pacific Coast Hwy., Malibu,
310-457-1519; www.geoffreysmalibu.com
California menu. Lunch, dinner. Bar. Casual attire. Reservations recommended. Valet parking. Outdoor seating. **$$$**

★★Moonshadows
20356 W. Pacific Coast Hwy., Malibu,
310-456-3010;
www.moonshadowsmalibu.com

American menu. Lunch, dinner. Bar. Casual attire. Valet parking. Outdoor seating. **$$$**

★★★Nobu
3835 Cross Creek Rd., Malibu,
310-317-9140;
www.nobumatsuhisa.com
The plain wooden interior may not look spectacular, but the minimalist style serves to put the focus on the Chilean-Japanese cuisine that made Nobu into a mini-empire, known more for miso-marinated black cod and rock shrimp with spicy mayo than sushi.

Japanese, sushi menu. Dinner. Reservations recommended. **$$$$**

★Reel Inn
18661 Pacific Coast Hwy., Malibu,
310-456-8221
Seafood menu. Lunch, dinner. Children's menu. Casual attire. Outdoor seating. **$$**

MANHATTAN BEACH

This once-quiet beach enclave has become a vibrant neighborhood that is constantly buzzing with new construction and an influx of increasingly wealthy inhabitants. The rolling hills just blocks from the beach are dotted with quaint homes and the mini-mansions of such luminaries as Tiger Woods.

Still, a mellow beach atmosphere prevails. You'll still see groups of surfers walking down the street or families in flip flops from the beach shopping in the local markets. The main zone of activity is Manhattan Beach Boulevard and the Pier, which are crammed with trendy nightclubs, surf shops and restaurants. Along the strand, in-line skaters, beach volleyball players, bikers and dog lovers make for an active scene.
Information: www.ci.manhattan-beach.ca.us

HOTELS

★Springhill Suites Los Angeles LAX/ Manhattan Beach
14620 Aviation Blvd., Hawthorne,
310-727-9595, 800-228-9290;
www.marriott.com
164 rooms, all suites. Complimentary full breakfast. High-speed Internet access. Airport. **$$**

★★★Manhattan Beach Marriott
1400 Parkview Ave., Manhattan Beach,
310-546-7511, 800-228-9290;
www.marriott.com/laxmn

Located three miles south of LAX, this 26-acre property offers vacationers and business travelers a convenient South Bay location. The property is within walking distance of shopping, restaurants and theater, and is just a short ride to the local beaches. Newly renovated guest rooms feature the Marriott Revive bedding. Nine-hole golf course on site.

385 rooms. High-speed Internet access. Restaurant, bar. **$$**

RESTAURANTS

★Back Home in Lahaina
916 N. Sepulveda Blvd.,
Manhattan Beach, 310-374-0111;
www.backhomeinlahaina.com
Hawaiian menu. Breakfast, lunch, dinner.
Bar. Children's menu. Casual attire. **$**

★★★Mangiamo
128 Manhattan Beach Blvd.,
Manhattan Beach, 310-318-3434
This quiet, romantic restaurant is just steps
from the Pier 9 beach. Nab a table in the
intimate wine cellar or sit up front to catch
a view of the sunset. The northern Italian
menu features many seafood selections,
as well as dishes like osso buco and three-
mushroom farfalle.

Italian menu. Dinner. Bar. Business casual
attire. Reservations recommended. **$$$**

★★Reed's Restaurant
2640 N. Sepulveda Blvd.,
Manhattan Beach,
310-546-3299;
www.reedsrestaurant.com
California, French menu. Lunch, dinner.
Casual attire. Reservations recommended.
Outdoor seating. **$$**

★Uncle Bill's Pancake House
1305 Highland Ave., Manhattan Beach,
310-305-9545
American menu. Breakfast, lunch.
Children's menu. Casual attire. Outdoor
seating. No credit cards accepted. **$**

MARINA DEL REY

As its name suggests, this community, located next to Venice and only four miles from
LAX, attracts many boating and sport fishing enthusiasts. The dominate feature is the largest man-made harbor in the world, with more than 5,000 slips. Sail and power boat rentals,
ocean cruises and fishing expeditions are available. Besides boating, there's biking and
jogging in front of the marina, numerous restaurants, shops and beaches.
Information: Marina del Rey Convention & Visitors Bureau, 4701 Admiralty Way,
310-305-9545; www.visitthemarina.com

WHAT TO SEE AND DO
Fisherman's Village
13755 Fiji Way, Marina del Rey,
310-823-5411; www.visitthemarina.com
Modeled after a turn-of-the-century New
England fishing town and located on the main
channel of the largest man-made small craft
harbor in the country, this area and its well-
known lighthouse have appeared in many television and movie productions. Cobblestone
walks complement the nautical atmosphere
and provide a panoramic view of the marina.
Boat rentals, fishing charters, harbor cruises;
shops, boutiques and restaurants. Entertainment throughout the year, including free jazz
concerts on Saturdays and Sundays. Daily.

HOTELS
★Best Western Jamaica Bay Inn
4175 Admiralty Way, Marina Del Rey,
310-823-5333, 888-823-5333;
www.bestwestern-jamaicabay.com

42 rooms. Restaurant, bar. Beach. Pool.
Business center. **$$**

★★Courtyard Los Angeles Marina Del Rey
13480 Maxella Ave.,
Marina del Rey,
310-822-8555, 800-321-2211;
www.courtyard.com/laxcm
276 rooms. Wireless Internet access. Res-
taurant, bar. **$$**

★★★Marina Del Rey Marriott
4100 Admiralty Way,
Marina del Rey,
310-301-3000, 800-228-9290;
www.marriott.com/laxmb
All the rooms at this modern hotel overlook
the marina or have views of the Malibu
Mountains and the Pacific. Every measure
is taken to help guests relax, including a
calming scent that circulates throughout

★
★
★
★
★

the hotel and a candlelit lobby. This hotel is non-smoking.

370 rooms. High-speed Internet access. Restaurant, bar. Pool. Business center. **$$**

★★★The Ritz-Carlton, Marina Del Rey
4375 Admiralty Way, Marina del Rey,
310-823-1700, 800-241-3333;
www.ritzcarlton.com

This luxury hotel has it all, from its location occupying five acres on the marina to a new boutique spa to a waterfront pool. The spacious guest rooms are sprinkled with art and antiques and boast views of the marina. Every need is anticipated: dock slips and bikes are available for rental, access is given to the jogging trails on the waterfront and guests don't even have to leave the premises for some nightlife. The lobby features a house DJ mix Thursday through Sunday nights.

304 rooms. Restaurant, two bars. Pets accepted. Pool. Tennis. Business center. **$$$$**

SPECIALTY LODGINGS
Inn at Playa Del Rey
435 Culver Blvd., Playa Del Rey,
310-574-1920; www.innatplayadelrey.com

This inn is close to the beach and overlooks the main channel of Marina del Rey and the Ballona Wetlands bird sanctuary.

25 rooms. Complimentary full breakfast. **$$**

RESTAURANTS
★★Ballona Fish Market
13455 Maxella Ave., Marina del Rey,
310-822-8979

Seafood, sushi menu. Lunch, dinner. Bar. Casual attire. Reservations recommended. **$$$**

NEWPORT BEACH

This seaside community—sometimes referred to as the American Riviera—is famous for elegant waterfront villas, shops and restaurants and beautiful Pacific Coast scenery. With a six mile-long beach and a large harbor, it offers a variety of water activities. Vacation attractions are clustered around the Balboa peninsula, a six-mile finger of land running east and west. The Balboa Fun Zone, located on Balboa Peninsula, features a ferris wheel and an old-time merry-go-round. Behind Balboa is Newport Harbor, with 12 miles of waterways and eight islands. Back Bay is a wildlife sanctuary. .

Information: Newport Harbor Area Chamber of Commerce, 1470 Jamboree Rd., 949-729-4400; www.newportbeach.com

WHAT TO SEE AND DO
Balboa Fun Zone
600 E. Bay Ave., Newport Beach,
949-673-0408;
www.thebalboafunzone.com

Amusement area at the pier. Ferris wheel, rides, video games, arcade. Fee for rides. Sunday-Thursday 11 a.m.-9 p.m., Friday-Saturday until 10 p.m.

Orange County Museum of Arts
850 San Clemente Dr., Newport Beach,
949-759-1122;
www.ocma.net

Permanent and changing exhibits of modern and contemporary art, with an emphasis on Californian art since World War II.

Tuesday-Sunday 11 a.m.-5 p.m., Thursday until 8 p.m. Admission free on Tuesday.

Sherman Library & Gardens
2647 E. Pacific Coast Hwy.,
Corona del Mar, 949-673-2261;
www.slgardens.org

Botanical gardens set amid fountains and sculptures. Historical library has a research center for the study of Pacific Southwest. Daily 10:30 a.m.-4 p.m.

SPECIAL EVENTS
Christmas Boat Parade
Newport Beach Harbor, Newport Blvd.,
Newport Beach, 949-729-4400;
www.christmasboatparade.com

★
★
★
★

Hundreds of yachts, boats, kayaks and canoes sail around the harbor decked out in Christmas lights, and many go all out with Christmas scenes, music and costumed carolers. Mid-December.

Taste of Newport

Newport Center Dr., Newport Beach, 949-729-4400;

www.tasteofnewport.com

For three days, 75,000 people attend this festival to taste countless culinary creations from some of the area's best-loved restaurants. In addition to pizza, tacos, gyros and ribs, you'll find prime rib, crab cakes and sushi. The Sound Stage features live music throughout the festival. Sample wines from premium California wineries. Mid-September.

HOTELS

★★★Balboa Bay Club & Resort

1221 W. Coast Hwy.,

Newport Beach, 888-445-7153;

www.balboabayclub.com

Set on 15 waterfront acres, the rooms at this comfortable and whimsical resort feel like private bungalows with their furnished patios and plantation shutters. Sit back and watch the yachts in the bay, hit the spa or enjoy the numerous attractions nearby. The First Cabin Restaurant offers a seasonal menu of California cuisine in a cozy setting with panoramic views of the bay.

132 rooms. Wireless Internet access. Restaurant, bar. Pets accepted. **$$$**

★Bay Shores Peninsula Hotel

1800 W. Balboa Blvd., Newport Beach, 949-675-3463, 800-222-6675;

www.thebestinn.com

25 rooms Complimentary full breakfast. High-speed Internet access. Beach. Business center. **$**

★★★Fairmont Newport Beach

4500 MacArthur Blvd., Newport Beach, 949-476-2001

The hotel recently completed a $32 million renovation and the result is a new luxurious spa, a redesigned sky pool and luxurious new rooms with Egyptian cotton sheets

and flat-screen TVs. For a small fee sign up for the Executive Club, which offers access to free breakfast, afternoon snacks, evening hors d'oeuvres, late night dessert, the DVD/CD library and high-speed wireless Internet. Special Pageant of the Masters packages available.

435 rooms. High-speed, wireless Internet access. Two restaurants, bar. Airport transportation available. Airport. **$**

★★★Hyatt Regency Newport Beach

1107 Jamboree Rd., Newport Beach, 949-729-1234, 800-633-7313;

www.newporter.hyatt.com

This Spanish-style hotel is situated on 26 lush acres overlooking Newport beach. The rooms echo the surroundings with tropical-inspired décor, and there's plenty to do: golf, volleyball, a relaxing spa and three outdoor pools.

403 rooms. Restaurant, bar. Airport transportation available. **$$**

★★★Marriott Suites Newport Beach

500 Bayview Circle, Newport Beach, 949-854-4500, 800-228-9290;

www.marriott.com

This newly remodeled all-suite hotel features separate bedrooms and living areas, mini-refrigerators and wet bars. Some rooms have views of Upper Back Bay. There's also a brand-new spa. This hotel is non-smoking.

254 rooms, all suites. Restaurant, bar. Airport transportation available. Pool. **$$**

★★★★The Island Hotel, Newport Beach

690 Newport Center Dr.,

Newport Beach,

866-554-4620;

www.theislandhotel.com

This 20-story tower is angled toward the Pacific Ocean and is only minutes from the beach. All the rooms have private balconies or furnished patios and marble bathrooms with oversized towels. Guests may never want to leave the pool with its lush landscaping, 17-foot fireplace for chilly evenings and dataports and telephone jacks to stay in touch. Golf and shopping are nearby.

★

★

★

★

★

295 rooms. High-speed Internet access. Two restaurants, bar. Spa. Airport transportation available. Pets accepted. **$$$**

★★★Newport Beach Marriott Hotel and Spa
900 Newport Center Dr., Newport Beach, 949-640-4000, 800-228-9290;
www.marriott.com/laynb
A recent $70 million renovation turned this into a sleek and modern hotel. It's located just blocks from Newport Harbor and next door to the high-end Fashion Island mall.

532 rooms. High-speed internet access. Restaurant, bar. Spa. Airport transportation available. Pets accepted. **$$**

SPECIALTY LODGINGS
Doryman's Inn Bed & Breakfast
2102 W. Oceanfront, Newport Beach, 949-675-7300;
www.dorymansinn.com
This quaint bed-and-breakfast, confined to the second-story of a Victorian landmark built in 1921, charms with its classic design and historic, wharf-side Old Newport location. French and American antiques are sprinkled liberally throughout the guest rooms which feature fireplaces, sunken marble tubs and old-fashioned window seats.

10 rooms. Complimentary continental breakfast. **$$**

Newport Beach Hotel
2306 W. Oceanfront Blvd., Newport Beach, 949-673-7030, 800-571-8749;
www.newportbeachhotel.com
This restored oceanfront hotel has apartments as well as standard guest rooms. The Italian Renato Restaurant next door provides room service.

20 rooms. Complimentary continental breakfast **$$**

RESTAURANTS
★★21 Oceanfront
2100 W. Oceanfront, Newport Beach, 949-673-2100; www.21oceanfront.com
Seafood, steak menu. Dinner. Bar. Valet parking. Outdoor seating. **$$$**

★★El Torito Grill
951 Newport Center Dr., Newport Beach, 949-640-2875;
www.eltorito.com
Mexican menu. Lunch, dinner, Sunday brunch. Bar. Children's menu. Casual attire. Valet parking. Outdoor seating. **$$**

★★Newport Beach Brewing Company
2920 Newport Blvd., Newport Beach, 949-675-8449;
www.nbbrewco.com
American menu. Lunch, dinner. Bar. Children's menu. Casual attire. Outdoor seating. **$$**

★★★Pascal
1000 Bristol St., Newport Beach, 949-752-0107;
www.pascalnewportbeach.com
Much-lauded chef/restaurateur Pascal Olhats (as seen on *Oprah*) showcases his French countryside cuisine in this rose-filled, farmhouse-style space. Those who can afford to pay for the chef's perfectionism come here to enjoy dishes like lamb salad with apples and walnuts, foie gras with brandied cherries and dandelion greens and grilled pork with apricot and Spanish chorizo. A lavish five-course prix fixe meal is available.

French menu. Lunch, dinner. Closed Sunday. **$$$**

★★Sapori
1080 Bayside Dr., Newport Beach, 949-644-4220
Italian menu. Lunch, dinner. Bar. Reservations recommended. Outdoor seating. **$$$**

★★★The Ritz
880 Newport Center Dr., Newport Beach, 949-720-1800;
www.ritzrestaurant.com
No fewer than five distinctive, richly appointed indoor and outdoor dining spaces grace the premises, ranging from the Escoffier Room (a pavilion-style space with Georgian accents and portraits of the renowned Paris Ritz Hotel chef Auguste Escoffier) to the Wine Cellar (a vaulted brick chamber accessed through an oval

tunnel). The outstanding cuisine encompasses French, Italian and American styles.

American, French menu. Lunch, dinner. Bar. Valet parking. **$$$**

★★Tutto Mare
545 Newport Center Dr.,
Newport Beach, 949-640-6333;
www.tuttomare.com
Peach marble floors, burnished mahogany columns and expansive windows set the stage for casual upscale dining at Tutto Mare, where mesquite-grilled fish join a variety of homemade pastas and oak-fired pizzas. Sunday brunch is a big hit, presented to the sounds of live classical guitar.

Italian menu. Lunch, dinner, Sunday brunch. Bar. Outdoor seating. **$$$**

★★Villa Nova
3131 W. Coast Hwy., Newport Beach,
949-642-7880;
www.villanovarestaurant.com

Italian menu. Dinner. Bar. Children's menu. Valet parking. Outdoor seating. **$$**

SPAS
★★★★The Spa at the Island Hotel
690 Newport Center Dr., Newport Beach,
949-759-0808, 866-554-4620;
www.theislandhotel.com
Slip away to the Spa at the Island Hotel for a muscle-relieving massage or detoxifying volcanic clay treatment that is said to reenergize the body from head to toe. Spacious and modern, the spa's elegant touches—granite floors, silver tea pitchers and a calming water wall—instantly set a tranquil and tasteful tone. The spa's signature rituals use rejuvenating elements from India, Bali and the Hawaiian Islands to smooth, soften, and invigorate skin. The Island Tropical Splendor is a full-body scrub blending fresh coconut, rice, and vetiver—a perennial grass native to India known for its medicinal and aromatic properties **$$**

ORANGE

Information: Chamber of Commerce, 439 E. Chapman Ave., 714-538-3581; www.orangechamber.org

70

WHAT TO SEE AND DO
Tucker Wildlife Sanctuary
29332 Modjeska Canyon Rd.,
Orange, 714-649-2760;
www.tuckerwildlife.org
Twelve-acre refuge for native plants and animals, including several species of hummingbirds (seasonal); observation porch, nature trails; museum displays; picnic areas. Tuesday-Sunday 9 a.m.-4 p.m.

HOTELS
★★Country Inn by Ayres Orange
3737 W. Chapman Ave., Orange,
714-978-9168, 800-706-4885;
www.countrysuites.com
130 rooms. Complimentary full breakfast. Restaurant. Fitness room. Pool. **$**

★★Doubletree Hotel
100 The City Dr.,Orange,
714-634-4500, 800-528-0444;
www.doubletree.com

454 rooms. Restaurant, bar. Business center. Fitness room. Pool. Tennis. **$$**

★Hawthorn Suites
720 The City Dr. S., Orange,
714-740-2700;
www.hawthorn.com
123 rooms, all suites. Complimentary full breakfast. Pool. Business center. **$$**

★★★Hilton Suites Anaheim/Orange
400 N. State College Blvd., Orange,
714-938-1111;
www.anaheimsuites.hilton.com
This comfortable property is located within walking distance of Anaheim Stadium and minutes from Disneyland. Rooms feature plush beds and spacious bathrooms with separate tubs and Crabtree and Evelyn products. An indoor and outdoor pool, whirlpool, sundeck and dry sauna help guests relax.

230 rooms. Complimentary full breakfast. Restaurant, bar. **$$**

RESTAURANTS

★★★The Hobbit
2932 E. Chapman Ave., Orange,
714-997-1972;
www.hobbitrestaurant.com

The Hobbit has been an elegant dining destination in Orange County since 1972. Owners Michael and Debra Philippi offer guests a relaxed atmosphere and a menu of contemporary American cuisine that is served as a seven-course prix-fixe dinner, including such exquisitely prepared entrées as filet of beef en croute, prime filet mignon with morel mushrooms and tarragon-crusted rack of lamb. Between courses, take a tour of the wine cellar, visit the kitchen or take a stroll on the patio. Allow about three hours for a meal.

American menu. Dinner. Closed Monday. Bar. Jacket required. Reservations recommended. **$$$**

★★Yen Ching
574 S. Glassell St., Orange,
714-997-3300
Chinese menu. Lunch, dinner. **$$**

PASADENA

Home of the world-famous Tournament of Roses, Pasadena was first chosen as a health refuge for wintering Midwesterners, and later as a retreat for Eastern millionaires. Today, it is a cultural and scientific center with many research, development and engineering companies centered in Pasadena, including NASA's Jet Propulsion Laboratory.
Information: Convention & Visitors Bureau, 171 S. Los Robles, 626-795-9311; www.pasadenacal.com

WHAT TO SEE AND DO

Angeles National Forest
701 N. Santa Anita Ave.,
Arcadia, 626-574-1613;
www.fs.fed.us/r5/angeles

Since 1892, the Angeles National Forest has been Los Angeles' backyard. More than 650,000 acres of beautiful chaparral and pine-covered terrain, in altitudes ranging from 1,200 to 10,064 feet, provide endless opportunities for every outdoor activity. Enjoy fishing and jet-skiing on Pyramid Lake, more than 500 miles of hiking trails, skiing, horseback riding, hunting and more.

Arroyo Seco Trail
Ventura St. and Windsor Ave.,
Altadena

This 7.5-mile trail leads through a thick forest along the Arroyo Seco River in the foothills near Pasadena. The first part of the trail is a paved fire road with easy biking for less-experienced riders. As it winds farther north, the trail narrows and you'll cross the river, so expect to carry bikes across the rocky riverbed. Continue into the Angeles National Forest for a longer ride.

Brookside Men's Golf Club
1133 N. Rosemont Ave.,
Pasadena, 310-281-8877

Brookside has two 18-hole courses: the Koiner and the Nay. The Koiner course is the better but more difficult of the two. It plays considerably longer and the vistas are not to be missed. The Rose Bowl itself sits beyond hole 16, which is a medium-length dogleg par-four, and hole 8 offers a challenge off the tee with a par-three over a large water hazard.

Descanso Gardens
1418 Descanso Dr., La Cañada Flintridge,
818-949-4200;
www.descansogardens.org

The lush gardens here span 165 acres. Many types of beautiful plants thrive, but Descanso is especially known for growing more than 100,000 camellias outdoors. The roses are radiant—the All-America Rose Selections Garden showcases every variety

SOUTHERN CALIFORNIA

imagineable. Live music in summer Daily 9 a.m.-5 p.m.; tram tours Tuesday-Friday 1 p.m., 2 p.m., 3 p.m., Saturday-Sunday 11 a.m., 1 p.m., 2 p.m., 3 p.m.

Kidspace Children's Museum
480 N. Arroyo Blvd., Pasadena, 626-449-9144; www.kidspacemuseum.org
Kids can climb aboard raindrops as they travel through the water cycle, or dig up fossils and dinosaur eggs. Daily 9:30 a.m.-5 p.m.

Norton Simon Museum of Art
411 W. Colorado Blvd., Pasadena, 626-449-6840; www.nortonsimon.org
Many art lovers say this stellar museum in Pasadena tops the better-known Getty in Los Angeles. The 85,000-square-foot facility houses one of the world's finest private collections of European, American and Asian art spanning more than 2,000 years, including etchings by Rembrandt and Goya and a collection of Picasso graphics. Monday, Wednesday-Thursday noon-6 p.m., Friday to 9 p.m., Saturday-Sunday to 6 p.m.

Pacific Asia Museum
46 N. Los Robles Ave., Pasadena, 626-449-2742; www.pacificasiamuseum.org
Changing exhibits of traditional and contemporary Asian and Pacific Basin art; Chinese Imperial Palace-style building and Chinese courtyard garden; research library; bookstore. Docent tours available. Wednesday-Thursday, Saturday-Sunday 10 a.m.-5 p.m.

Pasadena Museum of History
470 W. Walnut St., Pasadena, 626-577-1660; www.pasadenahistory.org
Housed in the 18-room Fenyes Estate (1905) includes original furnishings, antiques, paintings and accessories, giving a glimpse of the elegant lifestyle that existed on Orange Grove Boulevard at the turn of the century. Tours. Wednesday-Sunday noon-5 p.m.

Rose Bowl
1001 Rose Bowl Dr., Pasadena, 626-577-3101; www.rosebowlstadium.com
Although no longer the home of the annual bowl game between the winners of the Pac-10 and the Big Ten conferences, the Rose Bowl still hosts Bowl Championship Series games every year. During the regular season, UCLA's Bruins football team plays at the venue.

SPECIAL EVENTS
Tournament of Roses
391 S. Orange Grove Blvd., Pasadena, 626-449-4100; www.tournamentofroses.com
Millions turn out each year on New Year's day to watch the gorgeous floral floats, high-stepping marching bands and beautiful equestrian units. After the parade, get an up-close look at the Showcase of Floats, which continues through January 2.

HOTELS
★★★Hilton Pasadena
168 S. Los Robles Ave., Pasadena, 626-577-1000, 800-445-8667; www.hilton.com
Located just steps from the Pasadena Convention Center and Old Town Pasadena and its hundreds of dining, shopping and entertainment options, the spacious guest rooms at this hotel are equipped with dataports, high-speed Internet access and comfortable ergonomic chairs for business travelers. The lively bar has a pool table and multiple video screens.
296 rooms. High-speed wireless Internet access. Restaurant, bar. Pets accepted. $$

★★★Sheraton Pasadena Hotel
303 E. Cordova St., Pasadena, 626-449-4000, 800-457-7940; www.starwoodhotels.com
Within walking distance of many of the city's attractions, this hotel is a nice spot for business and leisure travelers. In addition to pillow-top mattresses and large desks, guest rooms feature two-line phones,

SOUTHERN CALIFORNIA

★
★
★
★

dataports, voice mail and complimentary newspapers.

317 rooms. Restaurant, bar. Fitness center. Pool. Tennis. Business center. **$$**

★★★Westin Pasadena
191 N. Los Robles Ave., Pasadena, 626-792-2727; www.westin.com

This beautifully appointed hotel in the heart of downtown appeals to families and business travelers. An in-house kids' club supplies coloring books, bath toys and a phone line dedicated to bedtime stories. Office rooms come with a fax and printer, and all accommodations feature signature Heavenly Beds with pillow-top mattresses. Services include a concierge and a business center.

350 rooms. Two restaurants, bar. Airport transportation available. Fitness center. Pool. Business center. **$$**

SPECIALTY LODGINGS

Artists' Inn and Cottage
1038 Magnolia St., South Pasadena, 91030, 626-799-5668, 888-799-5668; www.artistsinns.com

This inn has a 1890s Victorian style. 10 rooms, 2 story. Children over 9 years only. Complimentary full breakfast. **$$**

RESTAURANTS

★Beckham Grill
77 W. Walnut St., Pasadena, 626-796-3399; www.beckhamgrill.com

American, Steak menu. Lunch, dinner. Bar. Children's menu. Casual attire. Reservations recommended. Valet parking. Outdoor seating. **$$**

★★★Bistro 45
45 S. Mentor Ave., Pasadena, 626-795-2478; www.bistro45.com

Located in an Art Deco building on a quiet Old Pasadena street, this top-ranked restaurant features a French-influenced California menu focused on fresh ingredients. Notable specialties include lobster bisque, roasted prime rib au jus with a mousseline of horseradish and potatoes, and grilled salmon drizzled with sun-dried tomato vinaigrette.

All dishes are presented with refined service and a wine list that should impress even the most discerning connoisseur.

California menu, French menu. Lunch, dinner. Closed Monday. Bar. Casual attire. Reservations recommended. Valet parking. Outdoor seating. **$$$**

★★Cafe Santorini
64 W. Union St., Pasadena, 626-564-4200; www.cafesantorini.com

Mediterranean menu. Lunch, dinner. Bar. Children's menu. Casual attire. Reservations recommended. Valet parking. Outdoor seating. **$$**

★Crocodile Cafe
140 S. Lake Ave., Pasadena, 626-449-9900; www.crocodilecafe.com

California menu. Lunch, dinner. Bar. Children's menu. Casual attire. Reservations recommended. Outdoor seating. **$$**

★★Maison Akira
713 E. Green St., Pasadena, 626-796-9501; www.maisonakira.com

French, Japanese menu. Lunch, dinner. Closed Monday. Bar. Business casual attire. Reservations recommended. Outdoor seating. **$$$**

★★Mi Piace
25 E. Colorado Blvd., Pasadena, 626-795-3131; www.mipiace.com

Italian menu. Breakfast, lunch, dinner. Bar. Children's menu. Casual attire. Outdoor seating. **$$$**

★Saladang Song
383 S. Fair Oaks Ave., Pasadena, 626-793-5200

Thai menu. Lunch, dinner. Casual attire. Outdoor seating. **$$**

★★The Raymond Restaurant
1250 S. Fair Oaks Ave., Pasadena, 626-441-3136; www.theraymond.com

American menu. Lunch, dinner. Closed Monday. Bar. Business casual attire. Valet parking. Outdoor seating. **$$$**

★
★
★
★
★

★★Twin Palms
101 W. Green St., Pasadena,
626-577-2567; www.twin-palms.com
California menu. Lunch, dinner, Sunday brunch. Bar. Children's menu. Business casual attire. Reservations recommended. Outdoor seating. **$$**

★★Yujean Kang's
67 N. Raymond Ave., Pasadena,
626-585-0855
Chinese menu. Lunch, dinner. Bar. Casual attire. Reservations recommended. Valet parking. Outdoor seating. **$$$**

POMONA
Information: Pomona Chamber of Commerce, 101 W. Mission Blvd., 909-622-1256; www.pomonachamber.org

WHAT TO SEE AND DO
Fairplex
1101 W. McKinley Ave., Pomona,
909-623-3111; www.fairplex.com
This is the home of the Los Angeles County Fair each September, but there are also more than 300 events here each year: dog shows, horse sales, antique auto shows, computer fairs, boat shows and more. The venue has 325,000 square feet of indoor exhibit space in eight exhibit halls, an equine complex, scenic plazas, picnic areas and carnival grounds.

SPECIAL EVENTS
Highland Gathering and Games
Fairplex, 1101 W. McKinley Ave.,
Pomona, 909-623-3111;
www.unitedscottishsociety.com
Scottish games; dancing; soccer, rugby; piping, drumming competition. Memorial Day weekend.

Los Angeles County Fair
Fairplex, 1101 W. McKinley Ave., Pomona,
909-623-3111; www.lacountyfair.com
The world's largest county fair includes elaborate floral and garden exhibits, thoroughbred horse racing, world-famous musical acts and much more. 17 days in September.

HOTELS
★Best Western Diamond Bar Hotel & Suites
259 Gentle Springs Lane, Diamond Bar,
909-860-3700, 800-780-7234;
www.bestwestern.com
97 rooms. Complimentary continental breakfast. Fitness room. Pool. Business center. **$**

★★Holiday Inn
21725 E. Gateway Center Dr.,
Diamond Bar, 909-860-5440, 800-988-3587;
www.holiday-inn.com
175 rooms. Restaurant, bar. Pool. **$**

REDONDO BEACH
This recreation and vacation center just south of LAX features a two-mile beach and the popular King Harbor which houses hundreds of watercraft. Once a commercial port, the historic beach town's pier now features shops, restaurants and marinas. Biking, fishing, surfing and all sorts of water sports are popular here.
Information: Chamber of Commerce and Visitors Bureau, 200 N. Pacific Coast Hwy., 310-376-6911, 800-282-0333; www.visitredondo.com

WHAT TO SEE AND DO
Galleria at South Bay
1815 Hawthorne Blvd., Redondo Beach,
310-371-7546;
www.southbaygalleria.com
The Galleria at South Bay includes Nordstrom and Robinsons-May department stores, as well as perennial favorites such as Banana Republic and Gap. Restaurants include California Pizza Kitchen.

SOUTHERN CALIFORNIA

Monday-Friday 10 a.m.-9 p.m., Saturday 10 a.m.-8 p.m., Sunday 11 a.m.-7 p.m.

Redondo Beach Pier
Torrance Blvd., Redondo Beach,
310-318-0631, 800-280-0333;
www.redondopier.com

With its laid-back atmosphere and white sandy beaches, Redondo is a beach bum's paradise. Surfing and volleyball are popular and there are many funky beach restaurants and bars. Daily, 24 hours.

HOTELS

★Best Western Sunrise at Redondo Beach Marina
400 N. Harbor Dr., Redondo Beach,
310-376-0746, 800-334-7384;
www.bestwestern-sunrise.com

111 rooms. Complimentary continental breakfast. $

★★Portofino Hotel & Yacht Club
260 Portofino Way, Redondo Beach,
310-379-8481, 800-468-4292;
www.hotelportofino.com

160 rooms. High-speed wireless Internet access. Restaurant, two bars. Fitness room. $$$

★★★Crowne Plaza
300 N. Harbor Dr., Redondo Beach,
310-318-8888, 800-368-9760;
www.crowneplaza.com

This oceanfront Crowne Plaza is seven miles from LAX and close to attractions and activities. Many restaurants are within walking distance and a free shuttle is offered to area shopping malls. Guests also get access to the adjacent Gold's Gym. Comfortable guest rooms feature a separate living room, work desks and refrigerators. Some guest rooms offer balconies with a water view.

339 rooms. High-speed Internet access. Restaurant, bar. $$

RESTAURANTS

★★★Chez Melange
1716 S. Pacific Coast Hwy.,
Redondo Beach, 310-540-1222

Chez Melange raised the bar for fine California cuisine in the beach cities years ago, and the upscale clientele is fiercely loyal to this day. The décor may scream 1985 with its peach walls, but the menu is up to the minute, offering a full sushi list as well as modern twists on classics like rabbit three ways, spicy fried oysters and steak tartare. The restaurant is always open and features holiday menus.

California menu. Breakfast, lunch, dinner, brunch. Bar. Casual attire. Reservations recommended. $$$

★★Kincaid's Bay House
500 Fisherman's Wharf,
310-318-6080

This chain's flagship restaurant is a popular stop for tourists and locals. You can't beat the location at the end of the pier offering great views of the Pacific, and the food won't disappoint either. Belly up to the raw bar for fresh shellfish or order a well-portioned entrée—black tiger prawns stuffed with blue crab and macadamia nuts is a favorite. Large booths comfortably accommodate big parties and the friendly staff will, weather permitting, steer diners toward the lovely outdoor waterfront tables.

Seafood, steak menu. Lunch, dinner, Sunday brunch. Bar. Casual attire. Reservations recommended. Outdoor seating. $$$

★★Zazou
1810 S. Catalina Ave.,
Redondo Beach,
310-540-4884

Nestled amid the art galleries and boutiques of this shore town's picturesque Riviera Village, Zazou offers delicacies such as sautéed frog legs and roasted rabbit alongside dishes like pan-roasted veal sweetbreads in an intimate, contemporary setting enhanced by soft jazz music, plenty of candles and Mediterranean artwork. The superior martinis, outstanding wine list and excellent service add to the fun.

Mediterranean menu. Lunch, dinner. Bar. Reservations recommended. Outdoor seating. $$

★
★
★
★
★

SAN PEDRO

Nestled in the Palos Verdes hills, this community is a neighborhood of Los Angeles.
Information: Chamber of Commerce, 390 W. Seventh St., 310-832-7272;
www.sanpedrochamber.com

WHAT TO SEE AND DO

Cabrillo Marine Aquarium
3720 Stephen White Dr., San Pedro,
310-548-7562; www.cabrilloaq.org
Thirty-four seawater aquariums display extensive marine life. Includes interpretive displays, environmental conservation and multimedia shows, as well as whale-watching. Access to beaches, picnic areas and fishing pier. Tuesday-Friday noon-5 p.m., Saturday-Sunday 10 a.m.-5 p.m.

Los Angeles Maritime Museum
Berth 84, San Pedro, 310-548-7618;
www.lamaritimemuseum.org
This educational museum features scale models of ships, including movie studio models from the films like *The Poseidon Adventure* and *Mutiny on the Bounty*, and numerous displays and artifacts from sailing vessels of all types. The Los Angeles Maritime Institute is also housed here. The Institute takes pride in its TopSail Youth Program, giving trips for schoolchildren and thousands of hours of free sailing lessons each year. Tuesday-Saturday 10 a.m.-5 p.m., Sunday noon-5 p.m.

Ports O' Call Village
San Pedro Waterfront, San Pedro,
310-568-8080
This quaint seaside village has a New England feel and cobblestone streets lined with shops and restaurants. The 15-acre village overlooks the Los Angeles Harbor, a busy port with cruise ships and other types of seagoing vessels used for commercial fishing, sailing, whale-watching, deep-sea fishing and more. Daily from 11 a.m.; some restaurants open earlier.

HOTELS

★Best Western Sunrise Hotel
525 S. Harbor Blvd., San Pedro,
310-548-1080, 800-356-9609;
www.bestwestern.com
110 rooms. Complimentary continental breakfast. Pool. **$**

★★Crowne Plaza Harbor Hotel
601 S. Palos Verdes St., San Pedro,
310-519-8200;
www.crowneplaza.com/laharbor
246 rooms. Complimentary continental breakfast. Restaurant, bar. Pool. **$$**

★★★Doubletree Hotel San Pedro
2800 Via Cabrillo Marina,
San Pedro, 310-514-3344;
www.marinahotelsanpedro.com
Just 19 miles from LAX and six miles from downtown Long Beach, this comfortable hotel overlooks Cabrillo Marina and is convenient to the World Cruise Center and Catalina Island.
226 rooms. Restaurant, bar. Pets accepted. **$$**

RESTAURANT

★★22nd Street Landing Seafood
141A W. 22nd St., San Pedro,
310-548-4400.
Seafood menu. Dinner. Bar. Children's menu. Casual attire. Outdoor seating. **$$$**

SANTA ANA

Slightly more than 27 square miles in area, Santa Ana is the largest city in Orange County and the ninth-largest city by population in California.

Home to a number of theatrical companies, art galleries and museums, Santa Ana's thriving downtown business district comes alive on the first Saturday of each month with an elaborate open house in which artists, actors and musicians perform for the public at the Artists'

Village (Second Street at Broadway). The Centennial Regional Park (3000 Centennial Rd.), includes an historic bike path following the original path of the Santa Ana River.
Information: Chamber of Commerce, 2020 N. Broadway, 714-541-5353; www.santaanacc.com

WHAT TO SEE AND DO

Bowers Kidseum
1802 N. Main St., Santa Ana,
714-480-1520;
www.bowers.org/kidseum/kidseum.asp
This museum for children ages 6-12 focuses on art and culture of the Americas, Pacific Rim and Africa. Tuesday-Sunday 11 a.m.-4 p.m.

Bowers Museum
2002 N. Main St., Santa Ana,
714-567-3600; www.bowers.org
More than 80,000 objects focusing on the artwork of pre-Columbian, Oceanic, Native American, African and Pacific Rim cultures. Tuesday-Sunday 10 a.m.-4 p.m.

Centennial Heritage Museum
3101 W. Harvard St., Santa Ana,
714-540-0404;
www.centennialmuseum.org
A hands-on museum geared toward families that helps make the history of Orange County come alive. Visitors can talk through a hand-cranked telephone, play a pump organ, try on Victorian clothing and more. Wednesday-Friday 1-5 p.m., Sunday 11 a.m.-3 p.m.

Discovery Science Center
2500 N. Main St., Santa Ana,
714-542-2823; www.discoverycube.org
Features more than 100 interactive exhibits with an emphasis on math, science and technology. Daily 10 a.m.-5 p.m.

The Santa Ana Zoo at Prentice Park
1801 E. Chestnut, Santa Ana,
714-836-4000; santaanazoo.org
Playgrounds, picnic area, zoo. Monday-Friday 10 a.m.-4 p.m.; also Saturday-Sunday from Memorial Day-Labor Day.

HOTELS

★★DoubleTree Club Orange County Airport
7 Hutton Centre Dr., Santa Ana,
714-751-2400, 800-528-0444;
http://www.dtclluborangeco.com
167 rooms. Restaurant, bar. Airport transportation available. Fitness center. Pool. $

★★Holiday Inn Orange County Airport
2726 S. Grand Ave., Santa Ana,
714-481-6300, 800-522-6478;
www.holiday-inn.com
178 rooms. Complimentary continental breakfast. Restaurant, bar. Fitness center. Pool. Business center. $

★Quality Suites
2701 Hotel Terrace Dr., Santa Ana,
714-957-9200, 800-638-7949;
www.qualityinns.com
177 rooms, all suites. Complimentary continental breakfast. Bar. Airport transportation available. Pets accepted. $

RESTAURANT

★★★Antonello Ristorante
3800 Plaza Dr., Santa Ana,
714-751-7153;
www.antonello.com
Antonello's has offered a taste of northern Italy in sunny California for the past 40 years. The terrific menu of homemade pasta and exceptional fish, poultry and beef dishes make it the perfect spot for a power lunch or romantic dinner al fresco.
　　Italian menu. Lunch, dinner. Closed Sunday. Bar. Jacket required. Reservations recommended. Valet parking. $$$

SOUTHERN CALIFORNIA

SANTA MONICA

Santa Monica is one of the more diverse and interesting of the beach cities that surround Los Angeles. The beach is wide, sandy and crowded. Santa Monica is a scene—if you want to spend time in a beach community that's buzzing with activity, this is it. The famous Santa Monica Pier has amusements and restaurants. Palisades Park stretches out among the bluffs and is a great walking area for enjoying the ocean. There's also great shopping in Santa Monica, including the famous Third Street Promenade, referred to as Three-Prom by the locals. This stretch of theaters, boutiques, restaurants, curbside vendors and street vendors occupying three pedestrian-only blocks from Wilshire to Broadway is the first place locals bring out-of-towners.

For an introduction to the pulse and variety of Santa Monica, approach it from Wilshire Boulevard. Head west until it appears to dead-end at Ocean Avenue and then move down the California Incline, which lands on the Pacific Coast Highway (the PCH to locals). Take in the coast and then turn around and head south toward the pier through the McClure Tunnel, which sends visitors careening onto the Santa Monica (I-10) freeway.

Information: Visitor Center, 1920 Main St., 310-319-6263; www.santamonica.com

WHAT TO SEE AND DO

California Heritage Museum
2612 Main St., Santa Monica, 310-392-8537; www.californiaheritagemuseum.org
Located on charming Main Street, the California Heritage Museum adds even more culture and flair to the neighborhood with its unique displays of American decorative art, fine art and folk art. This renovated Victorian house, built along the palisades in 1894, was moved to its present site and restored to represent four decades of design. The museum features unusual and entertaining themes and exhibits, such as "Aloha Spirit—Hawaii's Influence on the California Lifestyle." Wednesday-Sunday 11 a.m.-4 p.m.

Main Street
Main St., Santa Monica; www.mainstreetsm.com
The Third Street Promenade is not the only shopping district Santa Monica calls its own. For those looking for a slightly edgier, more urban feel, head just a few blocks south to Main Street. Here are dozens of restaurants ranging from Joe's Diner to the California-French cuisine at the Frank Gehry-designed Rockenwagner. Shops include everything from Betsey Johnson to Patagonia, plus locally-owned specialty shops and boutiques.

Palisades Park
Within walking distance of Third Street Promedande, this beautiful stretch of bluff-top lawn and walkways overlooking the Pacific offers some of the best spots to catch the California sunset.

Santa Monica Mountains National Recreation Area
401 W. Hillcrest Dr., Thousand Oaks, 805-370-2301; www.nps.gov/samo
A huge park incorporating federal lands (with a number of old ranch sites), four state parks ranging from Will Rogers State Historic Park to Point Mugu (also Topanga and Malibu Creek state parks) and state beaches (Topanga and Will Rogers among them). Surfing; hiking horseback riding, and mountain biking trails. Daily 9 a.m.-5 p.m.

Santa Monica Pier
Ocean and Colorado Avenues, Santa Monica, 310-458-8900; www.santamonicapier.org
Opened in 1909, the Santa Monica Pier is a Los Angeles landmark. Ride the Ferris wheel, roller coaster and antique carousel, visit the Playland video arcade or simply stroll the pier's 1,600 feet and marvel at the views of the Santa Monica Bay. Vendors shill everything from sunglasses to T-shirts. Restaurants range from food court-style snacks to sit-down fare. Daily.

Santa Monica Pier Aquarium
1600 Ocean Front Walk, Santa Monica,
310-393-6149
An innovative, interactive aquarium that's popular with local families. Hours vary seasonally.

Santa Monica Place
Fourth and Broadway,
Santa Monica, 310-394-1049;
www.santamonicaplace.com
With almost 150 shops, this three-level shopping center is located just a few blocks from the famous Santa Monica Pier. (Monday-Saturday 10 a.m.-9 p.m., Sunday 11 a.m.-6 p.m.

South Bay Bicycle Trail
Temescal Canyon Rd., Santa Monica,
Paved trail extends 22 miles along the beach from Will Rogers State Beach near Malibu to Torrance County Beach in Torrance. Numerous bike rentals along the beach.

Third Street Promenade
Third St., Santa Monica,
310-393-8355;
www.thirdstreetpromenade.com
This pedestrian-only street is lined with theaters, boutiques, restaurants, curbside vendors and street performers. On Wednesdays and Saturdays, check out the huge farmers' market (one of California's largest) on Arizona between Second and Fourth Streets. Wednesday 8:30 a.m.-1:30 p.m., Saturday 8:30 a.m.-1 p.m.

Venice Beach and Boardwalk
Pacific and Windward Avenues,
Venice, 310-396-7016;
www.venice.net
People-watching doesn't get any better than in this funky beach community. The boardwalk that fronts the ocean stretches for two miles and every inch of it is packed with a colorful cast of characters. In-line skaters, power-walkers, runners and bikers mingle with street performers, local artists, massage therapists, preachers, tattoo artists and anyone else who shows up for a day in the California sun.

Will Rogers State Historic Park
1501 Will Rogers State Park Rd.,
Pacific Palisades, 310-454-8212;
www.parks.ca.gov
Tour the 186-acre hilltop ranch where Will Rogers lived with his family from the late 1920s until his death in 1935. Also available are hiking trails, horseback riding, a polo field and pickning. Daily 8 a.m.-sunset.

HOTELS
★★Channel Road Inn
219 W. Channel Rd., Santa Monica,
310-459-1920; www.channelroadinn.com
This historic home is tucked away in the rustic Santa Monica Canyon, just one block from the beach.
16 rooms. Complimentary full breakfast. Whirlpool. $$

★★Delfina Sheraton
530 W. Pico Blvd., Santa Monica,
310-399-9344;
www.sheratonsantamonica.com
314 rooms. High-speed Internet access. Restaurant, bar. Pets accepted. Fitness center. Pool. $$

★★DoubleTree Guest Suites
1707 Fourth St., Santa Monica,
310-395-3332, 800-222-8733;
www.doubletree.com
253 rooms, all suites. High-speed Internet access. Restaurant, bar. Pool. $$

★★★Georgian Hotel
1415 Ocean Ave., Santa Monica,
310-395-9945, 800-538-8147;
www.georgianhotel.com
This Art Deco boutique hotel, built in 1933, was once the playground of celebrities like Clark Gable and Carole Lombard. It's located directly across from the beach and within a short walk of downtown. The striking guest rooms, decorated in warm colors, feature goose down comforters, hand-woven carpets and locally crafted furniture. Most rooms offer views of the Pacific.
84 rooms. High-speed wireless Internet access. Restaurant, bar. Pets accepted. $$$

SOUTHERN CALIFORNIA

★★★Hotel Casa Del Mar

1910 Ocean Way, Santa Monica,
310-581-5533, 800-898-6999;
www.hotelcasadelmar.com

This European-style resort captures the essence of an elegant 1920s Mediterranean villa with its graceful arches, tiled floors and swaying palms. A breezy, fresh style of understated luxury is evident throughout, especially in the delightful guest rooms with their mango-colored walls, gauzy curtains and sumptuous linens. All the rooms feature hydrothermal massage bathtubs. The spa offers other wonderful ways to unwind and the beachfront pool is a dream. The restaurant is a lovely spot for fine dining.

132 rooms. High-speed wireless Internet access. Restaurant, bar. Beach. Pets accepted. **$$$$**

★★★Hotel Oceana

849 Ocean Ave., Santa Monica,
310-393-0486, 800-777-0758;
www.hoteloceanasantamonica.com

The spacious accommodations in this all-suite hotel include 50" plasma TVs, game tables for backgammon, chess and checkers, magazines and books and iPod docking stations. Private work areas are adjacent to the living room, and suite-size bathrooms have Waterworks fixtures and L'Occitane products. There's also a gorgeous pool. The hotel is in a prime location, just blocks from the Third Street Promenade and Montana Avenue shopping district.

63 rooms, all suites. Pets accepted; restrictions, fee. High-speed Internet access. Beach. **$$**

★★★Le Merigot, A JW Marriott Beach Hotel and Spa

1740 Ocean Ave., Santa Monica,
310-395-9700; www.lemerigothotel.com

Recalling the grand hotels of the French Riviera, Le Merigot brings a touch of European panache to the Santa Monica coastline. Not far from the world-famous pier, the resort conveys quiet luxury. Guest rooms feature plush, oversized beds swathed in Frette linens and marble bathrooms, while the fantastic spa offers a wide variety of treatments and includes a eucalyptus steam room and redwood sauna. The restaurant, popular with locals and guests alike, relies on fresh ingredients from nearby farmers' markets.

175 rooms. Wireless Internet access. Restaurant, bar. Spa. Beach. Pets accepted. Pool. **$$$$**

★★★Loews Santa Monica Beach Hotel

1700 Ocean Ave., Santa Monica,
310-458-6700, 800-235-6397;
www.loewshotels.com

Enjoy magnificent sunset views from this SoCal beachfront haven. Relax in a doeskin robe in the guest rooms, lounge at the striking ocean-front pool and bliss-out in the luxurious spa, a favorite of West Side-dwelling celebrities.

342 rooms. Restaurant, two bars. Spa. Beach. Pets accepted. **$$$$**

★★★Renaissance Agoura Hills Hotel

30100 Agoura Rd., Agoura Hills,
818-707-1220;
www.renaissancehotels.com

Nestled at the foot of the Santa Monica Mountains (and just minutes from Malibu beach), the contemporary guest rooms at this hotel are beautifully decorated with warm, vibrant colors, European furnishings and plush bedding with extra pillows. The three on-site restaurants will satisfy any craving, from seafood to barbecue. Golf lovers can choose from five nearby courses.

280 rooms. Restaurant, bar. Exercise. Pool. Business center. **$$**

★★★Shutters on the Beach

1 Pico Blvd., Santa Monica,
310-458-0030, 800-334-9000;
www.shuttersonthebeach.com

The sunny rooms and suites here feature white walls and country-chic furnishings. Beds are piled high with fine linens, and oversize bathrooms feature Jacuzzi tubs. The beachfront pool and two restaurants are among the best places to see and be seen in greater Los Angeles.

198 rooms. High-speed wireless Internet access. Restaurant, bar. Spa. Beach. **$$$$**

SOUTHERN CALIFORNIA

★
★
★
★
★

★★The Fairmont Miramar Hotel
101 Wilshire Blvd., Santa Monica,
310-576-7777, 800-441-1414;
www.fairmont.com

This century-old landmark, situated atop Santa Monica's scenic beachfront bluffs just north of the world-famous pier, recently underwent a major renovation and now includes the 8,000 square-foot Willow Steam Spa, a fitness center featuring Techno Gym equipment (with built-in LCD monitors) and a heated sky pool and deck. Guest rooms, ranging from single- and double-story bungalows to tower suites, include luxury bedding, flat-screen TVs and (in most rooms) oversized tubs. The Third Street Promenade is around the corner.

302 rooms. High-speed Internet access. Restaurant, bar. Pets accepted. **$$$**

★★★Viceroy
1819 Ocean Ave., Santa Monica,
310-260-7500, 800-670-6185;
www.viceroysantamonica.com

Decorated by star interior designer Kelly Wearstler, the hotel's fashionably retro Cameo Bar is where the city's beautiful people mingle, and the award-winning restaurant Whist serves a killer Sunday Champagne brunch. Best of all is the cabana-ringed poolside. Afterward, retreat to your stunning guest room for spa treatments by Fred Segal Beauty.

162 rooms. High-speed wireless Internet access. Restaurant, bar. Pets accepted. **$$$$**

RESTAURANTS
★★Border Grill
1445 Fourth St., Santa Monica,
310-451-1655;
www.bordergrill.com

Mexican menu. Lunch, dinner. Bar. Casual attire. **$$**

★Broadway Deli
1457 Third Street Promenade,
Santa Monica, 310-451-0616

Deli menu. Breakfast, lunch, dinner. Bar. Children's menu. Casual attire. Valet parking. **$$**

★★Buffalo Club
1520 Olympic Blvd., Santa Monica,
310-450-8600; www.thebuffaloclub.com

American menu. Lunch, dinner. Closed Sunday. Bar. Business casual attire. Reservations recommended. Valet parking. Outdoor seating. **$$$**

★★★Capo
1810 Ocean Ave., Santa Monica,
310-394-5550

If money is no object, head to this rustic Italian farmhouse where hearty classics get a gourmet twist. Try rigatoni with truffled meat sauce and polenta with lamb sausage. Modern Italian menu. Dinner. Closed Sunday-Monday. Bar. Business casual attire. Valet parking. **$$$$**

★★★Catch
1910 Ocean Way, Santa Monica,
310-581-7714; www.hotelcasadelmar.com

Overlooking the wide, white sandy beach is Catch, the flagship restaurant of the European château-style Casa Del Mar hotel. The décor is modern, with crisp whites hues accented by chocolate and blue tones. Executive chef Michael Reardon crafts seafood offerings from the freshest ingredients—the day's catch. Before or after dinner, step out onto the veranda, relax under a star-blanketed sky, breathe in the salty sea air, and enjoy a cocktail or two.

Seafood, sushi menu. Breakfast, lunch, dinner. Bar. Casual attire. **$$$**

★★★Cézanne
1740 Ocean Ave., Santa Monica,
310-395-9700;
www.lemerigothotel.com

A bold décor sets the stage for the impeccable French California-style dishes served here, including roasted farm-raised pheasant breast with mushroom ravioli, and roasted striped bass with shallot confit and red wine sauce. All the plates are prepared with market-fresh ingredients. Try to snag one of the high-backed banquettes for the best people-watching.

California, French menu. Breakfast, lunch, dinner. Bar. Children's menu. Business casual attire. Reservations recommended. Valet parking. Outdoor seating. **$$$**

★★★Chinois on Main
2709 Main St., Santa Monica,
310-392-9025;
www.wolfgangpuck.com
Wolfgang Puck's West Side outpost features wild décor with modern chinoiserie, and the place is always a roar of energy, with tables jammed with dressed-up revelers celebrating birthdays. This party vibe meshes well with the family-style menu of shared dishes like lobster with spicy ginger curry and a whole sizzling catfish.

Chinese, French menu. Lunch, dinner. Bar. Casual attire. Valet parking. **$$$**

★Cora's Coffee Shop
1802 Ocean Ave., Santa Monica,
310-451-9562
American menu. Breakfast, lunch. Casual attire. Outdoor seating. **$**

★★★Drago Ristorante
2628 Wilshire Blvd., Santa Monica,
310-828-1585; www.celestinodrago.com
Modern impressionist paintings of Italian landscapes grace the cream-colored walls of this pleasant dining room where guests feast on fresh pastas and splurge on the encyclopedic wine list. The sleek marble and wood bar with floating glass shelves filled with fine cognacs is a nice spot to grab a bite, while private dining rooms are perfect for business meals.

Italian menu. Lunch, dinner. Bar. Children's menu. Casual attire. Reservations recommended. Valet parking. **$$$**

★★The Hump
3221 Donald Douglas Loop S.,
Santa Monica, 310-313-0977;
www.thehump-sushi.com
Sushi menu. Lunch, dinner. Reservations recommended. **$$$**

★★Il Ristorante di Giorgio Baldi
114 W. Channel Rd., Santa Monica Canyon, 310-573-1660;
www.giorgiobaldi.com

Italian menu. Dinner. Closed Monday. Bar. Casual attire. **$$$**

★★Ivy at the Shore
1535 Ocean Ave., Santa Monica,
310-393-3113
American menu. Lunch, dinner. Bar. Casual attire. Reservations recommended. Valet parking. Outdoor seating. **$$$**

★★JiRaffe
502 Santa Monica Blvd.,
Santa Monica, 310-917-6671;
www.jirafferestaurant.com
French menu. Dinner. Casual attire. Valet parking. **$$$**

★★★Josie
2424 Pico Blvd., Santa Monica,
310-581-9888;
www.josierestaurant.com
Located on an unforgettable strip of Pico Boulevard, Josie is an elegant dining oasis. With dark walls and a stone fireplace, the dining room resembles a warm and graceful lodge. Chef Josie Le Balch aims to bring continental comfort food to new gastronomic heights using exotic game like buffalo sirloin with Gruyère and venison with vegetable hash. Adventurous eaters from all corners of Los Angeles get dolled up to dine here for special occasions and romantic dates. Excellent selections of half bottles of wine are perfect for sharing and sampling.

American menu. Dinner. Bar. Casual attire. **$$$**

★★La Serenata de Garibaldi
1416 Fourth St., Santa Monica,
310-656-7017
Mexican menu. Lunch, dinner. Bar. Children's menu. Casual attire. **$$**

★★The Lobster
1602 Ocean Ave., Santa Monica,
310-458-9294;
www.thelobster.com
American, seafood menu. Lunch, dinner. Bar. Casual attire. Reservations recommended. Valet parking. Outdoor seating. **$$$**

★
★
★
★
★

★★★★Melisse
1104 Wilshire Blvd., Santa Monica,
310-395-0881; www.melisse.com
Classic French technique is the basis for the creative contemporary American menu at Melisse, an elegant, Provençal-style dining room. Warmed with fresh flower arrangements and paintings of rural French landscapes, the room at Melisse is lovely and intimate with tabletops set with fine linens and beautiful hand-painted china. Chef/owner Josiah Citrin weaves intricate dishes from stunning, seasonal ingredients procured from regional farmers. His notable creations served in four-, five-, seven- or eight-course menus, include seared Hudson Valley foie gras, sweet corn ravioli, Dover sole roasted on the bone (and filleted tableside) and dry-aged Cote de Boeuf for two, also carved tableside.

French menu. Dinner. Bar. Casual attire. Reservations recommended. $$$$

★★★Michael's
1147 Third St., Santa Monica, 310-451-0843; www.michaelssantamonica.com
Touted as the birthplace of California cuisine, Michael's continues to deliver plates that delight the senses with the freshest ingredients. Dine on the enchanting heated back patio if a table is free.

California, French menu. Lunch, dinner. Closed Sunday. Bar. Children's menu. Casual attire. Valet parking. Outdoor seating. $$$

★★Ocean Avenue Seafood
1401 Ocean Ave., Santa Monica,
310-394-5669; www.kingsseafood.com
Seafood menu. Lunch, dinner. Bar. Children's menu. Casual attire. Reservations recommended. Valet parking. Outdoor seating. $$$

★★★One Pico
1 Pico Blvd., Santa Monica,
310-587-1717;
www.shuttersonthebeach.com
Situated on the sand at the Shutters on the Beach Hotel, this dining room has the unfussy elegance of Cape Cod, with working fireplaces, beamed ceilings and pretty table settings. The contemporary American fare has a slightly exotic Southern California twist, with kicked-up corn chowder, truffle-kissed salmon and for dessert, gourmet s'mores.

California menu. Lunch, dinner, Sunday brunch. Bar. Business casual attire. Valet parking. $$$

★★Sushi Roku
1401 Ocean Ave., Santa Monica,
310-458-4771; www.sushiroku.com
This sushi place lives up to the hype, offering high-quality sushi, crisp tempura and mouthwatering entrées like asparagus wrapped in filet mignon and miso-glazed black cod. The dining room resembles a sexy Zen rock garden, where beautiful people sip cold sake poured from giant stalks of bamboo.

Japanese menu. Lunch, dinner. Bar. Children's menu. Business casual attire. Reservations recommended. Valet parking. Outdoor seating. $$$

★★★Valentino
3115 Pico Blvd., Santa Monica,
310-829-4313; www.pieroselvaggio.com
For almost three decades, Valentino's owner Piero Selvaggio has provided diners with premier Italian food accompanied by a wine list comprised of the best that both Italy and California have to offer. The food is classic with dishes like linguini with clams and sweet garlic, or a veal chop with prosciutto, cream and Marsala.

Italian menu. Dinner. Closed Sunday. Bar. Business casual attire. Reservations recommended. Valet parking. $$$$

★★★Whist
1819 Ocean Ave., Santa Monica, 310-260-7500; www.viceroysantamonica.com
Inside the Viceroy hotel, Chef Tim Goodell dishes up his contemporary fare focused on market produce, Asian accents and sweet and savory combinations, such as pineapple and foie gras.

Modern American menu. Breakfast, dinner, late-night. Bar. Casual attire. Reservations recommended. Valet parking. Outdoor seating. $$$

SOUTHERN CALIFORNIA

STUDIO CITY

Studio City is a four-square mile area in the San Fernando Valley about 12 miles northwest of Los Angeles (between Hollywood and Sherman Oaks). Many film studios are located here. The area is experiencing redevelopment and a surge in restaurants.
Information: www.studiocitychamber.com

WHAT TO SEE AND DO

Gibson Amphitheatre
100 Universal City Plaza, Universal City, 818-622-4440;
www.hob.com/venues/concerts/universal
Though this mammoth theater seats about 6,000, it's known for its good sight lines and acoustics. Every chart-busting music act has entertained here at one time or another. It's part of the Universal City complex, so you're just steps from Universal Studios Hollywood and Universal CityWalk, a popular entertainment center with an IMAX 3-D theater, restaurants, shops and nightclubs.

Universal Studios Hollywood
100 Universal City Plaza,
Universal City, 818-622-3801;
www.universalstudioshollywood.com
Universal Studios Hollywood opened its doors to the public in 1964, and since then more than 90 million people have visited this movie studio and theme park. Take a tour of the Universal Studios backlot, where you can see sets and learn how special effects work. Universal Studios Hollywood is an essential part of the Los Angeles experience, especially for those who love movies. Summer: Monday-Friday 9 a.m.-9 p.m., Saturday-Sunday 9 a.m.-10 p.m.; rest of year: daily 9 a.m.-6 p.m.

HOTELS

★★Sportsmen's Lodge Hotel
12825 Ventura Blvd., Studio City,
818-769-4700, 800-821-8511;
www.slhotel.com
200 rooms. Restaurant, bar. Airport transportation available. Pets accepted. Pool. $$

★★★Hilton Los Angeles/Universal City
555 Universal Hollywood Dr.,
Universal City,
818-506-2500, 800-445-8667;
www.losangelesuniversalcity.hilton.com

Across from the main entrance of Universal Studios and CityWalk, the Hilton features panoramic views of the Hollywood Hills, a heated pool and fitness room. The restaurant serves a big seafood and prime rib buffet on weekends.
483 rooms. Restaurant, bar. Fitness center. Pool. Business center. $$

★★★Sheraton Universal Hotel
333 Universal Hollywood Dr.,
Universal City,
818-980-1212, 877-599-9810;
www.sheraton.com
Overlooking the San Fernando Valley and Hollywood Hills, this hotel offers complimentary tram rides to Universal Studios Hollywood and Citywalk. For a break, kick back at the large pool or enjoy lunch on the terrace.
36 rooms. Restaurant, bar. Pool. Business center. $

RESTAURANTS

★★★Asanebo
11941 Ventura Blvd.,
Studio City,
818-760-3348
Forget the strip-mall ambience and concentrate on the jaw-dropping array of beautifully crafted delicacies served by a super-fast and helpful staff. Besides superior sushi, there are special dishes like Dungeness crab served sashimi-style and monkfish liver in ponzu sauce.
Japanese. Lunch, dinner. Closed Monday. Casual attire. $$

★★Firefly
11720 Ventura Blvd.,
Studio City,
818-762-1833
California menu. Dinner. Closed Sunday. Bar. Casual attire. Reservations recommended. Outdoor seating. $$

SOUTHERN CALIFORNIA

★★La Loggia
11814 Ventura Blvd., Studio City,
818-985-9222
Italian menu. Lunch, dinner. Bar. Casual attire. Reservations recommended. Valet parking. Outdoor seating. **$$**

★★★Pinot Bistro
12969 Ventura Blvd., Studio City,
818-990-0500; www.patinagroup.com
Los Angeles celebrity chef Joachim Splichal of Patina fame has spun off Pinot Bistro, a less expensive, more accessible taste of his signature French cooking. The menu hews to bistro classics such as duck confit and roast chicken, while the extensive wine list pleasingly defies French-only conventions. This Studio City favorite offers dining in several distinct areas, such as the Fireplace Room. The décor is warm and inviting throughout, with wood accents, checkered floors, art-covered walls and cozy banquettes.
California, French menu. Lunch, dinner. Bar. Children's menu. Reservations recommended. Valet parking. **$$**

★★Sushi Katsu-ya
11680 Ventura Blvd., Studio City,
818-985-6976
Japanese, sushi menu. Lunch, dinner. Casual attire. **$$$**

★★Tama Sushi
11920 Ventura Blvd., Studio City,
818-760-4585
Japanese menu. Lunch, dinner. Closed Sunday. Casual attire. **$$$**

★★Wine Bistro
11915 Ventura Blvd., Studio City,
818-766-6233;
www.winebistro.net
French bistro menu. Lunch, dinner. Closed Sunday. Bar. Casual attire. Reservations recommended. Valet parking. Outdoor seating. **$$$**

VENICE
Venice has its canals and beaches, but it is probably best known for its bohemian vibe and boardwalk. A visit here might feel like a flashback to the 1960s counterculture. Famous residents include Julia Roberts and architect Frank Gehry. Abbot Kinney Boulevard is the local center of town. This upscale and eclectic street is home to some of the best dining in Los Angeles, as well as art galleries, exclusive antique dealers and fashionable boutiques.

RESTAURANTS

★★Axe
1009 Abbot Kinney Blvd., Venice,
310-664-9787; www.axerestaurant.com
California menu. Lunch, dinner. Closed Monday. Children's menu. Casual attire. **$$**

★★Capri
1616 Abbot Kinney Blvd., Venice,
310-392-8777
Italian menu. Dinner. Casual attire. **$$$**

★★Hal's Bar and Grill
1349 Abbot Kinney Blvd.,
Venice, 310-396-3105;
www.halsbarandgrill.com
American menu. Lunch, dinner. Bar. Casual attire. Valet parking. **$$$**

★★James' Beach
60 N. Venice Blvd., Venice,
310-823-5396
American menu. Lunch, dinner. Bar. Casual attire. Reservations recommended. Valet parking. Outdoor seating. **$$**

★★Joe's
1023 Abbot Kinney Blvd., Venice,
310-392-5655;
www.joesrestaurant.com
French, California menu. Lunch, dinner, brunch. Closed Monday. Bar. Casual attire.

Reservations recommended. Valet parking. Outdoor seating. **$$**

★★**Primitivo**
1025 Abbot Kinney Blvd., Venice,
310-396-5353
Mediterranean, Spanish, tapas menu. Lunch, dinner. Bar. Casual attire. Reserva-

tions recommended. Valet parking. Outdoor seating. **$$$**

★★**Wabi-Sabi**
1635 Abbot Kinney Blvd.,
Venice, 310-314-2229
Japanese, sushi menu. Dinner. Bar. Casual attire. Valet parking. **$$**

WEST HOLLYWOOD

It doesn't get more fabulous than West Hollywood. This tiny city-within-a-city is home to stylish home design shops, fashionable boutiques and fine restaurants.

West Hollywood's side streets are lined with sweet Spanish haciendas and trendy apartment complexes within walking distance of vibrant urban shopping streets. Robertson Boulevard features antiques, designer duds and celeb-heavy lunch spots like the Ivy. La Cienega is home to restaurant row and the famed Beverly Center Mall. Santa Monica Boulevard is the center of the city's gay community, with hip fast-food joints, nightclubs, gyms and crowded streets at all hours.

Locals take advantage of the breakfast spots, cheap manicures, tiny boutiques and swanky cocktail lounges on Beverly Boulevard and Third Street. Those with an unquenchable thirst for fashion flock to Melrose Avenue, which is more couture west of Fairfax and more punk rock to the east.

Fairfax is the center of Los Angeles' Orthodox Jewish community, and historic Canter's Deli is beloved by all Angelenos. Nearby, the Grove is a poplar outdoor shopping mall. Foodies should plan a trip to the adjacent Farmers Market.
Information: www.visitwesthollywood.com

WHAT TO SEE AND DO
Hollywood Forever Memorial Park
6000 Santa Monica Blvd.,
Hollywood, 323-469-1181;
www.forevernetwork.com
Hundreds of movie stars are buried at this beautiful cemetery including Cecil B. DeMille, Douglas Fairbanks Sr., Douglas Fairbanks Jr., Jayne Mansfield, Tyrone Power and Rudolph Valentino. Daily.

Paramount Film and Television Studios
860 N. Gower Ave., Hollywood,
323-956-1777;
www.paramount.com/paramount.php
Tapings of sitcoms and talk shows (seasonal; usually Tuesday or Friday evenings). For television tapings, minimum age 18. Monday-Friday.

Pink's Hot Dogs
709 N. La Brea Blvd., West Hollywood,
323-931-4223; www.pinkshollywood.com

In 1939, Paul Pink opened a hot dog cart at the location where the famous Pink's hot dog stand still sits. Times may have changed but Pink's hot dog recipe hasn't. Eat inside (among dozens of autographed star photographs) or outside under the shade of an umbrella. Don't be deterred by the long line—it's constant, but the people behind the counter move customers through faster than you can say, "I'll have a Three-Peat L.A. Laker Dog, hold the onions." Sunday-Thursday 9:30-2 a.m., Friday-Saturday to 3 a.m.

Saddle Ranch Chop House
8371 Sunset Blvd., West Hollywood,
323-656-2007;
www.srrestaurants.com
Located on the Sunset Strip, the Saddle Ranch is a cheesy imitation of an Old West saloon. Brave wannabe cowboys can ride the mechanical bull, which has been featured in numerous movies and TV

shows, including *Sex and the City*. Daily 8-2 a.m.

Sunset Plaza
Sunset Blvd., West Hollywood

Dine at an outdoor café and look for celebs (everyone from Julia Roberts to Richard Gere has been spotted here). Stores include Armani A/X, Nicole Miller and Oliver Peoples.

The Viper Room
8852 Sunset Blvd., West Hollywood, 310-358-1881;
www.viperroom.com

The Viper Room gained national attention when actor River Phoenix died of a drug overdose on the sidewalk outside the club on Halloween night 1993. Owned by actor Johnny Depp, it's still a favorite with celebrities. Hear live music every night—sometimes from big-name performers who tend to drop by unannounced. Daily 9 p.m.-2 a.m.

HOTELS
★★★Argyle Hotel
8358 Sunset Blvd., West Hollywood, 323-654-7100; www.argylehotel.com

This glamorous Art Deco tower has been a Sunset Boulevard landmark since Hollywood's Golden Age when everyone from Clark Gable to Marilyn Monroe stayed here. The glitzy lobby is decorated in gold and black and the accommodations feature custom furnishings, marble bathrooms, high-tech entertainment gadgets and stunning city and Hollywood Hills views. The adjacent Fenix dining room, with its famous wrought-iron palm trees, is a frequent gathering spot for entertainment power-brokers and up-and-comers.

64 rooms. Wireless Internet access. Restaurant, bar. Pets accepted. Pool. **$$**

★Chamberlain West Hollywood
1000 Westmount Dr., West Hollywood, 310-657-7400, 800-201-9652;
www.wyndham.com

111 rooms, all suites. Complimentary continental breakfast. Pets accepted. **$$**

★★★Chateau Marmont
8221 Sunset Blvd., West Hollywood, 323-656-1010, 800-242-8328;
www.chateaumarmont.com

Known as the place where celebrities misbehave, it's as close to the action as normal folks can probably get. The poolside people-watching may be worth the room price alone.

63 rooms. Wireless Internet access. Restaurant. Pets accepted. Pool. **$$$**

★★Elan Hotel Modern
8435 Beverly Blvd., Los Angeles, 323-658-6663, 888-611-0398;
www.elanhotel.com

50 rooms. High-speed Internet access. Business center. **$$**

★★★Hyatt West Hollywood
8401 Sunset Blvd.,
West Hollywood,
323-656-1234, 800-633-7313;
www.hyatt.com

With its modern California décor and large rooftop pool, this hotel is a good choice for couples hitting the town. Large work desks also make it convenient for business travelers. Dine by the fireplace in the restaurant or grab a drink in the swanky red leather bar.

262 rooms. Restaurant, bar. Fitness center. **$$**

★★★Le Montrose Suite Hotel
900 Hammond St.,
West Hollywood,
310-855-1115, 800-776-0666;
www.lemontrose.com

The Art Nouveau-styled Le Montrose includes spacious suites with sunken living rooms, fireplaces and refrigerators, and many have kitchenettes and private balconies. Venture to the roof for a dip in the pool. The noteworthy restaurant, the Library, is reserved exclusively for guests and their friends. The hotel has a well-equipped health club and tennis courts.

133 rooms, all suites. High-speed Internet access. Restaurant. Pets accepted. Business center. **$$$**

87

SOUTHERN CALIFORNIA

★
★
★
☆
☆

★★★Le Parc Suite Hotel

733 N. West Knoll Dr., West Hollywood, 310-855-8888, 800-578-4837; www.leparcsuites.com

A stay at this hotel includes 650 square feet of guest room space with a balcony, living room (with sleeper sofa), fireplace, kitchenette (with microwave and refrigerator), two TVs, a VCR, a DVD player and a CD player. There's a lighted tennis court, heated swimming pool and sundeck, all with views of the surrounding Hollywood Hills. Book an appointment with a personal trainer or masseuse. And if the thought of driving (or finding parking) in Los Angeles brings a shiver, complimentary Town Car service is available for destinations within a 3-mile radius.

154 rooms, all suites. Pets accepted; fee. High-speed Internet access. Restaurant, bar. $$$

★★★Mondrian

8440 Sunset Blvd., West Hollywood, 323-650-8999; www.mondrianhotel.com

With its Philippe Starck design and two hot spots (Asia de Cuba and Skybay), it doesn't get any cooler than the Mondrian. And yet it somehow feels homey: the comfortable guestrooms all have a kitchen, large work desk stocked with supplies and oversized bathrooms.

238 rooms. High-speed Internet access. Restaurant, bar. $$$

★★★Sunset Marquis Hotel and Villas

1200 N. Alta Loma Rd., West Hollywood, 310-657-1333, 800-858-9758; www.sunsetmarquishotel.com

This Mediterranean-style hotel has been a second home to the music industry since it opened its doors in 1963. There's even a recording studio, which has drawn top musical acts like the Rolling Stones and U2. The music can then be piped into the velvet-lined Whiskey Bar adjacent to the lobby, where industry types can be found cutting deals every night of the week. (Guests can actually get in to the otherwise exclusive spot.) The deluxe villas and suites feature king-size beds, marble bathrooms

and plush bathrobes and are decorated in a clean, modern style with warm earth tones and rich mahogany. The villas also have private alarm systems and butler service. The hotel is located on a quiet cul de sac surrounded by gorgeous grounds with koi ponds.

114 rooms, all suites. High-speed Internet access. Restaurant, bar. Airport transportation available. $$$

★★★The Grafton Hotel

8462 W. Sunset Blvd., West Hollywood, 323-654-4600, 800-821-3660; www.graftononsunset.com

The Grafton looks looks more South Beach than Sunset, and the fashionable pool and Mediterranean gardens are more Lake Como. But the feng shui design and touches including organic bath products are all Los Angeles. The courtesy shuttle service to restaurants and businesses within two miles is a plus.

108 rooms. Wireless Internet access. Restaurant, bar. Pets accepted. $$

RESTAURANTS

★★Ago

8478 Melrose Ave., West Hollywood, 323-655-6333

Italian menu. Lunch, dinner. Bar. Casual attire. Reservations recommended. Valet parking. Outdoor seating. $$

★★★Asia de Cuba

8440 Sunset Blvd., West Hollywood, 323-848-6000; www.chinagrillmgt.com

Flowy, sheer curtains and a candlelit communal table provide a sexy atmosphere for enjoying the oversized martinis and family-style creations served at Asia de Cuba. Try the Cuban Spiced Chicken with Thai coconut sticky rice, avocado fruit salsa and tamarind sauce. The calamari salad—with hearts of palms, bananas, cashews, chicory and raddiccio with sesame orange dressing—is unique and delicious.

Asian, Latin menu. Breakfast, lunch, dinner. Bar. Children's menu. Casual attire. Reservations recommended. Valet parking. Outdoor seating. $$$$

★★★BOA Restaurant & Lounge
8462 W. Sunset Blvd., West Hollywood,
323-650-8383
If there were such a thing as a boutique steakhouse, this would be it. Floating glass floors, artful screens of foliage, modern stained glass and candlelit banquettes give this dining room a sexy, intimate aura. Superb steaks come with a choice of sauces, like pinot noir reduction, and sides like decadent creamed spinach. Don't miss the Caesar salad prepared tableside. Every bottle on the impressive list is half price on Sunday nights.
    Steak menu. Breakfast, lunch, dinner. Bar. Casual attire. Reservations recommended. Valet parking. Outdoor seating. $$$

★★Chaya Brasserie
8741 Alden Dr., West Hollywood,
310-859-8833; www.thechaya.com
French, Japanese menu. Lunch, dinner. Bar. Casual attire. Reservations recommended. Valet parking. Outdoor seating. $$$

★★Chin Chin
8618 Sunset Blvd., West Hollywood,
310-652-1818; www.chinchin.com
Chinese menu. Lunch, dinner. Casual attire. Outdoor seating. $$

★★Fat Fish
616 N. Robertson Blvd., West Hollywood,
310-659-3882
Japanese, sushi menu. Lunch, dinner. Closed Monday. Bar. Casual attire. Outdoor seating. $$

★Greenblatt's Delicatessen
8017 W. Sunset Blvd., West Hollywood,
323-656-0606
Deli menu. Breakfast, lunch, dinner. Casual attire. $

★★★La Boheme
8400 Santa Monica, West Hollywood,
323-848-2360;
www.global-dining.com
The lavish La Boheme does its California-French fusion act with operatic flair. The menu ranges from tuna tataki salad and charred ahi to traditional filet mignon and duck breast with confit. Choose from the downstairs dining room with a wood-burning fireplace, the patio with gurgling fountains or the mezzanine balconies for prime people-watching.
    California, French menu. Dinner. Bar. Business casual attire. Reservations recommended. Valet parking. Outdoor seating. $$$

★★Le Dome
8720 Sunset Blvd., West Hollywood,
310-659-6919
American menu. Dinner. Closed Sunday-Monday. Bar. Casual attire. Reservations recommended. Valet parking. Outdoor seating. $$$

★Le Petit Four
8654 Sunset Blvd., West Hollywood,
310-652-3863;
www.lepetitfour.com
French menu. Lunch, dinner. Bar. Casual attire. Reservations recommended. Outdoor seating. $$

★★Lola's
945 N. Fairfax Ave., West Hollywood,
213-736-5652; www.lolasla.com
California menu. Dinner. Bar. Casual attire. Reservations recommended. Valet parking. $$$

★★★Lucques
8474 Melrose Ave., West Hollywood,
323-655-6277; www.lucques.com
Chef Suzanne Goin launched the West Hollywood Lucques to national raves with flavor-packed dishes like blood orange-date-Parmesan salad, sweetbreads and wild mushrooms, chorizo-stuffed rabbit and pancetta-wrapped sea bass. Menus change seasonally. The Sunday night prix fixe served family-style is a weekly event. The setting, with brick walls, a fireplace, leather banquettes and suspended light cubes, manages to look both sleek and warm.
    California menu. Lunch, dinner. Bar. Casual attire. Reservations recommended. Valet parking. Outdoor seating. $$$

★

★

★

☆

☆

★★★Nishimura
8684 Melrose Ave., West Hollywood,
310-659-4770
Pass through the garden and enter the simple white dining room, where master chefs carve up seafood behind a small sushi bar. Skip the rolls and sample the sashimi specials, simply the cleanest, tastiest cuts of fish the city has to offer and thoughtfully garnished with a fleck of dried roe or a sliver of crispy garlic.

Japanese menu. Lunch, dinner. Closed Sunday. Children's menu. Casual attire. Reservations recommended. Valet parking. $$$

WOODLAND HILLS
This community, located in the San Fernando Valley, is a neighborhood of Los Angeles.

HOTELS

★★★Hilton Woodland Hills & Towers
6360 Canoga Ave., Woodland Hills,
818-595-1000, 800-445-8667;
www.hilton.com
The hotel's proximity to the 101 Freeway, Warner Center and attractions like the Getty Center, Universal Studios and Six Flags California appeals to business and leisure travelers alike. The in-house Brasserie Restaurant specializes in California cuisine. Free transportation within three miles and complimentary access to the adjacent L.A. Fitness Sports & Tennis Club are included in a stay.

325 rooms. High-speed Internet access. Restaurant, bar. Pool. $$

★★★Marriott Warner Center Woodland Hills
21850 Oxnard St.,
Woodland Hills,
818-887-4800, 800-228-9290;
www.marriott.com
This hotel is ideally located in the San Fernando Valley's Warner Center business park, adjacent to the 101 Freeway and within an easy drive of many of the Los Angeles' major attractions. The bar and grill specializes in California cuisine, and an array of shopping and entertainment options are within walking distance.

476 rooms. High-speed Internet access. Restaurant, bar. Pets accepted. $$

MORRO BAY
Located halfway between Los Angeles and San Francisco, Morro Bay is a peaceful, slow-paced waterfront retreat. Its most striking feature is a 576-foot volcanic dome discovered by Juan Rodriguez Cabrillo in 1542 at the entrance to the harbor. A number of tourist attractions are found here, including beaches, gardens and whale and seal watching. Enjoy water sports, golfing and winery tours nearby.
Information: Chamber of Commerce, 845 Embarcadero Rd., 805-772-4467, 800-231-0592; www.morrobay.org

WHAT TO SEE AND DO

Montana de Oro State Park
350 Pecho Valley Rd., Los Osos,
805-528-0513, 800-772-7434;
www.parks.ca.gov
Spectacular scenery along seven miles of shoreline with tidepools, beaches and camping. Hikers enjoy trails up the 1,350-foot Valencia Peak. The park is also popular for whale-watching and viewing harbor seals and sea otters along the shore.

Morro Bay Aquarium
595 Embarcadero,
Morro Bay, 805-772-7647;
www.morrobay.com/morrobayaquarium
Includes 300 live marine specimens. Daily.

Morro Bay State Park
Morro Bay, 805-772-7434;
www.parks.ca.gov
Approximately 2,400 acres on Morro Bay. Fishing, boating; 18-hole golf course,

SOUTHERN CALIFORNIA

picnicking, cafe; hiking; tent and trailer camping. Daily 10 a.m.-5 p.m.

Morro Rock
Embarcadero and Coleman Dr.,
Morro Bay, 805-772-4467
A 576-foot-high volcanic boulder often called "the Gibraltar of the Pacific," or simply "the Rock." Drive to the base of the rock for optimum viewing. Daily.

Museum of Natural History
State Park Rd., Morro Bay, 805-772-2694
Films, slide shows, displays; nature walks. Daily 10 a.m.-5 p.m.

SPECIAL EVENTS
Winter Bird Festival
880 Main St., Morro Bay, 800-231-0592; www.morro-bay.net/birds
Celebration of migrating birds. Includes birding and natural history field trips; workshops; guest speakers; banquet, ice cream social; art exhibit. Four days in mid-January.

HOTELS
★Blue Sail Inn
851 Market Ave., Morro Bay,
805-772-2766, 800-971-6410;
www.bluesailinn.com
48 rooms. Whirlpool. **$**

★★★The Inn at Morro Bay Hotel
60 State Park Rd., Morro Bay,
805-772-5651, 800-321-9566;
www.innatmorrobay.com

Located in Morro Bay State Park, this coastal hideaway made up of Cape Cod-style buildings is a destination itself. After a day of sightseeing, golf or bike riding, return to a gourmet meal before sinking into a feather bed. The inn also offers a full range of body treatments in the spa.

97 rooms. High-speed Internet access. Two restaurants, bar. **$$**

★La Serena Inn
990 Morro Ave., Morro Bay,
805-772-5665, 800-248-1511;
www.laserenainn.com
38 rooms. Complimentary continental breakfast. Whirlpool. **$**

SPECIALTY LODGINGS
Beachwalker Inn
501 S. Ocean Ave., Cayucos,
805-995-2133, 800-750-2133;
www.beachwalkerinn.com
This cozy inn is located opposite the beach. 24 rooms. Complimentary continental breakfast. **$$**

RESTAURANT
★Hofbrau
901 Embarcadero, Morro Bay,
805-772-5166;
www.hofbraurestaurant.com
American menu. Lunch, dinner. Children's menu. Casual attire. Outdoor seating. **$**

OJAI
Ojai is a quiet, charming place full of citrus groves just outside Santa Barbara. Citrus and cattle ranchers first farmed it after the Civil War. In the 1870s, publicity in Eastern newspapers initiated its popularity as a tourist haven and winter resort. Attracted by the quiet, rural beauty and proximity to urban centers, artists, writers and other creative types make their home in the Ojai Valley. Many celebrities also have homes here, including Anthony Hopkins and Bill Paxton.
Information: Ojai Valley Chamber of Commerce & Visitors Center, 201 S. Signal St., 805-646-8126; www.ojaichamber.org

WHAT TO SEE AND DO

Lake Casitas Recreation Area
11311 Santa Ana Rd., Ojai, 805-649-2233
Fishing, boating, picnicking, camping (fee; for reservations, call 805-649-1122). Pets on leash only. Nearby beaches, golf courses and tennis courts. Daily.

Ojai Center for the Arts
113 S. Montgomery, Ojai, 805-646-0117; www.ojaiartcenter.org
Rotating exhibitions of local artists and live theater productions. Tuesday-Sunday noon-4 p.m.

Ojai Valley Museum
130 W. Ojai Ave., Ojai, 805-640-1390; www.ojaivalleymuseum.org
Permanent and changing exhibits explore environmental, cultural and historical factors that shaped the Ojai Valley. Research library. Thursday-Friday 1-4 p.m., Saturday from 10 a.m., Sunday from noon.

SPECIAL EVENTS

Ojai Music Festival
Libbe Bowl, 201 S. Signal St., Ojai, 805-646-2094; www.ojaifestival.org
For four days in June, the Libby Bowl is host to talented classical musicians performing pieces from composers such as Mozart, Stravinsky and Beethoven. Early June.

Ojai Shakespeare Festival
Matilija JHS Auditorium, 703 El Paseo St., Ojai, 805-646-9455; www.ojaishakespeare.org
Outdoor evening and matinee performances of Shakespeare plays. July-August.

Ojai Studio Artists Tour
Ojai Art Center, 113 S. Montgomery St., Ojai, 805-646-8126; www.ojaistudioartists.com
Recognized artists open their studios to the public. Two days in mid-October.

Ojai Valley Tennis Tournament
Ojai, 805-646-7241; www.ojaitourney.org
Held since 1895, this is the oldest amateur tennis tournament in the nation. Games take place at a variety of venues, including Libby Park, the Ojai Valley Athletic Club and high schools and colleges. Late April.

HOTELS

★Best Western Casa Ojai
1302 E. Ojai Ave., Ojai, 805-646-8175, 800-255-8175; www.bestwestern.com
44 rooms. Complimentary continental breakfast. Pets accepted. Pool. $

★Hummingbird Inn
1208 E. Ojai Ave., Ojai, 805-646-4365, 800-228-3744; www.hummingbirdinnofojai.com
31 rooms. Complimentary continental breakfast. Pool. $

★★★Ojai Valley Inn & Spa
905 Country Club Rd., Ojai, 805-646-1111; www.ojairesort.com
This gorgeous resort sits on 220 acres and includes championship golf and tennis, lavish rooms, horseback riding and a spectacular spa. Guests are shuttled around the grounds on golf carts by the friendly and attentive staff, and the SoCal cuisine served at the resort is outstanding.
209 rooms. Five restaurants, bar. Children's activity center. Pets accepted. Golf. Tennis. Business center. $$$

RESTAURANTS

★★★L'Auberge
314 El Paseo St., Ojai, 805-646-2288; www.laubergeojai.com
Using lots of local and seasonal ingredients, this divine restaurant serves sublime dishes like lamb sirloin with grilled eggplant. Be sure to save room for the delicious, classic desserts.
Continental, French menu. Dinner, brunch. Outdoor seating. $$

★★★The Ranch House
102 Besant Rd., Ojai, 805-646-2360; www.theranchhouse.com
The Ranch House has made a name for itself by offering simple, made-from-scratch dishes—many of them vegetarian—that

SOUTHERN CALIFORNIA

★

★

★

★

★

burst with fresh flavors, such as wild mushroom strudel and grilled diver scallops with sweet corn sauce. Fresh herbs are picked from the garden and bread is made fresh daily (and is available for sale).

American menu. Dinner, Sunday brunch. Children's menu. Outdoor seating. **$$$**

SPAS

★★★★Spa Ojai
905 Country Club Rd., Ojai,
805-646-1111, 888-697-8780;
www.ojairesort.com

Golfers, hikers and couples on romantic getaways all come to this sophisticated 31,000-square-foot sanctuary of health and well-being for a spa experience like no other. Spa Ojai features signature services such as Kuyam—a treatment that combines the therapeutic effects of cleansing mud, dry heat, inhalation therapy and guided meditation. This communal experience (kuyam means "a place to rest together") accommodates up to eight men or women. There's also an extensive array of facial, skin and body treatments, as well as a variety of art classes in the adjacent studio. **$$**

ONTARIO

Information: Convention and Visitors Authority, 2000 Convention Center Way, 91764, 909-937-3000, 800-455-5755; www.ontariocvb.com

WHAT TO SEE AND DO

Air Museum: Planes of Fame
7000 Merrill Ave., 17 Chino,
909-597-3722;
www.planesoffame.org
Exotic collection of more than 60 operable historic military aircraft, including Japanese Zero, ME-109G and B-17. Aircraft rides. Daily 9 a.m.-5 p.m.

California Speedway
9300 Cherry Ave., Fontana,
909-429-5000, 800-944-7223;
www.californiaspeedway.com
Two-mile asphalt track is home to professional auto racing, including NASCAR Nextel Cup Series and PPG CART World Series races. Dates vary.

Fontana Skate Park
Juniper Park, Juniper Ave. and Filbert St., Fontana,
909-428-8360;
www.fontana.org/main/public_serv/skate_park.htm
Rated among the top skate parks, this site includes street action, intermediate bowl/banks and a three-bowl clover with an 8- to 9-foot vertical. Protective gear must be worn at all times. Friday-Wednesday 9 a.m.-9:30 p.m., Thursday noon-9:30 p.m.

Graber Olive House Tour
315 E. Fourth St., Ontario, 909-983-1761
Tour of sorting, canning and packaging areas. Mini-museum, gourmet food and gift shop. Daily.

Museum of History and Art, Ontario
225 S. Euclid Ave., Ontario, 909-983-3198
Regional history and fine arts exhibits. Wednesday-Sunday noon-4 p.m.

Ontario Mills
One Mills Circle, Ontario, 909-484-8301;
www.ontariomills.com
The size of 30 football fields, this is California's largest entertainment and outlet mall. And it's the kind of place where busloads of tourists pull up to mine stores like Nordstrom Rack and Off 5th Saks Fifth Avenue. (Monday-Saturday 10 a.m.-9:30 p.m., Sunday 10 a.m.-8 p.m.

Raging Waters
Dr. Frank G. Bonelli Regional Park,
111 Raging Waters Dr.,
San Dimas, 909-802-2200;
www.ragingwaters.com
Huge 50-acre water park with 50 million gallons of water in use. Largest flume ride in the United States and highest two-person

SOUTHERN CALIFORNIA

tube ride. Million-gallon wave cove. Separate area for young kids. Late April-late May: Saturday-Sunday 10 a.m.-6 p.m.; July-August: daily 10 a.m.-8 p.m.; September: 10 a.m.-5 p.m., days vary.

SPECIAL EVENTS

Grape Harvest Festival
Rancho Cucamonga Epicenter,
Rochester Ave.
Ontario.
Wine tasting, grape stomping contest, carnival, displays, entertainment. Early October.

HOTELS

★★Ayres Suites Ontario Airport Convention Center
1945 E. Holt Blvd., Ontario,
909-390-7778, 800-706-4881;
www.ayreshotels.com
166 rooms, all suites. Complimentary full breakfast. High-speed Internet access. Restaurant, bar. Airport transportation available. **$**

★★Best Western InnSuites
3400 Shelby St., Ontario,
909-466-9600, 800-642-2617;
www.bestwestern.com
Complimentary breakfast. Pets accepted, some restrictions. Pool. **$**

★★DoubleTree Hotel Ontario Airport
222 N. Vineyard Ave., Ontario,
909-937-0900, 800-222-8733;
www.doubletree.com
484 rooms. Restaurant, bar. Airport transportation available. Pets accepted. **$$**

★★★Hilton Ontario Airport
700 N. Haven, Ontario,
909-980-0400, 800-654-1379;
www.hilton.com

This newly renovated hotel located at the entrance to the Ontario airport caters to business travelers with a large work desk and dual phone lines with voicemail. Suites also feature spacious sitting areas. This hotel is non-smoking.
309 rooms. Complimentary continental breakfast. High-speed wireless Internet access. Restaurant, bar. Airport transportation available. **$**

★★★Marriott Ontario Airport
2200 E. Holt Blvd.,
Ontario,
909-975-5000, 800-284-8811;
www.marriott.com
This hotel is convenient to California Speedway and the Ontario Mills shopping area. It's also an hour drive away from local beaches, Palm Springs and snow skiing.
299 rooms. High-speed wireless Internet access. Restaurant, bar. Airport transportation available. **$**

RESTAURANTS

★★★Rosa's
425 N. Vineyard Ave.,
Ontario,
909-937-1220;
www.rosasitalian.com
Since 1988, Rosa's has been a destination for inventive Italian fare, including appetizers like golden crab cakes with tarragon and mustard and cream sauce, as well as entrées such as crab, shrimp and lobster ravioli in lemon cream sauce. The soft lights and piano music make it a cozy, romantic spot.
Italian menu. Lunch, dinner. Closed Sunday. Bar. Reservations recommended. **$$$**

94

SOUTHERN CALIFORNIA

★
★
★
★
★

OXNARD

Information: Oxnard Convention and Visitors Bureau, 1000 Town Center Rd., 805-385-7545, 800-269-6273; www.visitoxnard.com

WHAT TO SEE AND DO

Carnegie Art Museum

424 South C St., Oxnard, 805-385-8157; www.vcnet.com/carnart/default.html
Features changing exhibits of regional and international visual and fine arts. Thursday-Saturday 10 a.m.-5 p.m., Sunday 1-5 p.m.

CEC/Seabee Museum

Naval Base Ventura County, Port Hueneme, 805-982-5167; www.seabeehf.org
Memorabilia of the U.S. Navy Seabees, the construction battalions of the Navy. Antarctic display, South Pacific artifacts, underwater diving display, outrigger canoes, World War II dioramas, weapons, flags. By appointment.

Channel Islands Harbor

Visitor Center, 2741 S. Victoria Ave., Oxnard, 805-985-4852; www.channelislandsharbor.org
Public recreation includes boating, fishing, swimming, beaches; parks, barbecue and picnic facilities; playgrounds; tennis courts; charter boat and bicycle rentals.

Fisherman's Wharf

Oxnard, 805-985-4852, 800-269-6273.
A New England-style village with specialty shops, restaurants and transient docking.

Gull Wings Children's Museum

418 W. Fourth St., Oxnard, 805-483-3005; gullwings.org
Kids can explore the cockpit of a space shuttle, dig for fossils or put on their own puppet show. Tuesday-Saturday 10 a.m.-5 pm.

Heritage Square

715 S. A St., Oxnard, 805-483-7960
Created in 1985, Heritage Square in downtown Oxnard is a quaint block of historic homes and buildings. Dating from 1876 to 1912, the buildings include several homes, a church, a water tower and a storehouse. Free tours of the homes are offered through the visitor center on Saturdays from 10 a.m. to 2 p.m.

Ventura County Maritime Museum

2731 S. Victoria Ave., Oxnard, 805-984-6260
Nautical exhibits and model ships illustrate maritime history. Daily 11 a.m.-5 p.m.

SPECIAL EVENTS

California Strawberry Festival

1661 Pacific Ave., Oxnard, 805-385-4739, 888-288-9242; www.strawberry-fest.org
Wine tasting, entertainment, crafts, strawberries. Third weekend in May.

95

SOUTHERN CALIFORNIA

HOTELS

★★**Casa Sirena Hotel & Marina**
3605 Peninsula Rd., Oxnard,
805-985-6311, 800-447-3529;
www.casasirenahotel.com
273 rooms. Restaurant, bar. Airport transportation available. Pets accepted. Pool. Tennis. **$**

★**Country Inn & Suites by Carlson**
350 E. Hueneme Rd., Port Hueneme,
805-986-5353, 800-456-4000;
www.countryinns.com

135 rooms. Complimentary full breakfast. Pool. **$**

★★**Embassy Suites Mandalay Beach Resort**
2101 Mandalay Beach Rd., Oxnard,
805-984-2500, 800-362-2779;
www.embassysuites.com
250 rooms. Complimentary full breakfast. Restaurant, bar. Beach. Airport transportation available. Fitness center. Tennis. Business center. **$$**

PALM DESERT

Information: Chamber of Commerce, 73-710 Fred Waring Dr., 760-346-6111,
800-873-2428; www.palm-desert.org

WHAT TO SEE AND DO

Living Desert
47-900 S. Portola Ave.,
Palm Desert, 760-346-5694;
www.livingdesert.org
This 1,200-acre wildlife and botanical park contains interpretive exhibits from the world's deserts. Animals include mountain lions, zebras, bighorn sheep, coyotes, cheetahs, reptiles and birds. Native American exhibits; picnic areas; nature trails; gift shop; cafe; nursery. Special programs on weekends. September-mid-June: daily 9 a.m.-5 p.m.; mid-June-August 31: daily 8 a.m.-1:30 p.m.

SPECIAL EVENTS

Bob Hope Chrysler Classic
39000 Bob Hope Dr., Rancho Mirage,
760-346-8184; www.bhcc.com
Golf pros and celebrities play at four country clubs: Bermuda Dunes, La Quinta, Palm Desert and Indian Wells. Mid-January.

HOTELS

★★**Courtyard by Marriott**
74895 Frank Sinatra Dr.,
Palm Desert, 760-776-4150;
www.courtyard.com
151 rooms. High-speed Internet access. Restaurant, bar. **$**

★**Holiday Inn Express**
74-675 Hwy. 111, Palm Desert,
760-340-4303
129 rooms. Complimentary full breakfast. Fitness center. Pool. Tennis. **$**

★★★**JW Marriott Desert Springs Resort and Spa**
74855 Country Club Dr., Palm Desert,
760-341-2211, 800-255-0848;
www.desertspringsresort.com
Hit the links for 36 rounds of golf, pick up a game of tennis at the more than 20 courts (hard, clay and grass) or head over to the 30,000 square foot European-style spa. This resort also boasts a health club, jogging paths, saunas, sand volleyball and croquet. Restaurants serve everything from sushi to seafood to Italian. Rooms have luxury beds and granite, limestone and Italian marble bathrooms.
884 rooms. High-speed Internet access. Five restaurants, two bars. Golf. Tennis. Business. center. **$$$**

RESTAURANTS

★★★**Cuistot**
72595 El Paseo, Palm Desert,
760-340-1000
Chef/owner Bernard Dervieux serves up inventive dishes inspired by his upbringing in France. Look for quail stuffed with

★
★
★
★
★

sweetbreads with black rice and Chablis sauce, or skillet-roasted veal chop with mushrooms, roasted garlic and fresh thyme. The restaurant itself is reminiscent of a French farmhouse, with beamed cathedral ceilings, a large stone fireplace and candlelight.

California, French menu. Lunch, dinner. Closed Monday; also July-August. Bar. Business casual attire. Reservations recommended. Valet parking. Outdoor seating. **$$$**

★★★Jillian's
74-155 El Paseo, Palm Desert,
760-776-8242; www.jilliansfinedining.com
Housed in a 1948 hacienda, this restaurant features a beautiful garden through which guests pass to reach the dining area, where tables are set with fresh flowers and candles. Selections from the lengthy and impressive wine list perfectly accompany the eclectic menu, which includes creations like prime boneless short ribs braised in California cabernet and rack of Colorado lamb with a Dijon herb crust. Featured desserts, like chocolate brioche pudding and blueberry cheesecake, are made daily.

International/Fusion menu. Dinner. Closed Sunday; mid-June-early September. Bar. Business casual attire. Reservations recommended. Valet parking. Outdoor seating. **$$$**

★Le Donne Cucina Italiana
72624 El Paseo, Palm Desert,
760-773-9441
Italian menu. Dinner. Closed early July-mid-September. Children's menu. Casual attire. Outdoor seating. **$$**

★★LG's Prime Steakhouse
74-225 Hwy. 111, Palm Desert,
760-779-9799;
www.lgsprimesteakhouse.com
Steak menu. Dinner. Bar. Business casual attire. Reservations recommended. Valet parking. Outdoor seating. **$$$**

★★★Ristorante Mamma Gina
73-705 El Paseo, Palm Desert,
760-568-9898; www.mammagina.com
This sister restaurant to one in Florence carries on the decades-old tradition of serving freshly prepared, traditional Tuscan fare. Pappa al pomodoro (authentic Florentine-style thick tomato bread soup), spaghetti alla Bolognese and risotto Mamma Gina (Arborio rice with imported wild porcini mushroom sauce) are a few dishes on the menu that keep customers coming back. An award-winning wine list and a number of decadent desserts add to the authentic Tuscan experience.

Italian menu. Dinner. Bar. Casual attire. Reservations recommended. Outdoor seating. **$$$**

★★★Ruth's Chris Steak House
74-740 Hwy. 111, Palm Desert,
760-779-1998
Born from a single New Orleans restaurant that Ruth Fertel bought in 1965 for $22,000, the chain is a favorite among steak lovers. Aged prime midwestern beef is broiled at 1,800 degrees and served on a heated plate sizzling with butter and with sides like creamed spinach and au gratin potatoes.

Steak menu. Dinner. Bar. Business casual attire. Reservations recommended. Valet parking. **$$$**

★★★Tuscany
74855 Country Club Dr., Palm Desert,
760-341-2211;
www.desertspringsresort.com
One of the many restaurants in the JW Marriott Desert Springs Resort and Spa, this eatery has a seasonal menu that features dishes like ravioli stuffed with fresh Maine lobster, minestrone with pesto and house-made tiramisu. The mile-long wine list is comprehensive and has bottles from around the world. Soft music and frescoes add to the authentic vibe.

Italian menu. Dinner. Bar. Children's menu. Business casual attire. Valet parking. Outdoor seating. **$$$**

97

SOUTHERN CALIFORNIA

★
★
★
★
★

PALM SPRINGS

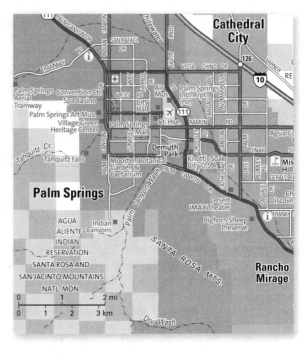

Located 120 miles east of Los Angeles and 135 miles north of San Diego, Palm Springs has long been the vacation getaway for Southern California's elite. The desert oasis is complete with spectacular resorts, fine dining and unique mid-century modern desert architecture. Recently, the town's resorts have been undergoing a renovation revival, with star designers such as Jonathan Adler and Kelly Wearstler called in to dream up funky, colorful and stylish interiors. There are nearly golf 90 courses within a 15-mile radius of the city. Originally the domain of the Cahuilla, the city has been laid out in a checkerboard pattern, with nearly every other square mile still owned by the tribe.

Information: Palm Springs Desert Resort Convention and Visitors Bureau, 70-100 Hwy. 111, Rancho Mirage, 760-770-9000, 800-967-3767; www.giveintothedesert.com

SOUTHERN CALIFORNIA

WHAT TO SEE AND DO

Indian Canyons
38520 S. Palm Canyon Dr.,
Palm Springs, 760-325-1862;
www.indian-canyons.com
The remains of the ancient Cahuilla people include rock art, mortars ground into bedrock, pictographs and shelters built atop high cliff walls. Spot bighorn sleep and wind ponies along the hiking trails. Rangers give interpretive walks. Daily 8 a.m.-5 p.m.

Knott's Soak City Water Park Palm Springs
1500 Gene Autry Trail,
Palm Springs,
760-325-7873;
www.knotts.com
This 22-acre water park has 13 water slides, an inner tube ride, and wave pool. Late March-Labor Day: daily; early September-late October: weekends.

Uprising Adventure Guides
Joshua Tree, 760-366-3799, 888-254-6266;
www.uprising.com
Outdoor rock-climbing gym offers training and climbing for all ages. Night climbing.

Moorten's Botanical Garden
1701 S. Palm Canyon Dr.,
Palm Springs, 760-327-6555
Approximately 3,000 varieties of desert plants, featuring the world's first "cactarium" which contains several hundred species of cactus and desert plants from around the world. Monday-Tuesday, Thursday-Satday 9 a.m.-4:30 p.m., Sunday 10 a.m.-4 p.m.

Palm Springs Aerial Tramway
1 Tramway Rd., Palm Springs,
760-325-1449, 760-325-1391;
www.pstramway.com
World's longest double-reversible, single-span aerial tramway. Two 80-passenger revolving cars make the 2 1/2-mile trip

(ascending to 8,516 feet) to the top of Mount San Jacinto. Picnicking; camping in summer; cafeteria at summit. Monday-Friday every half-hour from 10 a.m., Saturday-Sunday from 8 a.m.

Palm Springs Air Museum
745 N. Gene Autry Trail,
Palm Springs, 760-778-6262;
www.air-museum.org
Vintage World War II aircraft on display. Also period photographs and video documentaries. June-September: 9 a.m.-3 p.m., October-May: 10 a.m.-5 p.m.

Palm Springs Desert Museum
101 Museum Dr., Palm Springs,
760-325-7186;
www.psmuseum.org
Enjoy diverse art collections of world-renowned artists, science exhibitions with interactive elements and educational programs for the whole family. The Annenerg Performing Arts Theater features jazz, classical, dance and Broadway performances. Tuesday-Wednesday, Friday-Sunday 10 a.m.-5 p.m., Thursday noon-8 p.m.

Palm Springs Historical Society on Village Green
221 S. Palm Canyon Dr., Palm Springs,
760-323-8297;
www.palmspringshistoricalsociety.com
Comprised of two 19th-century houses exhibiting artifacts from early Palm Springs. McCallum Adobe (circa 1885) is the oldest building in the city and houses an extensive collection of photographs, paintings, clothes, tools, books and Native American ware. The Cornelia White House (circa 1893) was partially constructed of rail ties from the defunct Palmdale Railway and is furnished with authentic antiques. Mid-October-late May, Wednesday, Sunday noon-3 p.m.; Thursday-Saturday 10 a.m.-4 p.m.

Tahquitz Creek Golf Resort
1885 Golf Club Dr., Palm Springs,
760-328-1005;
www.tahquitzcreek.com

The resort consists of two 18-hole courses: the Legend course and the Resort course. Daily.

HOTELS

★Ballantines Hotel
1420 N. Indian Canyon Dr.,
Palm Springs, 92262,
760-320-1178,
800-485-2808;
www.ballantineshotels.com
14 rooms. No children allowed. Swim. **$$**

★Best Western Las Brisas
222 S. Indian Canyon Dr.,
Palm Springs, 92262,
760-325-4372, 800-346-5714;
www.bestwestern.com
90 rooms, 3 story. Complimentary full breakfast. Wireless Internet access. Pet. Swim. **$**

★★★Doral Desert Princess Resort
67-967 Vista Chino, Cathedral City,
760-322-7000, 888-386-4677;
www.doralpalmsprings.com
This 347-acre resort features panoramic mountain views and oversized guest rooms with in–room vanities. A PGA-rated 27-hole golf course, on-site spa and tennis courts provide plenty of recreation.
285 rooms. Restaurant, bar. Airport transportation available. **$**

★★★Hilton Palm Springs Resort
400 E. Tahquitz Canyon Way,
Palm Springs,
760-320-6868, 800-522-6900;
www.hiltonpalmsprings.com
From its dramatic setting at the foot of the steeply rising San Jacinto Mountains to the grand rooms with Italian travertine flooring, contemporary furnishings and cozy sitting areas, this is a popular resort for business travelers and vacationing families. It's less than two miles from the airport and within walking distance of cafés, galleries, boutiques, a casino and the Palm Springs Desert Museum.
260 rooms. High-speed Internet access. Two restaurants, bar. Spa. Pets accepted. **$**

★

★

★

★

★

★★★Hyatt Regency Suites Palm Springs
285 N. Palm Canyon Dr., Palm Springs,
760-322-9000, 800-223-1234;
www.palmsprings.hyatt.com
This Hyatt hotel is set in a prime downtown location overlooking the San Jacinto Mountains. Guest rooms feature separate sitting areas with pull-out sofas and dining tables, and furnished balconies give way to views of the mountains, pool or city. There are plenty of on-site activities including jogging paths, bicycle trails, a heated pool and putting green. The hotel's restaurant, the Palm Court Café, is located in the center of the six-story atrium and serves eclectic California cuisine in a casual setting.

193 rooms, all suites. High-speed Internet access, wireless Internet access. Restaurant, bar. Exercise. Swim. Busn. center. **$$**

★★★Ingleside Inn
200 W. Ramon Rd., Palm Springs, ,
760-325-0046, 800-772-6655;
www.inglesideinn.com
Everyone from Rita Hayworth to Arnold Schwarzenegger has stayed at this romantic inn fashioned from an early-1900s estate. It's only one block from the city's main drag, but hidden away within a residential neighborhood. The luxurious suites and villas combine old world décor with modern amenities like steam baths and whirlpool tubs. Melvyn's Restaurant specializes in continental cuisine, and the Casablanca Room is an intimate piano bar.

30 rooms. Restaurant, bar. Swim. **$$**

★★★Rancho Las Palmas Resort and Spa
41-000 Bob Hope Dr., Rancho Mirage,
760-568-2727, 866-423-1195;
www.rancholaspalmas.com
This family-friendly hotel is situated in the heart of Rancho Mirage on 240 acres surrounded by mountains, lakes and gardens. Activities include a Ted Robinson-designed golf course, a 25-court tennis center, a 100-foot water slide and a 20,000-square-foot European spa. The Spanish-style guest rooms feature furnished patios or balconies.

450 rooms. High-speed Internet access. Two restaurants, bar. Spa. **$$**

★★★Spa Resort Casino
100 N. Indian Canyon Dr.,
Palm Springs,
760-325-1461, 800-854-1279;
www.sparesortcasino.com
Though the entire resort underwent a renovation in 2003, the rooms are less luxurious than those found in other resorts in the area. The focus here is on gaming and nightlife. This is the only full-service resort/casino in Palm Springs, with all the dining options of a typical casino: two Asian restaurants, a New York-style deli, a large buffet-style restaurant and several bars. It's a block from Palm Canyon Drive where there are numerous shopping and dining options.

228 rooms. Wireless Internet access. Two restaurants, bar. Spa. Casino. **$**

★★★Viceroy Palm Springs
415 S. Belardo Rd., Palm Springs,
760-320-4117, 800-237-3687;
www.viceroypalmsprings.com
Built in 1929 and updated by star designer Kelly Wearstler to reflect old Hollywood glamour, this centrally located hotel lures a primarily adult clientele thanks to its seclusion. Luxurious rooms, suites and villas are surrounded by gorgeous gardens, and are outfitted with Italian linens. The full-service Estrella Spa offers aromatherapy and an array of body treatments, while the fitness center offers yoga and guided hikes. The gourmet restaurant, Citron, dishes up California cuisine.

68 rooms. High-speed Internet access. Restaurant, bar. Pets accepted. **$$**

★★★The Villa Royale Inn
1620 Indian Trail, Palm Springs,
760-327-2314, 800-245-2314;
www.villaroyale.com
Just a mile from downtown, this hotel combines the pampered privacy of a bed and breakfast with the amenities of a full-service hotel. Individually appointed Mediterranean-style suites and villas nestled amid

★
★
★
★
★

tranquil, lushly landscaped courtyards and two heated pools are decorated with European antiques and feature down duvets, luxurious robes and herbal bath products. Larger rooms also have fireplaces, open-beam ceilings, kitchens and private patios. The intimate restaurant, Europa, serves award-winning continental cuisine under the stars.

30 rooms. Complimentary full breakfast. Restaurant, bar. **$$**

★★★The Westin Mission Hills Resort and Spa
71333 Dinah Shore Dr.,
Rancho Mirage,
760-328-5955;
www.westin.com/missionhills
Set on 360 acres surrounded by mountains, palm trees and lush landscaping, there's almost no need to leave the resort. Activities are plentiful, with two championship golf courses, three swimming pools—one with a 60-foot water slide—a 14,000-square-foot spa with a state-of-the-art fitness center and seven lighted tennis courts. Guest rooms have private patio and sitting areas with couch and coffee table.

512 rooms. High-speed Internet access. Two restaurants, bar. Pets accepted. **$$$**

★★Wyndham Palm Springs Hotel
888 Tahquitz Canyon Way,
Palm Springs,
760-322-6000, 800-996-3426;
www.wyndham-palmsprings.com
Just eight blocks from the airport and adjacent to the convention center, the Wyndham anchors a 40-acre commercial development, making it a good choice for business travelers. The hotel's Spanish-colonial exterior gives way to a more contemporary décor inside the guest rooms, which feature oversized desks, high-speed Internet access and scenic mountain views. Amenities include a staffed health club, complete body spa and a large pool with an adjacent bar and barbecue.

410 rooms. High-speed Internet access. Restaurant, bar. Pets accepted. **$$**

★★★The Willows Historic Palm Springs Inn
412 W. Tahquitz Canyon Way,
Palm Springs, 760-320-0771;
www.thewillowspalmsprings.com
This legendary inn has hosted everyone from Marion Davies to Albert Einstein. The historic Mediterranean villa in the heart of Old Palm Springs has only eight guest rooms each with its own style, from the slate flooring in the Rock Room to the coffered ceiling in the Library, where Clark Gable and Carole Lombard spent their honeymoon.

8 rooms. Pool. **$$$**

SPECIALTY LODGINGS
Casa Cody Inn
175 S. Cahuilla Rd., Palm Springs,
760-320-9346, 800-231-2639;
www.casacody.com
27 rooms. Pets accepted; fee. Complimentary continental breakfast. **$**

RESTAURANTS
★★Blue Coyote Bar & Grill
445 N. Palm Canyon Dr., Palm Springs,
760-327-1196; www.bluecoyote-grill.com
Southwestern menu. Lunch, dinner. Closed August. Bar. Casual attire. Reservations recommended. Outdoor seating. **$$**

★★Cedar Creek Inn
1555 S. Palm Canyon Dr.,
Palm Springs, 760-325-7300;
www.cedarcreekinnps.com
Continental menu. Breakfast, lunch, dinner, brunch. Bar. Children's menu. Casual attire. Reservations recommended. Outdoor seating. **$$**

★★★Europa
1620 Indian Trail, Palm Springs,
760-327-2314; www.villaroyale.com
Housed in the Villa Royale Inn, this restaurant provides a romantic setting in which to enjoy continental dishes inspired by the flavors of France, Italy, Spain and Greece. Dine poolside by the fountains or by the fire in the cozy dining room.

101

SOUTHERN CALIFORNIA

★
★
★

Continental menu. Dinner. Closed Monday. Bar. Business casual attire. Reservations recommended. Outdoor seating. **$$$**

★Great Wall
362 S. Palm Canyon Dr., Palm Springs, 760-322-2209
Chinese menu. Lunch, dinner. Casual attire. **$$**

★★Kaiser Grill
205 S. Palm Canyon Dr., Palm Springs, 760-323-1003
California, Mediterranean menu. Lunch, dinner. Bar. Children's menu. Casual attire. Reservations recommended. Outdoor seating. **$$**

★★Las Casuelas Terraza
222 S. Palm Canyon Dr., Palm Springs, 760-325-2794
Mexican menu. Lunch, dinner. Bar. Children's menu. Casual attire. Reservations recommended. Outdoor seating. **$$**

★★★Le Vallauris
385 W. Tahquitz Canyon Way, Palm Springs, 760-325-5059; www.levallauris.com
Housed in a 1924 home with Louis XV furniture, rich tapestries and an enchanting tree-shaded garden surrounded by flowers, Le Vallauris transports you to the French countryside. Daily selections—from rack of lamb to Grand Marnier soufflé—are written on a board brought to the table. The impressive wine list includes bottles from France and California as well as Italy, New Zealand and Spain.
French menu. Lunch, dinner. Closed July-August. Bar. Business casual attire.

Reservations recommended. Valet parking. Outdoor seating. **$$$**

★★★Melvyn's
200 W. Ramon Rd., Palm Springs, 760-325-0046; www.inglesideinn.com
Located in the Ingleside Inn, this classic steakhouse is a long-standing Palm Springs tradition.
Continental menu. Lunch, dinner. Bar. Business casual attire. Reservations recommended. Valet parking. Outdoor seating. **$$$**

★★Palmie
44491 Town Center Way, Palm Springs, 760-341-3200
French menu. Dinner. Closed Sunday. Bar. Business casual attire. Reservations recommended. Valet parking. **$$**

★Rock Garden Cafe
777 S. Palm Canyon Dr., Palm Springs, 760-327-8840
American menu. Breakfast, lunch, dinner. Closed holidays. Bar. Children's menu. Casual attire. Outdoor seating. **$**

★★★St. James at the Vineyard
265 S. Palm Canyon Dr., Palm Springs, 760-320-8041; palmsprings.com/dine/stjames
Signature curries are offered alongside dishes like baked vegetarian cannelloni, bouillabaisse Burmese and grilled New-York Steak, while the award-winning wine list offers choices from California, Hungary, Portugal, Italy and Australia. The sophisticated Icon bar is a popular spot for cocktails and features live music Wednesday through Sunday.
International menu. Dinner. Bar. Business casual attire. Outdoor seating. **$$$**

PASO ROBLES
Franciscan Fathers named this city for the great oak trees in the area at the southern end of the fertile Salinas River Valley. Located between mountains on the west and barley and grape fields on the east, Paso Robles is also noted for its almond tree orchards.
Information: Chamber of Commerce, 1225 Park St., 805-238-0506, 800-406-4040; www.pasorobleschamber.com

SPECIAL EVENTS

California Mid-State Fair
2198 Riverside Ave., Paso Robles,
805-239-0655; www.midstatefair.com
Rodeo, horse show, amusements, entertainment. Late July-early August.

Wine Festival
805-239-8463; www.pasowine.com
Wine tasting, concerts and open houses. Third Saturday in May.

HOTELS

★Adelaide Inn
1215 Ysabel Ave., Paso Robles,
805-238-2770, 800-549-7276;
www.adelaideinn.com

67 rooms. Airport transportation available. Pool. $

★★Best Western Black Oak Motor Lodge
1135 24th St., Paso Robles,
805-238-4740, 800-780-7234;
www.bestwestern.com
110 rooms. Restaurant. Airport transportation available. Pool. Business center. $

RESTAURANTS

★F. McClintock's Saloon
1234 Park St., Paso Robles,
805-238-2233;
www.mclintocks.com
Steak menu. Lunch, dinner. Bar. Children's menu. $$

PISMO BEACH

Pismo Beach is famous for its 23 miles of scenic beaches. Ocean fishing, dunes, swimming, surfing, diving, golf, horseback riding and camping make the area popular with vacationers. Pismo Beach is also in a growing wine region. It is the last Pacific oceanfront community where autos can still be driven on the beach (access ramps are at two locations along the beach). A more dramatic and rugged coastline is found at Shell Beach to the north, which has been incorporated into Pismo Beach.
Information: Conference & Visitors Bureau, 581 Dolliver St., 805-773-7034, 800-443-7778; www.classiccalifornia.com

WHAT TO SEE AND DO

Lopez Recreational Area
6800 Lopez Dr.,
Arroyo Grande,
805-788-2381
This lake created by the Lopez Dam has swimming, water-skiing, water slide, windsurfing, fishing, boating, hiking, picnicking; camping, tent and trailer sites. Summer campfire programs, boat tours.

Monarch Butterfly Grove
Dolliver St.,
Pismo Beach,
800-443-7778;
www.monarchbutterfly.org
The state's largest winter site for Monarch butterflies. They can be seen in the grove located at the North Beach Campground. October-February, daily; dependent on butterfly migration.

SPECIAL EVENTS

Pismo Beach Clam Festival
581 Dolliver St., Pismo Beach, 93449,
805-773-4382, 800-443-7778.
Well-known festival held annually at Pismo Beach pier. Includes parade, clam chowder contest, sand sculpture contest, rubber duckie regatta, a clam dig, carnival rides and food booths. Mid-October.

HOTELS

★Oxford Suites Resort—Pismo Beach
651 Five Cities Dr., Pismo Beach,
805-773-3773, 800-982-7848;
www.oxfordsuites.com
133 rooms, all suites. Complimentary full breakfast. Bar. Pets accepted. Pool. Business center. $

★Sandcastle Inn
100 Stimson Ave., Pismo Beach,
805-773-2422, 800-822-6606;
www.sandcastleinn.com

SOUTHERN CALIFORNIA

75 rooms. Complimentary continental breakfast. Whirlpool. Pets accepted. **$$**

★★Sea Venture Resort
100 Ocean View Ave.,
Pismo Beach,
800-662-5543;
www.seaventure.com
50 rooms. Complimentary continental breakfast. Restaurant, bar. Beach. Whirlpool. **$$**

★★Spyglass Inn
2705 Spyglass Dr.,
Pismo Beach,
805-773-4855, 800-824-2612;
www.spyglassinn.com
82 rooms. Pets accepted. Pool. **$**

★★★The Cliffs Resort
2757 Shell Beach Rd.,
Pismo Beach,
805-773-5000, 800-826-7827;
www.cliffsresort.com
The cliff-top location overlooking the Pacific, inn-style hospitality and proximity to the local airport make this resort a good choice for both business travelers and vacationers. Guest rooms, having recently undergone a $2 million refurbishing, feature work desks, Italian marble baths and private balconies or patios with coastal or mountain views. Activities such as surfing, kayaking, hiking and golf are available on-site or nearby, and dozens of wineries are within driving distance.

165 rooms. Pets accepted, some restrictions, fee. Wireless Internet access. Restaurant, bar. Airport transportation available. **$$**

RESTAURANTS

★★F. McLintock's
750 Mattie Rd., Pismo Beach,
805-773-1892;
www.mclintocks.com
Steak menu. Dinner. Bar. Children's menu. Casual attire. Reservations recommended (Sunday-Thursday). **$$**

★★Rosa's
491 Price St., Pismo Beach,
805-773-0551;
www.rosasrestaurant.com
Italian menu. Lunch, dinner. Bar. Children's menu. Casual attire. Reservations recommended. **$$**

RANCHO SANTA FE

HOTELS

★★★Morgan Run Resort & Club
5690 Cancha de Golf, Rancho Santa Fe,
858-756-2471, 800-378-4653;
www.morganrun.com
The Morgan Run Resort & Club is both a club for area residents and a resort for guests. Guests can take full advantage of the club and its facilities, including a 27-hole championship golf course, tennis courts and fitness center offering Pilates and yoga classes. The guest rooms are traditional and elegant, and each has its own private patio or balcony. The resort is only five miles from the beach community of Del Mar with its beaches, boutiques and Del Mar Race Track, where's there's plenty of horse racing action.

90 rooms. Restaurant, bar. Spa. Golf. Tennis. **$$**

★★★★Rancho Valencia Resort & Spa
5921 Valencia Circle,
Rancho Santa Fe,
858-756-1123, 800-548-3664;
www.ranchovalencia.com
Located in the canyon of Rancho Santa Fe on 40 manicured acres of rolling hills, this relaxing retreat is just minutes from the charming boutiques and cafés of La Jolla. If you're looking for something secluded, this is it. The resort is made up of 20 pink casitas, which house only 49 suites, each featuring fireplaces with hand-painted tiles, beamed ceilings and private garden patios and large bathrooms, some with Jaccuzzi bathtubs and steam showers. There's also an award-winning tennis program, spa and privileges at local golf courses. An outstanding restaurant makes for a perfect stay.

49 rooms, all suites. Pets accepted, fee. High-speed Internet access. Restaurant, bar. Fitness room, fitness classes available. **$$$$**

★★★Inn at Rancho Santa Fe
5951 Linea Del Cielo, Rancho Santa Fe, 858-756-1131, 800-843-4661; www.theinnatranchosantafe.com

This historic spot doesn't fit the mold of a traditional inn. With several small cottages dotting the 20-acre property, guest accommodations are available in three varieties: deluxe rooms, suites and private cottages. The deluxe rooms have patios or decks, and many have fireplaces, wet bars, kitchenettes or sitting areas (some of the older rooms have hardwood floors). Suites are one- or two-bedrooms cottages, each with a living room, kitchen and fireplace, plus a patio or deck. The one-, two- and three-bedrooms private cottages have a full-sized kitchen and guest bath. A full-service spa, fitness program (offering guided runs and walks, swimming lessons, water aerobics and weight training classes), tennis courts (private lessons available), croquet lawn and walking and jogging trails provide plenty of recreation.

89 rooms. Restaurant. Pets accepted. Pool. Tennis. **$$**

RESTAURANTS

★★Delicias
6106 Paseo Delicias, Rancho Santa Fe, 858-756-8000

French, California menu. Dinner. Bar. Outdoor seating. **$$$**

★★★Mille Fleurs
6009 Paseo Delicias, Rancho Santa Fe, 858-756-3085; www.millefleurs.com

This newly remodeled restaurant serves such unforgettable dishes as vegetable ravioli with cave-aged Gruyère and venison

loin from New Zealand. Many of the fruits and vegetables come from a farm just down the road, which the chef visits every morning. An outdoor patio, seasonal music and a piano bar make for a perfect evening.

French menu. Lunch, dinner. Reservations recommended. Outdoor seating. **$$$**

★★★Valencia
5921 Valencia Circle, Rancho Santa Fe, 858-759-6216; www.ranchovalencia.com

Just off the Mission-style courtyard of the Rancho Valencia resort, you'll find Valencia, a romantic dining experience reminiscent of the French countryside, with whitewashed walls, beamed ceilings, live palms and a tiered patio. The menu features seafood, fresh vegetables and aged beef. Highlights include the Maryland Blue Lump Crab Cake, a Colorado Lamb Rib Eye with roasted vegetables and Merlot sauce and the Valencia Veal Picatto with crème fraiche-whipped potatoes and asparagus. Save room for one of the decadent desserts or the artisan cheese plate. The restaurant also offers an outstanding Sunday brunch.

Seafood menu. Breakfast, lunch, dinner, Sunday brunch. Bar. Casual attire. Reservations recommended. Valet parking. Outdoor seating. **$$$$**

SPAS

★★★Spa Rancho Valencia
5921 Valencia Circle, Rancho Santa Fe, 858-756-1123; www.ranchovalencia.com

This spa's mosaic-tiled décor echoes the Spanish mission-style look of the Rancho Valencia Resort. The 10 treatment rooms, outfitted with showers and private patios, are luxurious retreats where staff deliver massages, exfoliations, masques and wraps that make full use of the area's natural bounty, from Pacific sea salt to seaweed, sweet citrus fruits and cypress. **$$**

REDLANDS

Named for the color of the earth in the area and known for many years as the Navel Orange Center, Redlands still handles a large volume of citrus fruits.
Information: Chamber of Commerce, 1 E. Redlands Blvd., 909-793-2546; www.redlandschamber.org

WHAT TO SEE AND DO

Edward-Dean Museum and Gardens
9401 Oak Glen Rd., Cherry Valley, 951-845-2626;
www.edward-deanmuseum.org
European and Asian furniture, bronzes, porcelains, rugs, paintings from 17th and 19th centuries. Friday-Sunday 10 a.m.-5 p.m.

Kimberly Crest House and Gardens
1325 Prospect Dr., Redlands, 909-792-2111; www.kimberlycrest.org
Former estate of John Kimberly, founder of the Kimberly-Clark Corporation. The 1897 French chateau-style structure and accompanying carriage house on six and a half acres is representative of the "Mansion Era" of Southern California. The grounds also include Italian gardens and a citrus grove. Guided tours. September-July, Thursday-Sunday 1-4 p.m.; closed August.

Lincoln Memorial Shrine
125 W. Vine St., Redlands, 909-798-7632; www.lincolnshrine.org
Learn about the former president and the Civil War at this shrine featuring George Grey Barnard's Carrara marble bust of Lincoln, murals by Dean Cornwell and a painting by Norman Rockwell. Tuesday-Sunday 1-5 p.m.

Pharaoh's Lost Kingdom
1101 California St., Redlands, 909-335-7275;
www.pharaohslostkingdom.com
This family theme park features a race car complex with Indy, Grand Prix and kiddy cars, a water park with wave pools, miniature golf and 16 amusement rides. Arcade, indoor playground and amphitheater. Daily; schedule varies.

Redlands Bowl
25 Grant St., Redlands, 909-793-7316;
www.redlandsbowl.org
Locals call this amphitheater the "Little Hollywood Bowl" because of the free concerts held every Tuesday and Friday in summer.

San Bernardino County Museum
2024 Orange Tree Lane, Redlands, 909-307-2669;
www.co.san-bernardino.ca.us/museum
Check out the mounted collection of birds and bird eggs of Southern California, reptiles, mammals, rocks and more. Tuesday-Sunday 9 a.m.-5 p.m.

SPECIAL EVENTS

Cherry Festival
Stewart Park, Ninth St. and Orange Ave., Beaumont,
951-845-9541;
www.ci.beaumont.ca.us/cherryfestival.htm
This annual festival celebrates the area's cherry harvest. Activities include a parade, entertainment and carnival rides. Early June.

HOTELS

★Best Western Sandman Motel
1120 W. Colton Ave., Redlands, 909-793-2001, 800-780-7234;
www.bestwestern.com
65 rooms. Complimentary continental breakfast. Pets accepted. Pool. $

★★Best Western El Rancho Motor Inn
480 E. Fifth St., Beaumont, 951-845-2176;
www.bestwestern.com
52 rooms. Pets accepted, some restrictions; fee. Complimentary continental breakfast. Restaurant, bar. $

106

SOUTHERN CALIFORNIA

RESTAURANT

★★★**Joe Greensleeves**

220 N. Orange St., Redlands,
909-792-6969

This charming restaurant, housed in an historic 19th-century red brick building, is a favorite special occasion destination in the Inland Empire. Its rustic-themed dining room is inviting and features a stone fireplace and back booths that are perfect for private, romantic dinners. Although the menu is dominated by a number of tempting steak and seafood dishes, long-standing favorites include roasted Anaheim chile stuffed with venison and Sonoma goat cheese with smoked corn sauce and diced tomatoes. The wine list has been nationally recognized for its excellence, and house-made desserts are the perfect ending to a meal.

Seafood, steak menu. Lunch, dinner. **$$$**

RIVERSIDE

Riverside is known for the navel orange, which was introduced to America from Brazil by the first settlers in this area. It's home to the Parent Navel Orange tree, from which all North American navel oranges are descended. Vast navel orange groves make Riverside the center of the "Orange Empire."

Information: Greater Riverside Chambers of Commerce, 3985 University Ave., 951-683-7100; www.riverside-chamber.com

WHAT TO SEE AND DO

California Museum of Photography

3824 Main St., Riverside,
951-827-4787;
www.cmp.ucr.edu

Large collection of photographic equipment, prints and stereographs. Interactive gallery, walk-in camera; library. Tuesday-Saturday noon-5 p.m.

Castle Amusement Park

3500 Polk St., Riverside,
951-785-3000;
www.castlepark.com

Features 80-year-old Dentzel carousel with hand-carved animals. Park with 30 rides and attractions. Monday-Thursday 10 a.m.-11 p.m., Friday 10 a.m.-11 p.m., Saturday-Sunday 11 a.m.-11 p.m. Four 18-hole miniature golf courses and video arcade Monday-Thursday 10 a.m.-11 p.m., Friday to midnight, Saturday 11 a.m.-midnight, Sunday 11 a.m.-11 p.m. Fee for activities.

Heritage House

8193 Magnolia Ave., Riverside,
951-689-1333

(1891) Restored Victorian mansion. September-June, Friday noon-3 p.m., Saturday-Sunday to 3:30 p.m.

March Field Air Museum

22550 Van Buren Blvd.,
Riverside, 951-697-6602;
www.marchfield.org

This museum houses more than 60 historic aircraft, including the first operational jet used by the U.S. Air Force and the speed record-breaking SR-71 Blackbird. Take a spin in the G-force flight simulator or explore the collection of 2,000 artifacts dating back to 1918. Daily 9 a.m.-4 p.m.

Mount Rubidoux Memorial Park

4393 Riverview Dr., Riverside,
951-361-2090

According to legend, the mountain was once the altar of Cahuilla and Serrano sun worship. A cross rises on the peak in memory of Fray Junipero Serra, founder of the California missions. The World Peace Tower stands on the side of the mountain. Hiking. Daily.

Orange Empire Railway Museum

2201 South A St., Perris,
951-943-3020, 951-457-2605;
www.oerm.org

This free museum features more than 150 rail vehicles and pieces of off-rail equipment, railroad and trolley memorabilia.

SOUTHERN CALIFORNIA

Trolley rides run from 11 a.m. to 5 p.m. on Saturday, Sunday, and holidays. Daily 9 a.m.-5 p.m.

Parent Washington Navel Orange Tree
Magnolia and Arlington Avenues, Riverside
Propagated from one of the two original trees from Bahia, Brazil. Planted in 1873, all navel orange trees stem from this tree or from its offspring.

Riverside Art Museum
3425 Mission Inn Ave., Riverside, 951-684-7111; www.riversideartmuseum.org
Housed in a 1929 Mediterranean-style YWCA building designed by Julia Morgan, this museum features changing exhibits of historical and contemporary sculpture, painting and graphics. Monday-Saturday 10 a.m.-4 p.m.

Riverside Municipal Museum
3580 Mission Inn Ave., Riverside, 951-826-5273; www.riversideca.gov/museum
Area history, anthropology and natural history displays; changing exhibits. Tuesday-Friday 9 a.m.-5 p.m., Saturday 10 a.m.-5 p.m., Sunday 11 a.m.-5 p.m.

Rubidoux Drive-In
3770 Opal St., Riverside; www.rubidoux.icyspicy.com
The Rubidoux opened in 1948 and has three screens, each showing double features year-round.

University of California, Riverside
900 University Ave., Riverside, 951-787-1012; www.ucr.edu
The campus centers around a 161-foot Carillon Tower and has a 40-acre botanic garden featuring flora from all parts of the world and four miles of walking trails.

SPECIAL EVENTS
Easter Sunrise Pilgrimage
Mount Rubidoux Memorial Park, Riverside
First nonsectarian sunrise service in the United States, since 1909. Easter Sunday.

HOTELS
★Comfort Inn
1590 University Ave., Riverside, 951-683-6000, 800-228-5150; www.choicehotels.com
115 rooms. Complimentary continental breakfast. High-speed Internet access. **$**

★★Courtyard Riverside
1510 University Ave., Riverside, 951-276-1200, 800-321-2211; www.courtyard.com
163 rooms. High-speed Internet access. Restaurant, bar. Pool. **$**

★★★Marriott Riverside
3400 Market St., Riverside, 951-784-8000, 800-228-9290; www.marriott.com
Adjacent to the Riverside Convention Center and close to Ontario International Airport, this hotel attracts business and leisure travelers looking for a range of amenities. Spacious, elegant rooms offer comfort and practical business features including work desks, speaker phones and complimentary coffee. Olio Ristorante specializes in Italian food, while Martini's Lounge serves an eclectic menu. Antique stores, museums, shops and other attractions are within walking distance.
292 rooms. High-speed Internet access. Restaurant, bar. Pool. Business center. **$$**

★★★Mission Inn Hotel and Spa
3649 Mission Inn Ave., Riverside, 909-784-0300; www.missioninn.com
A National Historic Landmark, the Mission Inn is once hosted both Theodore Roosevelt and Andrew Carnegie in the early 20th century. After a period of mid-20th century decline, it was restored and reopened in the 1990s. Today, this stunning hotel has an ornately decorated lobby with dark wood floors, columns and ceramic tile. No two guest rooms are alike. The hotel features two chapels, perfect for weddings and other

SOUTHERN CALIFORNIA

occasions (Tiffany stained-glass windows adorn the larger of the two).

239 rooms. High-speed wireless Internet access. Restaurant, bar. Spa. Pool. **$$**

RESTAURANTS

★★Ciao Bella
1630 Spruce St., Riverside, 951-781-8840
Italian menu. Lunch, dinner. Closed Sunday. Bar. Casual attire. Reservations recommended. Outdoor seating. **$$$**

★★Gerard's
9814 Magnolia Ave., Riverside,
951-687-4882
French menu. Dinner. Closed Sunday. Casual attire. Reservations recommended. **$$$**

★Market Broiler
3525 Merrill Ave., Riverside, 909-276-9007;
www.marketbroiler.com
Seafood menu. Lunch, dinner. Bar. Casual attire. **$$**

SAN BERNARDINO

Set amid mountains, valleys and deserts, San Bernardino is a mixture of Spanish and Mormon cultures. The city takes its name from the valley and mountains discovered by a group of missionaries in 1810 on the feast of San Bernardino of Siena. In 1851, a group of Mormons bought the Rancho San Bernardino and laid out a town modeled after Salt Lake City. The group was recalled by Brigham Young six years later, but the city continued to thrive. The area has a vast citrus industry. In April, the fragrance and beauty of orange blossoms fill the nearby groves.

Information: San Bernardino Area Chamber of Commerce, 546 W. Sixth St., 909-885-7515; www.ci.san-bernardino.ca.us

WHAT TO SEE AND DO

Glen Helen Regional Park
2555 Glen Helen Pkwy.,
San Bernardino, 909-887-7540;
www.co.san-bernardino.ca.us/parks/glen.htm
Approximately 500 acres. Swimming, two flume water slides; fishing; nature trail; picnicking; playground. Daily.

Mountain High Ski Area
24510 Hwy. 2, Wrightwood,
888-754-7878;
www.mthigh.com
Three quad, three triple, six double chairlifts. Longest run 1 1/2 miles; vertical drop 1,600 feet. Night skiing. Mid-November-late April, daily.

Rim of the World Highway
Running Springs
Scenic 45-mile mountain road leading to Big Bear Lake, Snow Summit, Running Springs, Lake Arrowhead, and Skyforest. Beaches on the lakes with fishing, hiking and riding trails; picnic grounds.

San Bernardino National Forest
602 S. Tippecanoe Ave.,
San Bernardino, 909-382-2600;
www.fs.fed.us/r5/sanbernardino
Stretching east from San Bernardino to Palm Springs, this is of the most heavily used national forests in the country. Fishing, boating, hunting, hiking, horseback riding, skiing, picnicking, camping.

SPECIAL EVENTS

National Orange Show
Fairgrounds, 689 S. E. St.,
San Bernardino, 909-888-6788;
www.nationalorangeshow.com
Held annually since 1915 to mark the completion of the winter citrus crop harvest. Exhibits, sports events, entertainment. Memorial Day weekend.

Stater Brothers Route 66 Rendezvous
Downtown, San Bernardino, 909-388-2934;
www.route-66.org
During this annual four-day auto rally, more than 2,400 cars line the downtown streets. Mid-September.

SOUTHERN CALIFORNIA

★
★
★
★

HOTELS

★La Quinta Inn
205 E. Hospitality Lane, San Bernardino,
909-888-7571, 800-687-6667;
www.laquinta.com
153 rooms. Complimentary continental
breakfast. High-speed Internet access. **$**

★★Clarion Hotel & Convention Center
295 N. E St., San Bernardino,
909-381-6181; www.choicehotels.com

230 rooms. Complimentary continental
breakfast. High-speed wireless Internet
access. Restaurant, bar. **$**

RESTAURANT

★★Lotus Garden
111 E. Hospitality Lane, San Bernardino,
909-381-6171
Chinese menu. Lunch, dinner. Bar. Children's menu. Casual attire. Reservations
recommended. **$$**

SAN CLEMENTE

Information: Chamber of Commerce, 1100 N. El Camino Real, 949-492-1131;
www.scchamber.com

WHAT TO SEE AND DO

San Clemente State Beach
San Clemente; www.parks.ca.gov
Swimming, lifeguard; fishing; hiking trail;
picnicking; camping. Camping reservations
necessary. Daily.

Municipal Pier and Beach
100 Avenida Presidio,
San Clemente, 949-361-8200
Swimming, surfing; picnicking; playground; fishing, bait and tackle shop at the
end of the pier. Daily.

SPECIAL EVENTS

San Clemente Fiesta Street Festival
Ave. Del Mar, San Clemente,
949-492-1131
This giant block party provides fun for the
entire family: food, games, a classic car
and motorcycle show. Second Sunday in
August.

HOTEL

★★Holiday Inn San Clemente
111 S. Avenida De La Estrella,
San Clemente, 949-361-3000,
800-469-1161; www.ichotelsgroup.com
72 rooms. Restaurant. Pets accepted. Pool.
$$

110

SAN DIEGO

Can't decide between the city and the beach? You don't have to. In San Diego, there is plenty of culture, great shopping and wonderful restaurants—plus beaches with great surfing, snorkeling and sea lions that crawl to the shore to sun themselves. Weathermen here have it easy: every day is 70 degrees and sunny.

It wasn't too long ago that San Diego was a sleepy little town, a place where movie stars came to get away from it all. In the past 10 to 15 years, however, the city has grown by leaps and bounds. It now has a population of 1.3 million (2.8 million county-wide) and is the seventh-largest city in the United States. Much of the growth has come from people who want to shop in shorts all year. Other growth has come from companies that have relocated here because of the ease of recruiting workers. The area is also filled with Navy and Marine personnel from bases nearby.

San Diego is where California began. In 1542, explorer Juan Rodriguez Cabrillo was commissioned by the governor of Guatemala to take a voyage up the California coast under the flag of Spain. He reached "a very good enclosed port," now known as San Diego Bay (a Cabrillos statue stands at the edge of Cabrillo Park on the spot where he is believed to have anchored). In the mid-18th century, when it was feared that Russian interest in Alaska was a prelude to Southern expansion, Spanish missionaries came to California, and Father Junipera Serra built the first of his 31 famous California missions in San Diego.

San Diego is a city in which the arts flourish. Balboa Park, the largest urban cultural park in the country, features 15 museums, numerous art galleries, free outdoor concerts, the Tony Award-winning Globe Theatres and the world-famous San Diego Zoo. (The upscale community of La Jolla, a few miles up the coast, is the site of the La Jolla Playhouse, another Tony Award-winning theater.) There are quirky museums, like the Museum of Making Music. And kids won't know what to do first: swim in the ocean, visit SeaWorld, pan for gold in an old hard-rock gold mine, go to Legoland, explore the tidepools or visit the Aerospace Museum and Hall of Fame, where they can go on a motion simulator ride that takes them on different planes throughout time.

Information: Convention & Visitors Bureau, 401 B St., 619-236-1212; www.sandiego.org

WHAT TO SEE AND DO

Aerospace Museum and Hall of Fame
2001 Pan American Plaza,
San Diego, 619-234-8291;
www.aerospacemuseum.org
Learn about the extraordinary accomplishments of the world's leading aviation pioneers, including the Wright Brothers, Amelia Earhart, Neil Armstrong, Yuri Gagarin and Benjamin O. Davis, Jr., a Tuskegee airman and the first African-American graduate of West Point. Don't miss Wings, a motion simulator ride that takes you on different planes through time. Memorial Day-Labor Day: 10 a.m.-5:30 p.m.; rest of year: to 4:30 p.m.

SOUTHERN CALIFORNIA

Balboa Park

1549 El Prado, San Diego,
619-239-0512;
www.balboapark.org
Located in the heart of the city, this 1,200-acre park includes galleries, museums, theaters, restaurants, recreational facilities and miles of garden walks.

Balboa Park Golf Course

2600 Golf Course Dr., San Diego,
619-239-1660;
www.sannet.gov/park-and-recreation/golf/bpgolf.shtml
Municipal courses, 18 and 9 holes; pro shop; driving range, three putting greens; restaurant. Daily.

Barona Casino

1932 Wildcat Canyon Rd., Lakeside,
619-443-2300, 888-722-7662;
www.barona.com
Located amid rolling hills 25 miles north of San Diego and designed by the creative forces behind Las Vegas' Mirage Hotel and Casino, the Barona Casino is one of the most popular gaming destinations in California. It has 310,000 square feet of casino, including slots, tables and a poker room, plus an off-track betting facility and a bingo hall. The service here is legendary. The management promises, for example, to solve any slots problem within two minutes. Dining options range from a food court to a dinner-only steakhouse with buffalo on the menu. No liquor is allowed in the casino. Daily.

Belmont Park

3146 Mission Blvd., San Diego,
858-488-1549; www.belmontpark.com
Seaside amusement park with a vintage wooden roller coaster and other rides, as well as the largest indoor swimming pool in Southern California. Hours vary by season.

Cabrillo National Monument

1800 Cabrillo Memorial Dr.,
San Diego, 619-557-5450;
www.nps.gov/cabr
In late autumn of 1542, explorer Juan Rodriguez Cabrillo and his crew arrived at what he called a very good enclosed port, the San Diego Harbor. Today, his statue looks out over one of the most beautiful views in all of San Diego. The grounds of this national park include a historic lighthouse From late December through mid-March, natives come to this site to watch the annual migration of Pacific gray whales. Don't miss the coastal tide pools, particularly exciting during winter's low tides, when the sea pushes back to reveal a unique world of marine plants and animals in little pockets of the earth. Daily.

Café Sevilla

555 Fourth Ave., San Diego,
619-233-5979;
www.cafesevilla.com/sandiego
Have some paella as you watch a flamenco dinner show or a shrimp empanada as you enjoy a tango show. Enjoy free salsa and samba lessons on certain nights and listen to rock music by Latin bands. The tapas bar, which features live flamenco music every night, has been known to attract celebrities such as the Gypsy Kings. Daily 5 p.m.-1 a.m.

Casa de Estudillo

4002 Wallace St., San Diego,
619-220-5422
(1820-1829) Restored example of a one-story adobe townhouse with period furnishings. Daily 10 a.m.-5 p.m.

Coronado Island

619-435-5993;
www.coronadovisitorcenter.com
Coronado is a place for walkers. Once across the bridge, park your car and walk past homes with gardens of flowers native only to this part of the country, and through the quaint stores of Orange Street, which includes San Diego's largest independent bookstore (Bay Books). Hop the ferry to Ferry Landing Marketplace, a center of fine dining, specialty shops, art galleries and bike rentals. There's also a waterfront park, fishing pier, beach, bike path, family amusement center and Farmers' Market every Tuesday from 2:30 to 6 p.m.

★
★
★
★
★

Fashion Valley Mall

7007 Friars Rd., San Diego, 619-688-9113
This is a multilevel outdoor shopping center with stores including Neiman Marcus and Saks Fifth Avenue, as well as unique, one-of-a-kind boutiques. Monday-Saturday 10 a.m.-9 p.m., Sunday 11 a.m.-7 p.m.

Gaslamp Quarter

Downtown, 619-233-5227;
www.gaslamp.org
A 16 1/2-block national historic district bordered by Broadway on the north, Sixth Avenue on the east, Harbor Drive on the south, and Fourth Avenue on the west. This area formed the city's business center at the turn of the century, and many Victorian buildings are under restoration.

Horton Plaza

324 Horton Plaza, San Diego,
619-239-8180; www.westfield.com
Horton Plaza has reinvigorated downtown San Diego, and it's not difficult to see why. Sixteen years of research went into the design of this whimsical, multilevel shopping mall with more than 140 specialty shops, department stores and restaurants. The black concrete and narrow walkways were patterned after those found in European marketplaces, and many merchants display their goods on carts. Monday-Friday 10 a.m.-9 p.m., Saturday to 8 p.m., Sunday 11 a.m.-7 p.m.

Humphrey's Concerts by the Bay

2241 Shelter Island Dr., San Diego,
619-220-8497;
www.humphreysconcerts.com
The 1,295-seat venue, with palm tress on one side and the harbor on the other, has staged acts such as Smokey Robinson and Jay Leno.

Ken Cinema

4061 Adams Ave., San Diego,
619-819-0236;
www.landmarktheatres.com
This San Diego landmark has long been the local place for art films, foreign cinema and revivals.

Kobey's Swap Meet

3500 Sports Arena Blvd.,
San Diego, 619-226-0650;
www.kobeyswap.com
This is San Diego's largest and most popular open-air market, featuring furniture, fashion, electronics and fresh produce. The faithful come frequently and are usually in place when the doors open at 7 a.m. The back section, with its secondhand goods, is a bargain hunter's delight. Vendors sell food and beverages, and live entertainment gets shoppers ready to spend. Friday-Sunday 7 a.m.-3 p.m.

Mingei International Museum of World Folk Art

1439 El Prado, San Diego,
619-239-0003
Six galleries contain art exhibits of people from cultures around world. Many art forms, such as costumes, jewelry, dolls, utensils, painting and sculpture are shown in different collections and changing exhibitions. Also a theater, library, research center and educational facilities. Tuesday-Sunday 10 a.m.-4 p.m.

Mission Bay Park

2688 E. Mission Bay Dr.,
San Diego, 619-276-8200
This aquatic park on 4,600 acres provides swimming, water-skiing, fishing, boating, sailing (rentals, ramps, landings, marinas), golf, camping and more. Daily.

Mission San Diego de Alcala

10818 San Diego Mission Rd.,
San Diego, 619-281-8449;
www.missionsandiego.com
San Diego de Alcala marks the birthplace of Christianity in the Far West. It was California's first church and the first of the 21 great California missions. This remarkable shrine, still an active Catholic parish, provides an interesting look into San Diego's Spanish heritage, as well as an understanding of the beginning of Catholicism in this corner of the world. The San Diego Trolley makes a stop just half a block from the mission, which is a National Historic

113

SOUTHERN CALIFORNIA

★
★
★
★

Landmark. Gift shop, visitor center. (Daily 9 a.m.-4:45 p.m.)

Mount Woodson Rock Climbing

Poway. Mount Woodson lies along Hwy. 67 between Poway and Ramona. Park about 3 miles N. of the Hwy. 67/Poway Rd. junction in the vicinity of the state forestry fire station. A short dirt trail passes through the trees until it hits a paved road, which winds all the way to the top of Mount Woodson, 760-789-1311.

Mount Woodson may be the best place for rock climbing in Southern California. There are super-thin cracks, super-wide ones, mantles, edging, low-angle climbs and friction climbing. You can bring your own equipment and practice leading cracks or climb walls with problems ranging in difficulty levels. For simpler climbs, bring a chalk bag and you're off. To explore, make sure that you're with someone who knows these routes. Many are not in any guide.

Museum of Contemporary Art San Diego

1001 Kettner Blvd., San Diego, 92101, 619-234-1001; www.mcasd.org

Permanent and changing exhibits of contemporary painting, sculpture, design, photography and architecture. Bookstore. (Monday-Tuesday, Thursday-Sunday 11 a.m.-5 p.m.)

Museum of Man

1350 El Prado, San Diego, 619-239-2001

Permanent exhibits explore the Maya, ancient Egypt, human evolution and more. One of the newest exhibits is "Footsteps Through Time," which takes visitors through four million years of human evolution. Don't miss the Children's Discovery Center, where kids can experience aspects of royal and ordinary Egyptian life in the 18th Dynasty by bartering in an Egyptian market, navigating a small boat on the Nile and dressing in costume. Daily 10 a.m.-4:30 p.m.

Museum of Photographic Arts

1649 El Prado, San Diego, 619-238-7559; www.mopa.org

Changing exhibitions featuring works by world-renowned photographers from the early 19th century to today. Monday-Wednesday, Friday-Sunday 10 a.m.-5 p.m., Thursday to 9 p.m. Free guided tours Sunday.

Ocean Beach Farmers' Market

Newport Ave., San Diego, 619-224-4906; www.oceanbeachsandiego.com

Ride a llama around this farmer's market in Ocean Beach, or shop for fresh produce and flowers, and sample delicious treats well into the early evening. Winter: Wednesday 4-7 p.m., summer: Wednesday 4-8 p.m.

Old Globe Theatre

1363 Old Globe Way, San Diego, 619-239-2255; www.theoldglobe.org

This 581-seat venue, a replica of Shakespeare's theater in London, is frequently used for pre-Broadway tryouts. Many new works are also produced here. The Old Globe is one of three associated theaters on a grassy complex in Balboa Park, the other two being the Cassius Carter Center, an intimate, 225-seat theater, and the 612-seat Lowell Davies Festival Theater, used in the summer primarily for Shakespeare. Tours Saturday-Sunday 10:30 a.m.

Old Town

Mason St. and San Diego Ave., San Diego

Historic section of city with many restored or reconstructed buildings including old adobe structures. Restaurants, shops. Guided walking tours.

Old Town San Diego State Historic Park

San Diego Ave. at Twiggs St., San Diego, 619-220-5422; www.parks.ca.gov

An area within Old Town that is bounded by Congress, Wallace, Twigg and Juan streets. Daily 10 a.m.-5 p.m.

SOUTHERN CALIFORNIA

Presidio Park
2811 Jackson St., San Diego,
Inside is site of the first mission in California. Mounds mark the original presidio and fort. Daily 6 a.m.-10 p.m.

Reuben H. Fleet Science Center
1875 El Prado, San Diego, 619-238-1233; www.rhfleet.org
This science museum offers the latest in interactive and virtual reality exhibits. Check out planetarium shows and a collection of astronomical photography. The Explorazone 3 area offers a hands-on experience with such concepts as wind, illusion and turbulence. Monday-Thursday 9:30 a.m.-5 p.m., Friday to 9 p.m., Saturday to 8 p.m., Sunday to 6 p.m.

San Diego Hall of Champions Sports Museum
2131 Pan American Plaza, San Diego, 619-234-2544; www.sdhoc.com
Exhibits on more than 40 sports in the area. Daily 10 a.m.-4:30 p.m.

San Diego Bay and the Embarcadero
1300 N. Harbor Dr., San Diego
Port for active Navy ships, cruise ships, commercial shipping and tuna fleet. Sailing, powerboating, water-skiing and sportfishing at Shelter Island, Harbor Island, the Yacht Harbor and America's Cup Harbor.

San Diego Chargers (NFL)
Qualcomm Stadium, 9449 Friars Rd., San Diego,
858-874-4500, 877-242-7437; www.chargers.com
Professional football team.

San Diego-Coronado Ferry
1050 N. Harbor Dr., San Diego,
619-234-4111; www.sdhe.com
Hourly departures from San Diego Harbour Excursion dock to Ferry Landing Marketplace in Coronado. Daily.

San Diego Early Music Society
3510 Dove Court, San Diego,
619-291-8246; www.sdems.org

The San Diego Early Music Society, a group dedicated to preserving European medieval, Renaissance and baroque music, brings musicians from all over the world to play six times a year at the lovely St. James-by-the-Sea Church. Performers frequently play on authentic instruments such as a harpsichord or a baroque guitar. The group also holds concerts featuring local musicians six Sundays each year at the San Diego Museum of Art in Balboa Park.

San Diego Harbor Excursion
1050 N. Harbor Dr., San Diego,
619-234-4111, 800-442-7847; www.sdhe.com
One-hour (12-mile) narrated tour highlights Harbor Island, Coronado and the Navy terminals at North Island and 32nd Street. Two-hour (25-mile) narrated tour also includes Shelter Island, Ballast Point (where Cabrillo is believed to have first landed in 1542), the harbor entrance, the ship yards and the Navy's submarine base. Daily.

San Diego Junior Theatre at the Casa Del Prado Theater
1650 El Prado, San Diego, 619-239-1311; www.juniortheatre.com
Few children's theater groups have entertained one million people or boast alums like Raquel Welch. This San Diego institution, founded in 1947, has put on Broadway standards like *Guys and Dolls* and *Oliver!* The company has also adapted kids' literature like *Nancy Drew* and *James and the Giant Peach*. Children not only perform but also work on costumes and lighting, serve as the stage crew and even staff the ticket windows. Friday 7 p.m., Saturday-Sunday 2 p.m.

San Diego Maritime Museum and *Star of India*
1492 N. Harbor Dr., San Diego,
619-234-9153; www.sdmaritime.com
The Maritime Museum of San Diego has one of the world's finest collections of historic ships, including the world's oldest active ship, *Star of India*, which hosts movies in the summer on the ship's deck.

The maritime museum uses a state-of-the art digital projector to display the films on a special sail rigged to the main mast. Friday nights are date nights, while Saturdays are family nights with popular children's movies. Daily 9 a.m.-8 p.m.; movies start after sundown.

San Diego Museum of Art
1450 El Prado, San Diego, 619-232-7931; www.sdmart.org
See collections of art from all over the world. Includes European and American paintings and decorative arts; Japanese, Chinese and other Asian art; and contemporary sculpture. Tuesday-Wednesday, Friday-Sunday 10 a.m.-6 p.m., Thursday to 9 p.m. Free admission the third Tuesday of each month.

San Diego Natural History Museum
1788 El Prado, San Diego, 619-232-3821; www.sdnhm.org
Exhibits of flora, fauna and mineralogy of the southwestern United States and Baja California. Daily 10 a.m.-5 p.m.

San Diego Opera
202 B St., San Diego, 619-533-7000; www.sdopera.com
The San Diego Opera Company was born in 1965 and has grown to become one of the most respected opera companies in America. Between January and May, the company presents five productions and several concerts. Brief English translations of the operas lyrics are projected onto the stage.

San Diego Padres (MLB)
Qualcomm Stadium, 9449 Friars Rd., San Diego, 619-881-6500, 877-374-2784; www.padres.com
Professional baseball team.

San Diego Scenic Tours
San Diego,
858-273-8687;
www.sandiegoscenictours.com
Narrated bus and harbor tours, including tours of Tijuana, Mexico. Daily.

San Diego Trolley
707 F St., San Diego,
www.sdcommute.com
The 47-mile light rail system goes east to Santee and north through Old Town from downtown, serving many major shopping centers in Mission Valley and Qualcomm Stadium for easy access to San Diego Padres and Chargers games. Daily.

San Diego Zoo
2920 Zoo Dr., San Diego, 619-234-3153; www.sandiegozoo.org
Widely considered the nation's top zoo, this space houses more than 4,200 rare and exotic animals representing 800 species, many of which are displayed in natural habitats. The children's zoo features a petting paddock and animal nursery. Walk-through aviaries. Animal shows daily; 40-minute guided tour aboard double-deck bus; aerial tramway. Daily 9 a.m.-4 p.m.; to 9 p.m. in summer; to 5 p.m. for two weeks in April.

Seaport Village
849 W. Harbor Dr.,
San Diego, 619-235-4014;
www.spvillage.com
Designed to look like a 100-year-old fishing village, this area provides a place to sit at the water's edge and sip a glass of wine or wander through the 75 specialty stores. Also includes four restaurants. Don't miss the Broadway Flying Horses Carousel, originally built at Coney Island in 1890. Daily 10 a.m.-10 p.m.

SeaWorld San Diego
500 SeaWorld Dr., San Diego,
800-257-4268; www.seaworld.com
Check out the more than 400 penguins or sit and watch in amazement as orca whales Shamu, Baby Shamu and Namu entertain. Open since 1964, SeaWorld has continued to add attractions and animals and has even ventured beyond the sea: its newest section Pets Rule! is devoted to dogs and cats. The park has four different shows, four rides and more than 20 exhibits and attractions. In summer, don't miss Cirque de la Mer, an

★
★
★
★
★

over-water acrobatic performance. Daily; hours vary by season.

Serra Museum
2727 Presidio Dr., San Diego,
619-297-3258
This museum, which interprets the Spanish and Mexican periods of the city's history, stands on top of the hill recognized as the site where California's first mission and presidio were established in 1769. Daily 10 a.m.-4:30 p.m.

Spanish Village Center
1770 Village Place, San Diego,
619-233-9050; www.spanishvillageart.com
Observe artists and craftspeople working. Daily 11 a.m.-4 p.m.

Spreckels Organ Concerts
Spreckels Organ Pavilion,
Pan American Way, San Diego,
619-702-8138
The magnificent Spreckels organ, nestled in an ornate pavilion in the heart of Balboa Park, is a sight to see and hear with its 4,446 individual pipes ranging from less than 1/2 inch to more than 32 feet in length. The organ has been in almost continuous use since brothers John and Adolph Spreckels gave it to the city in 1914. Free hour-long concerts are held on Sundays at 2 p.m., with seating for 2,400. In summer, a 12-week Organ Festival takes place on Monday evenings. Sunday 2 p.m.

Starlight Bowl/Starlight Theatre
2005 Pan American Dr., San Diego,
619-544-7827; www.starlighttheatre.org
Since the first strands of *The Naughty Marietta* played in 1946, the San Diego Civic Light Opera Association has staged 120 musicals in this open-air theatre. The company employs union actors, musicians and stagehands, but also hires local actors and technicians who are able to get a start in Starlight's apprentice and internship programs. The season runs from mid-June through September. If you attend a performance, be sure to look for the legendary red box: on opening night in 1946, a the costume designer took her red sewing box, tied it with a gold tassel, and gave it to the stage manager as something regal for the bride to carry when she ran off to get married in a performance of *The Mikado*. The show was so successful the red box has been on stage ever since. Thursday-Sunday 8 p.m.; box office: Monday-Wednesday 10 a.m.-4 p.m., Thursday-Friday 10 a.m.-9:30 p.m., Saturday-Sunday noon-9:30 p.m.

Tavern Brick by Brick
1130 Buenos Ave., San Diego,
619-275-5483; www.brickbybrick.com
This neighborhood music club features everything from techno, rock, and pop to heavy metal (buy tickets in advance). There's also a relaxing lounge in the back with round, white cocktail tables and matching swivel stools and a small bar. Daily 8 p.m.-2 a.m.

Timken Museum of Art
1500 El Prado, San Diego, 619-239-5548;
www.timkenmuseum.org
Collection of European Old Masters, 18th- and 19th-century American paintings, and Russian icons. Tuesday-Saturday 10 a.m.-4:30 p.m., Sunday from 1:30 p.m.; closed September.

Veterans Memorial Center Museum
2115 Park Blvd., San Diego, 619-239-2300;
www.veteranmuseum.org
The memorial/museum is housed in a building that was once the chapel of the U.S. Naval Hospital. It almost became a parking lot extension for the San Diego Zoo, but is now on the National Register of Historic Places. See historical objects, artifacts, documents and memorabilia dating to the Civil War. Tuesday-Saturday 9:30 a.m.-3 p.m.

Villa Montezuma/Jesse Shepard House
1925 K St., San Diego,
619-239-2211
Lavish Victorian mansion built for Jesse Shepard, musician and author, during the city's Great Boom (1886-1888). More than 20 stained-glass windows reflect Shepard's interest in art, music and literature. Includes

SOUTHERN CALIFORNIA

a restored kitchen and antiques. Friday-Sunday 10 a.m.-4:30 p.m.

Whale-Watching Trips
San Diego
For three months each year (mid-December-mid-February), California gray whales make their way from Alaska's Bering Sea to the warm bays and lagoons of Baja, passing only a mile or so off the San Diego shoreline. As many as 200 whales a day have been counted during the peak of the migration period. Trips to local waters and Baja lagoons are scheduled by the San Diego Natural History Museum. For information on other whale-watching trips, inquire at local sportfishing companies (try: San Diego Harbor Excursion, 619-234-4111, www.sdhe.com), or at the International Visitors Information Center.

The Whaley House
2476 San Diego Ave., San Diego,
619-297-7511; www.whaleyhouse.org
In the mid-19th century, New Yorker Thomas Whaley came to San Diego via San Francisco, where gold beckoned. This home, which was built for him in 1856, was the first brick building in San Diego County. The bricks were made in his own kiln, while the walls were finished with plaster made from ground seashells. The inside of the house has an illustrious heritage as well. Not only have five generations of the Whaley family lived here, but apparently so have a few spirits. This is one of two authenticated haunted houses in California. Thursday-Tuesday 10 a.m.-4 p.m.

Wild Animal Park
15500 San Pasqual Valley,
Escondido, 760-747-8702;
www.sandiegozoo.org/wap
More than 3,500 exotic animals wander in herds and packs through this 1,800-acre wild animal preserve, which was opened to the public in 1972 and still operates as a preservation area for endangered species. Go on the Kilimanjaro Safari Walk or journey through the Heart of Africa. Several different tours are conducted daily, such as the highly popular Photo Caravan Tours, which travel right into the field exhibits where visitors can feed the animals. Special events are also held all summer, including sleepovers. Winter and spring: daily 9 a.m.-4 p.m., to 8 p.m. in early and late December; summer: daily 9 a.m.-8 p.m.

William Heath Davis Home
410 Island Ave., San Diego, 619-233-4692; www.gaslampquarter.org
The William Heath Davis House, the oldest structure in the Gaslamp Quarter, was shipped from Portland, Maine in 1850. The structure of the house has remained unchanged for 120 years and is an excellent example of a prefabricated saltbox family home—a small, square structure with two stories in front and one in back. A museum occupies the first and second floors. The house is also home to the Gaslamp Quarter Historical Foundation, which gives daily walking tours of the historic area. Call ahead for tour times. Tuesday-Sunday 10 a.m.-6 p.m.

SPECIAL EVENTS
Artwalk
734 W. Beech St., San Diego,
619-615-1090; www.artwalkinfo.com
Those in town in April should check out this lively, self-guided multimedia tour that travels into artists studios, through galleries and past exhibits of stained glass, sculpture, photography, electronic imaging and works of architecture and design. One popular exhibit has student artists use refrigerators as canvases for their projects, after which the refrigerators are sold to benefit local school art programs. Enjoy musical performances, short plays, dances and poetry readings. Last weekend in April.

Balboa Park December Nights-The Annual Celebration of Christmas on the Prado
Balboa Park, 1549 El Prado, San Diego, 619-239-0512;
www.balboapark.org/decembernights
On the first Friday or Saturday of December, Balboa Park is transformed into a winter

wonderland with walkways and buildings adorned with beautiful lights and decorations, including a 50-foot-tall tree and nativity scenes. All the museums are open until 9 p.m. and are free. Entertainment includes an eclectic mix of bell choirs, Renaissance and baroque music, African drums and barbershop quartets. Early December.

Cabrillo Festival
Cabrillo National Monument, 1800 Cabrillo Memorial Dr., San Diego, 619-557-5450
Celebration of discovery of the West Coast. Early October.

Corpus Christi Fiesta
Mission San Antonio de Pala, San Diego
Held annually since 1816, this festival includes an open-air mass and procession, games, dances and entertainment, plus a Spanish-style pit barbecue. First Sunday in June.

Ethnic Food Fair
10410 Corporal Way, San Diego, 619-234-0739
In the mood to sample something different? Perhaps Hungarian or Austrian or Lithuanian cuisine? Head for the International Cottages at Balboa Park's House of Pacific Relations during Memorial Day weekend. Each of these 32 tiny cottages representing a different nation is decorated and laid out with the traditional foods of that country. Each cottage is staffed with at least two people, one inside to explain customs and the other outside to talk about food and hand out recipes. Memorial Day weekend.

Festival of Bells
Mission Basilica San Diego de Alcala, 10818 San Diego Mission Rd., San Diego, 619-283-7319
Commemorates the July 16, 1769, founding of the mission. Weekend in mid-July.

San Diego Bay Parade of Lights
San Diego, www.sdparadeoflights.org
For two Sunday evenings each December, the San Diego Bay is flooded with color when at least 100 boats adorned with lights and other decorations follow one another on a semicircular path through the calm waters of the bay. Early December.

HOTELS

★★Balboa Park Inn
3402 Park Blvd., San Diego, 619-298-0823, 800-938-8181; www.balboaparkinn.com
Located in a quiet neighborhood bordering Balboa Park, this inn features themed rooms ranging from the escapist (Paris in the 1930s) to the erudite (Monet's) to the exceedingly romantic (Harlequin). Amenities include free coffee, tea and hot chocolate.
26 rooms. Complimentary continental breakfast. $

★Best Western Americana Inn
815 W. San Ysidro, San Diego, 619-428-5521, 800-553-3933; www.bestwestern.com
120 rooms. Pool. $

★★Best Western Cabrillo Garden Inn
840 A St., San Diego, 619-234-8477, 866-363-8388; www.bestwestern.com
30 rooms. Complimentary full breakfast. High-speed Internet access. Restaurant, bar. $$

★★Best Western Hacienda Suites-Old Town
4041 Harney St., San Diego, 619-298-4707, 800-888-1991; www.haciendahotel-oldtown.com
199 rooms, all suites. High-speed wireless Internet access. Restaurant, bar. Pool. $$

★Best Western Lamplighter Inn and Suites
6474 El Cajon Blvd., San Diego, 619-582-3088; www.bestwestern.com
61 rooms. Pets accepted. Complimentary breakfast. High speed Internet. Outdoor pool. $

★★★Bristol Hotel
1055 First Ave., San Diego, 619-232-6141, 800-662-4477; www.thebristolsandiego.com

119

★

★

★

★

This downtown boutique hotel lures young professionals and couples who are drawn to the funky, contemporary vibe. A pop art collection includes works by Andy Warhol, Roy Lichtenstein and Keith Haring. Rooms are decorated with bold colors and include free Internet access, salon-style hair dryers, honor bars and CD players. The top-floor ballroom features a retractable roof, and the bistro is a favorite among locals who come here for the signature martini, the Craizi Daizi.

102 rooms. High-speed Internet access. Restaurant, bar. Fitness room. Pets accepted. **$$**

★★Catamaran Resort Hotel
3999 Mission Blvd., San Diego, 858-488-1081, 800-422-8380; www.catamaranresort.com
315 rooms. High-speed Internet access. Restaurant, bar. Spa. Beach. **$$**

★★Courtyard San Diego Downtown
530 Broadway, San Diego, 619-446-3000, 800-321-2211; www.courtyard.com/sancd
246 rooms. High-speed Internet access. Restaurant, bar. Fitness room. **$$**

★★Dana Inn and Marina
1710 W. Mission Bay Dr., San Diego, 619-222-6440, 800-345-9995; www.thedana.com
271 rooms. High-speed wireless Internet access. Two restaurants, bar. Airport transportation available. Pool. **$$**

★★Doubletree Club Hotel
1515 Hotel Circle S., San Diego, 619-881-6900, 800-222-8733; www.doubletreeclubsd.com
217 rooms. High-speed Internet access. Restaurant, bar. Pets accepted. **$**

★★DoubleTree Golf Resort
14455 Penasquitos Dr., San Diego, 858-672-9100; www.sandiegogolfresort.doubletree.com
174 rooms. Restaurant, bar. Airport transportation available. Golf. Tennis. **$$**

★★★Doubletree Hotel Mission Valley
7450 Hazard Center Dr., San Diego, 619-297-5466, 800-222-8733; www.doubletree.com
This comfortable hotel is close to many major attractions including SeaWorld and the San Diego Zoo, and offers an indoor and outdoor pool as well as tennis and exercise facilities. The oversized guest rooms feature Sweet Dreams beds.

300 rooms. High-speed wireless Internet access. Restaurant, bar. Airport transportation available. Pets accepted. **$$**

★★Embassy Suites
601 Pacific Hwy., San Diego, 619-239-2400, 800-362-2779; www.embassysuites.com
337 rooms, all suites. Complimentary full breakfast. High-speed Internet access. Restaurant, bar. Airport transportation available. **$$**

★Hampton Inn Downtown
1531 Pacific Hwy., San Diego, 619-233-8408; www.hamptoninn.com
177 rooms. Outdoor pool. Business center. **$**

★★Heritage Park Inn
2470 Heritage Park Row, San Diego, 619-299-6832, 800-995-2470; www.heritageparkinn.com
This Queen Anne-style mansion features a wrap-around veranda, afternoon tea and an ongoing jigsaw puzzle in the parlor.

12 rooms. No children allowed. Complimentary full breakfast. **$$**

★★★Hilton Airport/Harbor Island
1960 Harbor Island Dr., San Diego, 619-291-6700, 800-774-1500; www.sandiegoairport.hilton.com
With its waterfront setting on Harbor Island, the rooms here feature views of Big Bay, Harbor Island marina and Point Loma. Sailboat and bicycle rentals are available nearby, as are golf courses and the beach.

SOUTHERN CALIFORNIA

★

★

★

★

★

There's a fully-equipped fitness center with sauna and outdoor headed pool.

211 rooms. High-speed Internet access. Restaurant, bar. Airport transportation available. **$$**

★★★Hilton San Diego Gaslamp Quarter
401 K St., San Diego,
619-231-4040, 800-774-1500;
www.hilton.com

This modern hotel is located in the heart of the historic Gaslamp Quarter—where you'll find nearly shopping, restaurants and nightclubs—and across the street from the San Diego Convention center. Opting to stay at the hotel's Lofts on 5th Avenue provides a residential space with 14-foot ceilings, Frette linens and robes, whirlpool tub and private entrance. Amenities include a spa and fitness room, outdoor heated pool and hot tub, and adjacent walking trails that border Big Bay. The outdoor fire pit is a nice spot for cocktails and appetizers or dessert.

282 rooms. High-speed Internet access. Restaurant, bar. **$$$**

★★★Hilton San Diego Mission Valley
901 Camino del Rio S., San Diego,
619-543-9000;
www.sandiegomissionvalley.hilton.com

This family-friendly hotel is set on the hillside of Mission Valley's business district, surrounded by trees and gardens. Popular Southern California tourist destinations are nearby, including SeaWorld, the historic Gaslamp Quarter and Balboa Park. Relax in spacious, modern rooms that feature Serta luxury mattresses and Crabtree & Evelyn bath products.

351 rooms. High-speed Internet access. Restaurant, bar. **$$**

★★★Hilton San Diego Resort
1775 E. Mission Bay Dr., San Diego,
619-276-4010, 800-345-6565;
www.sandiegohilton.com

The family-friendly Hilton San Diego Resort is located on Mission Bay, just steps from the beach and only one mile from SeaWorld. The hotel was recently remodeled,

and the result is an airy, beachy feel. There is also a new spa and state-of-the-art fitness center. Enjoy concerts while relaxing on the lawns of the garden by the bay in summer.

357 rooms. High-speed Internet access. Restaurant, bar. Spa. Beach. **$$$**

★Holiday Inn
1617 First Ave., San Diego,
619-239-9600, 800-366-3164;
www.holiday-inn.com

220 rooms. High-speed Internet access. Restaurant, bar. **$$**

★★Holiday Inn Select-Hotel Circle
595 Hotel Circle S., San Diego,
619-291-5720, 800-972-2802;
www.holidayinnselect.com

318 rooms. High-speed Internet access. Restaurant, bar. Pool. **$**

★★Horton Grand Hotel
311 Island Ave., San Diego,
619-544-1886, 800-542-1886;
www.hortongrand.com

132 rooms. Wireless Internet access. Restaurant, bar. Pets accepted. **$$**

★★Humphrey's Half Moon Inn & Suites
2303 Shelter Island Dr., San Diego,
619-224-3411, 800-345-9995;
www.halfmooninn.com

182 rooms. High-speed Internet access. Restaurant, bar. Airport transportation available. Pool. **$$**

★★★Hyatt Regency Mission Bay Spa and Marina
1441 Quivira Rd.,
San Diego,
619-224-1234;
www.missionbay.hyatt.com

This towering fixture in the heart of Mission Bay Park is the closest hotel to SeaWorld and offers panoramic views of the marina. A recent renovation resulted in a spa, water playground with multiple slides and new restaurants. Downtown San Diego and the airport are six miles away.

421 rooms. Restaurant, bar. Fitness room. Pool. Business center. **$$**

SOUTHERN CALIFORNIA

★★★The Ivy Hotel
600 F St., San Diego,
619-814-1000;
www.ivyhotel.com

A boutique hotel located in San Diego's Gaslamp Quarter, the Ivy has rooms decorated with contemporary furniture and outfitted with plasma TVs, luxury linens and iPod docking stations. The Quarter Kitchen serves dressed-up comfort food like caviar tacos and mini kobe hot dogs, while the rootop Eden bar and pool is a prime spot for after-dinner drinks. For those who want to zoom around town in style, the hotel offers chauffered Escalade service.

Pets accepted. Wireless Internet. Fitness center. Restaurant. $$$

★★★The Keating
432 F St., San Digeo,
619-814-5700;
www.thekeating.com

Housed in a historic building in San Diego's Gaslamp Quarter, the interior of this boutique hotel is completely of-the-moment. Italian design firm Pinanfarina, the force behind Ferrari and Maserati, dreamed up the look of this property from the stylish lobby to the luxe guest rooms. Plasma TVs, cutting-edge sound systems, Frette linens and espresso machines are some of the in-room amenties. The lounge, with its Saarinen-inspired chairs and cozy couches, is a good spot for cocktails, which are poured by personal hosts (a shade more attentive than your standard waiter).

35 rooms. Wireless Internet access. Pets accepted. Restaurant, bar. $$$

★★★Kona Kai Hotel & Spa
1551 Shelter Island Dr., San Diego,
619-221-8000, 800-566-2524;
www.shelterpointe.com

Just five minutes from SeaWorld and downtown, this hotel on the tip of Shelter Island strikes a balance between offering convenience and being a quiet retreat for travelers of all types. Rooms feature elegant, contemporary décor with amenities including dataports and coffeemakers as well as patios or balconies with bay or coastal views.

206 rooms. Pets accepted. High-speed Internet access. Restaurant, bar. Fitness room, spa. Outdoor pool. $$

★★★Manchester Grand Hyatt San Diego
1 Market Place, San Diego,
619-232-1234, 800-223-1234;
www.manchestergrandhyatt.com

Combining a resort-like atmosphere with the convenience of a downtown location, this luxury property on San Diego Bay is adjacent to the convention center and Seaport Village. The full-service Regency Spa and Salon staffs skilled therapists, estheticians and stylists.

1,625 rooms. High-speed Internet access. Six restaurants, two bars. $$$

★★★Marriott San Diego Hotel & Marina
333 W. Harbor Dr., San Diego,
619-234-1500, 800-228-9290;
www.marriott.com

Adjacent to the convention center and the Seaport Village, this waterfront hotel is conveniently situated. Rooms offer bay and marina views along with amenities complimentary coffee, work desks, refrigerators and full kitchens.

1,358 rooms. High-speed Internet access. Four restaurants, bar. Pets accepted. $$$

★★★Marriott San Diego Mission Valley
8757 Rio San Diego Dr., San Diego,
619-692-3800, 800-842-5329;
www.sandiegomarriottmissionvalley.com

This resort-style hotel with Spanish accents is about seven miles northwest of downtown and less than two miles from Qualcomm Stadium. It features a host of amenities for both business travelers and vacationers. Many of the modern and whimsical guest rooms overlook the hotel's beautiful courtyard pool and tropical landscaping, and include conveniences like high-speed Internet. Concierge, secretarial and child-care services are available. The downtown trolley stop is just steps way. This hotel is non-smoking.

352 rooms. High-speed Internet access. Restaurant, bar. Fitness center. Pool. $$

★
★
★
★
★

★Old Town Inn
4444 Pacific Hwy., San Diego,
800-643-3025; www.lamplighter-inn.com/
oldtown.htm
Complimentary breakfast. Pool. **$**

★Quality Suites San Diego
9880 Mira Mesa Blvd., San Diego,
858-530-2000, 800-822-6692;
www.qualitysuitessandiego.com
132 rooms, all suites. Complimentary continental breakfast. Pool. **$**

★★★Pacific Terrace Hotel
610 Diamond St., San Diego,
858-581-3500, 800-344-3370;
www.pacificterrace.com
This seaside hotel in northern San Diego is the perfect place to revel in the Southern California beach atmosphere. Old Spanish style characterizes the exterior and the common areas. The upscale guest rooms feature cheery prints and rattan furnishings with private patios or balconies and fully stocked minibars. Some rooms have fully equipped kitchenettes, and most have fabulous views of the ocean.
74 rooms. Complimentary continental breakfast. High-speed Internet access. Beach. **$$$**

★★★Paradise Point Resort & Spa
1404 W. Vacation Rd., San Diego,
858-274-4630, 800-344-2626;
www.paradisepoint.com
This 44-acre private island on Mission Bay offers cabana-style accommodations, making it the perfect spot for those looking for a little relaxation. The spa incorporates gentle Indonesian body treatments, while those looking for some recreation can enjoy tennis, volleyball and basketball courts, marina rentals, an 18-hole putting green and bike trails.
462 rooms. High-speed Wireless Internet access. Two restaurants, two bars. Beach. **$$$**

★★Radisson Suite Hotel Rancho Bernardo
11520 W. Bernardo Court, San Diego,
858-451-6600, 866-593-4267;
www.radissonranchobernardo.com

180 rooms, all suites. Complimentary full breakfast. Restaurant. Pool. **$$**

★★Sheraton Hotel
1433 Camino Del Rio S., San Diego,
619-260-0111
261 rooms. Restaurant, bar. Pets accepted. Pool. **$**

★★★Sheraton San Diego Hotel and Marina
1380 Harbor Island Dr., San Diego,
619-291-2900, 877-734-2726;
www.sheraton.com
This dual-tower waterfront landmark offers panoramic views and was recently updated with fresh, contemporary furnishings. Rooms have custom-designed beds with pillow-top mattresses, oversized desks and private patios or balconies. The East Tower has four restaurants and lounges, including Tapatinis, which serves a tapas menu and martinis. The West Tower features an outdoor heated pool and the restaurant Alfiere's, which specializes in Mediterranean cuisine.
1,044 rooms. High-speed Internet access. Three restaurants, three bars. Spa. Airport transportation available. **$$**

★★★Rancho Bernardo Inn
17550 Bernardo Oaks Dr.,
San Diego, 858-675-8500;
www.ranchobernardoinn.com
The newly remodeled guest rooms at this inn are warm and inviting, with antiques, original artwork and private patios or balconies. Suites also have wood-burning fireplaces. The hotel also offers two excellent options for dining: the Veranda Grill, an outdoor restaurant that overlooks the on-site golf course, and El Bizcocho, known by locals for its French cuisine.
287 rooms. Two restaurants, bar. Airport transportation available. Pets accepted. Golf. Tennis. **$$**

★★★Sheraton Suites San Diego
701 A St., San Diego,
619-696-9800, 800-962-1367;
www.sheraton.com/sandiego

123

SOUTHERN CALIFORNIA

★
★
★
★
★

Sharing a roof with Symphony Hall, this downtown all-suite hotel offers rapid access to the convention center, baseball stadium and the historic Gaslamp District. The spacious and contemporary rooms feature living rooms, minibars and custom-designed beds with pillow-top mattresses. The Sky Lobby lounge, with views of the skyline, is a nice spot for a cocktail.

264 rooms, all suites. High-speed Internet access. Restaurant, bar. Pets accepted. Pool. Business center. **$$**

★★★Tower 23
4551 Ocean Blvd., San Diego,
866-869-3723; www.tower23hotel.com
Perched on Pacific Beach just north of San Diego, this boutique hotel makes the most of its waterfront location with rooms (here, dubbed pads) that open to the surf and sand below. Decorated in cool tones of blue and green, guest rooms have beds swathed in Anichini linens and flat-screen TVs and X-Box entertainment centers. Suites are spacious and feature Kohler whirlpool tubs with chromatherapy lighting (which means you can turn your bath bubbles violet, aqua and other colors according to your mood). Jordan restaurant serves breakfast, lunch and dinner in a chic setting, while Eight sushi bar is a perfect spot for a post-surf nosh.

44 rooms. Restaurant, bar. Beach. **$$$**

★★★★U.S. Grant Hotel
326 Broadway, San Diego,
866-837-4270, 800-237-5029;
www.usgrant.net
This nearly 100-year-old hotel (opened in 1910 by Ulysses S. Grant, Jr. and his wife Fannie, and now part of Starwood's Luxury Collection) recently underwent a multi-million dollar renovation that restored the polish to this historic, grand building. The opulent new interiors, from the lobby to the Grant Grill, blend updated Art Deco furniture and decorative objects seamlessly with the belle époque bones of the hotel. Rooms feature original French art, custom imported wool carpets and marble bathrooms. The staff tends to guests' desires with old-world

aplomb. Spa treatments, from hot stone to deep tissue massage, are available in-room through a local spa.

317 rooms. Restaurant, bar. Fitness center. **$$$$**

★★★W San Diego
421 W. B St., San Diego,
619-398-3100;
www.whotels.com
Taking its cues from the city's beachfront location, this downton W hotel is lighter and brighter in design than others in the chain. The rooftop Beach bar (though located far from the sand) has a pool and cabanas ideal for lounging and sipping cocktails, while the hotel's living room is filled with rattan arm chairs and board games. Rooms have sea-blue walls and down duvets, flat screen TVs with CD/DVD players and Bliss bath products. The onsite Rice restaurant is a favorite with locals for its sultry look and spicy Asian-influenced food.

Restaurant, bar. Pool. Wireless Internet access. **$$$**

★★★Westgate Hotel
1055 Second Ave., San Diego,
619-238-1818, 800-221-3802;
www.westgatehotel.com
Located in downtown in the Gaslamp District, this sumptuous hotel is a treasure trove of antiques, French tapestries, crystal chandeliers and Persian carpets. The accommodations have Richelieu furniture, distinctive artwork and a bounty of fresh flowers. The dining is top-notch, particularly at Le Fontainebleau, a favorite choice for special occasions where afternoon tea is a tradition.

223 rooms. Complimentary continental breakfast. High-speed Internet access. Three restaurants, two bars. Spa. Pets accepted. **$$$**

★★★Westin Horton Plaza
910 Broadway Circle, San Diego,
619-239-2200;
www.westin.com/hortonplaza
This Westin hotel is adjacent to the Horton Plaza shopping mall, which features 182

SOUTHERN CALIFORNIA

stores and restaurants. It's also within minutes of the historic Gaslamp Quarter, San Diego Convention Center, Balboa Park, SeaWorld and the San Diego Zoo. Spacious guest rooms are decorated in neutral tones and feature mahogany furnishings, pillow-top mattresses with all-white bedding, sitting areas and minibars.

450 rooms. High-speed Internet access. Two restaurants, bar. Pets accepted. **$$**

★★★Westin San Diego
400 W. Broadway, San Diego,
619-239-4500; www.westin.com
Designed with an urban flair, the Westin San Diego offers a retreat to business and leisure travelers in the heart of downtown. The location means this hotel is minutes away from just about everything: SeaWorld, the zoo, conventions, Old Town, the Padres. This hotel is non-smoking.

436 rooms. High-speed wireless Internet access. Two restaurants, bar. Fitness room, spa. Outdoor pool, whirlpool. **$$**

SPECIALTY LODGINGS
Elsbree Beach Area Bed & Breakfast
5054 Narragansett Ave.,
San Diego, 619-226-4133;
www.bbinob.com
New England architecture and hospitality characterize this charming country house located in a quiet, seaside neighborhood just half a block from the beach. Guest rooms overlook beautiful gardens and offer the soothing sound of rolling surf.

6 rooms. Complimentary continental breakfast. **$**

RESTAURANTS
★★3rd Corner Wine Shop & Bistro
2665 Bacon St., San Diego, 619-223-2700;
www.the3rdcorner.com
Continental, French menu, wine bar. Lunch, dinner. Closed Monday. Bar. Casual attire. Outdoor seating. **$$**

★★Afghanistan Khyber Pass
523 University Ave., San Diego,
619-294-7579;
www.khyberpasscuisine.com

Middle Eastern menu. Lunch, dinner. Bar. Casual attire. Outdoor seating. **$$**

★Athens Market Taverna
109 W. F St., San Diego,
619-234-1955;
www.athensmarkettaverna.com
Greek menu. Lunch, dinner. Closed Sunday. Bar. Casual attire. Reservations recommended. Outdoor seating. **$$$**

★★★Baci
1955 W. Morena Blvd., San Diego,
619-275-2094;
www.bacicucina.com
This local favorite, which serves classic Northern Italian fare, has lots of old world charm, from the tuxedo-clad waiters to the romantic dining room and elegant patio.

Italian menu. Lunch, dinner. Closed Sunday. Bar. Children's menu. Business casual attire. Reservations recommended. Valet parking. **$$$**

★★Bella Luna
748 Fifth Ave., San Diego,
619-239-3222
Italian menu. Lunch, dinner. Bar. Casual attire. Reservations recommended. **$$$**

★★★Bertrand at Mister A's
2550 Fifth Ave., San Diego,
619-239-1377;
www.bertrandatmisteras.com
This restaurant is located on the 12th floor of a financial building just a few minutes from downtown San Diego. The attractive interior features pale walls, light woods, fresh floral arrangements and framed artwork. Diners come here not for the interior, but for the stunning views of the San Diego skyline. Chef de Cuisine Stephane Voitzwinkler and his staff create a wonderful assortment of modern American dishes with French and Mediterranean influences such as Mediterranean-style Cioppino, Maine lobster strudel and pan-seared Kobe flat-iron steak.

American menu. Lunch, dinner. Bar. Reservations recommended. Valet parking. Outdoor seating. **$$$**

★
★
★
★

★★★Blue Point

565 Fifth Ave., San Diego, 619-233-6623;
www.cohnrestaurants.com

Lounge on the black banquettes inside this oyster bar and seafood restaurant, or enjoy dinner—and people watching—at one of the intimate sidewalk tables.

Seafood menu. Dinner. Bar. Children's menu. Reservations recommended. Valet parking. Outdoor seating. **$$$**

★★★Busalacchi's

3683 Fifth Ave., San Diego, 619-298-0119;
www.busalacchis.com

Enjoy the authentic Southern Italian cuisine in one of the gems in the Busalacchi family-owned group of Italian eateries in the area. This site occupies a Victorian-style home.

Italian menu. Lunch, dinner. Bar. Business casual attire. Reservations recommended. Valet parking. **$$$**

★Cafe Coyote

2461 San Diego Ave., San Diego,
619-291-4695;
www.cafecoyoteoldtown.com

Mexican menu. Breakfast, lunch, dinner. Bar. Children's menu. Casual attire. Outdoor seating. **$$**

★★Cafe Pacifica

2414 San Diego Ave., San Diego,
619-291-6666;
www.cafepacifica.com

Seafood menu. Lunch, dinner. Bar. Children's menu. Casual attire. Reservations recommended. Valet parking. Outdoor seating. **$$$**

★★★California Cuisine

1027 University Ave., San Diego,
619-543-0790;
www.californiacuisine.cc

The chefs here mine the local markets daily to find the freshest ingredients. Dine on dishes like Niman Ranch pork chops with sweet potato gratin, or filet mignon with roasted garlic smashed Yukon potatoes and gorgonzola-pinot noir glaze. This elegant restaurant showcases new artwork each season from local artists.

California menu. Dinner. Business casual attire. Reservations recommended. Outdoor seating. **$$$**

★★Chateau Orleans

926 Turquoise St., Pacific Beach,
858-488-6744; www.chateauorleans.com

Cajun/Creole menu. Dinner. Closed Sunday. Children's menu. Casual attire. **$$**

★City Delicatessen

535 University Ave., San Diego,
619-295-2747

Deli menu. Breakfast, lunch, dinner. Bar. Children's menu. Casual attire. Outdoor seating. **$$**

★Corvette Diner

3946 Fifth Ave., San Diego, 619-542-1476;
www.cohnrestaurants.com

American menu. Lunch, dinner. Children's menu. Casual attire. **$**

★★Croce's Restaurant & Bar

802 Fifth Ave., San Diego, 619-233-4355;
www.croces.com

American menu. Lunch, dinner. Bar. Casual attire. Valet parking. Outdoor seating. **$$$**

★D.Z. Akin's

6930 Alvarado Rd., San Diego,
619-265-0218; www.dzakinsdeli.com

Deli menu. Breakfast, lunch, dinner. Children's menu. Casual attire. **$$**

★★Dakota Grill and Spirits

901 Fifth Ave., San Diego, 619-234-5554;
www.dakotagrillandspirits.com

Located in the Gaslamp Plaza Suite Hotel. Southwestern menu. Lunch, dinner. Bar. Children's menu. Casual attire. Reservations recommended. Valet parking. Outdoor seating. **$$$**

★★Dobson's

956 Broadway Circle, San Diego,
619-231-6771;
www.dobsonsrestaurant.com

California menu. Lunch, dinner. Closed Sunday. Bar. Casual attire. Reservations recommended. Valet parking. **$$**

★Edgewater Grill
861 W. Harbor Dr., San Diego,
619-232-7581; www.edgewatergrill.com
Seafood, steak menu. Breakfast, lunch, dinner. Bar. Children's menu. Casual attire. Reservations recommended. Outdoor seating. **$$**

★★★El Bizcocho
17550 Bernardo Oaks Dr., San Diego,
858-487-1611;
www.ranchobernardoinn.com
Prepare for an unforgettable experience at this elegant restaurant that's been earning raves in San Diego for three decades. The place is full of old-world charm but the menu is definitely new, with lots of locally grown produce and handcrafted artisan products.
  French menu. Dinner, Sunday brunch. Bar. Jacket required. Reservations recommended. Valet parking. **$$$**

★El Indio Mexican
3695 Indian St., San Diego,
619-299-0333; www.el-indio.com
Mexican menu. Breakfast, lunch, dinner. Casual attire. Outdoor seating. No credit cards accepted. **$**

★Fairouz Cafe and Gallery
3166 Midway Dr., San Diego,
619-225-0308;
www.alnashashibi.com/cafe.htm
Mediterranean menu. Lunch, dinner. Bar. Children's menu. Casual attire. **$$**

★★French Market Grille
15717 Bernardo Heights Pkwy.,
San Diego, 858-485-8055;
www.frenchmarketgrille.com
French menu. Breakfast, lunch, dinner. Casual attire. Reservations recommended. Outdoor seating. **$$$**

★★★Greystone—the Steakhouse
658 Fifth Ave., San Diego,
619-232-0225;
www.greystonesteakhouse.com
Located in an historic theater building in the Gaslamp district, the prime-aged meat,

pasta and seafood—as well as an extensive wine list—are the real stars of this elegant restaurant's menu.
  Steak menu. Dinner. Bar. Business casual attire. Reservations recommended. Valet parking. Outdoor seating. **$$$**

★★Harbor House
831 W. Harbor Dr., San Diego,
619-232-1141;
www.harborhouse-sandiego.com
Seafood menu. Lunch, dinner. Bar. Children's menu. Casual attire. Reservations recommended. Outdoor seating. **$$**

★★Hob Nob Hill
2271 First Ave., San Diego, 619-239-8176;
www.hobnobhill.com
American menu. Breakfast, lunch, dinner. Bar. Children's menu. Casual attire. **$$**

★★Imperial House
505 Kalmia St., San Diego, 619-234-3525
Continental menu. Lunch, dinner. Bar. Children's menu. Business casual attire. Reservations recommended. Valet parking. **$$$**

★★Jack and Giulio's
2391 San Diego Ave., San Diego,
619-294-2074; www.jackandgiulios.com
Italian menu. Lunch, dinner. Bar. Children's menu. Casual attire. Reservations recommended. Outdoor seating. **$$$**

★★Jasmine
4609 Convoy St., San Diego,
858-268-0888
Chinese menu. Lunch, dinner. Bar. Casual attire. **$$**

★Karl Strauss' Brewery and Grill
1157 Columbia St., San Diego,
619-234-2739;
www.karlstrauss.com
American menu. Lunch, dinner. Bar. Children's menu. Casual attire. Outdoor seating. **$$**

★★Kelly's Steakhouse
500 Hotel Circle N., San Diego,
619-291-7131

★
★
★
★
★

Steak menu. Dinner. Bar. Children's menu. Casual attire. Reservations recommended. Valet parking. **$$$**

★★La Vache and Company
420 Robinson Ave., San Diego,
619-295-0214; www.lavacheandco.com
French menu. Lunch, dinner, brunch. Casual attire. Reservations recommended. Outdoor seating. **$$**

★★Lamont Street Grill
4445 Lamont St., San Diego,
858-270-3060; www.lamontstreetgrill.com
Seafood, steak menu. Dinner. Bar. Outdoor seating. **$$**

★★★★Laurel
505 Laurel St., San Diego, 619-239-2222;
www.laurelrestaurant.com
Make a grand entrance down a sweeping, wrought-iron staircase into this sleek and sexy 3,200-square-foot dining room and packed bar. The rustic, contemporary French food includes signature dishes such as onion and Roquefort tart, and chicken cooked in a clay pot. The restaurant's stellar wine list emphasizes the Rhone region of France. Laurel also hosts some of the best live jazz musicians in town, making the bar a lively spot to unwind and make new friends.
French, Mediterranean menu. Dinner. Bar. Casual attire. Valet parking. **$$$**

★★★Le Fountainebleau
1055 Second Ave., San Diego,
619-238-1818;
www.westgatehotel.com
This glitzy dining room in the Westgate Hotel is all about romance—there's even a pianist who plays while diners bite into chateaubriand.
California, French menu. Lunch, dinner. Bar. Jacket required. Reservations recommended. Valet parking. Outdoor seating. **$$$**

★★The Linkery
3382 30th St., San Diego, 619-255-8778;
www.thelinkery.com

American menu. Dinner. Reservations not accepted. **$$**

★★Nick's at the Beach
809 Thomas Ave., San Diego,
858-270-1730; www.nicksatthebeach.com
Seafood menu. Breakfast, lunch, dinner. Bar. Children's menu. Casual attire. Reservations recommended. Outdoor seating. **$$**

★Old Town Mexican Cafe and Cantina
2489 San Diego Ave., San Diego,
619-297-4330, 888-234-9823;
www.oldtownmexcafe.com
Mexican menu. Breakfast, lunch, dinner. Bar. Children's menu. Casual attire. **$$**

★★Panda Inn
506 Horton Plaza, San Diego,
619-233-7800; www.pandainn.com
Chinese menu. Lunch, dinner. Bar. Casual attire. Outdoor seating. **$$**

★★★Prego
1370 Frazee Rd., San Diego,
619-294-4700; www.pregoristoranti.com
Prego brings a piece of the Italian countryside to San Diego with its Tuscan-inspired dining room with arches and columns. The bustling open kitchen turns out authentic pizzas baked in a brick-fired oven, and fresh pasta and seafood.
Italian menu. Lunch, dinner. Bar. Children's menu. Business casual attire. Reservations recommended. Valet parking. Outdoor seating. **$$$**

★★★Rainwater's
1202 Kettner Blvd., San Diego,
619-233-5757; www.rainwaters.com
Prime midwestern beef and fresh seafood are among the specialties at this clubby chophouse with cherry wood accents, leather seating and crisp white linens. The superb wine list, with selections from around the world, and the professional, personalized service make this the perfect spot for a power lunch or elegant dinner.
American, steak menu. Lunch, dinner. Bar. Business casual attire. Reservations

SOUTHERN CALIFORNIA

★

★

★

★

★

recommended. Valet parking. Outdoor seating. **$$$$**

★Red Sails Inn
2614 Shelter Island Dr., San Diego,
619-223-3030
Seafood menu. Breakfast, lunch, dinner. Bar. Children's menu. Casual attire. Outdoor seating. **$$**

★★★Ruth's Chris Steak House
1355 N. Harbor Dr., San Diego,
619-233-1422; www.ruthschris.com
Born from a single New Orleans restaurant that Ruth Fertel bought in 1965 for $22,000, the chain is a favorite among steak lovers. Aged prime midwestern beef is broiled at 1,800 degrees and served on a heated plate sizzling with butter and with sides like creamed spinach and au gratin potatoes.
Steak menu. Dinner. Bar. Business casual attire. Reservations recommended. Valet parking. **$$$**

★Saffron
3737 India St., San Diego, 619-574-7737;
www.sumeiyu.com
Thai menu. Lunch, dinner. Children's menu. Casual attire. Outdoor seating. Picnic baskets available. **$$**

★★★Sally's
1 Market Place, San Diego, 619-358-6740;
www.manchestergrand.hyatt.com
Although it's located on the Boardwalk adjacent to the Manchester Grand Hyatt, this is no tourist trap. Lots of locals come here to enjoy the beautiful waterfront views and ultra-fresh seafood, which includes pan-fried diver scallops with lychee relish and ahi tuna with miso-mustard. The crab cakes, which are grilled (not fried), are said to be some of the best in the city. For those looking for something besides seafood, dishes like Asian-style tofu lasagna and Colorado lamb loin marinated in Chinese black beans are a sure bet.
American menu. Lunch, dinner. Bar. Casual attire. Reservations recommended. Valet parking. Outdoor seating. **$$$**

★★★Salvatore's
750 Front St., San Diego, 619-544-1865;
www.salvatoresdowntown.com
A longtime favorite for elegant dining, Salvatore's has been the model for what a refined Italian restaurant should be since 1987. Perfectly prepared plates of homemade lasagna or eggplant- and mushroom-filled ravioli are delivered to tables swathed in crisp white linens and set with fine china by a friendly and efficient staff.
Italian menu. Dinner. Bar. Business casual attire. Valet parking. **$$$**

★San Diego Pier Cafe
885 W. Harbor Dr., San Diego,
619-239-3968; www.piercafe.com
Seafood menu. Lunch, dinner. Bar. Children's menu. Casual attire. Reservations recommended. Outdoor seating. **$$**

★★★Taka
555 Fifth Ave., San Diego, 619-338-0555;
www.takasushi.com
This gem in San Diego's Gaslamp District is popular for its traditional, no-frills sushi and fresh seafood that's brought in fresh everyday.
Japanese, sushi, fusion menu. Dinner. Bar. Children's menu. Casual attire. Reservations recommended. Outdoor seating. **$$**

★★★The Oceanaire Seafood Room
400 J St., San Diego, 619-858-2277;
www.theoceanaire.com
The stuffed fish on the walls and blackboards marked with daily specials set the stage for a delicious, super-fresh (delivered daily) seafood dinner prepared every way imaginable. The lounge is a nice locale for a pre- or post-dinner drink and a few oysters.
Seafood menu. Dinner. Bar. Casual attire. Reservations recommended. Valet parking. **$$$**

★★★The Prado at Balboa Park
1549 El Prado Way, San Diego,
619-557-9441
This lively, eclectic restaurant is located in the historic 1915 Spanish Colonial House of Hospitality building. The attractive interior

SOUTHERN CALIFORNIA

★
★
★
★
★

features colorful glass-blown sculptures, mosaic-tiled tables and beautiful chandeliers. Chef Jeff Thurston offers a delicious menu focusing on Italian and Latin American cuisine. The outdoor patio is lovely for kicking back and enjoying the surrounding views and a mojito.

Italian, Latin American menu. Lunch, dinner. Bar. Children's menu. Jacket required. Reservations recommended. Outdoor seating. $$$

★★★Thee Bungalow
4996 W. Point Loma Blvd., San Diego, 619-224-2884; www.theebungalow.com
Chef/owner Ed Moore continually strives to please his loyal beach following with his famous crispy roast duck (served with a choice of sauces), sampler platter featuring house-made pâtes and swoon-worthy dessert soufflés.

American, French menu. Dinner. Bar. Business casual attire. Reservations recommended. Outdoor seating. $$$

★★Tom Ham's Lighthouse
2150 Harbor Island Dr., San Diego, 619-291-9110;
www.tomhamslighthouse.com
Seafood menu. Lunch, dinner. Bar. Casual attire. Reservations recommended. Outdoor seating. $$$

★★★Top of the Market
750 N. Harbor Dr., San Diego, 619-234-4867; www.thefishmarket.com
The seafood is indeed fresh at this fish market/restaurant, which operates its own fishery and has a partnership with an oyster farm. The elegant, wood-paneled dining room, with large windows offering views of the bay, is the perfect place to indulge.

Seafood menu. Lunch, dinner. Bar. Children's menu. Business casual attire. Reservations recommended. Valet parking. Outdoor seating. $$$

★★★Winesellar and Brasserie
9550 Waples St., San Diego, 858-450-9576; www.winesellar.com
With crisp white linens and a candlelit atmosphere, this is the perfect destination for a romantic dinner of fine French cuisine. Don't forgot to stop at the lower level wine shop to browse the large selection of fine wines.

French menu. Dinner. Closed Sunday. Bar. Casual attire. $$$

★★Zocalo Grill
2444 San Diego Ave., San Diego, 619-298-9840; www.zocalogrill.com
California menu. Lunch, dinner, Sunday brunch. Bar. Children's menu. Casual attire. Reservations recommended. Outdoor seating. $$$

SAN DIEGO AREA CITIES AND TOWNS

BORREGO SPRINGS
Although prospectors and cattle ranchers had driven through this desert area in the late 19th century, it wasn't until 1906 that the first permanent settler arrived. In the winter and spring, wildflowers transform the desert's valleys, canyons and washes into a rainbow of colors, creating an oasis in the midst of the desert.
Information: Chamber of Commerce, 786 Palm Canyon Dr., Borrego Springs, 760-767-5555, 800-559-5524; www.borregospringschamber.org

WHAT TO SEE AND DO
Anza-Borrego Desert State Park
200 Palm Canyon Dr., Borrego Springs, 760-767-5311; www.parks.ca.gov

The largest state park in California, with approximately 600,000 acres of desert wilderness. The best time to visit is November through mid-May, when 600 species of flowering plants are in bloom. Elephant trees reach the northernmost limits of their

★
★
★
★
★

range and rare smoke trees and fan palms grow here around natural seeps and springs. The park also provides a refuge for wildlife including roadrunners, rare bighorn sheep and kit foxes. There are miles of hiking trails and campsites are scattered throughout the park. Naturalist programs, tours, and campfire programs are offered on weekends November-May.

HOTELS

★★Borrego Springs Resort
1112 Tilting T Dr., Borrego Springs,
760-767-5700, 888-826-7734;
www.borregospringsresort.com
100 rooms. Complimentary continental breakfast. Restaurant. Airport transportation available. Golf. Tennis. **$$**

★★★La Casa Del Zorro
3845 Yaqui Pass Rd.,
Borrego Springs,
760-767-5323, 800-824-1884;
www.lacasadelzorro.com
This historic resort dates back to 1937 and is located in the heart of San Diego County's majestic Anza Borrego Desert. The region's Spanish history inspires the décor at this serene resort. The 44 deluxe poolside rooms include marble baths and sitting areas with fireplaces and patios or balconies. The private casitas, each with its own pool or spa, range from one to four bedrooms.
79 rooms. Restaurant, bar. Children's activity center. Spa. Pool. Tennis. Business center. **$$$**

★★★The Palms at Indian Head
2220 Hoberg Rd., Borrego Springs,
760-767-7788, 800-519-2624;
www.thepalmsatindianhead.com
This historic hotel was built in classic mid-century style with Mondrian influences. The lobby features floor-to-ceiling windows,

terrazzo floors and historical photos of the property and its famous former guests, including Marilyn Monroe, Bing Crosby and Cary Grant. The cozy guest rooms are minimalist—no phones, no TVs. Warm cookies are delivered around sunset. Enjoy the Zen garden or go for an invigorating hike. The restaurant Krazy Coyote is a fun place to meet friends for dinner and drinks.
12 rooms. Complimentary continental breakfast. Restaurant. Pool. **$**

SPECIALTY LODGINGS

Borrego Valley Inn
405 Palm Canyon Dr., Borrego Springs,
760-767-0311, 800-333-5810;
www.borregovalleyinn.com
15 rooms. Closed June-September (weekdays). Children over 14 years only. Complimentary continental breakfast. Airport transportation available. Pets accepted. Pool. **$$**

RESTAURANTS

★★★Butterfield Room
3845 Yaqui Pass Rd., Borrego Springs,
760-767-5323;
www.lacasadelzorro.com
Beautiful oil paintings of the Old West Butterfield Stageline adorn the white-washed adobe walls of this elegant restaurant. Candlelight and sparkling table settings create a romantic atmosphere in which to enjoy creative California cuisine. The menu changes throughout the year, taking advantage of the freshest seasonal ingredients. Previous offerings include a grilled ahi tuna sandwich with cucumber-cilantro salad or Colorado rack of lamb glazed with Dijon mustard, wildflower honey and Provencal herbs.
American menu. Breakfast, lunch, dinner. Bar. Jacket required. Reservations recommended. Outdoor seating. **$$$**

131

SOUTHERN CALIFORNIA

★
★
★
✩
✩

CARLSBAD

Named for a famous European spa in Karlsbad, Bohemia (now in the Czech Republic), this beach-oriented community is a playground for golfers, tennis players, water-skiers and fishing enthusiasts.

Information: Convention & Visitors Bureau, 400 Carlsbad Village Dr., 760-434-6093, 800-227-5722; www.carlsbadca.org

WHAT TO SEE AND DO

Legoland

1 Legoland Dr., Carlsbad, 760-918-5346; www.legoland.com

Visitors are greeted by a 9-foot dinosaur of bright red blocks at the entrance to Legoland, and that's just the start. Everything here is made of Legos, from the characters along Fairy Tale Brook to the horses that kids ride through an enchanted forest. Designed for children ages 2 through 12, the 128-acre park has 60 family rides, hands-on attractions and shows, plus a special area designed for toddlers. The park's centerpiece is Miniland, which replicates areas of New York, Washington, D.C., the California coastline, New Orleans and an interactive New England harbor scene using 20 million Lego bricks. Daily, opens at 10 a.m.

Leo Carrillo Ranch Historic Park

6200 Flying LC Lane, Carlsbad, 760-476-1042; www.carrillo-ranch.org

This 27-acre park, once part of a working ranch, was dreamt up by actor Leo Carrillo, best known for his role as Pancho on the television show *The Cisco Kid*. Carrillo participated in a number of conservation efforts in southern California and conceived this ranch in the 1930s as a tribute to his Mexican ancestors who helped settle the area. (Carrillo's great-grandfather was the first provisional governor of California.) A number of buildings have been restored, including the main hacienda, cantina, barn, wash house and foundry. Guided tours are given Saturday and Sunday. Summer: Tuesday-Saturday 9 a.m.-6 p.m., Sunday 11 a.m.-6 p.m.; fall, winter, and spring: Tuesday-Saturday 9 a.m.-5 p.m., Sunday 11 a.m.-5 p.m.

Museum of Making Music

5790 Armada Dr., Carlsbad, 760-438-5996; www.museumofmakingmusic.org

A century of music is put into a historical perspective and made fun for every age level;.While the kids are making their own music with guitars, drums and pianos, adults can try their hands at a theremina wooden box, which has two antennas and works when sound waves are interrupted with a wave of the palm. See more than 450 vintage instruments, watch multimedia presentation and use the interactive listening stations to tune into some of the most influential music in history. Tuesday-Sunday 10 a.m.-5 p.m.

SPECIAL EVENTS

Carlsbad Village Street Faire

Grand Ave., Carlsbad.

More than 850 arts, crafts and antiques vendors; food and entertainment. First Sunday in May and first Sunday in November.

Flower Fields at Carlsbad Ranch

5704 Paseo Del Norte, Carlsbad, 760-431-0352; www.theflowerfields.com

From its roots as a family-owned flower operation, the annual Flower Fields at Carlsbad Ranch has bloomed into a local phenomenon, thanks to the beautiful Tecolote Giant Ranunculus. A British immigrant and horticulturist brought this Asian relative of the buttercup to California, where it now grows on 50 acres. Locals consider the March flowering to be a harbinger of spring, and more than 150,000 visitors per year come to check it out. March-May, daily.

SOUTHERN CALIFORNIA

★
★
★
★
★

HOTELS

★Best Western Beach Terrace Inn
2775 Ocean St., Carlsbad,
760-729-5951, 800-443-5415;
www.beachterraceinn.com
49 rooms, all suites. Beach. Pool. **$**

★Carlsbad Inn Beach Resort
3075 Carlsbad Blvd., Carlsbad,
760-434-7020, 800-235-3939;
www.carlsbadinn.com
56 rooms. Children's activity center. Fitness center. **$$**

★★Hilton Garden Inn Carlsbad Beach
6450 Carlsbad Blvd., Carlsbad,
760-476-0800, 800-774-1500;
www.hiltongardeninn.com
161 rooms. High-speed Internet access. Restaurant, bar. Beach. Airport transportation available. Fitness center. Pool. Business center. **$$**

★★★★Four Seasons Resort Aviara, North San Diego
7100 Four Seasons Point, Carlsbad,
760-603-6800, 800-819-5053;
www.fourseasons.com/aviara
Avid golfers come to play the 18-hole golf course designed by Arnold Palmer. But that's just one reason to come to this splendid resort on 200 lush acres overlooking the Batiquitos Lagoon, the Pacific Ocean and a nature preserve that's home to a variety of wildlife. The architecture pays homage to the region's history with its Spanish colonial design, and guest rooms feel luxurious and homey, with sumptuous sitting areas, sliding French doors opening up to private patios or balconies and marble bathrooms with deep soaking tubs. Dining choices range from Italian to California cuisine and the lively wine bar, with dramatic floor-to-ceiling windows offering views of the Pacific.
349 rooms. Two restaurants, bar. Children's activity center. Spa. Pets accepted. Fitness center. Pool. Golf. Tennis. Business center. **$$$$**

★★★La Costa Resort and Spa
2100 Costa Del Mar Rd., Carlsbad,
760-438-9111, 800-854-5000;
www.lacosta.com
Guests come to La Costa Resort and Spa to hit the links, relax in the spa, feast on mouthwatering meals and lounge by the pool. Designed to resemble a Spanish Colonial village, La Costa has a warm, inviting spirit. Golfers love the two PGA 18-hole courses, while the 21-court tennis center is a favorite of players. The resort is also home to the renowned Chopra Center, which helps guests achieve wellbeing through Ayurvedic principles. The dazzling spa with a Roman waterfall offers a variety of pampering treatments.
480 rooms. Restaurant, bar. Children's activity center. Airport transportation available. Fitness center. Pool. Golf. Tennis. Business center. **$$$**

RESTAURANTS

★★Tuscany
6981 El Camino Real, Carlsbad,
760-929-8111;
www.tomasos.com/carlsbadhome.htm
Italian menu. Lunch, dinner. Bar. **$$**

★★★Vivace
7100 Four Seasons Point, Carlsbad,
760-603-6800; www.fourseasons.com/aviara
Chef Bruce Logue puts his own twist on Central Italian cuisine, with dishes such as black spaghetti with rock shrimp and calabrese sausage, and hand-made orecchiette with braised capon. A large light stone fireplace fills the dining room with warmth while the floor-to-ceiling windows allow breathtaking views of the ocean and lagoon.
Italian menu. Dinner. Children's menu. Valet parking. Outdoor seating. **$$$**

SPAS

★★★★Spa at Four Seasons Resort Aviara, North San Diego
7100 Four Seasons Point, Carlsbad,
760-603-6800, 800-819-5053;
www.fourseasons.com/aviara

SOUTHERN CALIFORNIA

The newly renovated 15,000-square-foot spa has both indoor and outdoor treatment rooms and a solarium lounge. Pamper your skin with an avocado body wrap and customized facials. Water shiatsu (watsu) treatments involve massage and stretching while you float in a heated pool. The on-site José Eber Salon provides hair, nail and makeup services. **$$**

CORONADO

Known as the Crown City, Coronado lies across the bay from San Diego and is connected to the mainland by a long, narrow sandbar called the Silver Strand and by the beautiful Coronado Bridge. It is the site of the famous Hotel del Coronado.

Information: Coronado Chamber of Commerce, 875 Orange Ave., 619-435-9260; www.coronadochamber.com

WHAT TO SEE AND DO

Art in the Park

www.coronadoartassn.com

More than 50 top artists from throughout San Diego County set up their treasures in the center of Coronado Village. January-December, first and third Sundays.

HOTELS

★Best Western Suites Hotel Coronado Island

275 Orange Ave., Coronado, 619-437-1666; www.bestwestern.com

63 rooms. Complimentary continental breakfast. Pool. **$**

★★Crown City Inn & Bistro

520 Orange Ave., Coronado, 619-435-3116, 800-422-1173; www.crowncityinn.com

33 rooms. Restaurant. Pets accepted. Pool. **$**

★★El Cordova Hotel

1351 Orange Ave., Coronado, 619-435-4131, 800-229-2032; www.elcordovahotel.com

9 rooms. Restaurant. Pool. **$**

★★★Hotel Del Coronado

1500 Orange Ave., Coronado, 619-435-6611, 800-468-3533; www.hoteldel.com

Few hotels have earned a place in American history like the Hotel del Coronado. Charles Lindbergh was honored here after his first transatlantic flight, and it was at the Del that Marilyn Monroe romped on the beach in *Some Like It Hot*. It's even rumored that the Duke of Windsor met his future wife, Wallis Simpson, here. Set on 31 acres on the island of Coronado just off San Diego, this beachfront, Victorian-style hotel is the ultimate sand and surf getaway. The recently remodeled rooms are housed in three different areas: the Victorian Building, the Ocean Towers and the California Cabanas.

688 rooms. Three restaurants, bar. Children's activity center. Spa. Business center. **$$$**

★★★Loews Coronado Bay Resort

4000 Coronado Bay Rd., Coronado, 619-424-4000, 800-235-6397; www.loewshotels.com

Situated on a 15-acre peninsula overlooking San Diego Bay, this romantic yet family-friendly resort's lush tropical landscaping is freshened by ocean breezes that sweep through its private marina. Casual, Mediterranean-style elegance and expansive water views define the décor, from the sunny lobby to the luxe accommodations, where pillow-top mattresses, oversized tubs and spacious balconies are featured. Year-round activities include gondola rides, complimentary sailing lessons and dive-in movies, which play poolside on a large screen.

450 rooms. Pets accepted. Restaurant. Children's activity center. Spa. Beach. Pets accepted. **$$**

★★★Marriott Coronado Island Resort

2000 Second St., Coronado, 619-435-3000; www.marriott.com

★

★

★

★

★

This waterfront resort, just across the bay from downtown San Diego, sits on 16 tropical acres dotted with waterfalls, koi ponds and strolling flamingos. For a special getaway, reserve a villa with a private entrance and pool.

300 rooms. Pets accepted. High-speed Internet access. Two restaurants. **$$**

★★★The Mansion at Glorietta Bay
1630 Glorietta Blvd., Coronado,
619-435-3101, 800-283-9383;
www.gloriettabayinn.com
Built in 1908 by one of San Diego's earliest developers, the mansion was converted to a hotel in the mid-1970s. You can choose to stay in the mansion itself, which offers more luxurious accommodations, or in the surrounding inn buildings, which have more modern rooms perfect for families or business travelers. While there's no restaurant, the hotel is close to dining, shopping and the beach.

183 rooms. Complimentary continental breakfast. Pool. Business center. **$$**

RESTAURANTS
★★★Azzura Point
4000 Coronado Bay Rd., Coronado,
619-424-4000;
www.loewshotels.com
The Mediterranean menu features a fusion of Northern Italian and French cuisines, and uses locally caught seafood and fresh herbs from the resort's private herb garden. The huge curved windows, dressed in leopard print, frame the bay.

California menu. Dinner. Closed Monday. Bar. Children's menu. Valet parking. **$$$**

★★Brigantine
1333 Orange Ave., Coronado,
619-435-4166; www.brigantine.com
California menu. Lunch, dinner. Bar. Children's menu. Casual attire. **$$**

★★Chez Loma
1132 Loma Ave., Coronado, 619-435-0661;
www.chezloma.com
French menu. Dinner. Bar. Casual attire. Reservations recommended. **$$$**

★★Peohe's
1201 First St., Coronado, 619-437-4474;
www.peohes.com
American, seafood. Lunch, dinner, Sunday brunch. Bar. Children's menu. Casual attire. Outdoor seating. **$$$**

★★Primavera
932 Orange Ave., Coronado,
619-435-0454;
www.primavera1st.com
Italian menu. Dinner. Bar. **$$$**

DEL MAR
This village by the sea offers beautiful white beaches and brilliant sunsets. It's also an attractive area for year-round ballooning.
Information: Greater Del Mar Chamber of Commerce, 1104 Camino Del Mar, 858-793-5292; www.delmar.ca.us

SPECIAL EVENTS
Del Mar Thoroughbred Club
County Fairgrounds,
2260 Jimmy Durante Blvd., Del Mar,
858-755-1141; www.dmtc.com
Thoroughbred horse racing from July-mid-September.

HOTELS
★Best Western Stratford Inn
710 Camino del Mar, Del Mar,
858-755-1501, 800-780-7234;
www.bestwestern.com
94 rooms. Complimentary continental breakfast Pool. **$$**

★Clarion Hotel
720 Camino Del Mar, Del Mar,
858-755-9765, 800-451-4515;
www.delmarinn.com
81 rooms. Complimentary continental breakfast. Pets accepted. Pool. **$**

★★★Hilton San Diego/Del Mar
15575 Jimmy Durante Blvd.,
Del Mar, 619-792-5200; www.hilton.com

★
★
★
★
★

This comfortable hotel is located next to the Del Mar Thoroughbred Club and just minutes from the beach, though the pool may tempt guests to skip the sand. The rooms include high speed Internet, new Serenity Bed Collection and Web TV.

256 rooms. Restaurant, bar. Pets accepted. Fitness center. Pool. Business center. **$$**

★★★L'Auberge Del Mar Resort and Spa
1540 Camino del Mar, Del Mar,
858-259-1515,
800-245-9757;
www.laubergedelmar.com

This hideaway occupies more than five lush acres on the coast. Play a round of golf on the celebrated Tom Fazio-designed course, go up in a hot air balloon or take a long walk on the beach. The cheery cottage-style rooms blend Art Deco with antique pieces and feature marble bathrooms. The spa is a destination in its own right.

120 rooms. Restaurant, bar. Spa. Fitness center. Pool. Tennis. **$$$$**

RESTAURANTS
★★Epazote
1555 Camino del Mar, Del Mar,
858-259-9966;
www.epazote.signonsandiego.com

Southwestern menu. Lunch, dinner, Sunday brunch. Bar. Casual attire. Valet parking. Outdoor seating. **$$**

★★Il Fornaio
1555 Camino del Mar, Del Mar,
858-755-8876; www.ilfornaio.com
Italian menu. Lunch, dinner, Sunday. brunch. Bar. Children's menu. Casual attire. Outdoor seating. **$$**

★★J. Taylor's of Del Mar
1540 Camino del Mar, Del Mar,
858-793-6460; www.jtaylors.com
California menu. Breakfast, lunch, dinner. Bar. Valet parking. Outdoor seating. **$$$**

★★Jake's Del Mar
1660 Coast Blvd., Del Mar, 858-755-2002;
www.jakesdelmar.com
Seafood, steak menu. Lunch Tuesday-Sunday, dinner, Sunday brunch. Bar. Valet parking. Outdoor seating. **$$$**

★Pacifica Del Mar
1555 Camino del Mar, Del Mar,
858-792-0476;
www.pacificadelmar.com
Seafood menu. Lunch, dinner. Children's menu. **$$$**

ESCONDIDO
A Ranger District office of the Cleveland National Forest is located here.
Information: San Diego North Convention and Visitors Bureau, 360 N. Escondido Blvd., 92025, 760-745-4741, 800-848-3336; www.sandiegonorth.com

WHAT TO SEE AND DO
California Center for the Performing Arts
340 N. Escondido Blvd., Escondido,
760-839-4100, 800-988-4253;
www.artcenter.org
Designed by renowned architect Charles Moore, this 12-acre campus of postmodern buildings includes two theaters, an art museum and conference center. The center's museum presents works by upcoming and established Mexican and American artists, particularly those who live in and around Southern California. Other facilities include the Concert Hall and Center Theater. Tuesday-Saturday.

Escondido Heritage Walk
321 N. Broadway,
Escondido,
760-743-8207
History museum. Victorian ranch house. Working blacksmith shop. Early 1900s barn and windmill. 1888 Santa Fe train depot and model train replica of the Oceanside to Escondido run (circa 1920). Tuesday-Saturday.

Ferrara

1120 W. 15th Ave., Escondido,
760-745-7632

Producers of wine and grape juice. Self-guided tours, wine tasting. Daily 10 a.m.-5 p.m.

Orfila

13455 San Pasqual Rd., Escondido,
760-738-6500, 800-868-9463;
www.orfila.com

Guided and self-guided tours, wine tasting room. The picnic area beneath the grape arbor overlooks the vineyards and San Pasqual Valley. Daily 10 a.m.-6 p.m.

Palomar Observatory

35899 Canfield Rd.,
Escondido, 760-742-2119;
www.astro.caltech.edu/observatories/palomar

Check out the 200-inch Hale telescope (the second-largest in the United States). Self-guided tours. Daily.

San Pasqual Battlefield State Historic Park and Museum

15808 San Pasqual Valley Rd.,
Escondido, 760-737-2201;
www.parks.ca.gov

One of the deadliest battles of the Mexican-American War took place here on December 6, 1846. Twenty-one Americans died, 16 more were wounded and the Americans were forced to retreat. A short video at the visitor center places the battle in the context of the war. Every December, a reenactment of the battle takes place to mark its anniversary. Friday-Monday 10 a.m.-5 p.m.

Welk Resort Center Theatre-Museum

8860 Lawrence Welk Dr.,
Escondido, 760-749-3448

Houses memorabilia from Lawrence Welk's career. Daily.

HOTELS

★★Castle Creek Inn & Spa

29850 Circle R Way, Escondido,
760-751-8800, 800-253-5341;
www.castlecreekinn.com

30 rooms. Restaurant. Pets accepted. Pool. Tennis. $

★Comfort Inn

1290 W. Valley Pkwy., Escondido,
760-489-1010, 800-541-6012;
www.choicehotels.com

93 rooms. Complimentary continental breakfast. Fitness center. $

★★Lake San Marcos Resort

1025 La Bonita Dr., San Marcos,
760-744-0120, 800-447-6556;
www.lakesanmarcosresort.com

140 rooms. Pets accepted. Fitness center. Pool. $

★★★Welk Resort San Diego

8860 Lawrence Welk Dr., Escondido,
760-749-3000, 800-932-9355;
www.welksandiego.com

This sprawling, 600-acre resort is minutes from downtown San Diego. One-and two-bedrooms villas feature sitting and dining areas, kitchens, patios or balconies, and views of the mountain or golf course. Whirlpools and fireplaces are available in some suites. There are two 18-hole championship courses, dinner theater and scheduled activities such as jewelry making, painting and table tennis tournaments. Guests also have resort privileges at three sister properties: Boulder Springs, Harmony Hill and Broadway Hill. The Canyon Grille restaurant is a great spot for a casual dinner.

100 rooms. Restaurant, bar. Children's activity center. Fitness center. Tennis. $$

SPECIALTY LODGINGS

Zosa Gardens Bed and Breakfast

9381 W. Lilac Rd.,
Escondido,
760-723-9093, 800-711-8361;
www.zosagardens.com

This quiet retreat sits on 22 meticulously landscaped acres, about a 45-minute drive from downtown San Diego. Enjoy wine and cheese in the afternoon.

10 rooms. Complimentary full breakfast. Tennis. $

SOUTHERN CALIFORNIA

★
★
★
★
★

RESTAURANTS

★★★150 Grand Cafe
150 W. Grand Ave., Escondido,
760-738-6868;
www.150grandcafe.com

This health-conscious café uses all-natural meat, free range chicken and locally grown and organic produce. Starters include house-made liver paté with pistachios. Entrées include dishes like whole grain Dijon-braised rabbit. Desserts such as a banana boat sundae with avocado ice cream and cashews, pineapple and coconut provide a fresh finish. There's a New Orleans-style brunch on Saturday and Sunday.

American menu. Lunch, dinner. Bar. Outdoor seating. **$$**

★★Sandcrab Cafe
2229 Micro Place, Escondido,
760-480-2722; www.sandcrabcafe.com
Seafood menu. Lunch, dinner. Bar. Children's menu. Casual attire. **$$**

★★★Vincent's Sirino's
113 W. Grand Ave., Escondido,
760-745-3835; www.vincentssirinos.com
This converted pasta factory serves up dishes like Kobe-braised short ribs and sweet potato ravioli in a warm and friendly atmosphere.

California, French menu. Lunch, dinner. Closed Monday. Bar. Children's menu. Reservations recommended. Outdoor seating. **$$$**

JULIAN

Julian was born following the Civil War when Confederate veterans headed west to seek their fortunes. The gold rush lasted about a decade but the pioneers stayed and began farming the land, which became a good place to grow apples.

Information: Chamber of Commerce, 2129 Main St., 760-765-1857; www.julianca.com

138

WHAT TO SEE AND DO

The Road to Julian
Take this 100-mile route from San Diego to the picturesque mountain town of Julian, a popular site for exploring antique stores. There are many state parks along the way for hiking. From San Diego, take Interstate 8 (east) to Route 67 (north) to Highway 78 (east) to Julian. (Anza-Borrego Desert State Park lies to the east, but don't try to drive there unless two days are available for touring). Highway 79 then heads south from Julian (passing Cuyamaca Reservoir and rugged Cuyamaca Rancho State Park) to Interstate 8, which leads west back to San Diego. Julian is filled with restaurants and bed and breakfasts.

Eagle and High Peak Mines
C St., Julian, 760-765-0036
Tour the former gold mine tunnels where miners worked by candlelight a century ago and learn about the one-time economic mainstay of this historic little town. Tours, which last about one hour, travel into a 1,000-foot hard-rock tunnel where gold mining and milling processes can be seen.

Julian Pioneer Museum
2811 Washington St., Julian,
760-765-0227
Learn more about the mid-19th century gold town and check out what's said to be the finest lace collection in California. Nearby restaurants and shops sell the famous Julian apple pie. April-November Friday-Sunday 10 a.m.-4 p.m.; December-March Saturday-Sunday 10 a.m.-4 p.m.

SPECIALTY LODGINGS

Julian Gold Rush Hotel
2032 Main St., Julian,
760-765-0201, 800-734-5854;
www.julianhotel.com
Built in 1897 and lovingly restored, this tree-shaded landmark—the oldest continuously operating hotel in Southern California—maintains the Victorian-era flavor of the old mining town. All rooms feature private baths and are decorated with antiques and authentic period furniture. The adjoining

patio cottage and honeymoon house offer additional privacy with romantic amenities like fireplaces, verandas and claw-foot tubs.

16 rooms. Complimentary full breakfast. **$**

Orchard Hill Country Inn
2502 Washington St., Julian,
760-765-1700, 800-716-7242;
www.orchardhill.com

Opened in 1994, the Orchard Hill Country Inn has the feel of a rustic mountain lodge. The large inn has 22 individually decorated guest rooms. The deluxe cottage rooms have porches, patios or decks and include fireplaces.

22 rooms. Complimentary full breakfast. **$$**

LA JOLLA

This upscale community is known as the "Jewel of San Diego." Sandstone bluffs laced with white sand and sparkling ocean evoke the French Riviera. La Jolla is also a recognized center for scientific research.
Information: La Jolla Town Council, 858-454-1444; www.lajolla.com

WHAT TO SEE AND DO

Birch Aquarium at Scripps
2300 Expedition Way, La Jolla,
858-534-3474; aquarium.ucsd.edu
See undersea creatures in realistic habitats at this aquarium situated on a hill with spectacular ocean views. Tidepool exhibit. Beach and picnic areas nearby. At Scripps Institution of Oceanography, University of California, San Diego. Daily 9 a.m.-5 p.m.

The Comedy Store
916 Pearl St., La Jolla, 858-454-9176;
www.thecomedystore.com/2000/lajolla.htm
David Letterman got his start at this branch of the Los Angeles club franchise. Sunday is open-mike night (two drink minimum). Wednesday-Thursday, Sunday 8 p.m.; Friday-Saturday 8 p.m. and 10:30 p.m.

Kellogg Park
8200 Camino Del Oro, La Jolla,
619-235-1169
Swimming, snorkeling, surfing, beach, small-boat landing. Boardwalk, picnic areas. Daily dawn-dusk.

La Jolla Cove
1100 Coast Blvd., La Jolla, 619-221-8901;
www.sannet.gov/lifeguards/beaches/cove.shtml
Located at the southern edge of the San Diego-La Jolla Underwater Park, the cove is an ecologically protected area. The tiny

beach is a great place to sunbathe, snorkel or scuba dive and check out the seals. Divers can enjoy visibility of more than 30 feet—the waters are ideal for photography and videography. Every year around Halloween, divers participate in an underwater pumpkin-carving contest held by local diving company Ocean Enterprises. Daily.

La Jolla Playhouse
2910 La Jolla Village Dr., La Jolla,
858-550-1010; www.lajollaplayhouse.com
This Tony Award-winning venue has long been one of America's premier regional theatres. Gregory Peck, Dorothy McGuire and Mel Ferrer founded it in 1947. Located on the campus of the University of California, San Diego, the playhouse puts on six shows per season. Although *Thoroughly Modern Millie* and *Rent* played here, the playhouse is best known for taking chances on new works. Performances Monday noon-6 p.m., Tuesday-Saturday noon-8 p.m., Sunday noon-7 p.m.

Museum of Contemporary Art
700 Prospect St., La Jolla,
858-454-3541;
www.mcasd.org
Permanent and changing exhibits of contemporary paintings, sculptures, design, photography and architecture. Sculpture garden, bookstore, films, lecture programs. Monday-Tuesday, Friday-Sunday 11 a.m.-5 p.m., Thursday to 7 p.m.

139

SOUTHERN CALIFORNIA

Torrey Pines State Reserve
12000 N. Torrey Pines Rd., La Jolla,
858-755-2063;
www.torreypine.org

The 1,750-acre Torrey Pines State Reserve was established to protect the world's rarest pine tree, the gnarly, malformed Torrey Pine, which hundreds of years ago covered Southern California. Today, they are found only on Santa Rosa Island off the coast of Santa Barbara and in the La Jolla reserve. There are miles of unspoiled beaches and eight miles of hiking trails here. Visitor center and museum daily 9 a.m.-sunset, guided nature walks weekends and holidays, 10 a.m. and 2 p.m. and educational programs. Daily 8 a.m.-sunset

Torrey Pines Gliderport
2800 Torrey Pines Scenic Dr.,
La Jolla, 858-452-9858;
www.flytorrey.com

Soar 50 to 150 feet above the pines. Instructors give 20 minutes of paragliding lessons on the ground before sending guests up in tandem with their teachers. Hang gliding is offered as well, but eight lessons are needed to earn a beginner rating before taking flight. Daily.

University of California, San Diego
9500 Gilman Dr., La Jolla,
858-534-2230;
www.ucsd.edu

Scattered around campus is an outdoor collection of contemporary sculpture. Campus tours.

Windansea Surfing
6800 Neptune Place, La Jolla,
619-221-8874;
www.sannet.gov/lifeguards/beaches/
windan.shtml

Windansea boasts intense breaks created by underwater reefs. The only drawback: Everyone knows about it. On the best days, Windansea's concentrated surf breaks get crowded very quickly and even ambitious amateurs are advised to stay out of the way.

SPECIAL EVENTS
Wine and Roses Charity Tasting Event
The Westgate Hotel, 1055 Second Ave.,
San Diego, 619-583-9463;
www.wineandroses.net

Taste the gold, silver and bronze medal winners from the largest wine competition held each year in San Diego. Proceeds from the event go to charity. Wines available for purchase. Mid-June.

HOTELS
★★★★Best Western Inn by the Sea
7830 Fay Ave., La Jolla,
858-459-4461, 800-462-9732;
www.bestwestern.com

134 rooms. Complimentary continental breakfast. Restaurant. Tennis. $$

★★★★Embassy Suites Hotel San Diego-La Jolla
4550 La Jolla Village Dr., San Diego,
858-453-0400, 800-362-2779;
www.embassysuites.hilton.com

335 rooms, all suites. Complimentary full breakfast. High-speed Internet access. Restaurant, bar. Fitness center. Pool. $$

★★Grande Colonial Hotel
910 Prospect St., La Jolla,
858-454-2181, 888-530-5766;
www.thegrandecolonial.com

75 rooms. Restaurant. Pool. $$

★★Hotel La Jolla
7955 La Jolla Shores Dr., La Jolla,
858-459-0261, 800-666-0261;
www.hotellajolla.com

108 rooms. Complimentary continental breakfast. Restaurant, bar. Fitness center. Pool. $$

★★★La Jolla Shores Hotel
8110 Camino Del Oro, La Jolla,
858-459-8271, 800-640-7702;
www.ljshoreshotel.com

This beautiful 1970 Spanish-style hotel is located on the beach. The spacious rooms are decorated with white paneled walls and bamboo furniture and offer garden, coastal

★
★
★
★
★

and oceanfront views. Hit the beach for some kayaking or just to lounge (the hotel provides chairs and umbrellas). The Shores restaurant specializes in steak and seafood and has a romantic oceanfront setting with beautiful sunset views. Another dining option is the nightly beach barbecue, available by reservation.

129 rooms. Restaurant, bar. Fitness center. Pool. Tennis. **$$**

★★★Empress Hotel of La Jolla
7766 Fay Ave., La Jolla,
858-454-3001, 888-369-9900;
www.empress-hotel.com

This elegant hotel is located near the Birch Aquarium and the University of California, San Diego. The rooms are large and comfortable. There's fantastic food on-site: Manhattan's is located just off the lobby and is one of the most popular fine-dining restaurants in the area.

77 rooms. Complimentary continental breakfast. Restaurant, bar. Fitness center. **$$**

★★★Hotel Parisi
1111 Prospect, La Jolla,
858-454-1511, 877-472-7474;
www.hotelparisi.com

This hotel goes above and beyond to help visitors relax, from the award-winning feng shui design to the wide range of Eastern-inspired bodywork in the spa—there's even an on-call psychologist. The elegant rooms have goose down comforters, Egyptian cotton sheets and gourmet coffee makers. Luxury apartments with full-size kitchens are also available for extended stays.

20 rooms. Complimentary continental breakfast. **$$$**

★★★Hyatt Regency La Jolla at Avertine
3777 La Jolla Village Dr., San Diego,
858-552-1234; www.hyatt.com

Situated on 11 acres, this elegant hotel is minutes away from beaches, golf and museums. The rooms have been recently remodeled and include down comforters and Portico bath products. The biggest draw may

be the Sporting Club and the Spa, a 32,000-square-foot fitness center that includes a full-sized basketball court, two lighted tennis courts and a variety of classes, in addition to pampering treatments.

419 rooms. Restaurant, bar. Business center. **$$$**

★★★La Valencia
1132 Prospect St., La Jolla, 858-454-0771,
800-451-0772; www.lavalencia.com

Perched on a bluff overlooking the Pacific in the center of town, the "pink lady," as this hotel is called, has been a popular choice since it opened in 1926. The hotel effortlessly blends old-world charm with modern-day conveniences. In the rooms, large windows open out to views of the flourishing gardens, ocean or village. Locals adore the Whaling Bar and Grill, while couples head for the tiny Sky Room with 180-degree ocean views.

115 rooms. High-speed Internet access. Three restaurants, two bars. Beach. Pets accepted. **$$$$**

★★Sheraton La Jolla Hotel
3299 Holiday Court, La Jolla,
858-453-5500, 800-325-3535;
www.sheraton.com

252 rooms. Restaurant, bar. Airport transportation available. Business center. **$$**

★★★Hilton La Jolla Torrey Pines
10950 N. Torrey Pines Rd., La Jolla,
858-558-1500, 800-762-6160;
www.hilton.com

This full-service resort overlooks the famed oceanfront links of the Torrey Pines Golf Course in the heart of La Jolla. Advance reservations at the coveted course are available to guests. Rooms and suites feature plush bathrobes, luxury beds and Crabtree and Evelyn products, and all boast a private balcony or deck overlooking the links, ocean or garden. The Torreyana Grille serves up steaks and seafood prepared in a Pacific Rim style.

394 rooms. Restaurant, bar. Children's activity center. Fitness center. Golf. Tennis. Business center. **$$**

★

★

★

★

★

★★★★Lodge at Torrey Pines
11480 N. Torrey Pines Rd.,
La Jolla, 858-453-4420;
www.lodgetorreypines.com
The Lodge sits on a rocky cliff overlooking the Pacific Ocean and is surrounded by protected forest and unspoiled beaches. The view is gorgeous, but many are drawn by another aspect of the location: the lodge neighbors the 18th hole of one of the world's most acclaimed golf courses. Tee times are guaranteed for guests who want to try their hand at the championship course. The resort itself is a celebration of the American Craftsman period, from its stained glass and handcrafted woodwork to its Stickley-style furnishings. The warm guest rooms offer views of the golf course and ocean courtyard, and many have fireplaces.

170 rooms. High-speed Internet access. Two restaurants, two bars. Fitness room, fitness classes available, spa. Tennis. Airport transportation available. **$$$**

★★★Bed and Breakfast Inn at La Jolla
7753 Draper Ave., La Jolla,
858-456-2066, 800-582-2466;
www.innlajolla.com
Constructed in 1913 using "Cubist" architecture, this inn offers sunny guest rooms with either ocean or garden views. Personalized touches, including terry robes, fresh flowers and fine sherry in a crystal decanter in each room round out the experience.

16 rooms. Children over 12 years only. Complimentary full breakfast. Beach nearby. **$$**

SPECIALTY LODGINGS

La Jolla Inn
1110 Prospect St., La Jolla,
858-454-0133, 888-855-7829;
www.lajollainn.com
22 rooms. Complimentary continental breakfast. **$$**

Scripps Inn
555 Coast Blvd. South, La Jolla,
858-454-3391; www.scrippsinn.com
14 rooms. Complimentary full breakfast. Beach. **$$**

RESTAURANTS

★★★★A.R. Valentien
11480 N. Torrey Pines Rd., La Jolla,
858-453-4220; www. lodgetorreypines.com
La Jolla's Lodge at Torrey Pines may be best known for its golf, but its much-lauded restaurant, A.R. Valentien, gives the sport a run for its money. Named after a Craftsman-style California artist, the dining room is a showcase of stained glass lighting and Mission-style furnishings. It also shows off its pride of place with large windows overlooking the 18th hole and a clubby, timbered style. The quality of the ingredients is a focus of Chef Jeff Jackson, who delivers stand-out traditional American cooking. It isn't just happenstance that the restaurant is on the 18th hole – it does serve as the ideal 19th hole.

American menu. Dinner. Reservations recommended. **$$$**

★Ashoka
8008 Girard Ave., La Jolla, 858-454-6263
Indian menu. Dinner. Closed Monday. Casual attire. Outdoor seating. **$$**

★★★Azul
1250 Prospect St., La Jolla, 858-454-9616;
www.azul-lajolla.com
Nibble on sweet warm crab and artichoke palmieres or grilled Nebraska corn-fed beef ribeye maki roll while taking in the sweeping views of the Pacific. The menu features fresh seafood and local ingredients.

California menu. Lunch, dinner. Bar. Children's menu. Casual attire. Valet parking. Outdoor seating. **$$$**

★★Brockton Villa
1235 Coast Blvd., La Jolla,
858-454-7393;
www.brocktonvilla.com
American menu. Breakfast, lunch, dinner. Casual attire. Outdoor seating. **$$$**

★★Cafe Japengo
8960 University Center Lane, La Jolla,
858-450-3355
Japanese menu. Lunch, dinner. Casual attire. Valet parking. Outdoor seating. **$$$**

SOUTHERN CALIFORNIA

★The Cottage
7702 Fay Ave., La Jolla,
858-454-8409;
www.cottagelajolla.com
California menu. Breakfast, lunch, dinner.
Children's menu. Casual attire. **$$**

★Daily's Fit and Fresh
8915 Towne Centre Dr., La Jolla,
858-453-1112; www.dailysrestaurant.com
Vegetarian menu. Lunch, dinner. Closed
Sunday. Children's menu. Casual attire.
Outdoor seating. **$$**

★★★★The Dining Room at Jack's
7863 Girard Ave., La Jolla,
858-465-8111;
www.jackslajolla.com
Part of a cluster of restaurants and lounges all
under one roof in downtown La Jolla (Jack's
Grille and Jack's Ocean Room are the other
two dining outlets and there are multiple
lounges), the Dining Room is undoubtedly
the star of the group. Chef Tony DiSalvo
gives San Diegoans some of the best food in
the area. The menu looks traditional at first,
but look again—dishes include lobster with
Kaffir lime juice and sticks of Fuji apple, or
spice-crusted black sea bass with Japanese
eggplant. The room is crisp and elegant, with
tall banquettes to snuggle up in as well as
white-linen topped tables for lingering over
decadent desserts like chocolate caramel cus-
tard.
   Seafood menu. Dinner. Reservations rec-
ommended. **$$$**

★★Elarios
7955 La Jolla Shores Dr., La Jolla,
858-551-3620; www.elarios.com
California menu. Breakfast, lunch, dinner,
Sunday brunch. Bar. Casual attire. **$$**

★★★Fleming's Prime Steakhouse & Wine Bar
8970 University Center Lane, La Jolla,
858-535-0078;
www.flemingssteakhouse.com
In addition to the usual steaks (Porterhouse,
New York), you'll find some delicious sur-
prises on the menu, such as the smoked

salmon flatbread with goat cheese and dill
spread and the Australian lamb chops.
   American, steak menu. Dinner. Bar.
Casual attire. Outdoor seating. Reserva-
tions accepted. **$$$**

★★Manhattan
7766 Fay Ave., La Jolla, 858-459-0700
Italian menu. Lunch, dinner. Closed Saturday-
Monday. Bar. Casual attire. **$$$**

★★★Marine Room
2000 Spindrift Dr., La Jolla, 858-459-7222;
www.marineroom.com
In operation since 1941, this restaurant
owned by the La Jolla Beach & Tennis
Club features seafood dishes such as spin-
ach-wrapped oysters and abalone mush-
room-crusted organic salmon.
   French, International menu. Dinner. Bar.
Casual attire. **$$**

★★★Piatti Ristorante
2182 Avenida de la Playa, La Jolla,
858-454-1589; www.piatti.com
With its open kitchen and stone pizza
hearth, this warm restaurant resembles an
Italian trattoria. Sit in the terra cotta dining
room or out on the fountain patio.
   Italian menu. Lunch, dinner. Bar. Casual
attire. Outdoor seating. **$$**

★★★Roppongi
875 Prospect St., La Jolla, 858-551-5252;
www.roppongiusa.com
Restaurateur Sami Ladeki has hit the jackpot
with this popular dining spot. The tapas—
Polynesian crab stack, crispy buttermilk
onion rings and local halibut carpaccio are
just a few—are irresistible. There's also a
sushi and regular dinner and lunch menus.
   Asian fusion menu. Lunch, dinner. Bar.
Reservations recommended. Valet parking.
Outdoor seating. **$$$**

★★Sammy's California Wood-Fired Pizza
702 Pearl St., La Jolla,
858-456-5222;
www.sammyspizza.com
California menu. Lunch, dinner. Casual
attire. Outdoor seating. **$$**

★
★
★
★
★

★★★Sante Ristorante

7811 Herschel Ave., La Jolla,
858-454-1315; www.santeristorante.com
After a popular run in New York at La
Fenice, Tony Buonsante brought his authentic Northern Italian cooking to La Jolla in this intimate, elegant space. Dishes include eggless ricotta dumplings with Gruyère cheese and hearty lasagna Bolognese. Dine on the sidewalk terraces, in the elegant dining room with white tablecloths or at the cozy bar where you can browse the celebrity photographs.

Italian menu. Lunch, dinner. Bar. Casual attire. Outdoor seating. **$$**

★★★Sky Room Restaurant

1132 Prospect St., La Jolla, 858-454-0771;
www.lavalencia.com
If you're looking for a romantic dinner spot, the Sky Room is the place to go. Located in the elegant La Valencia Hotel, this intimate restaurant (there are only 12 booths and tables), offers breathtaking, 180-degree views of the Pacific Ocean. Formal, attentive service and a seasonal menu of contemporary French cuisine complement the scenery.

French menu. Dinner. Jacket required. **$$$**

★★★Tapenade

7612 Fay Ave., La Jolla, 858-551-7500;
www.tapenaderestaurant.com
The first item to arrive at your table when you dine at this restaurant is, of course, tapenade. What follows is expertly prepared southern French food meant to evoke a summer day in Provence. Dishes include aged sirloin with black peppercorn sauce made with cognac and pommes frites and roasted duck breast with Yukon gold garlic mashed potatoes. Be sure to save room for the cheese plate or coconut crème brûlée.

French menu. Lunch, dinner. Bar. Casual attire. Outdoor seating. **$$$**

★★Trattoria Acqua

1298 Prospect St., La Jolla, 858-454-0709;
www.trattoriaacqua.com
Italian, seafood menu. Lunch, dinner. Casual attire. **$$**

SPAS

★★★★The Spa at Torrey Pines

11480 N. Torrey Pines Rd., La Jolla,
858-453-4420, 800-656-0087
This spa at the Lodge at Torrey Pines has an oceanfront setting and surrounding forest that influence many of the treatments. There are numerous water treatments, including balneotherapy, a seawater bath in a hydrotherapy tub. Body scrubs use coastal sage and pine for exfoliation. Several facials combat aging, including a Champagne facial that uses yeast extracts and bubbly. The spa also has a list of rituals on the menu, which blend body treatments with massage. The Aromasoul Ritual, for instance, uses Chinese massage techniques to increase the flow of energy and replenish vitality.

OCEANSIDE

Oceanside is the third largest city in San Diego County. Together with Vista and Carlsbad, it makes up a tri-city area. It's just south of Camp Pendleton, the busiest U.S. Marine base in the country (Interstate 5 goes through the camp property for about 18 miles). The Oceanside Pier, first built in 1888, is the longest wooden pier on the western coastline. The bungalow house featured in *Top Gun* is located on South Pacific Street.

Information: Chamber of Commerce, Visitor Information Center, 928 N. Coast Hwy.,
800-350-7873, 760-722-1534; www.oceansidechamber.com

WHAT TO SEE AND DO

Antique Gas & Steam Engine Museum

2040 N. Santa Fe Ave., Vista,
760-941-1791, 800-587-2286;
www.agsem.com
Located in Guajome Regional Park in north San Diego County, this museum, working farm and restoration area will fill you in on agriculture, construction and early industrial trades between 1849 and 1949. Daily 10 a.m.-4 p.m.

California Surf Museum
223 N. Coast Hwy., Oceanside,
760-721-6876; www.surfmuseum.org
Learn everything about the sport through various exhibits and presentations. Tours by appointment. Daily 10 a.m.-4 p.m.

HOTELS
★Best Western Marty's Valley Inn
3240 E. Mission Ave., Oceanside,
760-757-7700, 800-747-3529;
www.bestwestern.com

111 rooms. Complimentary continental breakfast. Bar. Pool. $

★Best Western Oceanside Inn
1680 Oceanside Blvd.,
Oceanside,
760-722-1821, 800-443-9995;
www.bestwestern.com
80 rooms. Complimentary continental breakfast. Pool. $
   Lplants and animals in little pockets of the earth. Daily.

SAN JUAN CAPISTRANO
San Juan Capistrano developed around the Catholic mission for which it was named. Many of the buildings in town resemble the Spanish architecture of the church.
Information: Chamber of Commerce, 31421 La Matanza St., 92675,
949-493-4700;
www.sanjuanchamber.com

WHAT TO SEE AND DO
Mission San Juan Capistrano
Ortega Highway & Camino Capistrano, San Juan Capistrano, 949-234-1300;
www.missionsjc.com
Founded by Fray Junipero Serra in 1776 and named for the crusader St. John of Capistrano, the church was built in the form of a cross and was one of the most beautiful of all California missions. A self-guided tour includes the Serra Chapel, which is one of the oldest buildings in California, the padres' living quarters and three museum rooms exhibiting artifacts from Native American and early Spanish cultures. The mission is also famous for its swallows, which depart each year on St. John's Day (October 23) and return on St. Joseph's Day (March 19). Daily 8:30 a.m.-5 p.m.

O'Neill Museum
31831 Los Rios St.,
San Juan Capistrano,
949-493-8444;
www.sjchistoricalsociety.com/museum.html
Housed in a restored Victorian house, this museum features collections of historical photographs, rare books, Native American artificats and period furniture and clothing.

Tuesday-Friday 9 a.m.-4 p.m.; Saturday-Sunday noon-3 p.m.

Ronald W. Caspers Wilderness Park
33401 Ortega Hwy., San Juan Capistrano,
949-923-2210;
www.ocparks.com/caspers
This wilderness on 8,060 acres includes a nature center, and riding and hiking trails. Camping. Inquire in advance for camping and trail use information and restrictions. No pets. Daily 7 a.m.-sunset.

San Juan Capistrano Regional Library
31495 El Camino Real,
San Juan Capistrano, 949-493-1752;
www.ocpl.org/15brnch.asp
This postmodern building designed by Michael Graves combines Spanish, Egyptian, Greek and pre-Columbian American influences in its design. Monday-Wednesday 10 a.m.-8 p.m., Thursday to 6 p.m., Saturday to 5 p.m., Sunday noon-5 p.m.; tours by appointment.

Tour of Old Adobes
31831 Los Rios St., San Juan Capistrano,
949-493-8444;
www.sjchistoricalsociety.com/tour.html

SOUTHERN CALIFORNIA

Sponsored by the San Juan Capistrano Historical Society. Sunday 1 p.m.

SPECIAL EVENTS
Festival of Whales
Dana Point Harbor, 34675 Golden Lantern, San Juan Capistrano,
949-472-7888, 888-440-4309;
www.dpfestivalofwhales.com
Educational and entertainment events celebrating the return of the California gray whales each season. Mid-March, weekends.

Fiesta de las Golondrinas
Downtown San Juan Capistrano,
949-493-1976;
www.swallowsparade.com
This fiesta celebrates the return of the swallows to the mission with a dance pageant, art exhibits and a parade. Mid-March.

HOTELS
★Best Western Capistrano Inn
27174 Ortega Hwy., San Juan Capistrano,
949-493-5661, 800-441-9438;
www.bestwestern.com
108 rooms. Pets accepted. Pool. **$**

RESTAURANTS
★★El Adobe de Capistrano
31891 Camino Capistrano,
San Juan Capistrano, 949-493-1163
Mexican menu. Lunch, dinner, Sunday brunch. Bar. Children's menu. Outdoor seating. **$$**

★★L'Hirondelle
31631 Camino Capistrano,
San Juan Capistrano,
949-661-0425
French menu. Lunch, dinner, Sunday brunch. Outdoor seating. **$$**

SAN LUIS OBISPO

San Luis Obispo (Spanish for St. Louis, the Bishop) is located about halfway between San Francisco and Los Angeles on the Central Coast. The city, referred to locally as SLO or "San Luis," is the home of California Polytechnic State University. One of California's oldest communities, it was built around the Mission San Luis Obispo de Tolosa, founded by Father Fray Junipero Serra in 1772. After the thatched mission roofs burned several times, a tile-making technique was developed that soon set the style for all California missions. Located in a bowl-shaped valley, the town depends on government employment, tourism, agriculture and its university population.
Information: Chamber of Commerce, 1039 Chorro St., 93401, 805-781-2777;
www.slochamber.org

WHAT TO SEE AND DO
Ah Louis Store
800 Palm St., San Luis Obispo,
805-543-4332
A leader of the Chinese community, Ah Louis was an extraordinary man who achieved prominence at a time when Asians were given few opportunities. The two-story 1874 building, which served as the Chinese bank, post office and general merchandise store, was the cornerstone of the Chinese community. Monday-Saturday.

California Polytechnic State University
San Luis Obispo, 805-756-1111;
www.calpoly.edu

On the campus are three art galleries; working livestock and farm units; and horticultural, architectural and experimental displays. Campus tours Monday-Friday, 11:10 a.m.-12:30 p.m.; reservations required.

Performing Arts Center of San Louis Obispo
1 Grand Ave., San Luis Obispo,
805-756-2787; www.pacslo.org
Professional dance, theater, music and other performances.

Shakespeare Press Museum
California Polytechnic State University,
Graphic Communications Bldg.,
San Luis Obispo, 805-756-1108

Features a collection of 19th-century printing presses, type and related equipment; demonstrations for prearranged tours. Monday, Wednesday.

Mission San Luis Obispo de Tolosa
751 Palm St., San Luis Obispo,
805-781-8214;
www.missionsanluisobispo.org
The fifth of the California missions founded in 1772 still serves as the parish church. An eight-room museum also contains an extensive Chumash collection and artifacts from early settlers. The first olive orchard in California was planted here, and two original trees still stand. Daily 9 a.m.-5 p.m.

San Luis Obispo County Museum and History Center
696 Monterey St., San Luis Obispo,
805-543-0638; www.slochs.org
(1905) Local history exhibits and decorative arts. Wednesday-Sunday 10 a.m.-4 p.m.

SPECIAL EVENTS
Madonnari Italian Street Painting Festival
Mission Plaza, Monterey and
Chorro Streets, San Luis Obispo,
805-781-2777
Local artists decorate the streets around the mission with chalk drawings. Music, Italian cuisine and open-air market. Mid-September.

Mozart Festival
3165 Broad St., San Luis Obispo,
805-781-3008; www.mozartfestival.com
Recitals, chamber music, orchestra concerts and choral music held at various locations throughout the county—including Mission San Luis Obispo de Tolosa and California Polytechnic State University campus. Mid-July-early August.

Renaissance Festival
1087 Santa Rosa St., San Luis Obispo
Celebration of the Renaissance with period costumes, food booths, entertainment, arts and crafts. July.

SLO International Film Festival
San Luis Obispo,
805-546-3456;
www.slofilmfest.org
This festival showcases the history and art of filmmaking with screenings of new releases, classics, short films and documentaries. Additional events include seminars, a film competition and the annual sing-along, where moviegoers dress as characters from the featured musical and channel their inner Julie Andrews. Early-mid-March.

HOTELS
★Best Western Royal Oak Hotel
214 Madonna Rd., San Luis Obispo,
805-544-4410, 800-545-4410;
www.bestwestern.com
99 rooms. Complimentary continental breakfast. Pets accepted. Pool. $

★★Embassy Suites
333 Madonna Rd., San Luis Obispo,
805-549-0800;
www.embassysuitesslo.com
196 rooms, all suites. Complimentary full breakfast. High-speed Internet access. Restaurant, two bars. $$

★Holiday Inn Express
1800 Monterey St., San Luis Obispo,
805-544-8600, 800-465-4329;
www.hiexpress.com
100 rooms. Pets accepted. Pool. $

★★Quality Suites
1631 Monterey St., San Luis Obispo,
805-541-5001, 800-228-5151;
www.qualitysuites.com
138 rooms, all suites. Complimentary continental breakfast. High-speed Internet access. $

★Sands Suites & Motel
1930 Monterey St.,
San Luis Obispo,
805-544-0500, 800-441-4657;
www.sandssuites.com
70 rooms. Complimentary continental breakfast. Pets accepted. $

★
★
★
★
★

★★★Apple Farm Trellis Court
2015 Monterey St., San Luis Obispo,
805-544-2040, 800-255-2040;
www.applefarm.com
This quaint hotel combines the charm of a Victorian Inn with the conveniences of a luxury hotel. Rooms feature four-poster beds, fireplaces and high speed Internet. There are free treats, including an evening wine reception and welcome basket.
69 rooms. Restaurant. Airport transportation available. Pool. **$**

SPECIALTY LODGINGS
Garden Street Inn
1212 Garden St., San Luis Obispo,
805-545-9802, 800-488-2045;
www.gardenstreetinn.com
Restored Victorian house (1887) furnished with antiques.
13 rooms. Complimentary full breakfast. **$$$**

Madonna Inn
100 Madonna Rd., San Luis Obispo,
800-543-9666; www.madonnainn.com
Picture ornately carved hardwood, brightly-colored leather, gold plating and uniquely decorated rooms with everything from hot-pink carpeting to antique-car wallpapering. Even those not staying the night may want to grab a drink in the famous horseshoe-shaped bar.
109 rooms. Restaurant, bar. Airport transportation available. **$$**

RESTAURANTS
★★1865 Restaurant
1865 Monterey St., San Luis Obispo,
805-544-1865; www.1865.com
Seafood, steak menu. Lunch, dinner. Closed Sunday. Bar. Business casual attire. Reservations recommended. **$$**

★Apple Farm
2015 Monterey St., San Luis Obispo,
805-544-6100; www.applefarm.com
American menu. Breakfast, lunch, dinner. Children's menu. Casual attire. **$$**

★★Cafe Roma
1020 Railroad Way., San Luis Obispo,
805-541-6800
Italian menu. Lunch, dinner. Closed Sunday. Bar. Casual attire. Reservations recommended. **$$**

★Cisco's
778 Higuera St., San Luis Obispo,
805-543-5555; www.cisco-slo.com
American menu. Lunch, dinner. Children's menu. Casual attire. Outdoor seating. **$**

SAN SIMEON
San Simeon is an historic whaling village where sea lion-, otter- and whale-watching are all popular during northward migration in March-May, as well as in December-January, when southward migration occurs. Deep-sea fishing is popular all year.
Information: Chamber of Commerce, 250 San Simeon Ave., Ste. 3A, 93452, 805-927-3500; www.sansimeon-chamber.org

HOTELS
★★Best Western Cavalier Oceanfront Resort
9415 Hearst Dr., San Simeon,
805-927-4688, 800-826-8168;
www.cavalierresort.com
90 rooms. Restaurant, bar. Pets accepted. Pool. **$**

SANTA BARBARA

Spanish charm hangs over this city, with its colorful street names, adobe buildings and beautiful homes and gardens on the slopes of the Santa Ynez Mountains. It faces east and west on the Pacific Ocean along the calmest stretch of the California coast. Many wealthy people call this home—including Oprah. The large harbor can accommodate many boats (boat rentals and excursions are available). A Ranger District office of the Los Padres National Forest is located in Santa Barbara.

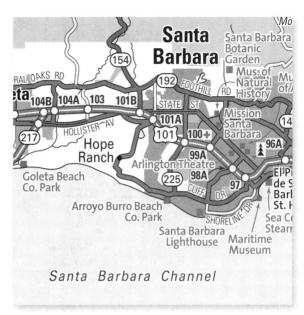

Information: Conference and Visitors Bureau & Film Commission, 1601 Anacapa St., 93101, 805-966-9222, 800-676-1266; www.santabarbaraca.com

WHAT TO SEE AND DO

Beach Areas
Santa Barbara East Beach (E. Cabrillo Blvd., next to Stearns Wharf), West Beach (W. Cabrillo Blvd., between Stearns Wharf and Harbor), and Ledbetter Beach (Shoreline Dr. and Loma Alta Dr.) are some of the outstanding beaches in Santa Barbara, known for great sand and surf, plus bike paths, picnicking and play areas. Daily.

Carpinteria State Beach
5361 Sixth St., Carpinteria,
805-968-1033; www.parks.ca.gov
Swimming, lifeguard (summer), fishing; picnicking; camping. Daily dawn-dusk.

El Paseo
Central Ave. and Main St., Santa Barbara
Courtyards and passageways similar to old Spain, with shops, art galleries and restaurants.

El Presidio de Santa Barbara State Historic Park
123 E. Canon Perdido St.,
Santa Barbara, 805-965-0093;
www.sbthp.org/presidio.htm
Original and reconstructed buildings of the last presidio (military and government outpost) built by Spain in the New World. Museum displays, slide show. Daily.

Island and Coastal Fishing Trips
301 W. Cabrillo Blvd.,
Santa Barbara,
805-963-3564
Scuba diving trips, fishing, whale-watching in season; dinner cruises.

Los Padres National Forest
3505 Paradise Rd.,
Santa Barbara,
805-967-3481;
www.fs.fed.us/r5/lospadres
This forest occupies 1,724,000 acres encompassing La Panza, Santa Ynez, San Rafael, Santa Lucia and the Sierra Madre mountains. The vegetation ranges from chaparral to oak woodlands to coniferous forests, which include the Santa Lucia fir, the rarest and one of the most unusual firs in North America. Also contains the mountainous 149,000-acre San Rafael Wilderness, the 64,700-acre Dick Smith Wilderness, the

149

SOUTHERN CALIFORNIA

★
★
★
★
★

SANTA BARBARA TO SAN SIMEON

Two days are needed to complete the entire route, but it combines exceptional coastal and mountain scenery, several interesting towns, wineries and vineyards and historic sites, including old missions and Hearst Castle. From Santa Barbara, head north into the Santa Ynez Mountains via Hwy. 154. The road passes Native American painted caves and a recreational lake. Follow Hwy. 246 west through the Santa Ynez wine country to the Danish-influenced town of Solvang, where you'll find lots of charming shops.

Continue on 246 to Hwy. 1. Near this junction is La Purisima, one of the most interesting of the state's old Franciscan missions. Hwy. 1 then goes north to dune-swept Pismo Beach, where there are plenty of restaurants to stop for lunch. Hwy. 1 (joining Hwy. 101) then veers back inland to the town of San Luis Obispo, site of another historic mission.

Travelers with only one day to tour might consider it time to head back (return to Santa Barbara via Hwy. 101). If continuing, follow Hwy. 1 (not 101) north back to the coast at Morro Bay, which is a nice place to spend the night. The seafront is lined with restaurants, many with views of Morro Rock, a bird sanctuary known as the "Gibraltar of the Pacific." The area has a number of good beaches. Montana de Oro State Park, a few miles south of Morro Bay, is one of the great undiscovered Central Coast gems.

From Morro Bay, Hwy. 1 leads north to Hearst Castle (tours take about two hours, make a reserveration). To return, take Hwy. 46 east off Hwy. 1 and then head to Hwy. 101, follow that south back to Santa Barbara. (Approximately 300 miles.)

SOUTHERN CALIFORNIA

21,250-acre Santa Lucia wilderness, as well as the Sespe Condor Refuge. Fish for trout in 485 miles of streams; hunting; hiking and riding on 1,750 miles of trails; camping.

Mission Santa Barbara
2201 Laguna St., Santa Barbara,
805-682-4713; www.sbmission.org
Founded in 1786, the present church was completed in 1820. Known as "Queen of the Missions" because of its architectural beauty, this tenth California mission stands on a slight elevation and at one time served as a beacon for sailing ships. Its twin-towered church and monastery represent the earliest phase of Spanish Renaissance architecture. Self-guided tours. Display rooms exhibit mission building arts, mission crafts and examples of Native American and Mexican art. Daily 9 a.m.-5 p.m.; closed holidays.

Moreton Bay Fig Tree
Chapala St. and Hwy. 101, Santa Barbara

Planted in 1877, this is believed to be the largest fig tree in the United States. It is considered possible for the tree to attain a branch spread of 160 feet, and a Santa Barbara city engineer estimated that 10,450 persons could stand in its shade at noon.

Santa Barbara Botanic Garden
1212 Mission Canyon Rd., Santa Barbara,
805-682-4726; www.sbbg.org
Native trees, shrubs and wildflowers of California on 65 acres; Old Mission Dam (1806). Guided tours. March-October: daily 9 a.m.-5 p.m.; November-February: Monday-Friday 9 a.m.-4 p.m., Saturday-Sunday to 5 p.m.

Santa Barbara County Courthouse
1100 Anacapa St., Santa Barbara,
805-962-6464; www.sbcourts.org
Resembles a Spanish-Moorish palace. Considered one of the most beautiful buildings in the West. Daily. Guided tours

Monday-Tuesday, Friday 10:30 a.m.; Monday-Saturday 2 p.m.

Santa Barbara Historical Museum
136 E. de la Guerra St.,
Santa Barbara, 805-966-1601;
www.santabarbaramuseum.com
Rich collections interpret the city's artistic and multicultural history from the Native American period to Spanish settlement to present day. Large, gilded Chinese Tong shrine. Library Tuesday-Friday. Museum Tuesday-Saturday 10 a.m.-5 p.m., Sunday noon-5 p.m.

Santa Barbara Maritime Museum
113 Harbor Way, Santa Barbara,
805-962-8404; www.sbmm.org
This museum at the harbor features interactive maritime-related exhibits, including historic vessels, whales, shipwrecks and a virtual-reality submarine ride. Labor Day-Memorial Day: daily 10 a.m.-5 p.m.; rest of year: to 6 p.m.

Santa Barbara Museum of Art
1130 State St., Santa Barbara,
805-963-4364; www.sbmuseart.org
Collections of ancient and Asian art, 19th-century French art, American and European paintings and sculpture, 20th-century art, photography; lectures; guided tours. Tuesday-Sunday 11 a.m.-5 p.m.

Santa Barbara Museum of Natural History
2559 Puesta del Sol Rd.,
Santa Barbara, 805-682-4711;
www.sbnature.org
Exhibits of fauna, flora, geology and pre-historic life of the Pacific coast; lectures; planetarium. Daily 10 a.m.-5 p.m.; closed first Friday in August.

Santa Barbara Zoo
500 Niños Dr., Santa Barbara,
805-962-6310;
www.santabarbarazoo.org
Zoo with walk-through aviary, monkeys, big cats, elephants and other exhibits; miniature railroad. Daily 10 a.m.-5 p.m.

Stearns Wharf
219 Stearns Wharf, Santa Barbara,
www.stearnswharf.org
Oldest operating wharf on the West Coast, with beautiful views of the harbor and city. Sport fishing piers. Restaurants and shops.

Truth Aquatics
301 W. Cabrillo Blvd., Santa Barbara,
805-962-1127; www.truthaquatics.com
Direct boat service to Channel Islands National Park (one departure daily). Call for fee information and reservations.

University of California, Santa Barbara
U.C. Santa Barbara,
Santa Barbara, 805-893-8000;
www.ucsb.edu
An 815-acre seaside campus. Tours Monday-Friday. For current performing arts activities on campus, phone 805-893-3535.

SPECIAL EVENTS
Old Spanish Days Fiesta
Carriage Western Art Museum,
129 Castillo St., Santa Barbara,
805-962-8101; www.oldspanishdays-fiesta.org
Re-creates the city's history from Native American days to arrival of American troops. Early August.

Santa Barbara International Orchid Show
Earl Warren Fairgrounds, 3400 Calle Real,
Santa Barbara, www.sborchidshow.com
Growers from around the world display their orchids. March.

Santa Barbara National Horse Show
Earl Warren Fairgrounds, 3400 Calle Real,
Santa Barbara, 805-687-0766;
www.earlwarren.com
One of the most impressive and well known horse shows in the United States, featuring champion jumpers, American Saddle Breds, Tennessee Walking horses and Welsh ponies. Mid-July.

Summer Sports Festival (Semana Nautica)
Santa Barbara, www.semananautica.com
Choose from more than 50 land and water sports, including water polo, beach

SOUTHERN CALIFORNIA

★ ★ ★ ★

volleyball, softball, running and canoeing. Late June or early July.

HOTELS

★★★★Bacara Resort & Spa
8301 Hollister Ave., Santa Barbara, 805-968-0100, 877-422-4245; www.bacararesort.com

With its spectacular setting overlooking the Pacific and dash of old-time Hollywood glamour, this resort is a jetsetter's fantasy. The luxurious rooms include Frette linens and private balconies. There are three infinity-edge pools on the grounds with 26 private cabanas. And the spa has everything to help guests relax and feel pampered, from citrus-avocado body polishes to earth crystal therapies. There's also golf, tennis, yoga, meditation and delicious California cuisine in the restaurant.

360 rooms. Restaurant, bar. Children's activity center. Pets accepted. Golf. Tennis. Business center. **$$$$**

★★Best Western Encina Lodge and Suites
2220 Bath St., Santa Barbara, 805-682-7277, 800-526-2282; www.bestwestern.com

121 rooms. High-speed Internet access. Restaurant, bar. Pool. **$$**

★★Best Western Pepper Tree Inn
3850 State St., Santa Barbara, 805-687-5511, 800-338-0030; www.bestwestern.com

150 rooms. Wireless Internet access. Restaurant, bar. Fitness center. Pool. **$$**

★★Coast Village Inn
1188 Coast Village Rd., Santa Barbara, 805-969-3266, 800-257-5131; www.coastvillageinn.com

28 rooms. Complimentary continental breakfast. High-speed Internet access. Restaurant. Pool. **$$**

★★★Fess Parker's Doubletree Resort
633 E. Cabrillo Blvd., Santa Barbara, 805-564-4333, 800-222-8733; www.fpdtr.com

This grand oceanfront resort surrounded by gardens offers world-class service, from the complimentary airport transportation to the fresh baked cookies offered upon arrival. The guest rooms are elegant, and the sprawling whitewashed property, with red-tile roofs and arched walkways, offers plenty of recreation.

360 rooms. High-speed wireless Internet access. Two restaurants, bar. **$$$**

★★★★Four Seasons Resort the Biltmore Santa Barbara
1260 Channel Dr., Santa Barbara, 805-969-2261; www.fourseasons.com

Situated on 20 lush acres on the Pacific Ocean, the resort pays tribute to the region's Spanish colonial history with its red-tiled roof, arches and hacienda-style main building. The guest rooms, located both in the main building and in separate cottages, include down pillows and luxe bathrobes. Crisp white cabanas line the sparkling pool. The world-class spa uses botanicals from the gardens.

211 rooms. High-speed Internet access. Two restaurants, bar. Spa. Pets accepted. Tennis. Business center. **$$$$**

★Franciscan Inn
109 Bath St., Santa Barbara, 805-963-8845; www.franciscaninn.com

53 rooms. Complimentary continental breakfast. **$**

★★★Harbor View Inn
28 W. Cabrillo Blvd., Santa Barbara, 800-755-0222; www.harborviewinnsb.com

It would be hard to beat the location of this upscale motor inn—it's right where the city meets the shore near Stearn's Wharf, and is just steps from the ocean. The comfortable rooms have views and private patios, and the complex includes a pool, adults-only fitness center and beautiful gardens.

96 rooms. High-speed wireless Internet access. Restaurant, bar. **$$$**

★★★Hotel Andalucia
31 W. Carrllio St., Santa Barbara,
805-884-0300, www.andaluciasb.com
Offering boutique luxury in a downtown location, this small hostelry has rooms outfitted with antiques and duvet-topped beds. A rooftop pool and deck is a prime spot for cocktails and taking in the view of the ocean. The onsite 31 West restaurant serves upscale classics like Kobe beef flat iron steak with frites or an Albacore tuna nicoise salad.

   97 rooms. Outdoor pool. Restaurant, bar. Wireless Internet access. **$$$**

★★Hotel Oceana
202 W. Cabrillo Blvd., Santa Barbara,
805-965-4577, 800-965-9776;
www.hoteloceana.com
122 rooms. Complimentary full breakfast. Wireless Internet access. Pool. **$$**

★Hotel Santa Barbara
533 State St., Santa Barbara,
805-957-9300, 888-259-7700;
www.hotelsantabarbara.com
75 rooms. Complimentary continental breakfast. **$$**

★Marina Beach Motel
21 Bath St., Santa Barbara,
805-963-9311, 877-627-4621;
www.marinabeachmotel.com
32 rooms. Complimentary continental breakfast. Pets accepted. **$**

★★★Montecito Inn
1295 Coast Village Rd., Santa Barbara,
805-969-7854, 800-843-2017;
www.montecitoinn.com
Originally built by Charlie Chaplin as a vacation spot for his Hollywood pals, the tradition of the silver screen legend lives on here with photos, memorabilia and an entire video library available for rental. While there are beautiful touches throughout the hotel, such as hand-crafted tiles, the bathrooms are small. It's just two blocks from gorgeous Butterfly Beach and convenient to local galleries and restaurants.

61 rooms. Complimentary continental breakfast. Wireless Internet access. Restaurant, bar. Exercise. Busn. center. **$$$**

★Pacifica Suites
5490 Hollister Ave., Santa Barbara,
805-683-6722, 800-338-6722;
www.pacificasuites.com
87 rooms, all suites. Complimentary full breakfast. Spa. Pets accepted. Pool. Business center. **$**

★★Santa Barbara Inn
901 E. Cabrillo Blvd., Santa Barbara,
805-966-2285
71 rooms. Restaurant, bar. Pool. Business center. **$$**

★★★★San Ysidro Ranch
900 San Ysidro Lane, Montecito,
805-969-5046, 800-368-6788;
www.sanysidroranch.com
John and Jackie Kennedy spent part of their honeymoon on this 550-acre resort, tucked away in the foothills of Montecito. Lushly planted acres are filled with fragrant flowers and plants, and stunning vistas of the Pacific Ocean and the Channel Islands can be seen in the distance. Scattered among the paths are the bungalows, which provide luxuries like wood-burning fireplaces and Frette linens. Gifted cuisine is a hallmark of this resort, and the two restaurants provide charming settings for the imaginative food.

40 rooms. High-speed Internet access. Restaurant, bar. Pets accepted. Pool. Tennis. **$$$$**

★★★Santa Ynez Valley Marriott
555 McMurray Rd., Buellton,
805-688-1000, 800-638-8882;
www.marriott.com
This Spanish-style hotel, located in the Santa Ynez Valley at the gateway to the Santa Barbara Wine Country, is near more than 60 vineyards and wineries. The spacious guest rooms are stocked with Starbucks coffee and other amenities. Enjoy the heated outdoor pool or lap pool or hit the spa or steam room. The casual buffet

SOUTHERN CALIFORNIA

breakfast in the hotel's restaurant is the perfect beginning to a busy day, and a friendly game of billiards in the Winner's Circle Pub is the perfect ending.

149 rooms. Pets accepted; restrictions. Restaurant, bar. Fitness room, spa. Outdoor pool. Tennis. Business center. **$$**

SPECIALTY LODGINGS

Cheshire Cat Inn
36 W. Valerio St., Santa Barbara,
805-569-1610;
www.cheshirecatinn.com
This intimate inn is rife with old-world Victorian charm. Each room is unique, with private balconies, whirlpools, fireplace and shabby chic decor. 17 rooms. No children allowed in main house, only cottages. Complimentary continental breakfast. Wireless Internet access. Whirlpool. **$$**

Inn on Summer Hill
2520 Lillie Ave., Summerland,
805-969-9998, 800-845-5566;
www.innonsummerhill.com
Located between Montecito and Santa Barbara, this cozy inn offers suites with views of the Pacific.

16 rooms. Complimentary continental breakfast. Whirlpool. **$$$**

Old Yacht Club Inn
431 Corona Del Mar Dr.,
Santa Barbara,
805-962-1277, 800-676-1676;
www.oldyachtclubinn.com
A perfect retreat for a romantic weekend, this huge California Craftsman inn is shaded by trees and surrounded by lush gardens and a white picket fence. Enjoy a gourmet breakfast, walk a block to the beach, then return to cocktails on the large patio.

15 rooms. Complimentary full breakfast. **$$**

Prufrock's Garden Inn by the Beach
600 Linden Ave., Carpinteria,
805-566-9696, 877-837-6257;
www.prufrocks.com
8 rooms. No children allowed. Complimentary full breakfast. **$$$**

Simpson House Inn
121 E. Arrellaga St.,
Santa Barbara,
805-963-7067, 800-676-1280;
www.simpsonhouseinn.com
Delicious country breakfasts are a highlight at this charming bed and breakfast, as are early-evening wine and hors d'oeuvres. Period furnishings and antiques characterize the rooms in the mansion. The English gardens, filled with towering oaks, blooming magnolias and tranquil fountains, are the centerpiece of this East Lake-style Victorian estate.

15 rooms. Wireless Internet access. **$$$$**

Tiffany Country House
1323 de la Vina St., Santa Barbara,
805-963-2283, 800-999-5672;
www.tiffanycountryhouse.com
Built in 1898, this restored Victorian is now one of the most unique bed and breakfasts in the area. Antique furnishings grace every room and most have fireplaces. Breakfast is served outside in the garden, while cocktails and hors d'oeuvres are served by the fire every evening.

7 rooms. Complimentary full breakfast. **$$**

White Jasmine Inn
1327 Bath St., Santa Barbara,
805-966-0589;
www.whitejasmineinnsantabarbara.com
Choose from individually decorated rooms, like the pink and flowery French Rose, the wooden-beamed Craftsman or the nautical-themed Captain's Quarters. A large living room acts as a common parlor,.

14 rooms. Complimentary full breakfast. Whirlpool. **$$**

RESTAURANTS

★★★Bella Vista
1260 Channel Dr., Santa Barbara,
805-969-2261;
www.fourseasons.com/santabarbara
Besides incredible views of the Pacific from the open-air patio or the window-lined dining room, this restaurant inside the Four Seasons Santa Barbara offers expertly prepared, locally sourced fresh and organic

SOUTHERN CALIFORNIA

food. Chef Martin Frost's specialities include free-range chicken breast filled with goat cheese, truffles, potato, eggplant and red pepper, or honey-cilantro glazed sea bass. The outdoor patio has several open-air fireplaces, perfect for cozying up to for dessert and after-dinner drinks.

California cuisine. Breakfast, lunch, dinner. Reservations recommended. Outdoor dining. Valet parking. **$$$$**

★★★Bouchon
9 W. Victoria St., Santa Barbara,
805-730-1160;
www.bouchonsantabarbara.com
Chef Josh Brown has taken advantage of the bounty of fresh ingredients from local farmers by creating a menu that draws rave reviews. This restaurant, with its farmhouse setting, open kitchen and gracious staff, is beloved by locals, and you'll taste why. Try the lemon- and thyme-glazed sea scallops or bourbon- and maple-glazed duck, paired with any number of local wines.

California, French menu. Dinner. Business casual attire. Reservations recommended. Outdoor seating. **$$$**

★★★Downey's
1305 State St., Santa Barbara,
805-966-5006; www.downeyssb.com
This unpretentious restaurant is housed in a converted storefront, providing a relaxing backdrop for the seasonal fare. Chef John Downey changes the menu each day to reflect the best of what the market has to offer. Expect simple dishes that let the ingredients speak for themselves, like porcini soup and grilled local swordfish. Well-selected California wines round out the meal.

California, French menu. Dinner. Closed Monday. Bar. Casual attire. Reservations recommended. **$$$**

★★El Paseo
10 El Paseo Place, Santa Barbara,
805-962-6050
Mexican menu. Lunch, dinner. Bar. Children's menu. Casual attire. Reservations recommended. Valet parking. Outdoor seating. **$$**

★★Harbor
210 Stearns Wharf, Santa Barbara,
805-963-3311
Seafood menu. Breakfast, lunch, dinner. Bar. Children's menu. Casual attire. Reservations recommended. Valet parking. **$$$**

★★★★Miró at Bacara Resort
8301 Hollister Ave., Santa Barbara,
805-968-1800, 877-422-4245;
www.bacararesort.com
Santa Barbara's luxurious Bacara Resort is home to the delightful Miró Restaurant. Joan Miró-style artwork, deep red dining chairs, a contemporary carpet and fantastic views of the Pacific Ocean set the scene, while behind the scenes, the chef creates masterful renditions of traditional Spanish cooking. From oak-grilled lamb chops with aged Sherry and pan-roasted lobster with oven-roasted tomatoes, the dishes are rooted in the classics but given a fresh twist. The 12,000-bottle wine cellar has something to match each meal. For a more casual alternative, the Miró Bar and Lounge features homemade sangria and tapas.

Mediterranean menu. Dinner. **$$$**

★★Opal's Restaurant & Bar
1325 State St., Santa Barbara,
805-966-9676;
www.opalrestaurantandbar.com
California menu. Lunch, dinner. Bar. Casual attire. Reservations recommended. Valet parking. **$$**

★★Palace Grill
8 E. Cota St., Santa Barbara,
805-963-5000; www.palacegrill.com
Cajun, Creole menu. Lunch, dinner. Bar. Casual attire. Outdoor seating. **$$**

★★Palazzio Downtown
1026 State St., Santa Barbara,
805-564-1985; www.palazzio.com
Italian menu. Lunch, dinner. Bar. Children's menu. Casual attire. Outdoor seating. **$$**

★★★Sage & Onion
34 E. Ortega St., Santa Barbara,
805-963-1012; www.sageandonion.com

155

SOUTHERN CALIFORNIA

★
★
★
★
★

A star on the Central Coast, this upscale bistro in downtown Santa Barbara offers a winning combination of food from the kitchen of co-owner/chef Steven Giles and friendly, attentive service under the amiable direction of his partner, Norbert Furnee. Seasonal menus take full advantage of the freshest local and regional ingredients, and the wine bar is a popular gathering place.

American, European menu. Lunch, dinner. Closed holidays. Bar. Casual attire. Reservations recommended. Outdoor seating. **$$$**

★★★Wine Cask
813 Anacapa St., Santa Barbara, 805-966-9463, 800-436-9463; www.winecask.com

An outgrowth of the neighboring wine shop, Wine Cask serves California fare alongside 40 by-the-glass pours and a 65-page wine list. The contemporary menu includes duck confit salad, seared foie gras and wasabi-crusted salmon. In addition to the handsome dining room, which sports an oversized fireplace and hand-painted beams, the restaurant also serves meals on its secluded patio.

American menu. Lunch, dinner. Bar. Casual attire. Reservations recommended. Outdoor seating. **$$$**

SPAS

★★★★Bacara Spa
8301 Hollister Ave., Santa Barbara, 805-968-1800, 877-422-4245; www.bacararesort.com

With the Pacific Ocean on one side and the Santa Ynez Mountains on the other, Bacara is all about location. A fitness center, a saline-filled pool and secluded nooks for sunbathing flank more than 30 treatment rooms and indoor and outdoor massage stations. The spa offers an intriguing selection of global healing regimens, and an Eastern Origin menu, which features options such as reiki and shiatsu massage. The rugged terrain of the Santa Ynez Mountains is the perfect place for a rigorous walk, run or hike. Clay tennis courts, pools almost too pretty to swim in and yoga on the beach are just a few of the other fitness options. **$$**

★★★★Spa at Four Seasons Resort Santa Barbara
1260 Channel Dr., Santa Barbara, 805-969-2261, 800-819-5053; www.fourseasons.com

This spa captures the essence of its oceanfront setting. The avocado citrus wrap is a spa signature that combines fruit extracts with sea salts and clay to hydrate and heal. The caviar facial is another signature therapy, and the Thai coconut scrub uses coconut and rice and includes a Thai foot massage. Or try a JAMU massage, which combines Chinese, Hindu and European techniques of acupressure, long strokes and rolling motions. Hair and styling services, manicures, pedicures and makeup are also available. **$$**

SOLVANG

Founded by Danes from the Midwest in 1911, a corner of Denmark has been re-created here. The picturesque scene includes Danish-style buildings and windmills, and shops full of pastries and imports.

Information: 1511-A Mission Dr., P.O. Box 70, 93464, 800-468-6765, 805-688-6144; www.solvangusa.com

WHAT TO SEE AND DO

Lake Cachuma Recreation Area
Hwy. 154, Solvang. 805-686-5054; www.sbparks.org/docs/Cachuma.html

Swimming pool (summer), fishing, boating (rentals); camping. Daily.

Old Mission Santa Ines
1760 Mission Dr., Solvang, 805-688-4815; www.missionsantaines.org

Established in 1804 by Fray Estevan Tapis ias the 19th mission in California. The gold adobe building with red-tiled roof, garden and arched colonnade in front is still used as a church, and many artifacts, manuscripts and vestments are on exhibit. Daily 9 a.m.-5:30 p.m.

SPECIAL EVENTS

Danish Days Festival

1511 Mission Dr., Solvang, 805-688-6144
Danish folk dancing, singing, band concerts and parade. Third weekend in September.

Solvang Theaterfest

420 Second St.,
Solvang, 805-686-1789;
www.solvangtheaterfest.org
The Pacific Conservatory of the Performing Arts (PCPA) presents musicals, dramas, new works and classics in an outdoor theater. Early June-early October.

HOTELS

★Royal Copenhagen Inn

1579 Mission Dr., Solvang,
805-688-5561, 800-624-6604;
www.royalcopenhageninn.com
48 rooms. Pets accepted. Pool. $

★★★Royal Scandinavian Inn

400 Alisal Rd., Solvang,
805-688-8000, 800-624-5572;
www.royalscandinavianinn.com
133 rooms. Restaurant, bar. Pool. $$

★★★Petersen Village Inn

1576 Mission Dr., Solvang,
805-688-3121, 800-321-8985;
www.peterseninn.com
Replica of an old Danish village with 28 shops on the premises and a garden area.

39 rooms. Complimentary full breakfast. Restaurant. $$$

SPECIALTY LODGINGS

Alisal Guest Ranch and Resort

1054 Alisal Rd., Solvang,
805-688-6411, 800-425-4725;
www.alisal.com
73 rooms. Restaurant, bar. Children's activity center. Golf. Tennis. $$$$

Wine Valley Inn & Cottages

1564 Copenhagen Dr., Solvang,
805-688-2111, 800-824-6444;
www.chimneysweepinn.com
Located in a tranquil neighborhood just minutes from the Santa Barbara wine region, this inn is full of old-world charm. Rooms feature canopy beds and oversized tubs. Choose one of the cottages, inspired by those in the gardens of the Palace of Versailles. Each has a kitchen, private patio and spacious living room with wood-burning fireplace. Some have lofts and private outdoor whirlpools.
56 rooms. Complimentary full breakfast. Whirlpool. Pets accepted. $$

RESTAURANTS

★Mustard Seed

1655 Mission Dr., Solvang,
805-688-1318
American menu. Breakfast, lunch, dinner. Closed Monday. Children's menu. Casual attire. Outdoor seating. $$

TEHACHAPI

Tehachapi was founded when the railroad made its way through the pass between the San Joaquin Valley and the desert to the east. The area is known for its electricity-generating wind turbines—5,000 of the approximately 15,000 wind turbines in the state are located here. The best time to see the turbines spinning is late afternoon, when heat on the nearby Mojave Desert is greatest. Historians believe the name Tehachapi is derived from a Native American word meaning "windy place." About 120 miles from Los Angeles, the area maintains a rural atmosphere with its many large ranches.
Information: Greater Tehachapi Chamber of Commerce, 209 E. Tehachapi Blvd., 93561, 661-822-4180; www.tehachapi.com/chamber

WHAT TO SEE AND DO
Tehachapi Loop
Tehachapi; www.tehachapi.com/loop
Watch trains (with 85 or more boxcars) pass over themselves when rounding the "Tehachapi Loop." Built in 1875, the loop makes it possible for trains to gain needed elevation in a short distance. It can be seen by taking Woodford-Tehachapi Road to a viewpoint just above the loop.

SPECIAL EVENTS
Indian PowWow
Tehachapi, 661-822-1118
Native American cultural and religious gathering of various tribes, open to public viewing. Dance competition, arts and crafts, museum display of artifacts. Usually last weekend in June.

Mountain Festival and PRCA Rodeo
Tehachap, 661-822-4180
Includes arts and crafts, food booths, parade, events. Third weekend in August.

HOTELS
★Best Western Mountain Inn
418 W. Tehachapi Blvd., Tehachapi, 661-822-5591, 800-780-7234; www.bestwestern.com
74 rooms, 2 story. Restaurant. $

★★The Lodge at Woodward West
18100 Lucaya Way, Tehachapi, 661-822-5581; www.stallionsprings.com
63 rooms. Restaurant, bar. Golf. Tennis. $

TEMECULA
Most people associate winemaking in California with Napa and Sonoma valleys. But there's serious Southern California wine tasting in the Temecula Valley, about two hours away. The Temecula Valley, bordered on the west by Camp Pendleton Marine Corps Base and the Cleveland National Forest, is also home to five championship golf courses and casino gambling at the local resorts.
Information: Temecula Valley Chamber of Commerce, 26790 Ynez Court Temecula, 92591 Suite 124, 909-676-5090; www.temecula.org

WHAT TO SEE AND DO
California Dreamin'
33133 Vista Del Monte Rd., Temecula, 800-373-3359; www.californiadreamin.com
This company offers sunrise balloon rides over Temecula wine country, as well as spectacular daytime forays over the Pacific and the Del Mar bluffs. The baskets accommodate six, nine or 12 people, making it perfect for families. Adrenaline junkies may prefer to schedule a ride in a World War I-style biplane. Daily.

Callaway Vineyard and Winery
32720 Rancho California Rd., Temecula, 800-472-2377; www.callawaycoastal.com
Taste the coastal wines, then grab a bite at Allies, the on-site restaurant. Daily 10 a.m.-5 p.m.

Filsinger Winery
39050 De Portola Rd., Temecula, 951-302-6363
This family-owned-and-operated winery produces about 7,000 cases of wine a year. Tours are available by appointment, or simply stop by for a tasting. Friday 11 a.m.-4 p.m., Saturday-Sunday 10 a.m.-5 p.m.

Stuart Cellars
33515 Rancho California Rd., Temecula, 888-260-0870; www.stuartcellars.com
This family-run winery is a wonderful retreat from Los Angeles. Bring a picnic lunch and enjoy it on the winery grounds, with views of the Temecula Valley. Daily 10 a.m.-5 p.m.

★
★
★
★
★

Temecula Valley Wineries

Rancho California Rd.,
Temecula, 800-801-9463;
www.temeculawines.org

More than 15 wineries produce award-winning cabernet sauvignon, chardonnay, merlot, syrah, sauvignon blanc and viognier. Each has a tasting room where you can sample the goods, and most offer tours.

SPECIAL EVENTS

Balloon and Wine Festival

Lake Skinner, 37701 Warren Rd.,
Temecula, 951-676-6713; www.tvbwf.com

Wine tasting, hot air balloon race, musical entertainment and children's activities. Early June.

HOTELS

★Ramada Inn Old Town

28980 Old Town Front St., Temecula,
951-676-8770, 888-298-2054;
www.ramada.com

70 rooms. Complimentary continental breakfast. $

★★Embassy Suites

29345 Rancho California Rd., Temecula,
951-676-5656, 800-362-2779;
www.embassysuites.com

136 rooms, all suites. Complimentary full breakfast. Restaurant, bar. $

★★★Pala Casino Resort Spa

11154 Hwy. 76, Pala,
877-946-7252, 877-725-2766;
www.palacasino.com

There's something for everyone at this resort, from shopping to theaters. Or sit down in front of one of the casino's 2,292 slot machines or 87 table games. Choose from one of eight restaurants. Spacious guest rooms feature minibars, three telephones, work desks and views of the mountains or pool.

425 rooms. Eight restaurants. Casino. $$

★★★Pechanga Resort & Casino

45000 Pechanga Pkwy., Temecula,
888-732-4264, 951-643-1819;
www.pechanga.com

Designed in the Prairie School style, this resort has spacious rooms with floor-to-ceiling windows and large bathrooms. One-bedroom suites include a wet bar, separate sleeping quarters and one and a half baths. The 188,000 square foot gaming floor makes this the biggest casino in California. Dining options abound.

522 rooms. High-speed Internet access. Seven restaurants, four bars. Airport transportation available. Casino. $

★★★Temecula Creek Inn

44501 Rainbow Canyon Rd., Temecula,
877-517-1823; www.temeculacreekinn.com

This hotel offers the perfect combination of work and play, with ample meeting space and a 27-hole golf course. Guest rooms overlook the golf course or mountains. The hotel's Temet Grill offers cuisine to complement wine from the area's many vineyards.

80 rooms. Restaurant, bar. Golf. Tennis. $

SPECIALTY LODGINGS

Loma Vista Bed and Breakfast

33350 La Serena Way, Temecula,
951-676-7047;
www.lomavistabb.com

Mission-style house surrounded by citrus groves and vineyards.

10 rooms. Complimentary full breakfast. $$

RESTAURANTS

★★Baily's

28699 Old Town Front St., Temecula,
951-676-9567; www.baily.com

American menu. Dinner. Outdoor seating. $$

★The Bank

28645 Front St., Temecula, 951-676-6160

Mexican menu. Lunch, dinner. Children's menu. Outdoor seating. $$

★★Cafe Champagne

32575 Rancho California Rd., Temecula,
951-699-0088; www.thorntonwine.com

French menu. Lunch, dinner, Sunday brunch. Bar. Outdoor seating. $$$

SOUTHERN CALIFORNIA

THOUSAND OAKS

Information: Thousand Oaks/Westlake Village Regional Chamber of Commerce, 600 Hampshire Rd., Suite 200, Westlake Village, 91361, 805-370-0035; www.towlvchamber.org

WHAT TO SEE AND DO
Camarillo Factory Stores
740 Ventura Blvd., Camarillo,
805-445-8520;
www.premiumoutlets.com
More than 100 outlet stores. Daily.

Channel Islands Aviation
305 Durley Ave., Camarillo,
805-987-1301;
www.flycia.com
Provides transportation to a number of the California Channel Islands located just off the coast from Ventura and Santa Barbara counties. Daily.

Los Robles Golf Course
299 S. Moorpark Blvd.,
Thousand Oaks, 805-495-6421;
www.losroblesgreens.com
Redesigned three times since opening in 1963, the course is constantly changing for the better. Lots of native California wildlife can be found along the course, which is only 6,304 yards from the back tees, so even the long shots should be accessible to most golfers.

HOTELS
★Best Western Camarillo Inn
295 E. Daily Dr., Camarillo, 805-987-4991;
www.bestwestern.com
58 rooms. Complimentary continental breakfast. $

★Country Inn & Suites by Carlson
1405 Del Norte Rd., Camarillo,
805-983-7171, 800-456-4000;
www.countryinns.com
100 rooms. Complimentary full breakfast. $

★★★★Four Seasons Hotel Los Angeles, Westlake Village
2 Dole Dr., Westlake Village,
818-575-3000, 800-819-5053;
www.fourseasons.com
Set on expansive, landscaped grounds, this hotel in suburban Los Angeles offers a tranquil escape from the city. Connected to the California Longevity and Health Institute, a premier medical spa, the hotel provides serenity-seeking Angelenos a place to rest up and rejuvenate themselves in style. Rooms are traditionally decorated with classic touches like mahogany furniture, chintz-covered sofas and marble bathrooms. The onsite Onyx restaurant serves light, healthful Asian cuisine.
269 rooms. Pool. Spa. $$$$

★Holiday Inn Express
4444 Central Ave., Camarillo,
805-485-3999;
www.holiday-inn.com
110 rooms. Complimentary continental breakfast. Pool. $

★★★Hyatt Westlake Plaza
880 S. Westlake Blvd.,
Westlake Village, 805-557-1234,
800-633-7313;
www.hyattwestlake.com
Spanish mission-style architecture can be found at this comfortable hotel. Amenities include a fitness center, pool and business center.
262 roomsRestaurant, bar. $$

★★★Westlake Village Inn
31943 Agoura Rd., Westlake Village,
818-889-0230, 800-535-9978;
www.westlakevillageinn.com
The property is dotted with gardens. Relax by the Mediterranean-style pool or hit the links. For practice at night, try the area's only lighted driving range. Enjoy live entertainment at Bogies, the hotel's nightclub, or dine at Le Café, the well-known bistro and wine bar on site. The inn is the perfect retreat for those wanting a quieter pace outside Los Angeles.
144 rooms. Complimentary continental breakfast. Restaurant, bar. Golf. Tennis. $$

SOUTHERN CALIFORNIA

★
★
★
★

RESTAURANTS

★**Corrigan's Steak House**
556 E. Thousand Oaks Blvd.,
Thousand Oaks, 805-495-5234
Seafood, steak menu. Breakfast, lunch,
dinner. Bar. **$$**

★★**Money Pancho**
3661 Las Posas Rd., Camarillo,
805-484-0591
Mexican menu. Breakfast, lunch, dinner.
Children's menu. **$$**

★★**Ottavio's**
1620 Ventura Blvd., Camarillo,
805-482-3810; www.ottavio.com
Italian menu. Lunch, dinner. Bar. **$$**

SPAS

★★★★**The Spa at Four Seasons Los
Angeles, Westlake Village**
2 Dole Dr., Westlake Village, 818-575-3000;
www.fourseasons.com
A 40,000 square-foot space with Asian-
influenced décor, this spa in the Four Sea-
sons Los Angeles, Westlake Village is
a tranquil spot for top-notch pampering.
Treatments also take their cue from Asian
traditions, with everything from shiatsu
to reiki making an appearance on the spa
menu. Couples can opt for a traditional
massage in the outdoor spa cabanas, which
include a private plunge pool. Or book a
spa suite for your treatment, which features
a fireplace and plunge pool. **$$$**

VALENCIA

Information: Santa Clarita Valley Chamber of Commerce,
28460 Avenue Stanford, Ste. 100, Santa Clarita, 91355, 661-702-6977;
www.scvchamber.org

WHAT TO SEE AND DO

Six Flags Magic Mountain
26101 Magic Mountain Pkwy.,
Valencia, 661-255-4100;
www.sixflags.com/parks/magicmountain
This 260-acre amusement park bills itself
as the world's only Xtreme Park. It now
has 16 megacoasters. In all, the park has
more than 100 rides, games and attractions
divided into nine themed lands. The adjacent water park, Hurricane Harbor, features
75-foot-tall enclosed speed slides, pool and
body slides, a 7,000-square-foot lagoon
with water sport and a children's Castaway
Cove. September-March: Friday-Sunday
10 a.m.-6 p.m.; April-May: Monday-Friday
10 a.m.-6 p.m., Saturday-Sunday to 8 p.m.;
June-August: daily 10 a.m.-10 p.m.

HOTELS

★**Hampton Inn**
25259 The Old Rd., Santa Clarita, 91381,
661-253-2400, 800-426-7866;
www.hampton-inn.com
130 rooms, 4 story. Complimentary continental breakfast. Pool. Busn. center. **$**

★★**Hilton Garden Inn Valencia Six Flags**
27710 The Old Rd., Valencia,
661-254-8800, 877-782-9444;
www.hiltongardeninn.com
152 rooms. Restaurant, bar. **$**

★★★**Hyatt Valencia**
24500 Town Center Dr., Valencia,
661-799-1234, 800-633-7313;
www.hyatt.com
This elegant hotel, adjacent to the Santa
Clarita Conference Center and within walking distance of great shopping, includes a
heated pool, outdoor lounge with fireplace,
a 27-hole putting course and a newly renovated fitness center. Rooms feature granite
baths with Portico products.
244 rooms. Restaurant, bar. **$$**

SOUTHERN CALIFORNIA

★
★
★
★
★

VENTURA

What was once a mission surrounded by huge stretches of sagebrush and mustard plants is now the busy city of Ventura. Today, uncrowded beaches, harbor cruises and whale-watching lure visitors here. The city is in the center of the largest lemon-producing county in the United States.

Information: Visitor & Convention Bureau Information Center, 89 S. California St., Suite C, 93001, 805-648-2075, 800-483-6214; www.ventura-usa.com

WHAT TO SEE AND DO

Albinger Archaeological Museum
113 E. Main St., Ventura, 805-648-5823
This preserved archaeological exploration site and visitor center downtown showcases evidence of Native American culture that's 3,500 years old. Audiovisual programs. Wednesday-Sunday 10 a.m.-4 p.m.

Camping
Ventura, 805-968-1033; www.parks.ca.gov
Emma Wood State Beach and McGrath State Beach: Swimming, fishing; nature trail; 170 developed campsites. North Beach: Swimming, surfing, fishing; two RV group camping sites, 61 primitive camp sites. Daily dawn-dusk.

Channel Islands National Park Visitors Center
1901 Spinnaker Dr., Ventura, 805-658-5730; www.nps.gov/chis
Scale models of the five islands; marine life exhibit; observation tower; film of the islands. Daily 8:30 a.m.-5 p.m.

Island Packer Cruises
1691 Spinnaker Dr., Ventura, 805-642-1393; www.islandpackers.com
Hop on a boat from Ventura Harbor to Channel Islands National Park. Reservations required. Memorial Day-September, five islands; rest of year, two islands.

Mission San Buenaventura
211 E. Main St., Ventura, 805-643-4318; www.sanbuenaventuramission.org
(1782) The ninth California mission and the last founded by Father Junipero Serra. Museum (enter through the gift shop at 225 E. Main St.) features the original wooden bell in the tower. Museum. Monday-Friday 10 a.m.-5 p.m., Saturday from 9 a.m., Sunday 10 a.m.-4 p.m. Church and gardens. Daily.

Olivas Adobe
4200 Olivas Park Dr., Ventura, 805-644-4346
(1847) Restored adobe with antique furnishings; displays; gardens; visitor center; video. Tours (by appointment). House open for viewing. Saturday-Sunday 10 a.m.-4 p.m. Special programs monthly.

Ortega Adobe
215 W. Main St., Ventura, 805-658-4726
(1857) Restored and furnished adobe built on the Camino Real. Furnished with rustic handmade furniture from the 1850s. Tours by appointment.

Ronald Reagan Presidential Library and Museum
40 Presidential Dr., Simi Valley, 805-577-4000, 800-410-8354; www.reaganfoundation.org
This 150,000-square-foot tribute to the 40th president occupies 100 acres atop a hill with ocean views and includes 22,000 square feet of exhibit space packed with retrospective displays. It is also the site where the former president is buried. View a full-scale replica of the Oval Office and Cabinet Room, a nuclear missile that was deactivated after the President and Mikhail Gorbachev signed the INF treaty, a section of the Berlin Wall, more than 400 magazine covers of both the President and Nancy Reagan and presidential memorabilia dating as far back as the Andrew Jackson administration. Daily 10 a.m.-5 p.m.

★
★
★
★
★

San Buenaventura State Beach
Harbor Blvd. and San Pedro, Ventura,
805-968-1033; www.parks.ca.gov
Approximately 115 acres on a sheltered sweep of coast. Offers swimming, lifeguard (summer), surf fishing; coastal bicycle trail access point; picnicking, concession. Daily dawn-dusk.

Ventura County Museum of History and Art
100 E. Main St., Ventura, 805-653-0323;
www.venturamuseum.org
See a collection of Native American, Spanish and pioneer artifacts and changing exhibits of local history and art. Outdoor areas depict the county's agricultural history. Tuesday-Sunday 10 a.m.-5 p.m.

Ventura Harbor
1583 Spinnaker Dr., Ventura,
805-642-8538, 877-894-2726;
www.venturaharbor.com
Accommodates more than 1,500 boats. Sportfishing and island boats, sailboat rentals, cruises, guest slips. Swimming, fishing; hotel, shops, restaurants. Channel Islands National Park headquarters.

SPECIAL EVENTS
Ventura County Fair
Seaside Park, 10 W. Harbor Blvd.,
Ventura, 805-648-3376;
www.seasidepark.org/fair
Parade, rodeo, carnival, entertainment and livestock auction. August.

Whale-watching
1867 Spinnaker Dr., Ventura,
805-642-1393; www.islandpackers.com
Gray whales, December-March; blue whales, July-September.

HOTELS
★★Clocktower Inn
181 E. Santa Clara St., Ventura,
805-652-0141, 800-727-1027;
www.clocktowerinn.com
49 rooms. Complimentary continental breakfast. Restaurant, bar. $

★Country Inn & Suites by Carlson
298 Chestnut St., Ventura,
805-653-1434, 800-456-4000;
www.countryinns.com
120 rooms. Complimentary full breakfast. Beach. Pool. $

★★★Marriott Ventura Beach
2055 E. Harbor Blvd., Ventura,
805-643-6000;
www.marriott.com
A good choice for business travelers or families taking in Ventura. The comfortable rooms feature the new Revive Marriott bedding. The pool, with tropical landscaping, is a nice spot to relax. The restaurant serves flavorful Baja coastal cuisine. This hotel is 100 percent non-smoking.
284 rooms. Restaurant, bar. $

SPECIALTY LODGINGS
La Mer European Bed & Breakfast
411 Poli St., Ventura,
805-643-3600
5 rooms. Children over 13 years only. Complimentary full breakfast. $

Pierpont Inn
550 SanJon Rd., Ventura,
805-643-6144, 800-285-4667;
www.pierpontinn.com
Established in 1928, this inn overlooks Pierpont Bay. 77 rooms. Complimentary continental breakfast. Restaurant, bar. Pool. $

163

VICTORVILLE
Victorville looks familiar even to newcomers, as it has been the setting for hundreds of cowboy movies. On the edge of the Mojave Desert, the town serves as a base for desert exploration.
Information: Chamber of Commerce, 14174 Green Tree Blvd., 92395,
760-245-6506;
www.vvchamber.com

WHAT TO SEE AND DO
California Route 66 Museum
16825 D St., Victorville, 760-951-0436;
www.califrt66museum.org
A tribute to the first national highway connecting Chicago with Los Angeles. Exhibits on different artists' views of Route 66 and its history. Thursday-Monday 10 a.m.-4 p.m.

Mojave Narrows Regional Park
18000 Yates Rd., Victorville, 760-245-2226;
www.co.san-bernardino.ca.us/parks/
mojave.htm
Fishing, boating; hiking, bridle trails; picnicking, snack bar; camping. Daily.

SPECIAL EVENTS
Huck Finn Jubilee
Mojave Narrows Regional Park,
18000 Yates Rd., Victorville, 760-245-2226;
www.huckfinn.com
River-raft building, fence painting, bluegrass and clogging activities, food. Father's Day weekend.

San Bernardino County Fair
14800 Seventh St., Victorville,
760-951-2200;
www.sbcfair.com
Rodeo, livestock and agricultural exhibits, carnival. May.

RESTAURANTS
★★Chateau Chang
15425 Anacapa Rd.,
Victorville, 92392,
760-241-3040.
Chinese, French menu. Lunch, dinner. Closed Sunday. Bar. $$$

VISALIA

Information: Convention and Visitors Bureau, 220 N. Santafe St., 93292, 559-713-0141; www.cvbvisalia.com

WHAT TO SEE AND DO
Chinese Cultural Center
500 S. Akers Rd., Visalia, 559-625-4545
Chinese artifacts, paintings, rare archaeological findings. Chinese garden. Confucius Temple. Wednesday-Sunday 8 a.m.-4 p.m.

Tulare County Museum
27000 S. Mooney Blvd., Visalia,
559-733-6616;
www.tularecountyhistoricalsociety.org
Ten buildings set in a 140-acre park house historical exhibits. Thursday-Monday, admission times vary by season, call for information.

HOTELS
★★Radisson Hotel Visalia
300 S. Court, Visalia,
559-636-1111, 800-333-3333;
www.radisson.com
201 rooms. Restaurant, bar. Airport transportation available. $

SPECIALTY LODGINGS
The Spalding House
631 N. Encina, Visalia, 559-739-7877;
www.thespaldinghouse.com
Fully restored Colonial Revival house built 1901. 3 rooms. Complimentary full breakfast. $

RESTAURANT
★★★The Vintage Press
216 N. Willis, Visalia,
559-733-3033; www.thevintagepress.com
Since 1966, a loyal clientele has been coming to this well-known central California restaurant to celebrate special occasions. The elegant, old-world ambience with rustic antiques complements classic dishes like New York strip. Organic, locally produced ingredients are used whenever possible, and an extensive wine list features a number of impressive selections by the glass and half-bottle.
French menu. Lunch, dinner, Sunday brunch. Bar. Children's menu. Reservations recommended. Outdoor seating. $$$

SOUTHERN CALIFORNIA

WHITTIER

This Quaker-founded community was named for John Greenleaf Whittier, the Quaker poet. At the foot of the rolling Puente Hills, this residential city was once a citrus empire. It is the home of Whittier College.

Information: Chamber of Commerce, 8158 Painter Ave., 90602, 562-698-9554; www.whittierchamber.org

WHAT TO SEE AND DO

Richard Nixon Library and Birthplace
18001 Yorba Linda Blvd.,
Yorba Linda, 714-993-5075;
www.nixonfoundation.org

This tribute to the 37th president includes a gallery devoted to the Watergate scandal. Many other exhibits fill the 52,000-square-foot main gallery. The World Leaders section showcases priceless gifts the Nixons received from governments around the world. The complex also includes the farmhouse in which Nixon was born in 1913, and the memorial burial sites of both the President and his wife. Monday-Saturday 10 a.m.-5 p.m., Sunday from 11 a.m.

Rose Hills Memorial Park and Mortuary
3888 S. Workman Mill Rd., Whittier, 562-699-0921; www.rosehills.com

Gardens and cemetery covering 2,500 acres. The Pageant of Roses Garden has more than 7,000 rose bushes of over 600 varieties in bloom most of the year. Also includes a Japanese garden with a lake, arched bridge and meditation house. Daily sunrise-sunset.

HOTELS

★★★Radisson Hotel Whittier
7320 Greenleaf Ave., Whittier,
562-945-8511, 800-333-3333;
www.radisson.com

This comfortable hotel provides high-speed Internet, a fitness center and a pool. The restaurant offers California cuisine and the bar includes live entertainment on weekends.

202 rooms. Restaurant, bar. $

165

HAWAII

ABOUT SEVEN MILLION SUN-SEEKERS HOP ABOARD PLANES EACH YEAR TO REACH HAWAII'S warm rays. But there's more to this chain of mostly volcanic islands than beaches and great weather.

It's believed that Polynesians from the Marquesas Group, north of Tahiti, first came to Hawaii between the third and seventh centuries A.D. In 1778, Captain James Cook arrived introducing the island to Europeans (or vice versa). Soon thereafter the islands were united by King Kamehameha and became the Republic of Hawaii. Statehood was granted in 1959.

Of Hawaii's more than 130 isles and atolls, eight are considered major islands: the Big Island, Kahoolawe, Kauai, Lanai, Maui, Molokai, Niihau and Oahu. Six of the eight have tourism industries. Of the two that do not, Niihau is privately owned and Kahoolawe is uninhabited.

All the main islands have a mixture of attractions, and each has its own appeal. Oahu, where more than 70 percent of the state's population lives, is the most cosmopolitan thanks to Honolulu and its Waikiki Beach. Maui, where development has boomed over the last quarter-century, offers a luxury escape. With its many natural attractions, Kauai is for those who love the outdoors. With its large size, the Big Island has something for everyone, including erupting volcanoes and snowcapped peaks. Lanai pampers the wealthy in a private, secluded setting. Molokai, where time has seemingly stood still, showcases the real Hawaiian lifestyle.

Information: www.gohawaii.com

BIG ISLAND OF HAWAII

The Big Island of Hawaii is just that: big. It covers 4,038 square miles and runs 95 miles north to south and 80 miles east to west. Even though it is the youngest of all the Hawaiian Islands (about 800,000 years old), it's twice the size of all the other major islands combined and accounts for 63 percent of the total land in the archipelago.

Hawaii is growing bigger by the day as lava continues to flow from Kilauea, the world's most active volcano. Since Kilauea's latest eruption began in 1983, more than 560 acres of new land have been added.

The Big Island is diverse and much of the west side looks barren with miles and miles of black-colored lava fields. But green dominates the east side, where tropical plants and trees flourish. Inland, sandwiched between both coasts, Mauna Kea

 SPOTLIGHT

★ Hawaii's Llolani Palace is the only royal residence in the U.S.

★ Hawaiian is the most widely studied Native American language.

★ Hawaii is the only U.S. state that grows coffee.

★ More than one-third of the world's commercial supply of pineapples comes from Hawaii.

introduces an alpine twist with peaks that sometimes have enough snow for downhill skiing.

Visitors typically arrive in Kailua-Kona, the major city on the sunny west side, and check into the many hotels that dot the 70-mile coastline that runs north and south of the airport. The island's most luxurious resorts, gorgeous beaches and best golf courses are north along the Kohala Coast.

Information: Big Island Convention and Visitor Bureau, 250 Waikoloa Beach Dr., Waikoloa, 808-886-1655; www.gohawaii.com/bigisland

HILO AND THE HAMAKUA COAST (THE EAST SIDE OF THE BIG ISLAND)

Not only is Hilo on the opposite coast from Kailua-Kona, it's different in almost every way. Lush and not as dry, Hilo is one of the wettest spots in the United States, with an average rainfall of about 130 inches.

Hilo is the largest city on the Big Island, with a population approaching 50,000. Its main boulevard along the bayfront, Banyan Drive, is lined with tall banyan trees, and the downtown has been partially restored.

When visitors venture east to Hilo, most take the scenic drive along the dramatic Hamakua Coast. Hilo is also home to a lush rain forest, numerous waterfalls, tropical gardens and tall coastal cliffs that overlook the ocean below. The six-mile-long Waipio Valley and the fern-filled Akaka Falls are two popular attractions on this coast. Despite its charm, Hilo is markedly lacking in good hotels, so consider the city for a day trip.

Information: Big Island Visitors Bureau, 250 Keawe St., 808-961-5797; www.downtownhilo.com

WHAT TO SEE AND DO

Akaka Falls State Park
Hwy. 220, Honomu, 808-974-6200; www.hawaii.gov/dlnr/dsp/hawaii.html
You have to make your way along a half-mile loop trail to see Akaka Falls, but the view is worth the effort. Water free-falls more than 442 feet into a stream-eroded gorge. Thousands of ferns and other plants add to Akaka's beauty. Before you come upon Akaka, you'll see Kahuna Falls, where the water cascades down 100 feet. The park has no facilities, just the trail. Daily dawn-dusk.

Hawaii Tropical Botanical Garden
27-717 Old Mamalahoa Hwy., Papaikou, 808-964-5233; www.htbg.com
More than 2,000 species of plants from around the world flourish at the Hawaii Tropical Botanical Garden, a privately owned 40-acre beauty in the Omomea Valley, about eight miles north of Hilo. The various trails in this natural greenhouse take you across streams and by waterfalls and gorgeous ocean views. Daily 9 a.m.-5 p.m.

Hilo Farmers' Market
Mamo St. and Kamehameha Ave., Hilo, 808-933-1000; www.hilofarmersmarket.com
Every Wednesday and Saturday since 1988, island vendors have gathered at this outdoor market to sell fresh produce, crafts, gifts and tropical flowers. Over the years, the market has grown from a handful of vendors to more than 120. Here you can buy everything from bongo drums and jewelry to pareos and puka shell necklaces. Wednesday and Saturday from dawn until everything is sold.

Laupahoehoe Beach Park
Hwy. 19, Hamakua Coast , www.hawaii-county.com/parks/laupahoehoe.htm
Come to this grassy park to watch the surf pound large lava rocks on the coastline. The Great Tsunami of 1946 slammed ashore here, killing 20 students and four teachers. A monument in the park honors the victims of the disaster. You can also camp here with a county permit. Daily dawn-dusk.

LEI OF THE LAND

People associate the Aloha State with leis, which are colorful mixtures of flowers, bark and vines either braided, twisted, wrapped or strung together. They' re so iconic that the state celebrates Lei Day every year on May 1. Locals throughout the islands drape the fragrant handiwork on their necks, there are lei-making contests and schools crown Lei Day kings and queens. Different types of leis suit different occasions. The Hawaiian maile lei, an open lei about four feet long, is standard wedding gear for brides and grooms.

Giving and receiving leis comes with rules of etiquette. When you give someone a lei, accompany it with a kiss on the cheek. It's considered poor form to refuse a lei, so always accept one when offered. Wear it draped over your shoulders, with portions of it hanging in the front and back, and don't remove the lei in the presence of the person who gave it to you. Leis are considered a symbol of love, so never throw a lei in the trash. Hang it from a tree or place it somewhere outside so that it can return to the earth instead.

Leleiwi Beach Park
Kalanianaole Ave., Keaukaka,
808-961-8311
When you want to snorkel on the Hilo side of the island, this small black-sand beach is your best bet. Not only will you see lots of sea life, the water here tends to attract green sea turtles and sometimes even dolphins. Daily dawn-dusk.

Muliwai Trail
Hwy. 240, Honokaa, 808-974-4221;
www.hawaiitrails.org
Although it's a breathtakingly beautiful hike, this zigzagging, 18-mile trail is for seasoned fit hikers only. Climb more than 1,200 feet up the western edge of Waipio Valley to a plateau that leads to gorgeous Waimanu Valley. A round-trip hike takes two or three days and requires a camping permit from the Division of Forestry and Wildlife office. Daily.

Panaewa Rainforest Zoo and Gardens
Stainback Hwy., Hilo, 808-959-7224,
www.hilozoo.com
More than 80 animal species live at Panaewa, the country's only tropical rain forest zoo. At the 12-acre facility there are a white Bengal tiger, feral goats, pygmy hypos, water buffalo, spider monkeys and more. Daily: 9 a.m.-4 p.m.

Wailuku River State Park
Waianueue Ave., Hilo
A short drive from downtown Hilo, the park encompasses 16 acres along the Wailuku River. Highlights include Rainbow Falls and a basalt lava formation known as the Boiling Pots. Water flows over Rainbow Falls and drops 80 feet, creating a mist in which often produces a rainbow (particularly on sunny mornings). Legend holds that Hina, mother of the demigod Maui, lived beneath the falls in a cave. Two miles upstream, at the end of Peepee Falls Drive, a short trail leads to the Boiling Pots. The river water bubbles and foams as it cascades through the Boiling Pots, a succession of pools formed during the gradual cooling of basalt lava.

HOTELS
★★Hilo Bay Hotel
87 Banyan Dr., Hilo,
808-935-0861; 800-367-5102;
www.unclebilly.com
150 rooms. Restaurant, bar. Outdoor pool.
$

★★Hotel Hilo Hawaiian
71 Banyan Dr., Hilo,
808-935-9361; 800-367-5004;
www.castleresorts.com

286 rooms. Restaurant, bar. Outdoor pool. $

SPECIALTY LODGINGS

At the Beach with Friends Bed and Breakfast

369 Nene St., Hilo, 808-934-8040;
www.bed-and-breakfast-hilo-hawaii.com
Before coming to Hawaii, the owners of this inn ran a construction and landscaping company in their native Oregon, so every detail in the gardens and architecture of this house has been well thought-out. Rooms have DVD/CD players, wireless Internet and refrigerators.
3 rooms. Complimentary continental breakfast. $

Luana Ola B&B Cottages

Hwy. 19, Honokaa,
808-775-1150, 800-357-7727;
www.island-hawaii.com
The artsy town of Honokaa is located within walking distance from these cottages, which feature views of the ocean and large kitchens stocked with fresh island fruits and breads.
Complimentary continental breakfast. $

Shipman House Bed & Breakfast Inn

131 Kaiulani St., Hilo,
808-934-8002, 800-627-8447;
www.hilo-hawaii.com
This Victorian mansion once hosted Queen Liliuokalani, who loved to play the Shipmans' Steinway concert grand piano (which still sits in the living room along with many other heirloom pieces). Writer Jack London stayed here for a month in 1907. In the main house are three bedrooms and a 1910 guest house holds the other two, which share a large, screened lanai.
5 rooms. Children are restricted; inquire when making reservations. Complimentary continental breakfast. $$

The Bay House B&B

42 Pukihae St., Hilo,
808-961-6311, 888-235-8195;
www.bayhousehawaii.com

Located on the east side of the Big Island, this white ranch-style house with a wrap-around porch has three oceanview rooms furnished with ceiling fans and private lanais.
3 rooms. Complimentary continental breakfast. $

The Old Hawaiian Bed & Breakfast

1492 Wailuku Dr., Hilo,
808-961-2816, 877-961-2816;
www.thebigislandvacation.com
The quiet neighborhood surrounding this white 1950s two-story structure is only a half-hour drive from the Liliuokalani Japanese Gardens, the famous farmers market of Hilo and Rainbow Falls. The three guest rooms vary in size. Breakfast each morning is hearty and homemade, as one of the owners is a skilled and passionate baker.
3 rooms. Complimentary continental breakfast. $

The Palms Cliff House Inn

28-3514 Mamalahoa Hwy., Honomu,
96728, 866-963-6076;
www.palmscliffhouse.com
Perched on a cliff overlooking Pohakumano Bay, this Victorian mansion has something for everyone: massages at the inn's spa, cooking classes with the inn's chef or hiking at nearby Akaka Falls. Suites have hot tubs and private lanais.
8 rooms. Complimentary full breakfast. Whirlpools. $$$$

Waianuhea B&B

45-3505 Kahana Dr., Honokaa,
808-775-1118, 888-775-2577;
www.waianuhea.com
This inn pairs the luxury of a hotel with the seclusion and intimacy of a bed-and-breakfast. All the power in the house, from Internet to satellite TV is supplied by solar panels, making this bed-and-breakfast an eco-friendly escape.
5 rooms. Complimentary full breakfast. $$$

HAWAII

★
★
★
★
★

Waipio Wayside Bed and Breakfast Inn
Hwy. 240, Honokaa,
808-775-0275, 800-833-8849;
www.waipiowayside.com
Enjoy an organic breakfast at this quaint inn, which includes the owners' specialty, scrambled eggs Waipio Wayside.
5 rooms. Complimentary full breakfast. **$$**

Waterfalls Inn Bed & Breakfast
240 Kaiulani St., Hilo, 96720,
808-969-3407, 888-808-4456;
www.waterfallsinn.com
This stately plantation-style house is located just across a one-lane bridge from downtown Hilo. The guest rooms (named after waterfalls) are simply furnished in pastel Hawaiian prints and there is wireless Internet throughout the house.
5 rooms. Children over 6 years only. Complimentary continental breakfast. Wireless Internet access. **$$**

RESTAURANTS

★**Black Rock Cafe**

287 Government Beach Rd., Pahoa,
808-965-1177
American menu. Lunch, dinner. Children's menu. Casual attire. **$**

★★**Cafe Pesto**
308 Kamehameha Ave., Hilo,
808-969-6640; www.cafepesto.com
Italian menu. Lunch, dinner. Bar. Children's menu. Casual attire.**$$**

★★**Harrington's**
135 Kalanianaole Ave., Hilo,
808-961-4966
Seafood, steak menu. Lunch, dinner. Bar. Children's menu. Casual attire. Reservations recommended.**$$**

★★★**Kaikodo**
60 Keawe St., Hilo,
808-961-2558;
www.restaurantkaikodo.com
This restaurant is located in downtown Hilo in a former bank. The bank's vault now serves as Kaikodo's wine cellar. The menu features elegant entrées such as sesame-crusted ahi and pan-roasted Sonoma duck breast.
Japanese menu. Lunch, dinner. Bar. Business casual attire. Reservations recommended.**$$$**

★**Ken's House of Pancakes**
1730 Kamehameha Ave., Hilo,
808-935-8711
American menu. Breakfast, lunch, dinner, late-night. Children's menu. Casual attire.
$

★**Miyo's**
400 Hualani St., Hilo, 808-935-2273
Japanese menu. Lunch, dinner. Bar. Casual attire. **$**

★**Pescatore**
235 Keawe St., Hilo, 808-969-9090
Italian menu. Lunch, dinner. Casual attire. Reservations recommended.**$$**

★**Reuben's Mexican Food**
336 Kamehameha Ave., Hilo,
808-961-2552
Mexican menu. Lunch, dinner. Bar. Casual attire. **$**

★★**Royal Siam**
70 Mamo St., Hilo,
808-961-6100
Thai menu. Lunch, dinner. Bar. Children's menu. Casual attire. **$**

KAILUA-KONA AND THE KONA COAST (THE WEST SIDE OF THE BIG ISLAND)

On the Big Island's sunny west side, Kailua-Kona is the anchor for the Kona Coast, which stretches for about 70 miles north and south of the city. This area includes other smaller seaside villages with some moderate to expensive hotels and condominiums, especially in Keauhou. There are a few good beaches and Kealakekua Bay, one of the island's best snorkeling spots and the place where Captain James Cook died in the 1700s.

When you've seen one corner of this coastal region, don't think you've seen it all. The landscape varies from dry and barren in some parts to green in others where plantation owners grow rich Kona coffee and macadamia nuts. The Kona Coast also has a reputation for great deep-sea fishing. Charter-boat captains leave the Honokohau Marina in Kailua-Kona every day with visitors hoping to reel in jumbo-size marlin.

Information: Kona-Kohala Chamber of Commerce, 75-5737 Kuakini Hwy., 808-329-1758; www.kona-kohala.com

WHAT TO SEE AND DO

Big Island Country Club
71-1420 Mamalahoa Hwy., Kailua-Kona, 96740, 808-325-5044

Expect to be wowed by this Perry Dye-designed golf course. Built at 2,000 feet above sea level on the slopes of Mauna Kea, this semi-private course offers great views of both the Pacific and inland areas. The 72 sand and numerous grass bunkers on this par 72 7,034-yard course demand accurate shots. Amenities include a golf shop and short-game practice area. Daily 7 a.m.-6 p.m.

Holualoa
Mamalahoa Hwy., Holualoa

Just up the Hualalai Road from Kailua-Kona sits the charming upcountry artists' haven of Holualoa. Inside the small, spruced up plantation homes that line its two-block-long main street are several art galleries and arts-and-crafts shops selling works by island artists. This is coffee country, with groves all over the mountainside leading up to Holualoa, so the town is a good place to sample a cup of strong Kona coffee or an espresso, especially at the Holuakoa Café.

Island Breeze Luau
King Kamehameha's Kona Beach Hotel, 75-5660 Palani Rd., Kailua-Kona, 808-329-8111, www.islandbreezeluau.com

This luau is held on the historic grounds of King Kamehameha's former estate on

Kamakahonu Bay. Festivities begin with a shell-lei greeting, followed by a torch-lighting ceremony and the arrival of the Royal Court—decked out in traditional Hawaiian dress—via outrigger canoe. After a 22-dish buffet, the drum-pounding entertainment begins. The revue features hula dancing, Fijian and Maori war dances and the Samoan fire-knife dance. Sunday and Tuesday-Thursday 5:30-8:30 p.m.; reservations required.

Kona Coast State Park (Kekaha Kai State Park)
Hwy. 19, Kailua-Kona, 808-327-4958

A little more than a mile off the highway down a bumpy road you'll find this state park. It's home to two beaches—Mahaiula and Kua Bay—connected by a four and a half-mile trail. The swimming is good when the ocean's calm. There are picnic facilities at Mahaiula. Daily dawn-dusk.

Puuhonua o Honaunau National Historical Park
Hwy. 160, Honaunau, 808-328-2288; www.nps.gov/puho

In the old days, Hawaiians who broke the law sought refuge here to avoid a punishment of death. Besides the refuge area, the 182-acre park includes coastal village sites, royal fish ponds, sledding tracks, temple platforms and reconstructed thatched buildings. Monday-Thursday 6 a.m.-8 p.m., Friday-Sunday 6 a.m.-11 p.m. Visitor center open daily 7:30 a.m.-5:30 p.m.

HAWAII

White Sands Beach County Park

Alii Dr., Kailua-Kona, 808-961-8311
In winter, the sand here disappears into high surf, which is why some people call this beach Magic Sands or Disappearing Sands. During this time, swimming is unsafe. When the water calms down, White Sands is a popular place for swimming, snorkeling, body surfing and riding boogey boards. Unlike many Hawaii beaches, this one usually has lifeguards in summer, making it good for families. Daily dawn to dusk.

SPECIAL EVENTS

Ironman Triathlon World Championship

Kailua-Kona, 808-329-0063;
www.ironmanlive.com
Each October, up to 2,000 athletes come to Kona to compete in this one-day grueling race. The event unfolds along the Kona Coast and consists of a 2.4-mile ocean swim, 112-mile bike ride and a marathon-length run (26.2 miles). The top 10 finishers pocket more than $400,000 in prize money. October.

Kona Coffee Cultural Festival

Kailua-Kona, 808-326-7820,
www.konacoffeefest.com
For more than 35 years, this 10-day festival has celebrated the annual coffee harvest. Events take place in various venues around coffee country and include bean-picking contests, tastings, art shows, tours of working farms and mills and the crowning of the year's best cup of joe. Early-mid-November.

HOTELS

★★King Kamehameha's Kona Beach Hotel

75-5660 Palani Rd., Kailua-Kona,
808-329-2911, 800-367-2111;
www.konabeachhotel.com
460 rooms. Two restaurants, bar. Outdoor pool. Business center. $$

★★Royal Kona Resort

75-5852 Alii Dr., Kailua-Kona,
808-329-3111, 800-919-8333;
www.royalkona.com
452 rooms. Restaurant, bar. Spa. Outdoor pool, children's pool. Tennis. Airport transportation available. Business center. $

★★★Kona Village Resort

Queen Kaahumanu Hwy., Kailua-Kona,
808-325-5555, 800-367-5290;
www.konavillage.com
This beachfront resort doesn't have standard hotel rooms. Instead, it offers 125 individual *hales,* or bungalows with thatched roofs. Though luxuriously decorated, none of the hales has air conditioning or televisions. The room rate includes meals at the resort's oceanfront restaurants and tickets to a luau that many consider the best on the island.
125 rooms. Closed one week following Thanksgiving. Complimentary full breakfast. Two restaurants, three bars. Children's activity center. Fitness room, fitness classes available. Beach. Outdoor pool, whirlpool. Tennis. Airport transportation available. Business center. $$$$

SPECIALTY LODGINGS

An Aloha Guest House

84-4780 Mamalahoa Hwy., Captain Cook,
808-328-8955, 800-897-3188;
www.alohaguesthouse.com
High in the jungles of Hawaii's Kona coast, this bed and breakfast is surrounded by a citrus and macadamia nut plantation. The individually designed and decorated rooms are furnished with refrigerators and coffee makers.
5 rooms. Complimentary continental breakfast. Whirlpool. $$

Hale Ho'ola Bed & Breakfast

85-4577 Mamalahoa Hwy., Captain Cook,
808-328-9117, 877-628-9117;
www.hale-hoola.com
This countryside bed and breakfast serves a homemade breakfast buffet, and has rooms with private lanais overlooking the Pacific.
3 rooms. $

Holualoa Inn

76-5932 Mamalahoa Hwy., Holualoa,
808-324-1121, 800-392-1812;
www.holualoainn.com

With commanding views of the Kona coast, this open-air house features eucalyptus-wood floors and oversized rattan furniture for an exotic, yet comfortable atmosphere. Around the property are secluded gazebos and an oceanfront swimming pool.

Nancy's Hideaway

75-1530 Uanani Place, Kailua-Kona,
808-325-3132, 866-325-3132;
www.nancyshideaway.com

This bed and breakfast, which rents both guest houses and a studio, has wireless Internet, TVs with DVD players and private lanais. Breakfast is served in room and includes fresh pastries and local juices. **$**

Pomaika'I "Lucky" Farm B&B

83-5465 Mamalahoa Hwy., Captain Cook,
808-328-2112, 800-325-6427;
www.luckyfarm.com

This small bed-and-breakfast has also functioned as a macadamia nut and coffee farm for more than a hundred years. Be sure to check availability in the Coffee Barn, a rustic cottage. **$**

RESTAURANTS

★Bianelli's

75-5653 Ololi St., Kailua-Kona,
808-329-7062

Italian menu. Lunch, dinner. Bar. Casual attire. Reservations recommended. Outdoor seating.**$$**

★Cassandra's Greek Tavern

75-5669 Alii Dr., Kailua Kona,
808-334-1066;
www.cassandraskona.com

Greek menu. Lunch, dinner. Bar. Casual attire.**$$**

★Holuakoa Cafe

76-5901 Mamalahoa Hwy., Holualoa,
808-322-2233

Continental menu. Breakfast, lunch. Closed Sundays. Casual attire. **$**

★Huggo's

75-5828 Kahakai Rd., Kailua-Kona,
808-329-1493;
www.huggos.com

American menu. Lunch, dinner. Bar. Casual attire. Outdoor seating.**$$**

★★Jameson's by the Sea

77-6452 Alii Dr., Kailua-Kona,
808-329-3195

Seafood menu. Lunch, dinner. Bar. Casual attire. Reservations recommended. Outdoor seating.**$$$**

★★Keei Cafe

79-7511 Mama., Kealakekua, 96750,
808-328-8451

International menu. Dinner. Closed Sunday-Monday. Business casual attire. Reservations recommended. No credit cards accepted. **$$**

★★★La Bourgogne Restaurant

77 Nalani St., Kailua-Kona,
808-329-6711

This small restaurant serves perfectly prepared French cuisine. Signature dishes include baked brie in puff pastry, fresh lobster salad with goat cheese and mango and roast duck breast with raspberries and pine nuts. Desserts include flourless chocolate cake or creme brulée.

French menu. Dinner. Closed Sunday-Monday. Bar. Business casual attire. Reservations recommended.**$$$**

★★★Pahu i'a

100 Ka'upulehu Dr., Ka'upulehu,
808-325-8000

Located at the Four Seasons Resort Hualalai, Pahu I'a has an outdoor dining area separated from the Pacific Ocean by just a few feet of sand. Pahu I'a means aquarium in the Hawaiian language, and this point is reinforced by a brilliant array of tropi-

HAWAII

cal fish swimming in an aquarium near the restaurant's entrance. Fish is also echoed on the seafood-heavy menu, in dishes such as steamed snapper with ginger or macadamia-crusted mahi mahi.

Pacific-Rim/Pan-Asian menu. Breakfast, dinner. Bar. Reservations recommended. Valet parking. Outdoor seating. $$$

KOHALA COAST

From the highway, this coastline doesn't seem all that impressive—endless fields of black-lava rock, mile after mile. That's because you can't see the four world-class resorts—Hualalai, Mauna Kea, Mauna Lani and Waikoloa—that sit out of sight just a mile or two off the road. The resorts are home to eight of Hawaii's most luxurious hotels and seven golf courses designed by legends like Robert Trent Jones, Sr., Jack Nicklaus and Arnold Palmer. This is the island's sunny side, so rain seldom keeps anyone off the beach or off the fairways.

The Kohala area is also rich in history, with ancient petroglyph fields and the Puukohola Heiau, a temple built by King Kamehameha the Great, who was born in this region in the 1700s.

WHAT TO SEE AND DO

Hapuna Beach State Park
Hwy. 19, Kohala Coast,
808-974-6200
Hapuna is considered one of the island's top beaches, as it stretches for about a half-mile, is wide (up to 200 feet in summer), and has calm water most of the year. But take note: stay out of the water in winters high surf, when riptides pose a danger. Lifeguards patrol the beach sometimes, but not necessarily daily. The 62-acre park has a picnic area with a pavilion, hiking trails, a camping area, and a few A-frame cabins that can be rented. Daily dawn to dusk.

Kaunaoa Beach
Mauna Kea Beach Resort, Hwy. 19,
Kohala Coast
Kaunaoa, also known as Mauna Kea Beach, isn't as long as nearby Hapuna Beach, but many people say this is still the island's best stretch of sand. Green turtles like to swim here, too, so be on the lookout. The hotel owns and operates most of the facilities up on the shore, and public parking is limited. Daily dawn to dusk.

Kohala Na'alapa Trail Rides
Kohala Mountain Rd., North Kohala,
808-889-0022;
www.naalapastables.com/kahua.html
At one of Hawaii's oldest working ranches, take your pick from two rides, one on horseback and the other by wagon. If you choose a horse, you'll ride through hilly pastures, views of the mountains and the Pacific Ocean. Opt for the other ride, and you'll explore the ranch in a farm wagon pulled by two Percheron geldings. The morning trip lasts 2 1/2 hours; the afternoon trip, 1 1/2 hours. Daily, various times.

Mookini Luakini Heiau
Upolu Airport, Hwy. 270, Hawi,
808-974-6200
Nearly the size of a football field, Mookini Luakini is Hawaii's largest temple. It's also the oldest one, built in A.D. 480 of water-worn basalt from the Pololu Valley. It took more than 18,000 workers to build it and they used no mortar. You'll need a four-wheel-drive vehicle to reach the temple, which is about 1 1/2 miles down a rough dirt road off the highway. Daily dawn to dusk.

Puako Archaeological District
Hwy. 19, Kohala Coast
Expect to spend about a half-hour walking along the Kalahuipuaa Trail, next to Holoholokai Beach Park. In this historic district, one of the state's largest petroglyph fields, you'll see about 3,000 ancient stone carv-

ings believed to have been created from about A.D. 1200 to the A.D. 1800s. Access the trail from the Fairmont Orchid Hawaii Hotel. Daily dawn to dusk.

Puukohola Heiau National Historic Site
62-3601 Kawaihae Rd., Kawaihae,
808-882-7218; www.nps.gov/puhe
King Kamehameha I had this large *heiau*, or place of worship, built in 1791 at the urging of a prophet. The king was told building it would please Kukailimoku, the war god. The site also includes the home of John Young, a British sailor and advisor to the king and a smaller *heiau* submerged offshore that's dedicated to the shark gods. Daily 7:30 a.m.-4 p.m.

HOTELS

★★★The Fairmont Orchid, Hawaii
1 N. Kaniku Dr., Kohala Coast,
808-885-2000;
www.fairmont.com/orchid
Rooms at this beachfront resort feature Italian marble bathrooms and private lanais with wonderful views. The hotel has eight bars and restaurants, including the Grill and Brown's Beach House, both of which serve up seafood dishes, and Norio's Sushi Bar and Restaurant, where the emphasis shifts to Japanese cuisine. The Spa Without Walls offers massages, pedicures and other treatments. The Keiki Aloha program keeps children occupied with activities such as cave explorations, lei-making, Hawaiian games and sand castle building.
540 rooms. Pets accepted; fee. High-speed Internet access. Five restaurants, bar. Fitness room, fitness classes available, spa. Beach. Outdoor pool, whirlpool. Golf. Tennis. $$$$

★★★★Four Seasons Resort Hualalai at Historic Ka'upulehu
100 Ka'upulehu Dr., Ka'upulehu,
808-325-8000, 800-332-3442;
www.fourseasons.com
Located at the southern end of the Kahala Coast, this property is 15 minutes from the Kona airport. The luxurious rooms, which reflect the island setting with their rattan chaises and batik fabrics, all have ocean views with a private lanai. Regional cuisine takes center stage at both Pahu i'a and the Hualalai Grille by Alan Wong. Laid-back island sophistication is the idea behind both restaurants, which serve creative dishes crafted from fresh fish and local ingredients. The Beach Tree Grill & Bar has a well-rounded menu and also offers Italian and beach barbecue buffet nights each week.
243 rooms. Pets accepted. High-speed, wireless Internet access. Three restaurants, two bars. Children's activity center. Fitness room, fitness classes available, spa. Beach. Five outdoor pools, children's pool, whirlpool. Golf, 18 holes. Tennis. Business center. $$$$

★★★Hapuna Beach Prince Hotel
62-100 Kauna'oa Dr., Kohala Coast,
808-880-1111;
www.princeresortshawaii.com
This hotel, which sits on 32 oceanfront acres, borders one of the top-rated beaches in the country, the lovely Hapuna Beach. The hotel's 350 rooms offer terrific ocean views. Dine in any of five restaurants, including the Coast Grille, which features regional Hawaiian cuisine, or the Hakone Steakhouse and Sushi Bar, which has an East-West menu of island-raised Kobe beef, shabu shabu and sukiyaki. Watch a colorful sunset at the open-air Reef Lounge, then dance the night away to the local entertainment.
351 rooms. High-speed Internet access. Five restaurants, four bars. Fitness room, fitness classes available. Beach. Outdoor pool, whirlpool. Golf, 18 holes. Tennis. Airport transportation available. Business center. $$

★★★Hilton Waikoloa Village
425 Waikoloa Beach Dr., Waikoloa,
808-886-1234;
www.hiltonwaikoloavillage.com
With 1,240 rooms in three buildings spread over 62 acres, the Hilton Waikoloa Village is a good choice for families. One of the most popular features is the Dolphin

★

★

★

★

★

Quest dolphin encounter program. This large resort has nine restaurants and eight lounges that serve a wide variety of cuisine. Boats traversing man-made canals and trams make getting around the spacious resort easier.

1,240 rooms. High-speed Internet access. Nine restaurants, eight bars. Children's activity center. Beach. Three outdoor pools, children's pool, whirlpool. Tennis. Airport transportation available. Business center. **$$$**

★★★The Mauna Lani Bay Hotel And Bungalows
68-1400 Mauna Lani Dr., Kohala Coast, 808-885-6622, 800-356-6652; www.maunalani.com

One of the premier resorts on the Big Island's Kohala Coast, the elegant Mauna Lani Bay Hotel has 350 guest rooms and private bungalows. Guests are greeted with leis and served fresh-squeezed juice during check in. The rooms have private lanais and, of course, the region's famous Kona coffee. Those staying in a private bungalow have access to a personal chef. Activities here include tennis, golf (two 18-hole courses) and a children's camp.

350 rooms. High-speed Internet access. Five restaurants, five bars. Children's activity center. Fitness room, fitness classes available, spa. Beach. Outdoor pool, whirlpool. Golf, 36 holes. Tennis. Airport transportation available. Business center. **$$$$**

★★★Waikoloa Beach Marriott Resort and Spa
69-275 Waikoloa Beach Dr., Waikoloa, 808-886-6789, 800-922-5533; www.marriott.com

The 545-room Marriott has an amazing location on Anaehoomalu Bay with a lovely crescent-shaped beach that borders an ancient fishpond. Fresh from a complete renovation, rooms are now sleek and contemporary with luxury beds and down duvets. The Hawaii Calls Restaurant serves Pacific Regional cuisine. Twice a week, the Marriott puts on one of the Big Island's better luaus.

545 rooms. High-speed Internet access. Two restaurants, two bars. Children's activity center. Fitness room, spa. Beach. Outdoor pool, children's pool, whirlpool. Tennis. Business center. **$$$**

RESTAURANTS

★★Bamboo
Akoni Pule Hwy., Hawi, 808-889-5555

Pacific-Rim/Pan-Asian menu. Lunch, dinner, Sunday brunch. Closed Monday. Bar. Children's menu. Casual attire. Reservations recommended. **$$**

★★Big Island Steakhouse
250 Waikoloa Beach Dr., Waikoloa, 808-886-8805

Steak menu. Dinner, late-night. Bar. Casual attire. Reservations recommended. Outdoor seating. **$$**

★★Cafe Pesto
Hwy. 270, Kawaihae, 808-882-1071; www.cafepesto.com

Italian menu. Lunch, dinner. Bar. Children's menu. **$$**

★★★CanoeHouse
1400 Mauna Lani Dr., Kohala Coast, 808-885-6622; www.maunalani.com

This restaurant couples spectacular views with outstanding Pacific-Rim cuisine for one of the Big Island's best fine-dining experiences. Located at the Mauna Lani Bay Hotel and Bungalows, CanoeHouse is elegant but unpretentious. Entrées include sake-steamed local fish and blackened ahi and scallops.

Pacific-Rim/Pan-Asian menu. Dinner. Bar. Children's menu. Casual attire. Reservations recommended. Valet parking. Outdoor seating. **$$$**

★★Kawaihae Harbor Grill
Hwy. 270, Kawaihae, 808-882-1368; www.theharborgrill.com

Seafood menu. Lunch, dinner, late-night. Bar. Children's menu. Casual attire. Reservations recommended. Outdoor seating. **$$**

★★Roy's Waikoloa Bar & Grill
250 Waikoloa Beach Dr., Waikoloa,
808-886-4321; www.roysrestaurant.com
Pacific-Rim/Pan-Asian menu. Lunch, dinner. Bar. Casual attire. Reservations recommended. Outdoor seating. **$$**

★Tres Hombres Beach Grill
Hwy. 270, Kawaihae, 808-882-1031
Mexican menu. Lunch, dinner. Bar. Children's menu. Casual attire. Outdoor seating. **$**

SPAS
★★★★Hualalai Sports Club and Spa, Four Seasons Resort Hualalai
100 Ka'upulehu Dr., Ka'upulehu-Kona, 808-325-8440, 800-983-3880; www.fourseasons.com

Featuring an open-air gym, a grass yoga and meditation courtyard, an Olympic-style lap pool, a sand volleyball court and eight tennis courts, the Hualalai Sports Club and Spa at the Four Seasons Resort has dozens of ways to stay fit. Try climbing the 24-foot climbing wall, join fitness hikes or take a kickboxing, tai chi or water aerobics class. After working up a sweat at the fitness center, unwind in the sensational spa. The facility offers a variety of massages, including lomi lomi, Swedish and sports. Signature body treatments include the Hualalai herbal wrap, which uses hibiscus (the state flower) to stimulate the release of toxins, while Hawaiian red clay, mineral-rich salts and essential oils make up the deep-cleansing Hualalai salt glow. **$$$**

HAWAII VOLCANOES NATIONAL PARK
Volcano, 96718, 808-985-6000; www.nps.gov/havo
More than a million visitors a year arrive to witness the tempestuous Kilauea, the world's most active volcano. Kilauea has erupted continuously since 1983, the volcano's longest rift-zone eruption in more than 600 years. As lava flows down Kilauea and into the ocean, new land mass is created, making the Big Island even bigger. The eruption has also had destructive consequences, wiping out nearly 200 homes, eight miles of highway, a park visitor center and a 700-year-old Hawaiian temple.

Most visitors arrive at the park hoping to observe from a distance flowing streams of red-hot lava. Kilauea doesn't always cooperate. While molten lava is consistently visible from the sky, it cannot always be observed safely from the ground. The good news is that, lava or no lava, there's no shortage of things to see and do within the park.

If you're only here for a few hours, visit the Holei Sea Arch, Thurston Lava Tube, Kilauea Iki Overlook and Jaggar Museum. If you're here for one night, park your car at the end of Chain of Craters Road and walk east along the coast, crossing the eerie but beautiful landscape of black frozen lava, formed in recent years as molten lava flowed across the road and into the sea, disappearing with a hiss and cloud of steam. If you're staying in the park for a few days, experience the region's diverse ecosystems by hiking the Kau Desert Trail, Puna Coast Trail and Crater Rim Trail. Only experienced trekkers should consider tackling the Mauna Loa Trail, which leads to the precipitous summit of the world's most massive volcano.

SPECIALTY LODGINGS
Aloha Junction
Old Volcano Hwy., Volcano, 808-967-7289, 888-967-7286; www.bbvolcano.com
With an elevation of 4,000 feet, this cabin-like house is a cool respite, built in 1927 as part of a sugar plantation, restored and furnished with modern amenities. Hiking trails and lava tubes at Volcano National Park are located less than a mile from the house.
4 rooms. Complimentary full breakfast. Whirlpool. **$**

★
★
★
★
★

Kilauea Lodge

19-3948 Old Volcano Rd., Volcano,
808-967-7366;
www.kilauealodge.com

Within a serene wooded area in Volcano Village, the Kilauea Lodge offers 12 charming, distinctly decorated guest rooms and two off-property vacation cottages. Room rates include breakfast in the lodge's restaurant, which is open to the public for lunch and dinner.

14 rooms. Complimentary full breakfast. Restaurant. Whirlpool. **$**

Volcano Cedar Cottage

11-3799 Seventh St., Volcano,
808-985-9020; www.volcanocc.com

The owner of this bed and breakfast is a native Hawaiian and is happy to give great recommendations for nearby restaurants and activities. After a day of hiking at the national park nearby, relax in the Great Room and take in views of the night sky through the floor-to-ceiling windows.

2 rooms. **$**

Volcano Rainforest Retreat

11-3832 Twelfth St., Volcano,
808-985-8696, 800-550-8696;
www.volcanoretreat.com

Situated in the thick of a rain forest adjacent to Hawaii Volcanoes National Park, these secluded cottages are constructed of red-

178

wood and cedar. The historic town of Hilo is about a half-hour away, with shopping, dining and botanical gardens.

4 rooms. Complimentary continental breakfast. **$**

RESTAURANTS

★★★Kilauea Lodge

19-3948 Old Volcano Rd., Volcano,
808-967-7366; www.kilauealodge.com

This restaurant offers a dining experience unlike any other on the Big Island. Built as a YMCA camp in the 1930s, the lodge is now a country inn and restaurant. Chef Albert Jeyte specializes in continental cuisine, and his menu ranges from Pacific Rim fish dishes to European favorites such as hasenpfeffer and venison.

American menu. Dinner. Casual attire. Reservations recommended. **$$$**

★★Mister Bell's

Mamalahoa Hwy., Kau,
808-929-7447

Seafood, steak menu. Lunch, dinner. Bar. Children's menu. Casual attire. Reservations recommended. Outdoor seating. **$$**

★Thai Thai

19-4084 Old Volcano Rd., Volcano,
808-967-7969

Thai menu. Lunch, dinner. Bar. Casual attire. **$$**

WAIMEA (KAMUELA)

This small city in the upcountry goes by two names. Waimea (which means "reddish water") is its original moniker, but because there is also a Waimea on the island of Kauai, the postal service requested a unique referent after Hawaii became a U.S. territory. The name that was chosen, Kamuela, means "Samuel" in Hawaiian and it honored a prominent citizen. This rapidly growing town set in the rolling green hills of South Kohala continues to capitalize on its heritage as a farming and cattle-ranching community. One of the area's earliest ranches was established by John Palmer Parker and Parker Ranch is still a dominant presence.

Information: www.kamuela.com

WHAT TO SEE AND DO

Parker Ranch

67-1435 Mamalahoa Hwy., Kamuela,
808-885-7655; www.parkerranch.com

Tucked between Mauna Kea and Mauna Loa is the Parker Ranch, which was founded in 1847 when John Palmer Parker bought two acres of land from King Kamehameha for

$10. Encompassing about 175,000 acres, it's one of the country's oldest and largest working ranches. A short drive from the visitors center are two historic homes you can tour: Puuopelu features European heirloom furniture and an impressive private art collection. At Mana Hale, you'll see native koa wood interiors, handmade furniture and Hawaiian quilts. The ranch also offers horseback riding, wagon rides, ATV rides and hunting. Visitor and Museum Center: Monday-Saturday 9 a.m.-5 p.m. Historic homes: Monday-Saturday 10 a.m.-5 p.m.

SPECIALTY LODGINGS

Jacaranda Inn
65-1444 Kawaihae Rd., Waimea,
808-885-8813;
www.jacarandainn.com
This historic ranch sits just off Waimea's main road. Some of the buildings once served as bunkhouses for the ranch hands at Parker Ranch. There's also a private three-bedroom, three-bath cottage that sleeps six. 8 rooms. Complimentary full breakfast. **$$**

RESTAURANTS

★★★Daniel Thiebaut
65-1259 Kawaihae Rd., Waimea,
808-887-2200;
www.danielthiebaut.com
This restaurant is housed in the historic Chock In Store, which served the local ranching community for nearly 100 years. Chef Daniel Thiebaut's French Asian menu includes dishes such as sautéed macadamia nut chicken breast, spiced with Dijon mustard sauce and served with pickled pineapple and potatoes. A prix fixe menu is also available.
Pacific-Rim/Pan-Asian menu. Lunch, dinner. Bar. Children's menu. Casual attire. Reservations recommended.**$$$**

MAUNA KEA SUMMIT

Mauna Kea is the world's highest mountain, if you measure from the base, which is about 17,000 feet under the ocean. You can drive almost to the top of this peak and hike the extra 200 feet to the official summit marker at 13,796 feet.

For some, driving Saddle Road, which passes between Mauna Loa and Mauna Kea, is thrill enough. Built in a hurry during World War II, Saddle Road is winding and hilly, with blind curves poorly banked. The saddle crests at 6,000 feet, almost half way to the top.

Once you reach the Onizuka Center for International Astronomy at 9,200 feet, you'll realize the enormity of driving to the summit. Mauna Kea still looms above, the summit invisible, while the city of Hilo is lost in clouds below. Air at the summit has only about 60 percent of the oxygen content of air at sea level. Perhaps most important is the weather, which is difficult to determine from anywhere on the island except the Onizuka Center. Between November and April, snow is not uncommon and freezing fog can occur at anytime.

The rewards of reaching the summit are many. The clarity of the air is spectacular, great for photography. The landscape is near enough to lunar conditions that *Apollo* astronauts trained here. Two dozen of the world's finest telescopes are sprinkled around the summit. Tours of the University of Hawaii's telescope are given on weekends. (Call 808-961-2180 for more information). To Native Hawaiians, Mauna Kea is sacred, and at the top it feels that way. Locals believe the mountain is the home of Poliahu, the Snow Goddess, as well as three other deities. Also atop Mauna Kea is Lake Waiau, found at 13,020 feet partly filling a cinder cone, which is green as a lawn in desert conditions.

★Maha's Cafe
Hwy 19., Waimea, 808-885-0693
American menu. Breakfast, lunch. Closed Tuesday-Wednesday. Casual attire. **$**

★★★Merriman's
65-1227 Opelo Rd., Waimea,
808-885-6822;
www.merrimanshawaii.com
Located in the Big Island's ranch country, Merriman's specializes in innovative Hawaiian cuisine. Chef/owner Peter Merriman uses fresh, locally produced ingredients. A popular entrée is Merriman's Mixed Plate, a sampling of the restaurant's signature fish including ponzu, mahi mahi, fresh island shrimp and wok-charred ahi.

Pacific-Rim/Pan-Asian menu. Lunch, dinner. Children's menu. Casual attire. Reservations recommended.**$$$**

★Paniolo Country Inn
65-1214 Lindsey Rd., Waimea,
808-885-5590
Continental menu. Breakfast, lunch, dinner. Children's menu. Casual attire. **$**

★★Parker Ranch Grill
67-1185A Mamalahoa Hwy., Kamuela,
808-887-2624;
www.parkerranchgrill.com
Steak menu. Lunch, dinner. Bar. Children's menu. Casual attire. Reservations recommended.**$$**

LANAI

Privacy is the draw on Lanai, the smallest of the accessible Hawaiian Islands and once the home to the world's largest pineapple plantation. Only about 3,000 people live on the island, and only about 100,000 visitors come ashore each year.

The island has only one town, Lanai City, a small but friendly inland place void of all pretension. Most tourist attractions require a true sense of adventure and a four-wheel-drive vehicle to reach. On Lanai, sightseeing usually means traveling down rugged roads.

Except for Hulopoe, many of the beaches are tricky to access and while good for sunbathing, many aren't safe for swimming due to strong currents and riptides.
Information: Destination Lanai, 808-244-3530, 800-947-4774; www.visitlanai.net

WHAT TO SEE AND DO
Spinning Dolphin Fishing Charter
1574 S. Ohohia Place, Lanai City,
808-565-6613
The 29-foot *Spinning Dolphin* is available for half-day and full-day deep-sea charters for up to six people. Captain Jeff Menze provides all you'll need for a day at sea except for food, so bring a picnic lunch. Charters on demand.

Adventure Lanai Eccentric
Lanai City, 808-565-0485;
www.adventurelanai.com
This company takes action-craving visitors hiking, biking, kayaking, snorkeling, scuba diving and exploring in four-wheel-drive Jeeps. The tours typically last from two to four hours. Adventure Lanai also rents

a wide range of equipment, such as All-Terrain Vehicles, camping gear, mountain bikes and kayaks. Daily, various times.

Central Bakery
1311 Fraser Ave., Lanai City,
808-565-3920
As the name implies, this sweet spot supplies baked goods, ice creams and desserts for most of the island's restaurants and hotels. Visitors can order everything from cookies to croissant. Opens daily at 4:30 a.m.; orders must be picked up by 3:30 p.m.

Hulope Beach
Manele Rd., Manele
Hulope is Lanai's top beach, and is a short walk from the posh Four Seasons Resort

180

HAWAII

Manele Bay. This beach is a Marine Life Conservation Area, so snorkeling is superb. To the left of the beach, there are tidepools and hiking trails. Camping is allowed with a permit. Daily dawn to dusk.

Kanepuu Preserve
Polihua Rd., North Shore Lanai,
808-537-4508
Kanepuu, now managed by the Nature Conservancy, is home to 49 plant species, including three federally endangered ones: the vine Bonamia menziesii, the Hawaii gardenia and the sandalwood. A self-guided tour on a specially marked trail that forms a loop takes only 10 to 15 minutes, though you'll need a four-wheel-drive vehicle to reach the preserve. Daily 9 a.m.-4 p.m.

Kaunolu Village
Manele Rd., South Lanai
Now a National Historic Landmark, this site used to be an ancient Hawaiian fishing village where it's believed King Kamehameha would come for recreation about 200 years ago. Among the 86 ruins are a temple and the remains of the king's retreat. At Kahekili's Leap, a steep drop to the ocean below, warriors would supposedly prove their courage to the king by plunging into the water. Daily dawn to dusk.

Keomoku Village
Keomoku Rd., East Shore Lanai
Visit this off-the-beaten-path village to see Hawaii's version of a ghost town. As the site of the Maunalei Sugar Company, Keomoku was a community of about 2,000 people until 1901, when the local water turned brackish and salty making it difficult to continue sugar production. According to legend, the gods tainted the water because sacred stones were moved to construct the village. All the buildings are decaying now except for a clapboard church, Ka Lanakila O Ka Malamalama, which has been partially restored. From here, the views of Maui are splendid. Daily dawn to dusk.

Lanai Art Program
339 Eighth St., Lanai City, 808-565-7503;

www.lanaiart.org
The Lanai Arts Center was founded in 1991 to provide artistic and cultural experiences to locals and visitors through art classes, workshops, gallery exhibitions and access to art studios. Visitors are welcome to join in classes as well as browse through the gallery/gift shop, which features the creativity of more than 20 Lanai artists. Class times vary. Gallery hours: Monday-Saturday noon-4 p.m.

Lanai Theater and Playhouse
456 Seventh St., Lanai City,
808-565-7500
This 153-seat, Art Deco theater dates back to the 1930s but underwent a major renovation in 1993 that updated the facility. It shows first-run films and occasionally hosts plays and special events. Nightly show times vary; matinees occasionally.

Luahiwa Petroglyphs
Manele Rd., South Central Lanai
Drive a couple of miles south of Lanai City, turn onto a dirt road, drive to a slope overlooking the Palawai Basin and you'll see a large field of boulders. On 34 of the largest rocks are petroglyphs depicting ancient symbols, animals and people dating to the 18th century. Luahiwa is difficult to reach and requires a four-wheel-drive vehicle. Daily dawn to dusk.

Munro Trail
Manele Rd., Central Lanai
Get behind the wheel of a four-wheel-drive and set out on this seven-mile-long trail that winds past pine forests to the summit of Mount Lanaihale (3,370 feet) then down to the Palawai Basin. On clear days, all of the major Hawaiian islands can be seen from the summit. The dirt road is rough and bumpy in spots, so the round-trip drive of about 15 miles will take up to three hours. Explore the trail on good-weather days—it gets muddy, slick and treacherous during rain. Daily dawn to dusk.

Shipwreck Beach
Keomoku Rd., North Shore

The strong currents at this windy beach on the northeast coast make it too dangerous for swimming, but those same currents make this a wonderful place for beachcombing. Shells and driftwood wash onto the beach, which is dotted with boulders and lava rocks. Shipwreck stretches for more than eight miles and offers superb hiking. Offshore, you'll see the remains of a large ship, and across the channel, the island of Molokai. Much of the road to this beach is paved, but not the last stretch, so rent a four-wheel-drive car to get here. Daily dawn to dusk.

HOTELS

★★★★Four Seasons Resort Lanai at Manele Bay

1 Manele Bay Rd., Lana'i City,
808-565-2000, 800-819-5053;
www.fourseasons.com

Perched atop red lava cliffs, this resort resembles a sprawling Mediterranean villa. The guest rooms have private lanais and countless other amenities, plus a prime location near Hulopoe, considered the island's best beach. Local musicians playing Hawaiian tunes accompany cocktail hour at the Hale Ahe Ahe Lounge. The Challenge, a gorgeous course designed by golf great Jack Nicklaus is located here.
249 rooms. High-speed Internet. Restaurant, bar. Children's activity center. Fitness room, spa. Beach. Outdoor pool, whirlpool. Golf, 18 holes. Tennis. Airport transportation available. Business center. $$$$

★★★★Four Seasons Resort the Lodge at Koele

1 Keomoku Hwy., Lanai City,
808-565-2000, 800-819-5053;
www.fourseasons.com

Located upcountry at the center of Lanai, this Victorian-style lodge has extensive and perfectly manicured grounds and a more sophisticated feel than its sister resort, the beachfront Four Seasons Manele Bay. The resort boasts one of the best championship golf courses in the world, designed by PGA legend Greg Norman. Other amenities include children's programs, babysitting services, a health club, yoga classes, tennis,

swimming pools and live evening music in the Great Hall.
102 rooms. High-speed Internet. Restaurant, bar. Fitness room. Outdoor pool, two whirlpools. Golf, 18 holes. Tennis. $$$$

SPECIALTY LODGINGS

Hale Moe Lanai Bed & Breakfast

502 Akolu Place, Lanai City,
808-565-9520, www.staylanai.com

Ideal for families, this three-bedroom house sits in a clearing of tropical fields. Nearby Manele Bay is great for a day outing with its restaurants, museums, art and golf.
3 rooms. Complimentary continental breakfast. $

Hotel Lanai

828 Lanai Ave., Lanai City,
808-565-7211, 877-665-2624;
www.hotellanai.com

Built in the 1920s during the plantation era, this hotel is set in a quiet setting on the edge of Lanai City. The rooms are basic but charming, and the rates are reasonable. Rooms are individually decorated with Hawaiian quilts and original local art. There are no TVs or resort activities, but golf, ocean beaches, hiking and other outdoor pursuits are nearby.
10 rooms. Complimentary continental breakfast. Restaurant, bar. Airport transportation available. $

Lanai Plantation Home

1168 Lanai Ave., Lanai City,
808-565-6961, 800-566-6961;
www.dreamscometruelanai.com

This guest house has been reincarnated as a contemporary hideaway. The four-bedroom, four-bath cottage features skylights, hardwood floors, Italian marble bathrooms and a gourmet kitchen. $

RESTAURANTS

★Blue Ginger Cafe

409 Seventh St., Lanai City,
808-565-6363

American menu. Breakfast, lunch, dinner. Children's menu. Casual attire. Outdoor seating. No credit cards accepted. $

182

HAWAII

★★★★The Dining Room at the Four Seasons Resort the Lodge at Koele

1 Keomoku Hwy., Lanai City,
808-565-7300, 800-819-5053;
www.fourseasons.com.

Located inside the Four Seasons Resort the Lodge at Koele, this fine-dining room is somewhat of an anachronism in laid-back Hawaii. The room is elegant and formal with white-linen topped tables, but there are distinct island influences as well. The food features American classics brought to life with local produce and seafood, showcased in dishes such as butter-poached lobster with salsify, fennel and caviar.
American menu. Breakfast, lunch, dinner. Bar. Children's menu. Jacket required. Reservations recommended. Valet parking. **$$$$**

★Pele's Other Garden

811 Houston St., Lanai City,
808-565-9628, 888-764-3354
Italian, Italian deli menu. Lunch, dinner. Closed Sunday. Casual attire. Reservations recommended (dinner). Outdoor seating. **$$**

SPAS

★★★★The Spa at Four Seasons Manele Bay

1 Manele Bay Rd.,
808-565-2000, 800-819-5053,
www.fourseasons.com

Signature treatments at this Hawaiian spa incorporate centuries-old native skin and beauty rituals. Revitalize skin with a full-body tropical fruit and sea salt scrub, or soothe tired feet with the hehi lani treatment, which uses hot eucalyptus towels, exfoliation and massage. Traditional or Hawaiian lomi lomi massages take place in the spa, the privacy of a guest room or poolside.

MAUI

Miles of beaches. An average temperature of 75 to 85 degrees. Humpback whales splashing around just offshore every winter. Some of the best windsurfing anywhere in the world. For these reasons and many more, Maui attracts more than two million visitors each year.

This tropical playground is called the Valley Isle because of its geography. Maui has two volcanoes, the 10,023-foot-high dormant Haleakala and the 5,788-foot-high extinct Puu Kukui, whose lava spills created a seven-mile-wide green valley between them centuries ago. This so-called Central Valley is home to the island's two major towns, Wailuku and Kahului, which are small by Mainland standards.

In west Maui, the West Maui Mountains rise over the old whaling village of Lahaina, which is packed with shops, restaurants and nightclubs. North of the city are the coastal resort areas of Ka'anapali, Napili and Kapalua.

On the Haleakala side of the island, which is much larger than West Maui, the terrain varies from lush to barren. A rain forest dominates Haleakala's north side, where most visitors make the 55-mile drive to Hana, a remote haven devoid of commercialism. On the volcano's sunny south side, the landscape looks more like a desert and is home to Wailea and Makena's luxury resorts, some of the islands most luxurious which front crescent-shaped beaches.

Venture up Haleakala's slopes into Upcountry Maui to experience art communities, farms, ranches, a winery and a national park. In the early morning hours, folks huddle in the park's chilly high altitude to watch a sunrise that warrants losing a few hours of sleep.
Information: Maui Visitors Bureau, 800-525-6284; www.visitmaui.com

183

HAWAII

★

★

★

★

★

CENTRAL VALLEY

The majority of Maui's residents live in this area in the neighboring towns of Wailuku, the county seat, and Kahului. Visitors to the island arrive at the airport in Kahului, then rent a car and make a beeline straight to coastal resorts.

The restaurants and shops in the Central Valley rely on the business of people who live on Maui year-round, so prices are often lower than the Mainland. In Wailuku, several antique stores and gift shops draw shoppers to Main and Market Streets.

WHAT TO SEE AND DO

Blue Hawaiian Helicopters
1 Kahului Airport Rd., Kahului,
808-871-8844, 800-745-2583;
www.bluehawaiian.com

The panoramic views of the island from one of this company's helicopters are hard to beat. Six regular tours run from a half-hour to 90 minutes and are packed with sights well worth seeing: ancient cinder cones, green valleys, knife-edged ridges, rain forests, mountain pools, rugged shoreline, waterfalls and more. Book its premier tour—the Maui Spectacular—and fly over West Maui and Hana/Haleakalaand and finish with refreshments on a ranch. Daily 7a.m.-10 p.m.

Hang Gliding Maui
32 Kuukama St., Kahului, 808-572-6557;
www.hangglidingmaui.com

Get a spectacular view of Maui aboard one of this outfitter's powered hang gliders. Each glider has two seats, so you'll be airborne with an instructor who will teach you how to fly. Opt for a 30-minute ($115) or 60-minute ($190) lesson. For an extra $25, your adventure can be captured on film with the help of a wing-mounted camera. All flights leave from the Hana airport. Flights are offered throughout the day and reservations are required.

Hawaiian Island Surf and Sport
415 Dairy Rd., Kahului,
808-871-4981, 800-231-6958;
www.hawaiianisland.com

This full-service aquatic shop specializes in anything and everything related to surf-ing, windsurfing, kiteboarding, skimboarding and boogie boarding. Buy or rent the best equipment and accessories available, or sign up for lessons. Instructors teach all levels, from novices to experts. Daily 8:30 a.m.-6 p.m.

Hawaiian Sailboarding Techniques
425 Koloa St., Kahului,
808-871-5423, 800-968-5423;
www.hstwindsurfing.com

Maui is known around the world for its top-rate windsurfing, so why not learn how to ride a board yourself while vacationing on the island? HST's experienced instructors teach all levels at Kanaha Beach Park in Kahului. Novice lessons take place in the morning when winds are calmest; gusts typically intensify by noon when the instructors shift their attention to more advanced riders. Choose from 2 1/2-hour group lessons or 90-minute private sessions. Monday-Saturday, various times.

Maui Arts and Cultural Center
1 Cameron Way, Kahului,
808-242-2787; www.mauiarts.org

The visual and performing arts take center stage at this 12-acre complex overlooking Kahului Harbor. Big-name entertainers such as Bob Dylan, Pearl Jam, Sting and others have performed at its 5,000-seat outdoor amphitheater. Two smaller theaters are used for other performances such as symphony concerts, and the centers museum-quality art gallery hosts traveling exhibitions. Daily 10 a.m.-5 p.m.

HAWAII

Maui Crafts Guild

43 Hana Hwy., Paia, 808-579-9697;
www.mauicraftsguild.com

Twenty-one Maui artists make everything
that's sold in this artist-owned cooperative
gallery. As you wander through the shop,
choose from baskets, beadwork (and other
jewelry), ceramics, framed art, glass creations, sculpture, textiles, wood products
and more. Daily 9 a.m.-6 p.m.

Mendes Ranch Trail Rides

3530 Kahekili Hwy., Wailuku,
808-871-5222;
www.mendesranch.com/rides.htm

This 3,000-acre working ranch (owned by
the Mendes family who first came to Maui
from Portugal in 1866) offers various horseback treks for visitors which last from 2 1/2
to 3 hours. From atop your horse, you'll
see a rain forest, Eki Crater, the West Maui
Mountains, waterfalls, taro patches and
more. Monday-Saturday, times vary.

Pacific Whale Foundation

300 Maalaea Rd., Wailuku,
808-249-8811, 800-942-5311;
www.pacificwhale.org

This foundation offers whale-watching
cruises between December and May. PWF
is all about being kind to the environment,
so its catamarans have been designed with
features that help protect sound-sensitive
whales and other sea creatures. The boats
use an alternative fuel made from recycled
vegetable cooking oils. The foundation
also offers several other tours including a
sunset dinner cruise and snorkeling trips
to Molokini and Lanai. Tours leave from
both Maalaea Harbor and Lahaina Harbor.
The foundation earmarks all of its profits
for programs that help save whales and the
planet's oceans. Daily, times vary.

SPECIALTY LODGINGS

The Old Wailuku Inn at Ulupono

2199 Kaho'okele St., Wailuku,
808-244-5897, 800-305-4899;
www.mauiinn.com

This historic house in the residential area
of Wailuku has 10 guest rooms decorated
with antiques and Hawaiian quilts. A full
breakfast is served every morning on the
veranda.

10 rooms. Complimentary full breakfast.
$$

RESTAURANTS

★★Manana Garage

33 Lono Ave., Kahului, 96732,
808-873-0220; www.mananagarage.com

Latin American menu. Lunch, dinner, late-
night. Closed holidays. Bar. Children's
menu. Casual attire. Reservations recom-
mended. Outdoor seating. $$

EAST MAUI

When you're ready for a road trip, explore East Maui via the Hana Highway. Fifty-two
miles separate Kahului from Hana (population about 700), and those miles take you
through a rain forest and some of the prettiest scenery anywhere in Hawaii. Sights include
waterfalls, freshwater pools, black-sand beaches and more. The drive can take up to three
hours one way, with much of it on two lanes with tons of curves and narrow bridges.

As you enter Hana, it's easy to see why the town is called Maui's Last Hawaiian Place.
None of the tourism-related development that has changed the landscape on other parts of
the island has occurred here. This island community, the birthplace of Queen Kaahumanu,
borders a crescent-shaped bay without a high-rise hotel in sight. At the Hana Cultural Center and Museum, you can learn more about this remote village.

Hana isn't the only city of interest on the east side. Near the Central Valley, at the beginning of the Road to Hana, sits the colorful town of Paia. It's home to a string of small shops
and restaurants located right on the highway. It's also a good place to pick up a picnic

lunch before heading to Hana. A little farther east of Paia, Haiku also has shops and a few bed-and-breakfasts.

WHAT TO SEE AND DO

Hamoa Beach
Hana Hwy., Hana, 96713
Hamoa Beach is remote and not at all touristy, though it's maintained by the Hotel Hana-Maui. It frequently has rip currents and the rolling surf is often high, which makes for dramatic viewing from the shoreline. Daily dawn to dusk.

Hana Coast Gallery
Hana Hwy., Hana,
808-248-8636, 800-637-0188;
www.hanacoast.com
This handsome upscale gallery specializes in local original fine art, including wood, stone and bronze sculptures, turned wood bowls, handcrafted furniture from rare and exotic Hawaiian woods and original prints from the 16th to 20th centuries. Daily, 9 a.m.-5 p.m.

Historic Paia
A sugar mill once defined this quaint little town where the Road to Hana begins. The village is now known for its colorful collection of about 50 eclectic shops and restaurants, located mostly along Hana Road. Come early and have a hearty breakfast at Charley's before you start shopping. Daily, times vary.

Wainapanapa State Park
Hana Hwy., Hana, 808-984-8109
This remote, 122-acre state park located just outside Hana has an impressive black-sand beach, but a strong current and rocky reef make it dangerous for swimming. Instead, hike along the park's coastal trail for great views of the landscape and sea caves. Tent-camping is allowed with reservations, and cabins are located nearby.

HOTELS

★Hana Kai-Maui Resort
1533 Uakea Rd., Hana,
808-248-8426, 800-346-2772;
www.hanakaimaui.com

18 rooms. Wireless Internet access. Beach. **$**

★★★Hotel Hana Maui
5031 Hana Hwy., Hana,
808-248-8211, 800-321-4262;
www. hotelhanamaui.com
Located at the end of the scenic but serpentine Road to Hana, this resort has a beachfront location and extensive, manicured grounds. Bay and Sea Ranch cottages are spacious with living areas and large bathrooms (but no TVs or radios). The resort's wellness center offers treatments, yoga and aerobics classes, tai chi lessons and a broad range of sports and recreation activities.
66 rooms. Three restaurants, bar. Fitness room, fitness classes available, spa. Beach. Two outdoor pools, whirlpool. Tennis. Airport transportation available. Business center. **$$$$**

SPECIALTY LODGINGS

Ala'aina Ocean Vista
Hwy. 184A, Hana,
808-248-7824, 877-216-1733;
www.hanabedandbreakfast.com
The seclusion of Hana is for those who seek a quiet retreat, and this guest house is ideal for that experience. The one-bedroom house is equipped with an open-air kitchen on a private lanai with a stone barbecue grill, a garden tub and outdoor shower and fresh in-room flowers.
1 room. Complimentary continental breakfast. No credit cards accepted. **$$**

Heavenly Hana Inn
Hana, 808-248-8442;
www.heavenlyhanainn.com
Japanese style dominates this bed-and-breakfast. The three guest suites are furnished with private entrances, sitting rooms and large baths. The grounds include Japanese gardens, tea rooms and meditation rooms, and the area's famed black, red and white sand beaches are nearby.
3 rooms. Breakfast available. **$$**

★
★
★
☆
☆

RESTAURANTS

★Charley's
142 Hana Hwy., Paia, 808-579-9453
American menu. Breakfast, lunch, dinner,
late-night. Bar. Casual attire. **$$**

★Jacques North Shore
120 Hana Hwy., Paia, 808-579-8844
Seafood. Dinner. Bar. Casual attire. Out-
door seating. **$$**

★★★Mama's Fish House
799 Poho Place, Paia, 808-579-8488;
www.mamasfishhouse.com

Located on Maui's Kuau Cove, several
miles north of Paia, this restaurant has
a large dining area perched above a crescent-shaped white-sand beach. Fish caught
locally each day make up most of the menu,
from fresh mahi mahi stuffed with lobster
and crab to ahi sashimi salad. Lending
authenticity to the experience are island-
print tablecloths, thatched ceilings, bamboo
walls and Hawaiian music playing in the
background.
Seafood menu. Lunch, dinner. Bar. Children's menu. Casual attire. Reservations
recommended. Valet parking. Outdoor
seating. **$$$**

LAHAINA AND WEST MAUI

Lahaina, an old whaling village, and several attractive resort areas hug the shoreline that
wraps around the base of the splendid West Maui Mountains. This region, called West
Maui, was the first on the island to be developed for tourism and remains one of its most
popular.

To the north of Lahaina are the upscale resorts of Ka'anapali and Kapalua. In Ka'anapali,
six luxury hotels and four condominium complexes front a beach with breathtaking views
of Lanai and Molokai. Complementing the accommodations are two championship golf
courses and Whalers Village, an open-air shopping center with upscale shops (such as
Louis Vuitton and Tiffany) and oceanfront restaurants.

Down the road, the more exclusive town of Kapalua spoils visitors in style with two
waterfront hotels and a group of villas spread out over the mountainside. The resort also
has three golf courses with gorgeous views and three beaches, the most notable being
Kapalua Beach, a crescent-shaped slice of sand with calm, clear water that's usually good
for swimming and snorkeling.

WHAT TO SEE AND DO

Expeditions Lanai
Lahaina Harbor, Lahaina,
808-661-3756, 800-695-2624;
www.go-lanai.com
Hop aboard this inter-island ferry when you
want to spend a day or so in the neighbor-
ing island of Lanai. From Lahaina, the trip
across the Auau Channel takes about one
hour, and you'll ends at Manele Harbor. If
it's whale season, you might also see some
of the humpbacks that frequent these waters
in winter. Daily: from Maui at 6:45 a.m.,
9:15 a.m., 12:45 p.m., 3:15 p.m., and 5:45
p.m.; from Lanai at 8 a.m., 10:30 a.m., 2
p.m., 4:30 p.m. and 6:45 p.m.

Aloha Toy Store
640 Front St., Lahaina,
808-661-1212, 888-628-4227;
www.maui.net/~toystore/harley.htm
Maybe touring Maui in a plain old rental
car isn't your style. This shop rents Har-
leys, Ferraris, Porsches and even humble
Vespa scooters by the hour or the day. The
Aloha Toy Store also has rental outlets in
Ka'anapali and Wailea. Daily 8 a.m.-5 p.m.

America II
Lahaina Harbor,
808-667-2133, 888-667-2133;
www.mauisailingadventures.com
Board this 65-foot yacht, the fast-mov-
ing vessel that raced in the 1987 Americas
Cup. Choose from a whale-watching tour,

an afternoon tradewind sail or a romantic sunset sail. Daily, times vary.

Banyan Tree Park
649 Wharf St., Lahaina
No trip to Lahaina is complete without stopping by this park to see one of the city's most famous landmarks—a banyan tree planted in 1873, the 50th anniversary of the city's first Christian mission. The tree now stands 50 feet tall and has at least 12 trunks with hundreds of sprawling limbs.

Lahaina Divers
143 Dickenson St., Lahaina,
808-667-7496, 800-998-3483;
www.lahainadivers.com
Choose from a variety of diving charters, including treks to Lanai, Molokini Crater, Molokini Backwall and Turtle Reef, frequented by endangered green sea turtles. Most of the trips are for certified divers only, but some allow non-certified divers. The charters range from one to four dives and run from about four to eight hours. Daily, times vary.

Old Lahaina Luau
1251 Front St., Lahaina,
808-667-2998, 800-248-5828;
www.oldlahainaluau.com
The Old Lahaina Luau, a nightly three-hour oceanfront feast, begins with a flower-lei greeting, a demonstration of Hawaiian arts and crafts by local artisans and authentic Hawaiian music. For dinner, there are traditional local dishes with entertainment on an outdoor stage. The fast-paced, award-winning production tells the story of Hawaii, beginning with the migration of the Polynesians to the islands. April-September: daily 5:45 p.m.; October-March: daily 5:15 p.m.

SPECIAL EVENTS
Kapalua Wine and Food Festival
Kapalua Resort, Kapalua,
800-527-2582;
www.kapaluawineandfood.com
More than 3,500 wine and food lovers come to Maui each July for this four-day culinary

event. A grand tasting spotlights the vintages of more than 150 wineries, and a seafood festival features the talents of some of Hawaii's top chefs. Events at various times and venues. Late June.

Mercedes-Benz Championships
500 Bay Dr., Kapalua, 808-669-2440;
www.pgatour.com
Each year in early January, the PGA Tour starts its season with a tournament played by champions from the previous year on the Kapalua Resort's beautiful Plantation Course. To alleviate parking problems, tournament officials offer shuttle service from several locations around the island. Early January.

HOTELS
★★Best Western Pioneer Inn
658 Wharf St., Lahaina,
808-661-3636, 800-457-5457;
www.pioneerinnmaui.com
34 rooms. Restaurant, bar. Outdoor pool. $

★★★Hyatt Regency Maui Resort and Spa
200 Nohea Kai Dr., Ka'anapali,
808-661-1234, 800-554-9288;
www.maui.hyatt.com
This luxurious hotel occupies one of the most enviable locations on Ka'anapali Beach. Diversions include golf, tennis, upscale boutiques and an onsite spa. Two other unique features are a rooftop observatory for stargazing and a full luau with performances and a buffet dinner.
806 rooms. Wireless Internet access. Six restaurants, five bars. Children's activity center. Fitness room, fitness classes available, spa. Beach. Outdoor pool, children's pool, whirlpool. Golf, 36 holes. Tennis. Business center. $$$

★★★Lahaina Inn
127 Lahainaluna Rd., Lahaina,
800-669-3444, 800-669-3444;
www.lahainainn.com
If you prefer a small, intimate inn to a large beach resort, the Lahaina Inn is a great choice. Housed in 1930s-era building in the center of Lahaina's old whaling port,

the inn is steps from the ocean. Rooms are located on the second floor above a small lobby and a first-class restaurant. Lahaina's shops and restaurants are outside the inn's front door, at the corner of Lahainaluna Road and Front Street.
12 rooms. Complimentary continental breakfast. Restaurant, bar. **$**

★Mauian Hotel
5441 Lower Honoapiilani Rd., Napili, 808-669-6205, 800-367-5034; www.mauian.com
44 rooms. Complimentary continental breakfast. Outdoor pool. **$$**

★★Napili Kai Beach Resort
5900 Lower Honoapiilani Rd., Napili, 808-669-6271, 800-367-5030; www.napilikai.com
163 rooms. Closed one week in December. Restaurant, bar. Fitness room. Beach. Four outdoor pools, whirlpool. Business center. **$$$**

★★Outrigger Napili Shores
5315 Lower Honoapiilani Rd., Napili, 808-669-8061, 888-859-7867; www.outrigger.com
97 rooms. High-speed Internet access. Two restaurants, bar. Beach. Two outdoor pools, whirlpool. Business center. **$$**

★★★★The Ritz-Carlton, Kapalua
1 Ritz-Carlton Dr., Kapalua, 808-669-6200, 800-262-8440; www.ritzcarlton.com
Fresh from a complete makeover, this resort has views of the Pacific stretching all the way to Molokai. Rooms have been updated with flatscreen TVs, marble bathrooms and Hawaiian artwork. Part of a 23,000-acre working pineapple plantation, the resort also has two championship golf courses a three-tiered swimming pool and beaches that are about 10 minutes away by foot (a complimentary shuttle transports guests to the beaches, restaurants and golf courses within the Kapalua Resort). A new 14,000 square foot spa has 15 private treatment rooms, treatments inspired by local ingre-

dients and several new couples cabanas. A sushi restaurant has been added to the hotel's collection of six eateries.
548 rooms. Pets accepted. High-speed Internet access. Four restaurants, four bars. Children's activity center. Fitness room, fitness classes available, spa. Beach. Outdoor pool, two whirlpools. Golf. Tennis. Airport transportation available. Business center. **$$$$**

★★★Sheraton Maui Resort
2605 Ka'anapali Pkwy., Ka'anapali, 808-661-0031, 866-716-8109; www.sheraton-hawaii.com
This large beach resort on Maui's northwest coast has an inviting location on a semi-sheltered cove. Most rooms have ocean views and duvet-topped beds. Resort activities run the gamut from snorkeling and whale-watching to tennis, croquet and a full-service spa. Two Ka'anapali Golf Club courses are a short walk away.
510 rooms. Wireless Internet access. Four restaurants, three bars. Children's activity center. Fitness room (fee), spa. Beach. Outdoor pool, children's pool, whirlpool. Tennis. Business center. **$$$$**

★★★Westin Maui Resort & Spa
2365 Ka'anapali Pkwy., Ka'anapali, 808-667-2525, 800-937-8461; www.westin.com/maui
This hotel is located within the expansive Ka'anapali resort complex on Maui's northwest coast. Guest rooms, located in two high-rise towers, have been updated with luxury bedding and beds and tropical-inspired décor. A huge aquatic playground has five pools, water slides and a swim-through grotto. The resort also has a new Reebok gym, a full-service spa with 16 treatment rooms and a yoga studio. The Kaanapali Golf Resort is adjacent to the property.
Pets accepted. Fitness room, spa. Beach. Five outdoor pool, one Jacuzzi. **$$$**

★★★Plantation Inn
174 Lahainaluna Rd., Lahaina, 808-667-9225, 800-433-6815;

189

HAWAII

www.theplantationinn.com
This bed and breakfast is housed in a historic, veranda-encased house dating to the 1900s. Rooms are individually decorated and most have private lanais or balconies. Guests of the inn have full privileges at the nearby Ka'anapali Beach Hotel, located on one of Maui's best beaches. Gerard's, the inn's acclaimed French restaurant, serves a complimentary breakfast.
19 rooms. Complimentary continental breakfast. Restaurant. Outdoor pool, whirlpool. $$

SPECIALTY LODGINGS
Blue Horizons Bed & Breakfast
3894 Mahinahina St., Lahaina,
808-669-1965, 800-669-1948;
www.bluehorizonsmaui.com
While still technically located in the delightful town of Lahaina, this bed and breakfast is slightly off the beaten path and has views of the Pacific, which is only 550 feet from the property.
4 rooms. Complimentary continental breakfast. $

Garden Gate Bed & Breakfast
67 Kaniau Rd., Lahaina,
808-661-8800, 800-939-3217;
www.gardengatebb.com
The garden at this bed-and-breakfast is practically a destination in itself, with a trickling stream winding through plantings of hibiscus, plumeria and birds of paradise. The amenities in the inn's suites and studios include wet bars, private baths and views of the ocean, mountains and neighboring islands.
8 rooms. Complimentary continental breakfast. Wireless Internet access. $

House of Fountains
1579 Lokia St., Lahaina,
808-667-2121, 800-789-6865;
www.alohahouse.com
This inn claims to be the most Hawaiian bed and breakfast on Maui, and with native Hawaiian artifacts adorning each room, its not hard to see why. Everything in each of the six rooms is handmade, including real

koa wood furniture and cozy Hawaiian quilts, and all rooms feature either an ocean or mountain view.
6 rooms. Outdoor pool, whirlpool. $

Old Lahaina House
407 Ilikahi St., Lahaina,
808-667-4663, 800-847-0761;
www.oldlahaina.com
Set in a quiet neighborhood, this bed and breakfast has a large patio courtyard and swimming pool for soaking up sun, and rooms decorated with tropical prints.
4 rooms. $$

Penny's Place in Paradise
1440 Front St., Lahaina,
808-661-1068, 877-431-1235;
www.pennysplace.net
This Victorian house in downtown Lahaina is located only 150 feet from the water's edge. Rooms have elegant period furniture and private baths.
4 rooms. $

Wai Ola Vacation Paradise
1565 Kuuipo St., Lahaina,
808-661-7901, 800-492-4652;
www.waiola.com
Situated in a neighborhood near Lahaina, this inn has five rooms. A pool, jacuzzi and barbecue area anchor the inn, and there are views of the ocean, where humpback whales can be spotted in winter.
5 rooms. $$

RESTAURANTS
★Cheeseburger in Paradise
811 Front St., Lahaina, 808-661-0830;
www.cheeseburgerland.com
American menu. Breakfast, lunch, dinner, late-night. Bar. Casual attire. $

★★Chez Paul
820B Olowalu Village, Lahaina,
808-661-3843; www.chezpaul.net
French menu. Dinner. Closed July 4. Business casual attire. Reservations recommended. $$$

★China Boat
4474 Lower Honoapiilani Rd., Kahana,
808-669-5089
Chinese menu. Lunch, dinner. Bar. Casual
attire. Reservations recommended. Outdoor
seating.**$$**

★★David Paul's Lahaina Grill
127 Lahainaluna Rd., Lahaina,
808-667-5117, 800-360-2606;
www.lahainagrill.com
American menu. Dinner. Bar. Children's
menu. Casual attire. Reservations recom-
mended.**$$$**

★★Erik's Seafood & Sushi
843 Wainee Rd., Lahaina, 808-669-4806
Seafood menu. Lunch, dinner, late-night.
Bar. Children's menu. Casual attire. Reser-
vations recommended.**$$$**

★★★★Gerard's
174 Lahainaluna Rd., Lahaina,
808-661-8939, 877-661-8939;
www.gerardsmaui.com
Chef Gerard Reversade is an internation-
ally recognized master of French cuisine,
but that doesn't mean his namesake res-
taurant doesn't also celebrate its Hawaiian
location. He uses ahi tuna in his Basque-
inspired fisherman's stew, and a poha
berry compote accompanies a seared duck
fois gras appetizer. The flourless chocolate
gateau is created with macadamia nuts and
Kona coffee liqueur, while the apple tarte
tatin includes tropical fruit. Gerard's décor
blends perfectly with the Victorian charm
of its host hotel, the Plantation Inn. Request
a table on the veranda or the garden patio—
they're often the best seats in the house.
French, Hawaiian menu. Dinner. Children's
menu. Business casual attire. Reservations
recommended. Outdoor seating.

★★★I'O
505 Front St., Lahaina, 808-661-8422;
www.iomaui.com
This stylish oceanside restaurant at the south
end of historic Old Lahaina has a modern,
tropical flair and gorgeous views. The menu

features dishes such as fresh sashimi tuna in
a nori and panko crust, Maine lobster tails
in a mango Thai curry sauce and grilled
baby-back ribs with a green apple confit.
Specialty martinis, tropical drinks and an
extensive selection of wines by the glass
and the bottle pair nicely with the cuisine.
French, Pacific-Rim/Pan-Asian menu. Din-
ner. Bar. Children's menu. Business casual
attire. Reservations recommended. Outdoor
seating.**$$$**

★★Kimo's
845 Front St., Lahaina, 808-661-4811;
www.kimosmaui.com
American, seafood menu. Lunch, dinner.
Closed holidays. Bar. Children's menu.
Casual attire. Outdoor seating.**$$**

★★Lahaina Fish Company
831 Front St., Lahaina, 808-661-3472;
www.lahainafishcompany.com
Seafood menu. Lunch, dinner. Bar. Chil-
dren's menu. Casual attire. Reservations
recommended.**$$**

★★Longhi's
888 Front St., Lahaina,
808-667-2288, 888-844-2288;
www.longhi-maui.com
International menu. Breakfast, lunch, dinner, late-night. Bar. Reservations recom-
mended. Valet parking.**$$**

★★Old Lahaina Luau
1251 Front St., Lahaina,
808-667-1998, 800-248-5828;
www.oldlahainaluau.com
Pacific-Rim/Pan-Asian menu. Dinner.
Closed one week in mid-December. Bar.
Casual attire. Reservations recommended.
Outdoor seating. **$$$$**

★★Pacific'O
505 Front St., Lahaina, 808-667-4341;
www.pacificomaui.com.
Pacific-Rim/Pan-Asian menu. Lunch, din-
ner. Bar. Children's menu. Business casual
attire. Reservations recommended. Outdoor
seating.**$$$**

191

HAWAII

★

★

★

★

★

★Pioneer Inn Bar and Grill
658 Wharf St., Lahaina, 808-661-3636;
www.pioneerinnmaui.com
American menu. Breakfast, lunch, dinner.
Bar. Children's menu. Casual attire. Outdoor seating.**$$**

★★★Plantation House Restaurant
2000 Plantation Club Dr., Kapalua,
808-699-6299;
www.theplantationhouse.com
The PGA Mercedes-Benz Championship is
played on the Plantation Golf Course each
year, and this restaurant offers an impressive 180-degree view of the links, the
Pacific Ocean and the island of Molokai.
The casual but sophisticated restaurant features contemporary island-inspired décor,
with two levels of dining rooms and terrace
and bar dining. On the menu is a selection
of creative salads and a variety of fresh seafood like seared scallops with orzo pasta.
Mediterranean, Pacific-Rim/Pan-Asian
menu. Breakfast, lunch, dinner, brunch.
Bar. Children's menu. Business casual
attire. Reservations recommended.**$$$**

★★★Roy's Kahana Bar & Grill
4405 Honoapiilani Hwy., Kahana,
808-669-6999;
www.roysrestaurant.com
The second in chef/owner Roy Yamaguchi's chain of contemporary Hawaiian
restaurants, this outpost is a sleek, upscale
space with a large, attractive dining room
and an impressive demonstration kitchen.
The cuisine is dubbed Hawaiian fusion,
and features Asian and European prepara-

tions of fresh seafood. Prix fixe meals are
available, and the wine list includes selections made by winemakers specifically for
Roy's.
Pacific-Rim/Pan-Asian menu. Dinner. Bar.
Children's menu. Casual attire. Reservations recommended. **$$**

★★Sansei
600 Office Rd., Kapalua, 808-669-6286;
www.sanseihawaii.com
Japanese, sushi menu. Dinner, late-night.
Closed Mon-Wed. Bar. Casual attire. Reservations recommended. **$$**

★Sunrise Cafe
693A Front St., Lahaina,
808-661-8558
American menu. Lunch, brunch. Casual
attire. Outdoor seating. No credit cards
accepted. **$**

SPAS

★★★Spa Moana
200 Nohea Kai Dr., Lahaina, 808-661-1234;
www.hyatt.com
Located in the Hyatt Regency Maui, this
relaxing retreat has 15 treatment rooms
where technicians deliver services such as
traditional Hawaiian lomi-lomi massage
or a decadent macadamia nut wrap. The
salon offers manicures and pedicures (with
a unique sugar scrub version for men). The
Moana Athletic Club has 5,000 square feet
of cutting edge exercise machines, weights
and classroom space for yoga, aerobics and
more. **$$**

UPCOUNTRY MAUI

From on top of Pu'u Ulla'ula (or Red Hill) mountain, the panoramic views of Maui and the
ocean beyond are nothing short of breathtaking. The sand and palm trees give way to green
pastureland and ranches as you snake your way up the 10,000-foot mountain. As the terrain
turns desert-like near the summit, be on the lookout for silversword plants, a member of the
yucca family that grows only here.

The major reason visitors come Upcountry is to make their way to the summit and
explore Haleakala National Park. But Upcountry also includes Tedeschi Vineyards, which
makes wine from tropical fruit, and Kula Botanical Gardens, six acres of blooming splendor at 3,300 feet. Shoppers stop in the little town of Makawao in the middle of Maui's
paniolo country, where talented artisans have opened galleries and shops.

WHAT TO SEE AND DO

Baldwin Avenue
Baldwin Ave., Makawao

Galleries line both sides of the street in this Upcountry artists' community, as do gift and souvenir shops and a few cozy restaurants. For something sweet, try any of the pastries at the Komoda Store and Bakery, a longtime Makawao favorite.

Bike tours of Haleakala
Haleakala

Every year, thousands of people ride nearly 40 miles down Haleakala, Maui's dormant volcano. It's one of the most popular activities on the island, and one of the most fun and scenic. Several companies offer tours, and most are guided. Tour companies that specialize in bike treks include Haleakala Bike Co. (888-922-2453), Maui Downhill (800-535-2453), Maui Mountain Cruisers (800-232-6284) and Mountain Riders Bike Tours (800-706-7700).

Haleakala National Park
Hwy. 378, Makawao, 808-572-4400;
www.nps.gov/hale

Originally a part of Hawaii Volcanoes National Park, this 30,183-acre park was established as a separate entity in 1961 to preserve the Haleakala Crater and the surrounding volcanic landscape. Often, you can see up to 115 miles out to sea from the summit. Dress warmly if you plan to travel to the summit (about a one and 1/2-hour drive from Kahului), especially if you come for a sunrise or stay in the park to watch the sun set. Between dusk and dawn, temperatures regularly drop below freezing.

Hui No'eau Visual Arts Center
2841 Baldwin Ave., Makawao,
808-572-6560; www.huinoeau.com

The striking Kaluanui mansion, built in the early 1900s, was once the home of Harry and Ethel Baldwin who made their fortune in the pineapple industry. The lovely estate is now an art center. View the exhibit galleries, participate in hands-on classes taught by visiting artists or tour the grounds. Monday-Saturday 10 a.m.-4 p.m.

Maui Polo Club
Makawao, 808-877-7744;
www.mauipolo.com

Each spring and summer (in April, May, and June), this club sponsors indoor polo matches at the Manduke Baldwin Polo Arena on Haleakala Highway. Come fall, the clubs play in the fresh air at the Olinda Outdoor Polo Field. If you play this game and are a rated player, you can lease horses for chukkers. Gates open 12:30 p.m.; games begin at 1:30 p.m.

Tedeschi Vineyards
Ulupalakua Ranch, Kula Hwy., Ulupalakua,
808-878-6058; www.mauiwine.com

Sample locally produced wine at Maui's only vineyard, located on a ranch on the southern slopes of Haleakala. Choose from red, white, sparkling and fruit wines. You'll do your tasting in a historic cottage built in the 1870s specifically for King Kalakaua. Pack a picnic lunch and find a spot to enjoy the views from 2,000 feet above sea level. Daily 9 a.m.-5 p.m.; free tours at 10:30 a.m. and 1:30 p.m.

SPECIALTY LODGINGS

Hale Ho'okipa Bed & Breakfast
32 Pakani Place, Makawao,
808-572-6698;
www.maui-bed-and-breakfast.com

Built in 1927 as a plantation house, this bed and breakfast is listed by both the Hawaii State and National Historic Registers. Decorated with local art and native wood furniture, the three guest rooms are located in the main house, while the Kipa Cottage, moss-green and two-story, has rustic furnishings and large windows framing views of the Haleakala Crater.
5 rooms. $

RESTAURANTS

★★★Haliimaile General Store
900 Haiimaile Rd., Haliimaile,
808-572-2666;
www.haliimailegeneralstore.com

Occupying the old general store of a former sugar plantation, this unique restaurant is the inspiration of chef/owner Beverly Gannon.

Despite the historical context, the dining room is contemporary. The menu features local seafood like blackened ahi with sweet Thai chili sauce, and heartier offerings like braised short ribs with truffle white cheddar macaroni and cheese.

Pacific-Rim/Pan-Asian menu. Lunch, dinner. Closed holidays. Bar. Children's menu. Casual attire. Reservations recommended. $$$

★**Makawao Garden Cafe**
3669 Baldwin Ave., Makawao, 808-573-9065
Vegetarian menu. Lunch. Casual attire. Outdoor seating. No credit cards accepted. $

★★**Makawao Steak House**
3612 Baldwin Ave., Makawao, 808-572-8711
Steak menu. Dinner, Sunday brunch. Closed holidays. Bar. Children's menu. Casual attire. Reservations recommended. Outdoor seating. $$

KIHEI AND SOUTH MAUI

Year-round good weather is the draw on this increasingly popular side of Maui, which runs down the south coast from Maalaea to Makena, with Kihei and Wailea between them. This well-manicured resort town has the island's most exclusive hotels and condominiums, most of them beachfront. The area has five crescent-shaped beaches, high end shopping and three championship golf courses.Neighboring Makena is more private, with just one luxury hotel and a few condominiums, as well as two Robert Trent Jones Jr. designed golf courses. Kihei, just north of Wailea, is a more laid back coastal community with budget-friendly hotels and condominiums, most an easy walk from the town's beaches. Up the coast a few miles, tiny Maalaea is beginning to grow, thanks to its small harbor. From here, you can climb aboard boats for everything form snorkeling trips to whale-watching cruises. The town is also home to the Maui Ocean Center, the island's aquarium.

WHAT TO SEE AND DO
Keawalai Congregational Church
190 Makena Rd., Makena, 808-879-5557; www.keawalai.org
Built with lava rock and coral mortar in 1855, this church sits on a quiet stretch of beach. On Sunday mornings at 7:30 and 10 a.m. it provides a Hawaiian-language service. In the cemetery, many tombstones feature ceramic pictures. Tuesday-Saturday 9 a.m.-5 p.m., Sunday during worship services.

Kihei Canoe Club
Kihei, 808-879-5505; www.kiheicanoeclub.com
The members of this club take the island tradition of outrigger canoeing seriously. They practice their paddling regularly and compete in fast-paced races throughout the islands. Twice a week they invite visitors to join them for a fun hour of recreational canoeing. The club provides the equipment, basic training and an experienced crew to ensure a smooth ride. Tuesday and Thursday at 7:30 a.m.

Maui Dive Shop
1455 S. Kihei Rd., Kihei, 808-879-3388, 800-542-3483; www.mauidiveshop.com
Hawaii's largest dive shop operates solely on Maui, where it has nine retail outlets spread across the island. It offers diving and snorkeling trips to the best sites, dive courses, rental gear and even a dive lodge. The activity desk can book other adventures from sailing and deep-sea fishing trips to horseback-riding and luaus. Daily 6 a.m.-9 p.m.

Maui Ocean Center
192 Ma'alaea Rd., Ma'alaea, 808-270-7000; www.mauioceancenter.com
This center highlights the beauty and wonder of Hawaii's marine life. More than 60

interactive exhibits describe the thousands of sea creatures that swim in the water beyond the shoreline and reef. The Underwater Journey exhibit features a 50-foot-long acrylic tunnel that offers a spectacular 240-degree view of sharks and other predators swimming in a 750,000-gallon saltwater aquarium. Daily 9 a.m.-5 p.m.

Molokini
Wailea-Makena, Off the South Shore; www.molokini.us

Most visitors to Maui take one of the many snorkeling or diving tours to this marine life park, located two and half miles off the South Shore between West Maui and Kahoolawe, an uninhabited island. The small, crescent-shaped Molokini is a volcanic cinder cone whose northern rim is beneath sea level, which causes its crater to be flooded. The underwater sightseeing is fabulous, with more than 250 species of fish playfully swimming in this area. The water depth around Molokini varies from just 35 feet to more than 350 feet, making this site perfect for all levels of snorkelers and divers. Daily; boat tours by multiple companies at various times, mostly in the mornings.

South Pacific Kayaks & Outfitters
2439 S. Kihei Rd., Kihei, 808-875-4848, 800-776-2326; www.southpacifickayaks.com

Maui's only full-service kayak shop offers tours on both the south and west sides of the island. On the south side, you'll explore the Ahihi Kinau Marine Reserve, Makena Bay, Turtle Reef or Turtle Town. On the west side, opt for a trip along the Ukumehame Valley shoreline or one that takes you from Ka'anapali to Lahaina. Daily, times vary.

SPECIAL EVENTS
Maui Film Festival
Wailea, 808-572-3456; www.mauifilmfestival.com

Each year, Hollywood comes to Maui's South Shore for five days in mid-June for this cinema festival. More than 50 films are screened by an array of celebrities, directors, producers, writers and movie buffs in three outdoor venues under the stars. The festival runs in conjunction with the Taste of Wailea. Mid-June.

HOTELS
★★★Fairmont Kea Lani Maui
4100 Wailea Alanui, Wailea, 808-875-4100, 800-441-1414; www.fairmont.com

Resting on the island's southwestern shore with Mount Haleakala as a backdrop, this 22-acre oceanfront property is Hawaii's only all-suite and villa luxury resort. All suites have private lanais, marble wet bars and DVD players. Shuttle service is available to nearby tennis facilities and the renowned Wailea Golf Club. The Spa Kea Lani features Hawaiian ingredients in treatments such as the sugar cane body polish. 450 rooms, all suites. Pets accepted. High-speed Internet access. Five restaurants, bar. Children's activity center. Fitness room, fitness classes available, spa. Beach. Outdoor pool, whirlpool. Airport transportation available. Business center. **$$$$**

★★★★★Four Seasons Resort Maui at Wailea
3900 Wailea Alanui, Wailea, 808-874-8000, 800-268-6282; www.fourseasons.com/maui.

Blessed with abundant sunshine and perfect white-sand beaches, Wailea is one of Maui's best destinations, and this resort is its most exclusive address. Guest rooms are studies in laid-back sophistication, with pastel colors, tropical patterns, rattan furnishings and oversized marble bathrooms. Lighted tennis courts, water sports, indoor and outdoor exercise facilities and off-site golf awaken the athlete in everyone, while shimmering pools provide a spot for lounging around. 380 rooms. Pets accepted, some restrictions. High-speed Internet access. Three restaurants, three bars. Children's activity center. Fitness room, fitness classes available, spa. Beach. Three outdoor pools, children's pool, whirlpool. Tennis. Airport transportation available. Business center. **$$$$**

★★★Grand Wailea Resort Hotel & Spa
3850 Wailea Alanui Dr., Wailea,
808-875-1234, 800-888-6100;
www.grandwailea.com

From its $50 million art collection to its nine pools on six levels, this lavish resort caters to both the sophisticate and the child in everyone. Tennis, golf and water sports are available, or the concierge can arrange excursions such as deep-sea fishing, helicopter tours, jeep adventures and horseback riding. There is an adults-only pool and a theme park-style Canyon Activity Pool with slides, waterfalls and the world's only water elevator.

780 rooms. High-speed Internet access. Five restaurants, five bars. Fitness room, fitness classes available, spa. Beach. Outdoor pool, whirlpool. Tennis. Business center. **$$$$**

★★★Wailea Beach Marriott Resort and Spa
3700 Wailea Alanui Dr., Wailea,
808-879-9122, 800-367-2960;
www.waileamarriott.com

The first resort built in the high-end Wailea resort complex, this hotel recently underwent a complete renovation. Built on a point of land with lava cliffs at the waters edge, there are two beautiful, sandy beaches on either side of the resort. In addition to the championship golf courses shared by all the Wailea resorts, the Marriott has five pools, a jogging trail, a putting green, ocean sports, a shopping arcade and a full-service spa and salon.

521 rooms. High-speed Internet access. Restaurant, bar. Fitness room, spa. Five outdoor pools, children's pool, whirlpool. Airport transportation available. Business center. **$$$**

★★Maui Coast Hotel
2259 S. Kihei Rd., Kihei,
808-874-6284, 800-895-6284;
www.mauicoasthotel.com

265 rooms. Two restaurants, two bars. Outdoor pool, children's pool, whirlpool. Tennis. Business center. **$$**

★★★Maui Prince Hotel
5400 Makena Alanui, Makena,
808-874-1111;
www.princeresortshawaii.com

Located on the far end of Maui's southwestern coast, this full-service golf and beach resort is set on a secluded expanse of oceanfront property. Overlooking crescent-shaped Makena Beach, the resort offers a wide range of outdoor activities, including tennis, snorkeling, jogging trails and a pool complex. It also has two 18-hole golf courses, one of which was designed by Robert Trent Jones. The hotel is built around a lushly landscaped, open-to-the-sky atrium with an attractive Asian meditation garden. The guest room wings are set up so that all rooms have ocean views.

310 rooms. Four restaurants, bar. Children's activity center. Fitness room. Beach. Outdoor pool, children's pool, two whirlpools. Golf, 36 holes. Tennis. **$$$$**

SPECIALTY LODGINGS
Kai's Bed & Breakfast
80 E. Welakahao Rd., Kihei,
808-874-6431, 800-905-8424;
www.mauibb.com

The hosts of this bed and breakfast fell in love with it when they came to stay here in 1997. The suites, which are named for the tropical fruits that grow just outside the door, are located a short walk from shopping, dining and tennis facilities. The owners also provide guests with beach chairs, umbrellas, body boards, bicycles, coolers and snorkel gear for days at the beach, which is two blocks from the house.

5 rooms. Complimentary continental breakfast. **$**

Maui What a Wonderful World B&B
2828 Umalu Place, Kihei,
800-943-5804;
www.amauibedandbreakfast.com

Located in dense island greenery, this house's four suites feel less like guest rooms and more like rooms you'd find at a friend's vacation house. The suites feature floor-to-ceiling windows and a common lanai with an outdoor grill.

★

★

★

★

★

4 rooms. Complimentary continental breakfast. **$**

RESTAURANTS

★★Greek Bistro
2511 S. Kihei Rd., Kihei, 808-879-9330;
www.restauranteur.com/greekbistro
Greek menu. Dinner. Bar. Children's menu. Business casual attire. Reservations recommended. Outdoor seating.**$$**

★★★★Spago
3900 Wailea Alanui, Wailea, 808-879-2999;
www.wolfgangpuck.com
With Spago at the Four Seasons Resort Maui at Wailea, Wolfgang Puck shows that, despite recent culinary forays into fast food and canned soups, he remains a master of the fine-dining experience. The Spago name, of course, isn't unique—Puck catapulted to international fame back in 1982 with the first Spago on Sunset Boulevard, and he currently operates three Spago outposts on the mainland: two in California and one in Las Vegas. Each Spago maintains its own identity, and that's good news for anyone who's hungry in Hawaii. The menu incorporates the best of the islands, fusing traditional Hawaiian tastes and locally sourced ingredients with Asian influences and Puck's signature California style. Hawaiian, Pacific-Rim/Pan-Asian menu. Dinner. Bar. Children's menu. Business casual attire. Reservations recommended. Valet parking. Outdoor seating. **$$$**

★Thailand Cuisine
1819 S. Kihei Rd., Kihei, 808-875-0839;
www.thailandcruisinemaui.com
Thai menu. Lunch, dinner. Casual attire. **$$**

SPAS

★★★★Spa Grande at Grand Wailea Resort
3850 Wailea Alanui Dr., Wailea,
808-875-1234, 800-888-6100;
www.grandwailea.com
The Grand Wailea's 50,000-square-foot spa has elegant interiors, a comprehensive fitness center and extensive spa menu. Visits begin with a one-hour Wailea hydrotherapy session, featuring five different aromatic baths to choose from including a bubbling Japanese furo bath, cascading waterfall, cold plunge pool, eucalyptus steam room and a redwood sauna, Roman Jacuzzi, or Swiss jet shower. Spa Grande's sizable menu includes a blend of classic treatments, Hawaiian favorites and eastern therapies. Experience pure pleasure with a deep shiatsu barefoot massage, or awaken your senses with an aromatherapy massage, just two of the 12 different types of massage available. **$$**

★★★★The Spa at Four Seasons Resort Maui at Wailea
3900 Wailea Alanui Dr., Wailea,
808-874-8000, 800-334-6284,
www.fourseasons.com
While the signature massages at this spa introduce guests to Hawaiian traditions, the body treatments expose them to the bounty of the islands. Using native and natural ingredients, these unique treatments rejuvenate skin, and smell and feel heavenly while doing so. The mango salt glow uses mango sorbet to exfoliate skin while the Hawaiian nut-sugar scrub employs a blend of macadamia, coconut and kukui nut to smooth skin. The papaya-pineapple body scrub combines those fruits with finely crushed grape seeds. With its orchid and sea salt bath, mango salt exfoliation, refreshing moisturizing treatment, and divine reflexology massage, the ultimate foot treatment delivers what it promises. **$$**

★★★Spa Kealani
4100 Wailea Alanui Dr., Wailea, 808-875-2229, 800-441-1414; www.fairmont.com
Poolside massages and lomi lomi massage are just some of the treats at this spa located in the Fairmont Kea Lani Maui. Body wraps make the most of local ingredients, including natural sugar cane, ginger and lime. Those who prefer to have their massages in private can opt for an in-room treatment. A full-service fitness center offers private yoga lessons or beach front workouts. **$$**

HAWAII

★
★
★
★
★

OAHU

Even though Oahu is only the third-largest Hawaiian Island, it's the most populous. Nearly 900,000 people, or about 80 percent of the state's population, live on the island.

Honolulu remains the island's business and state capital and home to most Oahu residents. More than 800,000 of them live on the South Shore, in sprawling neighborhoods in and around the city.

Nearly five million tourists crowd onto Waikiki Beach every year. Besides the world famous beaches, Honolulu's biggest attractions are Pearl Harbor and Diamond Head. Others include Iolani Palace, the home of Queen Liliuokalani until the monarchy fell in 1893, the state capitol building and Kawaihao Church, built in the 1830s and called the Westminster Abbey of Hawaii.

Away from the city, much of Oahu is rural, unspoiled and strikingly beautiful. Many little towns and villages sit between the ocean and two mountain ranges, Koolau and Waianae, which were formed by volcano eruptions. The mountains and their forests run parallel to one another down the eastern and western coasts with scenic hiking trails.

The North Shore is known for its many world-class surfing beaches, such as Banzai Pipeline and Sunset. On the Windward Coast, many locals consider Kailua Beach the island's best stretch of sand. Its strong gusts make it a haven for windsurfers and kitesurfers. Just up the road in Kanehoe is one of Hawaii's most gorgeous bays, where boating companies offer trips out to a sandbar for swimming and snorkeling. Farther north, several more secluded beaches add beauty to the coastline.

Information: Oahu Visitors Bureau, 877-525-6248; www.visit-oahu.com

HONOLULU AND THE SOUTH SHORE

Honolulu, on Oahu's South Shore, is the largest city in Hawaii. On the east side, the city begins at Diamond Head, where you can hike the 760 feet to its top for great panoramic views. From this volcano, Honolulu stretches westward for about 26 miles to Pearl Harbor. Every day, thousands go to the harbor to learn about the Japanese attack on December 7, 1941, which drew the U.S. into World War II.

About five million sun-seekers visit Honolulu every year, and most of them stay in famed Waikiki, where high-rise hotels line picturesque beaches. Although only a little more than two miles long, Waikiki overflows with restaurants, nightclubs and shops.

From Waikiki, Honolulu runs inland about 12 miles. In the middle of it all are attractions such as the Bishop Museum, Chinatown, Iolani Palace, Kawaihao Church, the Mission Houses Museum and the State Capitol Building.

Information: www.co.honolulu.hi.us

WHAT TO SEE AND DO

2100 Kalakaua
2100 Kalakaua Ave., Honolulu, 808-955-2878; www.2100kalakaua.com
A select group of high-end boutiques are housed here, including Chanel, Gucci, Tiffany, Tods, Boucheron and Yves Saint Laurent. Ongoing events promote Hawaii's arts and culture. Valet parking is available; complimentary validated self-parking is available next door at King Kalakaua Plaza. Daily 10 a.m.-10 p.m.

Ahupuaa O Kahana State Park
52-222 Kamehameha Hwy., Kahana, 808-237-7766; www.hawaii.gov/dlnr/dsp/oahu.html
This scenic 5,200-acre park, formerly known as Kahana Valley State Park, has become an archaeological dig. Researchers have found extensive remnants of Hawaiian culture here. Most sites are currently inaccessible to the public, but there are some that are open for viewing. Camping is available by permit; call 808-587-0300 for information. Daily dawn-dusk.

Ala Moana Beach Park
1201 Ala Moana Blvd., Honolulu
Located directly across from Oahu's largest shopping center, Ala Moana comprises more than a mile of sandy coastline stretching between Waikiki and downtown Honolulu. At the Waikiki end, jutting into Mamala Bay is Magic Island, a peninsula that has picnic areas, a swimming lagoon and paved paths for walkers, joggers and inline skaters.

Ala Moana Center
1450 Ala Moana Blvd., Honolulu,
808-955-9517;
www.alamoana.com
Within walking distance of most Waikiki hotels, this tri-level 240-store mall includes stores in every price range. Included here is Reyn's, which for 40 years has been the place to shop for men's Aloha wear. Reyn's Rack in Downtown Honolulu at 125 Merchant Street houses discounted merchandise from their collections.

American Institute of Architects Downtown Walking Tour
119 Merchant St., Honolulu,
808-545-4242; www.aiahonolulu.org
Honolulu's unique culture is reflected in both its contemporary and historic architecture. Take a walking tour of downtown Honolulu, led by a member of the American Institute of Architects and explore Hawaii's history. Call AIA Honolulu for tour times.

Anne Namba Designs
324 Kamani St., Honolulu, 808-589-1135;
www.annenamba.com
One of Hawaii's premier designers, Anne Namba creates contemporary women's and men's fashions using vintage kimono and obi fabrics from Japan. Her wedding couture line is the perfect marriage of East and West. Namba's designs also take center stage in the costuming for productions of Hawaii's Opera Theatre.

Bailey's Antiques and Aloha Shirts
517 Kapahulu Ave., Honolulu,
808-734-7628
Bailey's is a treasure trove of classic Aloha shirts, which were made popular in the 1930s, 40s and 50s and today come with serious collectors' price tags. There are also vintage souvenirs, memorabilia, photos spanning Hawaii's history from its most sublime to its touristy tacky. Daily 10 a.m.-6 p.m.

Battleship *Missouri* Memorial
501 Main St., Honolulu,
808-423-2263, 877-644-4896;
www.ussmissouri.com
Commissioned in 1940 and launched on January 29, 1944, this battleship served the United States for half a century before being retired and turned into a memorial. General Douglas MacArthur accepted Japan's surrender on the deck on September 2, 1945, ending World War II. Daily 9 a.m.-5 p.m.

Contemporary Museum
2411 Makiki Heights Dr., Honolulu,
808-526-1322, 866-991-2835;
www.tcmhi.org
The only thing here that dates before 1940 is the museum itself—it's housed in the historic Spalding House, which was built in 1925. Spend the afternoon pondering provocative pieces by some of the world's top contemporary artists including David Hockney, Jasper Johns and Deborah Butterfield. The museum's smaller downtown branch has local works and is located at the First Hawaiian Center. Tuesday-Saturday 10 a.m.-4 p.m., Sunday noon-4 p.m.

Diamond Head State Monument
Honolulu, 808-923-1811
Several short volcanic eruptions between 100,000 and 300,000 years ago created L'ahi, now known as Hawaii's most famous landmark, Diamond Head State Monument. The 1.4-mile hiking trail ends with a 560-foot climb up stairways and through dark tunnels leading to the crater. The reward: a 360-degree view of the island. Daily 6 a.m.-6 p.m.

HAWAII

Foster Botanical Garden

50 N. Vineyard Blvd., Honolulu,
808-522-7060;
www.co.honolulu.hi.us/parks/hbg/fbg.htm
After a German doctor and his wife leased
the land from Queen Kalama in 1853, they
planted trees that still stand on the site
today. Now more than 70 years old, the
Foster Botanical Garden features a wide
range of plants and flowers and herb and
spice gardens. Daily 9 a.m.-4 p.m.

Hans Hedemann Surf School

2586 Kalakaua Ave., Honolulu,
808-924-7778; www.hhsurf.com
In addition to surf school, Hedemann and
his instructors offer body surfing lessons
and surf camps at locations island-wide
with treks to Oahu's North and South
shores. Private surf lessons with Hedemann
are available upon request. Hedemann
accepts children five years and older, and
transportation is available from Waikiki to
North Shore locations.

Hawaii Geographic Society Downtown Tours

553 S. King St., Honolulu, 808-538-3952
The Hawaii Geographic Society offers
a variety of downtown guided walking
tours that include an archaeological tour of
Hawaii's rich historic downtown as well as
a temple tour of religious structures of various faiths found within downtown Honolulu. There is a minimum of three people
per tour.

Hawaii Nature Center

2131 Makiki Heights Dr., Honolulu,
808-955-0100;
www.hawaiinaturecenter.org
This nonprofit center helps children become
stewards of the *aina* (land) and offers weekend family outings and programs as well as
interpretive hikes, nature adventures and
projects.

Hawaii State Art Museum

250 S. Hotel St., Honolulu,
808-586-0300; www.hawaii.gov/sfca

Explore Hawaii's rich artistic tradition in
the museum's three galleries. The Diamond
Head, Ewa and Sculpture galleries house a
wide variety of art forms and styles, including traditional arts like quilting and pottery.
Tuesday-Saturday 10 a.m.-4 p.m.

Hawaii Theatre Center

1130 Bethel St., Honolulu, 808-528-0506;
www.hawaiitheatre.com
This historic downtown Honolulu theater
first opened in 1922 and hosted plays,
musical concerts and films. Almost left to
the wrecking ball in 1986, a group of theater preservationists and cultural patrons
spearheaded a restoration that took more
than a decade to complete. The Hawaii Theatre is now a 1,400-seat state-of-the-art performance venue. It presents local, national
and international artists in music, dance and
theatrical productions. To learn more about
the history, architecture and artwork, join a
weekly 60-minute guided tour, held Tues-
days at 11 a.m.

Hawaii Time Walk Tours

The Haunt, 2634 S. King St., Honolulu,
808-943-0371
A coffee shop and bookstore in Honolulu's
university neighborhood known as the
Haunt is the headquarters for two distinct
Hawaiian tours. Take the Ghost Hunters
Bus Tour Saturday evenings from 6:30 to
11 p.m. for a ride so spooky that kids under
13 are not allowed. On the last Friday of the
month, learn about the mysteries surrounding Oahu's historic Moilili neighborhood
in a walkabout evening tour. Kids 12 and
older are accepted for this tour. Guides are
costumed and full of stories of the legends
and ghosts of Hawaiian culture. New tours
and haunts are continually added, so call for
tour topics, schedules, times and rates.

Hawaiian Fire Surf School

3318 Campbell Ave., Honolulu,
808-737-3473, 888-955-7873;
www.hawaiianfire.com
The two-hour lessons offered by this outfitter include 45 minutes of land instruc-

tion followed by 75 minutes in the water. Group and private lessons provide foam-covered surfboards, reef shoes, accessories, shade tent and chair and transportation from Waikiki. Children 12 years and younger must have a private lesson. Daily 9 a.m.-6 p.m.

Heli USA Airways
155 Kapalulu Place, Honolulu,
808-833-3306, 866-936-1234;
www.heliusa.com
Many travelers opt to catch a view of Hawaii from a helicopter tour, and Heli USA is one of several companies to provide that service out of Honolulu International Airport. (Passengers are picked up at and returned to their hotels.) Tours include the nighttime Honolulu City Lights Flight, the Oahu Highlights Flight and the Oahu Deluxe Island Flight. You can also sign up for a day-long tour of Kauai, a good option if you'd like to see other islands but don't have much time to island-hop. Daily.

Honolulu Academy of Arts
900 S. Beretania St., Honolulu,
808-532-8700;
www.honoluluacademy.org
With a collection of more than 34,000 works, the Academy is Hawaii's premier art museum. Particularly strong is its Asian collection, which makes up almost half of the total collection. The museum also exhibits Western art from ancient Greece, Rome and Egypt to the present. The Doris Duke Theatre shows independent and foreign films and hosts lectures, concerts and theatrical performances. Tuesday-Saturday 10 a.m.-4:30 p.m., Sunday 1-5 p.m.

Shangri La
900 S. Beretania St., Honolulu,
866-385-3849;
www.shangrilahawaii.org
Shangri La was the home of socialite Doris Duke. For 60 years she collected Islamic art and filled her home with the works she amassed throughout her life. Today, the estate houses more than 3,500 pieces of art dating from 1500 B.C. to the 20th century,

including ceramics, decorative arts and furniture. The tour begins with a short film at the Honolulu Academy of Art followed by a 15-minute drive to Shangri La, where guests spend 1 1/2 hours on a guided walk through the main house and grounds. Make reservations as far in advance as possible, as demand is high and tour groups are small. Tickets are nonrefundable. Wednesday-Saturday 8:30 a.m.-1:30 p.m.; closed September.

Honolulu Zoo
151 Kapahulu Ave., Honolulu,
808-926-3191; www.honoluluzoo.org
This zoo features exhibits on the African Savanna, Tropical Forest, Islands of the Pacific and a children's zoo. The "Snooze in the Zoo" program gives families the chance to have a sleepover party at the zoo. Other programs include "Breakfast with a Keeper" and "Twilight Tours." Daily 9 a.m.-4:30 p.m.

Hoomaluhia Botanical Garden
45-680 Luluku Rd., Kaneohe,
808-233-7323;
www.co.honolulu.hi.us/parks/hbg/hmbg.htm
Built by the U.S. Army Corps of Engineers to provide flood protection for Kaneohe, this 400-acre botanical garden contains endangered and rare plants as well as a network of trails for hikers, bikers, and horseback riders. Daily 9 a.m.-4 p.m.

International Market Place
2330 Kalakaua Ave., Honolulu,
808-971-2080;
www.internationalmarketplacewaikiki.com
More than 130 shops and artisans' carts draw shoppers to this Waikiki fixture for Hawaiian gifts and souvenirs. Jewelry, clothing and handicrafts make up the majority of the offerings. You'll also find a variety of options for snacks and quick meals. On many evenings, local musicians perform. Daily 10 a.m.-10:30 p.m.

Iolani Palace State Monument
King and Richards Streets, Honolulu,
808-522-0824;

201

HAWAII

★
★
★
★
★
★

www.iolanipalace.org
A National Historic Landmark, this magnificent building served as Hawaii's capitol until 1969, as well as the home of Hawaiian royalty from 1882 to 1893, when Queen Liliuokalani was overthrown. The galleries tour, which does not include the palace itself but does include jewels, regalia and photographs, is self-guided. A 90-minute grand tour is also available. Reservations are recommended, and children under age five are not permitted. Galleries: Tuesday-Saturday 9 a.m.-4 p.m.; ticket office closes at 3:30 p.m.

Kawaiahao Church
957 Punchbowl St., Honolulu,
808-522-1333
The first permanent Western house of worship on the island, this 1842 church was built by Christian missionaries and Hawaiians working together for the first time. Kawaiahao, which means water of Hao, is where Hawaii's monarchs were baptized, wed, crowned and buried. Twenty-one royal portraits hang in the upper gallery, and the pews at the rear are still reserved for royal descendants. The public can attend Hawaiian-language services every Sunday. Tours follow the services. Sunday 10:30 a.m.

Manoa Falls Trail
Honolulu; www.hawaiitrails.org
Not even a mile long, the trail provides a 100 miles' worth of sights, including a grove of Eucalyptus trees and a rain forest before you arrive at a 100-foot-tall waterfall. Hop on the trail just shy of the entrance to the University of Hawaii's Lyon Arboretum.

★

Native Books/Na Mea Hawaii

★ Ward Warehouse,1050 Ala Moana Blvd.,
Honolulu, 808-596-8885;

★ www.nativebookshawaii.com
A hui (group) of local artists began this cooperative venture as an outlet for items made only in Hawaii. Here you can find rare Niihau shells, hand-painted fabrics, calabashes, fine art and prints and one of the island's most extensive Hawaiian book col-

lections. Monday-Saturday 10 a.m.-9 p.m., Sunday 10 a.m.-5 p.m.

National Memorial Cemetery of the Pacific
2177 Puowaina Dr., Honolulu,
808-566-1430
At once somber and serene, the National Memorial Cemetery of the Pacific (also known as the Punchbowl) is the site where the 776 servicemen killed during the December 7, 1941, attack on Pearl Harbor are interred. In addition to more than 13,000 soldiers killed at Iwo Jima, Guadalcanal and other World War II battles in the Pacific, the cemetery holds casualties from Korea and Vietnam and other U.S. servicemen. The solemn Courts of the Missing monument is made up of 10 stone walls inscribed with the names of more than 28,000 missing-in-action troops. Daily; closed federal holidays except for Memorial Day and Veterans Day.

Queen Emma Summer Palace
2913 Pali Hwy., Honolulu, 808-595-3167;
www.daughtersofhawaii.org
In the late 1800s, Queen Emma, wife of King Kamehameha IV and mother of Prince Albert Edward, inherited this royal retreat from her uncle John Young II, an advisor to King Kamehameha I. Run by the Daughters of Hawaii, the gardens and Hawaiian-Victorian home offer a unique way to spend an afternoon. Daily 9 a.m.-4 p.m.

Sunset on the Beach
Honolulu, Waikiki Beach,
www.sunsetonthebeach.net
On weekend evenings, recent and classic movies are projected onto a 30-foot screen right on Waikiki Beach. Locals and tourists gather to enjoy live music before the show and settle in for the main event, which usually begins at 7:30 pm. Food vendors provide snacks during the festivities. Saturday-Sunday at 4 p.m.

USS Arizona
Kamehameha Hwy., Honolulu,
808-422-2771;

www.nps.gov/usar
This memorial commemorates the 1,177 crewmen killed on December 7, 1941 when Japanese naval forces bombed the battleship *USS Arizona*. The interpretive program features a documentary film about the attack on Pearl Harbor. Survivors still come to tell visitors their stories of the attack. Avoid huge crowds at this popular tourist attraction by arriving early in the morning—tickets are distributed on a first-come, first-served basis. The last program of the day begins at 3 p.m. Daily 7:30 a.m.-5 p.m.

USS Bowfin Submarine Museum and Park
11 Arizona Memorial Dr., Honolulu, 808-423-1341; www.bowfin.org.
Now a National Historic Landmark, this submarine was used for nine war patrols after its launch on December 7, 1942. Take a tour of the sub, view artifacts in the 10,000-square-foot museum and watch a video about submarine history in the 40-seat theater. Children under age 4 are not allowed on the submarine. Daily 8 a.m.-5 p.m.

SPECIAL EVENTS
Hawaii International Film Festival
1001 Bishop St., Honolulu, 808-528-3456; www.hiff.org
Crouching Tiger, Hidden Dragon. The Piano. Shine. These are just some of the movies that have premiered at this film festival, which promotes understanding and cultural exchange among the peoples of Asia, the Pacific and North America. It's actually two festivals in one. The Spring Festival is held the first week of April each year and features more than 20 independent movies at several venues on the island of Oahu. The fall festival, held the last week of October, showcases up to 200 films at venues on every island in Hawaii. Early April and late October.

Honolulu Marathon
3435 Waialae Ave., Honolulu, 808-734-7200; www.honolulumarathon.org

One of the world's largest, the Honolulu Marathon hosts some 32,000 runners on the second Sunday each December on a marathon course designed to accommodate both novice and elite runners. Racers begin at Ala Moana Beach Park, travel through downtown Honolulu, wind their way past Waikiki, along the ocean to Hawaii Kai and return back to Kapiolani Park for the finish. Second Sunday in December.

King Kamehameha Celebration
Honolulu Harbour, 808-586-0333; www.hawaii.gov/dags/ king_ kamehameha_commission
King Kamehameha was the most famous—and best loved—king in Hawaii's history. This event celebrates his life and accomplishments with a floral parade complete with marching bands, parties and much more. The parade starts at King and Richards streets and ends at Queen Kapiolani Park. June.

NFL Pro Bowl
Aloha Stadium, 99-500 Salt Lake Blvd., Honolulu, 808-486-9300; www.nfl.com/probow
This all-star pro football game, held in Hawaii for more than 25 years, pits the best players of the NFC against the standouts of the AFC. Tickets are available through Ticketmaster. Early February.

World Invitational Hula Festival
Waikiki Shell, Kapiolani Park, Honolulu; www.worldhula.com
Hula dancers from around the world flock to Honolulu to take part in this annual event celebrating Hawaiian culture. Tickets are available through Ticketmaster and at the Blaisdell Center Box Office. Early November.

HOTELS
★★Doubletree Alana Hotel Waikiki
1956 Ala Moana Blvd., Honolulu, 808-941-7275, 800-744-1500; www.doubletree.com

313 rooms. Two restaurants, bar. Fitness room. Outdoor pool. Airport transportation available. Business center. **$$**

★★Holiday Inn Waikiki
1830 Ala Moana Blvd., Honolulu,
808-955-1111, 888-465-4329;
www.ichotelsgroup.com
200 rooms. Restaurant. Fitness room. Outdoor pool. Airport transportation available. **$**

★★★★Halekulani
2199 Kalia Rd., Honolulu,
808-739-8888, 800-367-2525;
www.halekulani.com
Located on the western side of Waikiki Beach, Halekulani's understated tropical elegance and exceptional service make it unforgettable. Guest rooms have deep soaking tubs and large lanais—handmade chocolates left in the rooms nightly by the staff are a reminder of the resort's attention to detail. Try surfing and snorkeling lessons on the beach, or take a bike ride around nearby Diamond Head. Besides occupying a prime spot on one of Hawaii's most popular beaches, the resort boasts the superb Spa-Halekulani, which celebrates the cultures of Hawaii, Asia and the South Pacific.
455 rooms. High-speed Internet access, wireless Internet access. Three restaurants, three bars. Children's activity center. Fitness room, spa. Beach. Outdoor pool. Airport transportation available. Business center. **$$$$**

★★★Hawaii Prince Hotel Waikiki
100 Holomoana St., Honolulu,
808-956-1111, 866-774-6236; www.
princeresortshawaii.com
All of the modern guest rooms have dramatic floor-to-ceiling windows that offer great views of the Ala Wai Yacht Harbor and the Pacific Ocean. The Prince has three restaurants and two bars, including the Prince Court, which specializes in contemporary island cuisine, and Hakone, which serves sushi and other Japanese dishes. The hotel is the only one in Waikiki with its own golf course, but reaching it requires about

a 45-minute trip by shuttle bus. Waikiki's beaches are a five-minute drive away, as is good shopping at the Ala Moana Shopping Center.
521 rooms. Three restaurants, two bars. Fitness room, spa. Outdoor pool, whirlpool. Airport transportation available. Business center. **$$$$**

★★★Hilton Hawaiian Village Beach Resort & Spa
2005 Kalia Rd., Honolulu,
808-949-4321, 800-445-8667;
www.hiltonhawaiianvillage.com
Vegas-like in size and scope, this hotel caters to families, with kids programs and a kid's pool. Rooms are spread throughout six towers and range from luxurious to low-key. Hula and surfing lessons, water aerobics and lei-making classes are offered. On Friday nights, the Super Pool is the setting for a Polynesian show that concludes with a fireworks display over Waikiki.
2,860 rooms. High-speed Internet access. 15 restaurants, 10 bars. Children's activity center. Fitness room, fitness classes available, spa. Beach. Outdoor pool, children's pool, whirlpool. Airport transportation available. Business center. **$$**

★★Hilton Waikiki Prince Kuhio
2500 Kuhio Ave., Honolulu,
808-922-0811; 800-445-8667;
www.hilton.com
606 rooms. High-speed internet access. Restaurant, bar. Fitness room. Outdoor pool, whirlpool. Business center. **$$$**

★★★Hyatt Regency Waikiki Resort
2424 Kalakaua Ave., Honolulu,
808-923-1234, 800-633-7313;
www.hyatt.com
With 1,230 rooms in two 40-story towers, this is a large hotel. Located across the street from Waikiki Beach near Diamond Head, the hotel has five restaurants and bars and more than 60 shops selling everything from apparel and jewelry to fine art. Send the kids off to Camp Hyatt (the children's program), then relax with a massage at the No Hoola Spa. If you book one of the rooms

★

★

★

★

★

on the Regency Floor, you'll have access to private rooftop sun decks with whirlpools, upgraded amenities and special services, such as complimentary continental breakfast and afternoon appetizers. 1,320 rooms. High-speed Internet access, wireless Internet access. Four restaurants, bar. Children's activity center. Fitness room, spa. Outdoor pool, children's pool, whirlpool. Airport transportation available. Business center. **$$$**

★★★Ilikai Hotel
1777 Ala Moana Blvd., Honolulu,
808-949-3811; 800-255-3811;
www.ilikaihotel.com
This hotel, built in 1964, is famous for being a film location of the TV series *Hawaii Five-O*. When it was built, it was Wakiki's first luxury high-rise hotel, and most of the rooms have ocean views. The hotel also has three restaurants, two pools, a fitness center, a tennis court, a massage center and boutiques and gift shops. Located on a marina, the Ilikai isn't a beachfront property, but the beach is within walking distance. 783 rooms. High-speed Internet access. Three restaurants, two bars. Fitness room. Two outdoor pools, whirlpool. Tennis. Airport transportation available. Business center. **$$$**

★★★JW Marriott Ihilani Resort & Spa at Ko Olina
92-1001 Olani St., Ko Olina,
808-679-0079; 800-228-9290;
www.ihilani.com
This resort borders a crescent-shaped beach, with the Waianae Mountains visible in the distance. The spa offers an array of treatments, including massages, water therapies, body scrubs and wraps. Among the hotel's four restaurants is Azul, which serves up Mediterranean fare in an elegant setting. Watch the sunset from the Hokulea Bar, which serves appetizers and cocktails. Other amenities include a Ted Robinson-designed golf course, tennis courts and an extensive children's program. 387 rooms. Four restaurants, two bars. Children's activity center. Fitness room, fitness

classes available, spa. Beach. Two outdoor pools, whirlpool. Golf, 18 holes. Tennis. Business center. **$$$**

★★★★Kahala Hotel and Resort
5000 Kahala Ave., Honolulu,
808-739-8888, 800-367-2525;
www.kahalaresort.com
Besides powdery beaches and beautiful views, this hotel offers a 26,000-square-foot lagoon occupied by Atlantic bottlenose dolphins. The Dolphin Quest program is a highlight, offering face-to-face encounters with dolphins. Complimentary surfing and scuba classes are available, while the Spa Suites at Kahala provide pampering. Rooms have plantation-style décor with canopied beds, luxury linens and deep soaking tubs. The resort has five restaurants which serve cuisine ranging from Hawaiian to Japanese. 364 rooms. Pets accepted, some restrictions. High-speed Internet access, wireless Internet access. Five restaurants, four bars. Children's activity center. Fitness room, fitness classes available, spa. Beach. Outdoor pool, children's pool, whirlpool. Airport transportation available. Business center. **$$$$**

★★★Marriott Resort Waikiki
2552 Kalakaua Ave., Honolulu,
808-922-6611, 800-367-5370;
www.marriottwaikiki.com
This hotel has some of the island's best views of Diamond Head and the Pacific Ocean. Swim at the beach or either of the hotel's two pools, browse through the boutiques in the shopping arcade or visit the Spa Olakino and Salon, which has 12 treatment rooms. The Euro-Asian treatment mixes a Thai massage with a lemongrass and honey body glow and a pesto body wrap. The Marriott's five restaurants and bars include the Kuhio Beach Grill, which features continental cuisine spiced with flavors of Hawaii, and the poolside Moana Terrace, which serves up live entertainment nightly. 1,310 rooms. High-speed, wireless Internet access. Six restaurants, three bars. Fit-

ness room, spa. Two outdoor pools. Airport transportation available. Business center. $$$$

★★Miramar at Waikiki
2345 Kuhio Ave., Honolulu,
808-922-2077, 800-367-2303;
www.miramarwaikiki.com
357 rooms. Four restaurants, two bars. Outdoor pool. $

★★★Moana Surfrider, A Westin Resort
2365 Kalakaua Ave., Honolulu,
808-922-3111, 800-325-3535;
www.starwood.com
This hotel, opened in 1901, was the first on Waikiki beach. Although it eventually merged with the neighboring Surfrider, guests checking in still access the lobby via the original colonial porte-cochere. The hotel was renovated and rebranded in 2007 from Sheraton to Westin, with rooms upgraded with Heavenly beds and flat-screen TVs. The hotel fronts the beach and there's also a pool for those who prefer freshwater swimming. Enjoy meals at the Beachside Café, or have afternoon tea and listen to Hawaiian music on the Banyan Veranda (named for the massive 100-year-old Banyan tree it overlooks). A beachfront spa is opening in 2008.
795 rooms. High-speed, wireless Internet access. Three restaurants, bar. Beach. Outdoor pool. Airport transportation available. $$$

★★New Otani Kaimana Beach Hotel
2863 Kalakaua Ave., Honolulu,
808-923-1555; 800-356-8264;
www.kaimana.com
124 rooms. Two restaurants, bar. Fitness room. Beach. $$

★★Outrigger Reef
2169 Kalia Rd., Honolulu, 808-923-3111;
www.outrigger.com
858 rooms. Two restaurants, four bars. Children's activity center. Fitness room. Beach. Outdoor pool, whirlpool. Airport transportation available. Business center. $$$

★★Outrigger Waikiki on the Beach
2335 Kalakaua Ave., Honolulu,
808-923-0711; 800-688-7444;
www.outriggerwaikiki.com
530 rooms. Three restaurants, five bars. Children's activity center. Beach. Outdoor pool, whirlpool. Airport transportation available. $$$

★★★The Royal Hawaiian
2259 Kalakaua Ave., Honolulu,
808-923-7311; 866-716-8109;
www.starwood.com
This classic Waikiki hotel, dubbed the Pink Palace of the Pacific because of its pink stucco exterior, is scheduled to close in the summer of 2008 for several months for a complete renovation. Until then, this Starwood-run hotel offers traditionaly decorated rooms and a prime location on Waikiki beach.
528 rooms. Two restaurants, bar. Children's activity center. Spa. Outdoor pool. Airport transportation available. $$$$

★★★Sheraton Princess Kaiulani
120 Kaiulani Ave., Honolulu,
808-922-5811, 800-782-9488;
www.princess-kaiulani.com
Located across the street from Waikiki beach on the former estate of Princess Kaiulani, Hawaii's last princess, this hotel has an outdoor pool, fitness center and business center. Among the many restaurants are Momoyama, where chefs prepare Japanese dishes tableside; Pikake Terrace, an open-air dining room that features buffets; and the Princess Food Court. Hawaiian performers entertain with island music nightly by the pool and in the Ainahau Showroom a talented cast presents a dinner show with fire-knife dancing, illusions and ancient and modern dances.
1,152 rooms. Pets accepted, some restrictions. Three restaurants, bar. Fitness room. Outdoor pool. Airport transportation available. Business center. $$

★★★Sheraton Waikiki
2255 Kalakaua Ave, Honolulu,

808-922-4422; 800-325-3535;
www.sheraton-waikiki.com

This hotel, located on Waikiki beach, is massive with 1,695 rooms in two 30-story towers. More than two-thirds of those rooms, all recently renovated, face the water and offer some sort of ocean view. The hotel has three restaurants, the most elegant of which is located on the 30th floor with views of the city.

1,695 rooms. Three restaurants, two bars. Children's activity center. Fitness room, fitness classes available, spa. Beach. Two outdoor pools, children's pool. Airport transportation available. Business center. **$$$$**

★★★W Honolulu Diamond Head

2885 Kalakaua Ave., Honolulu,
808-922-1700; 877-946-8357;
www.whotels.com

This hotel is small and modern, with just 49 rooms that feature attractive teak furniture and upgraded amenities. The lobby is designed without walls and resembles a chic living room in a very stylish house. The hotel's Diamond Head Grill is a mixture of Asian, Euro-American and Polynesian cuisine. The hotel is located on the quiet end of Waikiki at the base of Diamond Head, away from the water, but adjacent to two beaches.

51 rooms. Pets accepted, some restrictions; fee. High-speed Internet access. Restaurant, bar. Beach. Airport transportation available. **$$$**

RESTAURANTS

★★★3660 On the Rise

3660 Waialae Ave., Honolulu,
808-737-1177; www.3660.com

With its location on top of a hill above Honolulu's east side, this restaurant is appropriately named. 3660 on the Rise offers an eclectic blend of European, Pacific Rim and Island-style cuisine. Entrées include fire-roasted wild salmon or macadamia nut-crusted rack of lamb.

International, Pacific-Rim/Pan-Asian menu. Dinner. Closed Monday. Bar. Business casual attire. Reservations recommended. **$$$**

★★Bali by the Sea

2005 Kalia Rd., Honolulu, 808-941-2254;
www.hiltonhawaiianvillage.com

This dining room, inside the Hilton Hawaiian Village resort, overlooks Waikiki Beach. The menu emphasizes Pacific-Rim cuisine, with signature dishes such as scallion-crusted ahi tempura and sauteed island opakapaka.

Pacific-Rim menu. Dinner. Closed Sunday. Bar. Children's menu. Business casual attire. Reservations recommended. Valet parking. **$$$**

★★Brew Moon Restaurant and Microbrewery

1200 Ala Moana Blvd., Honolulu,
808-593-0088; www.brewmoon.com

Pacific-Rim menu. Lunch, dinner. Bar. Casual attire. Outdoor seating. **$$**

★★★★Chef Mavro

1969 S. King St., Honolulu,
808-944-4714; www.chefmavro.com

This restaurant is the creation of award-winning French chef George Mavrothalassitis, who moved to Honolulu in 1988 and ever since has focused his talents on perfecting a cuisine that couples French technique with fresh Hawaiian ingredients. The restaurant has no wine list—instead, each dish is served with a glass of wine that complements its ingredients. For special occasions, the six-course meal, priced at $220 with wine pairings, is an indulgence you won't forget.

Hawaiian menu. Dinner. Closed Monday. Business casual attire. Reservations recommended. Valet parking. **$$$**

★★★Diamond Head Grill

2885 Kalakaua Ave., Honolulu,
808-922-3734; www.w-dhg.com

While the food here is Hawaiian, the restaurant, located inside the W Diamond Head, is sleek and modern. Signature entrées include macadamia nut-crusted lamb chops, flavored with roasted garlic sauce and served with potato gratin. The restaurant's Wonder

★

★

★

☆

☆

Lounge, featuring a serpentine-style bar, is one of the hottest nightspots on Oahu. International/Fusion menu. Breakfast, dinner. Bar. Children's menu. Business casual attire. Reservations recommended. Valet parking. **$$$**

★Duke's Canoe Club Waikiki
2335 Kalakaua Ave., Honolulu, 808-922-2268; www.dukeswaikiki.com
American menu. Breakfast, lunch, dinner, late-night, brunch. Bar. Children's menu. Casual attire. Reservations recommended. Valet parking. Outdoor seating. **$$**

★★Golden Dragon
2005 Kalia Rd, Honolulu, 808-946-5336
Chinese menu. Dinner. Closed Monday. Bar. Casual attire. Reservations recommended. Valet parking. Outdoor seating. **$$$**

★★Hau Tree Lanai
2863 Kalakaua Ave., Honolulu, 808-921-7066, www.kaimana.com
Pacific-Rim menu. Breakfast, lunch, dinner, brunch. Bar. Children's menu. Business casual attire. Reservations recommended. Valet parking. Outdoor seating.**$$**

★★Indigo
1121 Nu'uanu Ave., Honolulu, 808-521-2900; www.indigo-hawaii.com
Eur-Asian menu. Lunch, dinner. Closed Sunday-Monday. Bar. Casual attire. Reservations recommended. Valet parking (dinner). Outdoor seating. **$$**

★★Keo's in Waikiki
2028 Kuhio Ave., Honolulu, 808-951-9355; www.keosthaicuisine.com
Thai menu. Breakfast, lunch, dinner. Bar. Casual attire.**$$**

★Kua Aina Sandwich Shop
1116 Auahi St, Honolulu, 808-591-9133
Burgers. Lunch, dinner. Casual attire. Outdoor seating. No credit cards accepted. **$**

★★★★La Mer
2199 Kalia Rd., Honolulu, 808-923-2311; www.halekulani.com
Pocketed along the coast on Waikiki's west side, La Mer makes good use of its enviable location inside the Halekulani hotel. Pocket doors open up to welcome in the tradewind breezes and the sound of the ocean. A private dining room accommodates up to 16 guests, ideal for celebrating a special occasion. A popular dish at this French restaurant is the medallions of milk-fed veal with golden brown Roquefort on a ragout of flageolet beans. For dessert, it's hard to pass on La Mer's Dreams of Chocolate, a decadent blend of cherry brandy chocolate mousse, white-and-dark chocolate tear drops and gianduja ice cream, all served in a chocolate cup.
French menu. Dinner. Bar. Children's menu. Reservations recommended. Valet parking. **$$$$**

★Mei Sum Dim Sum
65 N. Pauahi St, Honolulu, 808-531-3268
Chinese menu. Breakfast, lunch, dinner. Casual attire. **$**

★★★Nick's Fishmarket
2070 Kalakaua Ave., Honolulu, 808-955-6333; www.nickfishmarket.com
A cozy setting and an international, yet straightforward, menu of chowders, steaks, local seafood and desserts is what you will find at this Honolulu restaurant. Lobster is a specialty, with crustaceans served thermidor, grilled, steamed or with filet mignon.
Seafood menu. Dinner. Bar. Business casual attire. Reservations recommended. **$$$**

★★★Ocean House Restaurant
2169 Kalia Rd., Honolulu, 808-923-2277; www.outrigger.com
This seaside restaurant has the look and feel of a turn-of-the-century plantation home. Located in the Outrigger Reef hotel, this restaurant has spectacular views of the beach and Diamond Head. The atmosphere in this open-air restaurant is elegant but casual. The menu features a variety of

Pacific Rim favorites, such as crab-stuffed mahi mahi and pulehu prime rib.
American menu. Dinner. Bar. Children's menu. Casual attire. Reservations recommended. Valet parking.**$$$**

★Ono Hawaiian Foods
726 Kapahulu Ave., Honolulu,
808-737-2275
Pacific-Rim/Pan-Asian menu. Lunch, dinner. Closed Sunday. Bar. Casual attire. Outdoor seating. **$**

★★Pineapple Room
1450 Ala Moana Center, Honolulu,
808-945-6573
Pacific-Rim/Pan-Asian menu. Breakfast, lunch, dinner. Casual attire. Reservations recommended. **$$$**

★★★Roy's Honolulu
6600 Kalanianaole Hwy., Honolulu,
808-396-7697; www.roysrestaurant.com
Chef Roy Yamaguchi is known for his blending of European techniques with the flavors and ingredients of the Pacific Rim. His Hawaiian fusion cuisine focuses on seafood dishes, such as hibachi-style grilled salmon, flavored by citrus ponzu sauce and served with Japanese vegetables. The restaurant also prepares a variety of creative appetizers, such as crunchy lobster potstickers.
Pacific-Rim/Pan-Asian menu. Dinner. Business casual attire. Reservations recommended. **$$$**

★★Sam Choy's Breakfast, Lunch, Crab & Big Aloha Brewery
580 N. Nimitz Hwy., Honolulu,
808-545-7979; www.samchoy.com
American menu. Breakfast, lunch, dinner. Bar. Children's menu. Casual attire. **$$**

★Side Street Inn
1225 Hopaka St., Honolulu, 808-591-0253
Pacific-Rim/Pan-Asian menu. Lunch, dinner, late-night. Bar. Casual attire. No credit cards accepted. **$$**

★★Singha Thai Cuisine
1910 Ala Moana Blvd., Honolulu,
808-941-2898; www.singhathai.com
Thai menu. Dinner. Bar. Casual attire. Reservations recommended. **$$**

★★★Sushi Sasabune
1419 S. King St., Honolulu, 808-947-3800
Allow the sushi chef at this outpost of the Los Angeles Japanese favorite to guide you on a tour from impeccably fresh Pacific fish to regional catches. There's no menu, so order a flight of sake or a Japanese beer and enjoy the parade of seafood. The experience justifies the steep bill, as the quality and authenticity here are unparalleled.
Sushi menu. Lunch, dinner. Closed Sunday. Casual attire. Reservations recommended. **$$$**

★★Tiki's Grill & Bar
2570 Kalakaua Ave., Honolulu,
808-923-8454; www.tikisgrill.com
American menu. Lunch, dinner, late-night. Bar. Casual attire. Outdoor seating. **$$**

SPAS

★★★★Spa Suites at Kahala Hotel & Resort
5000 Kahala Ave., Honolulu,
808-739-8938, 800-367-2525;
www.kahalaresort.com
Named for different Hawaiian flowers, each of the five 550-square-foot spa suites is decorated in an authentic island style. All but one of the spa treatments begins with an ESPA welcoming foot ritual that uses Hawaiian sea salts and aromatic water. The spa's signature treatments include the pi'ha kino therapy, which uses a spearmint-aloe blend for a full-body exfoliation before a massage with aromatherapy oils. The kua lani back, face and scalp massage begins with a deep cleansing and exfoliation and continues with a massage, an energizing facial and a Hawaiian scalp massage with volcanic clay, apricot and watercress. **$$**

★★★★SpaHalekulani
2199 Kalia Rd., Honolulu,
808-931-5322, 800-367-2343;
www.halekulani.com
The healing traditions of the Pacific Islands, including Samoa, Tonga and Tahiti, inspire this spa's authentic treatments, which use only fresh island ingredients, such as coconut, orchid, hibiscus, seaweed and papaya. All of the spa's massages, body treatments and facials begin with a ritual foot pounding, an exotic way to treat neglected feet. In addition to traditional Swedish and shiatsu massages, Samoan-inspired nonu, Japanese amma and Hawaiian lomi lomi, hapai and pohaku massages are offered. Therapists will even customize a massage based on your needs and preferences. Facials are individually crafted for specific skin types, and the body scrubs and wraps come complete with a steam shower and a mini massage. **$$**

NORTH SHORE OAHU

This coastline is known as the Surfing Capital of the World thanks to its big, powerful winter waves. The swells sometimes soar as high as 30 or 40 feet. Any serious surfer in the world can name the North Shore's best-known surfing beaches: Banzai Pipeline, Sunset, Ehukai and Waimea Bay. Novices should stick to the beach between October and April, when the big breakers and strong currents are at their most intense.

In summer, the coastal scene changes dramatically. The waves calm (and the serious surfers move on), making them good for swimming, fishing and all types of water activities.

Puu o Mahuka Heiau State Park, near Sunset Beach, is home to Oahu's largest temple, believed to have been built in the 18th century. West of Waimea is Haleiwa, the area's main town, which has plantation-style buildings dating to the early 1900s. There are also restaurants, boutiques, gift shops, art galleries and, naturally, surf shops.

WHAT TO SEE AND DO
Barnfield's Raging Isle Surf and Cycle
North Shore Marketplace,
62-250 Kamehameha Hwy., Haleiwa,
808-637-7707;
www.ragingisle.com
Find custom surfboards by designer Bill Barnfield, as well as everything you need for a day of mountain biking Oahu's scenic North Shore. Barnfield's also carries sports apparel and accessories from Billabong, Oakley and Rip Curl. Daily 10 a.m.-6:30 p.m.

Haleiwa
At the turn of the 20th century, this sleepy seaside town was the endpoint of the railroad line and Oahu's first getaway destination. Not much has changed in 200 years. Haleiwa still exudes laid-back living. In winter months, Haleiwa swells with surfers who take on some of world's largest and most powerful waves, right down the road at Waimea Bay, Sunset Beach and the Banzai Pipeline. In summer, Haleiwa has shoppers exploring its eclectic galleries, boutiques and cafes (like the superlative Matsumoto's shave ice).

Hauula Loop Trail
Hauula Homestead Rd. and Maakua Rd., Hauula
This 2 1/2-mile hike (about three hours) features a fairly steep climb through fields dotted with ironwood trees and Norfolk pines and marked by switchbacks. The path loops around toward the ocean overlooking Kipaupau Valley and offers panoramic views of Oahu's windward coast and coastal waters.

North Shore Catamaran Charters
Haleiwa, 808-638-8279, 888-638-8279;
www.sailingcat.com
Depending on the time of year, this tour company will either take you snorkeling or out to watch for humpback whales. From

January to May, 2 1/2-hour whale-watching tours to Waimea Bay depart both in the morning and in the afternoon. In the mornings from May to October, the catamaran takes passengers out into the bay to snorkel, with a picnic lunch included. Tours depart from Haleiwa Harbor. Daily.

North Shore Eco-Surf Tours
Haleiwa, 808-638-9503;
www.ecosurf-hawaii.com
Stan Van Voorhis takes time out from his day job designing custom long boards to lead guided surf tours of Oahu's North Shore, and private and group surfing and windsurfing lessons. Learning to surf with Van Voorhis begins on the beach, discussing theory, safety, surf riding skills and on-land exercises.

North Shore Shark Adventures
Haleiwa, Tours depart from Haleiwa Small Boat Harbor, 808-228-5900;
www.sharktourshawaii.com.
This tour offers a chance to see sharks between five to 15 feet long at close range from the safety of a submerged cage in the middle of the ocean. During the two-hour trip, you're also likely to see green sea turtles, dolphins, and humpback whales in season. Daily 7 a.m.-3 p.m.

Polynesian Cultural Center
55-370 Kamehameha Hwy., Laie,
808-293-3333, 800-367-7060;
www.polynesia.com
With its multiple villages, each depicting life on one of the Polynesian islands, the Polynesian Cultural Center is the place to learn about native culture. People from these islands demonstrate ancient practices, like coconut cracking and spear tossing. The 90-minute *Horizons: Where the Sea Meets the Sky* dinner show features a cast of 100 dancers and musicians. Because the center is Hawaii's most popular attraction, reservations are essential. Ticket packages deliver varying levels of service, amenities, and dining options. Monday-Saturday 9 a.m.-6:30 p.m.; closed holidays.

Pu'u O Mahuka Heiau
Pupukea Rd., Haleiwa
Rock walls and stone floors mark the ruins of what was once the largest sacrificial temple on Oahu. In the 18th century, Kaopulu-pulu presided over the temple, which stood the length of two football fields. Built on the bluffs overlooking Waimea Bay, visitors who come to pray and pay homage to the gods often leave lei offerings.

Surf-N-Sea
62-595 Kamehameha Hwy., Haleiwa,
808-637-9887, 800-899-7873;
www.surfnsea.com
Besides being a great place to buy beachwear or rent surfboards, windsurfing boards and other gear, this surf shop offers lessons and tours. Learn how to surf, windsurf, bodyboard, scuba dive or snorkel or head out into deeper waters to fish or even swim with sharks (in a protected cage, of course). Daily 9 a.m.-7 p.m.

Waimea Valley Audubon Center
59-864 Kamehameha Hwy., Haleiwa,
808-638-9199;
www.waimea.audubon.org
This park, administered by the National Audubon Society, has natural habitats, botanical gardens and waterfalls. Walk along paths through the gardens and archaeological sites, or set off along the trails lined with endangered native Hawaiian greenery. Daily 9:30 a.m.-5 p.m.

211

HAWAII

HOTELS
★★★Turtle Bay Resort
57-091 Kamehameha Hwy., Kahuku,
808-293-6000, 800-203-3650;
www.turtlebayresort.com
The setting at this resort is gorgeous, with five miles of beaches on the northern tip of the island. All of its rooms, suites and beach cottages have good ocean views. There is not a lot of development on this side of the island, so the hotel offers a wide assortment of activities. The hotel's dining and entertainment options are plentiful, with on-site restaurants and lounges, including the 21

Degrees North, which serves contemporary island cuisine in an upscale setting. 443 rooms. Wireless Internet access. Restaurant, bar. Children's activity center. Fitness room, spa. Beach. Two outdoor pools, children's pool, whirlpool. Golf, 36 holes. Tennis. Airport transportation available. Business center. **$$$**

SPECIALTY LODGINGS
Santa's by the Sea
Ke Waena Rd., Haleiwa, 808-985-7488
This bed-and-breakfast is located on Oahu's famous Banzai Pipeline Beach. There is a one-bedroom ground level apartment that sleeps four and has a private entrance, bay window with an oceanfront views, outdoor breakfast gazebo and barbecue grill. **$**

WINDWARD COAST OAHU
Oahu's Windward Coast is a region of stark contrasts: It's home to the island's largest population outside of Honolulu as well as Oahu's rural areas.

This stretch of coastline is much more urban on it's south end, where more than 70,000 people live in the two cities of Kailua and Kaneohe. Many consider Kailua Beach, which runs for nearly two miles along the funky Kailua coastline, Oahu's best beach. It has become a favorite of windsurfers and kitesurfers. Just up the coast, Kaneohe fronts one of the loveliest bays in Hawaii. Residences, condominiums and a few private yacht clubs and marinas line the bayfront. Boating companies take visitors to a sandbar offshore for swimming and snorkeling. From there, the views of the Koolau Mountain Range are spectacular. Visitors also come for the many B&Bs which offer cheaper room rates than the hotels in Waikiki. North of Kaneohe, rural countryside begins. On one side of the highway are majestic-looking mountains, on the other, a shoreline dotted with several more beaches. The popular attraction on the Windward Coast is Hanauma Bay, one of Hawaii's best snorkeling spots.

WHAT TO SEE AND DO
Aaron's Dive Shop
307 Hahani St., Kailua, 808-262-2333;
www.hawaii-scuba.com
One of Oahu's oldest and largest dive outfitters, Aaron's offers both beach and boat dive excursions and takes dive charters in waters around the entire island. Whether you're a novice or expert diver, Aaron has a course that will get you in the water, including intro dives, refresher classes and three-day certification courses. Daily from 6:30 a.m.

Hanauma Bay State Underwater Park and Conservation District
Hawaii Kai, Hanauma Bay Beach Park
Hanauma Bay was formed by a series of underwater volcanic eruptions more than 30,000 years ago, creating an almost perfect crescent stretch of sand and an ocean playground teeming with colorful marine life. Hanauma's coral reefs protect the 50 species of fish here from their natural predators.

The fish are so tame that they swim right up to you, making Hanauma the most visited snorkeling destination in Hawaii. All visitors must enter through the park's marine education center and view the seven-minute video created to both educate and enlighten visitors about this delicate eco attraction. It's best to arrive early to avoid crowds. Monday, Wednesday-Sunday.

Kailua Beach Park
Steady year-round breezes from almost every direction make this beach Oahu's wind- and kite-surfing capital. If you rent a kayak, paddle out to the tiny Mokulua islands, a bird sanctuary. Volleyball courts, food concessions, lifeguards and parking are available as well.

Kualoa Ranch and Activity Club
49-560 Kamehameha Hwy., Kaaawa, 808-237-8515, 800-231-7321;
www.kualoa.com

Kualoa is a 4,000-acre working cattle ranch, recognzible as the setting for TV hits such as *Lost* and *Magnum P.I.* Take your pick from activities including a horseback ride complete with views of the Kualoa Mountains and the Pacific Ocean, an all-terrain vehicle ride into the Ka'a'awa Valley, kayaking along the shore of Secret Island, or touring the ranch by bus. Daily; closed holidays.

Naish Hawaii
155A Hamakua Dr., Kailua, 808-262-6068;
www.naish.com
This family-owned and operated business includes world championship windsurfer Robby Naish and his brother, Rick, one of the sport's premier windsurf and kiteboard designers. The company offers extensive windsurfing and kiteboarding lessons, board rentals and sales, as well as lodging advice for those eager to stay near Kailua Beach. Both private and group lessons are available. Private lessons last 90-minutes and include an additional 90 minutes of rental equipment use immediately following lessons at no extra charge.

Sea Life Park Hawaii
41-202 Kalanianaole Hwy., Waimanalo,
808-259-7933, 866-393-5158;
www.sealifeparkhawaii.com
Dolphins, stingrays, sea lions, monk seals and sea turtles are among the featured attractions here. See the shows and tour the exhibits, or splurge for a dolphin swim, a stingray encounter or one of several other interactive programs, which require advance reservations. Daily 9:30 a.m.-5 p.m.

Senator Fong's Plantation and Gardens
47-285 Pulama Rd., Kaneohe,
808-239-6775; www.fonggarden.com
Hiram Fong was the first Asian American to serve in the U.S. Senate. This sprawling spot was his home, and it includes extensive gardens. Daily 10 a.m.-4 p.m.

Twogood Kayaks Hawaii
345 Hahani St., Kailua, 808-262-5656;

www.twogoodkayaks.com
Twogood Kayaks offers a variety of tours, including an all-day adventure tour that's self-guided and includes kayak rental, a picnic lunch and hotel transportation.

SPECIALTY LODGINGS
Hawaii's Hidden Hideaway
1369 Mokolea Dr., Kailua,
808-262-6560, 877-443-2929;
www.ahawaiibnb.com
Located a short walk from Lanikai and Kailua beaches, this bed and breakfast was designed with Asian influences. Every unit has a private entrance, lanai and kitchenette.
3 rooms. Complimentary continental breakfast. **$**

Tee's at Kailua
771 Wanaao Rd., Kailua, 808-261-0771;
www.teesinn.com
This tiny inn has only two rooms, but both are decorated with top-notch furniture and luxury linens. Breakfast is served poolside and includes organic tea grown in the garden.
2 rooms. Complimentary continental breakfast. Outdoor pool. **$**

RESTAURANTS
★★Baci Bistro
30 Aulike St., Kailua, 808-261-2857;
www.restauranteur.com/baci
Italian menu. Lunch, dinner. Bar. Children's menu. Casual attire. Reservations recommended. Outdoor seating. **$$**

★Bueno Nalo
20 Kainehe St., Kailua, 808-263-1999
Mexican menu. Lunch, dinner. Children's menu. Casual attire. **$**

★★Crouching Lion Inn
51-666 Kamehameha Hwy., Kaaawa,
808-237-8511
American menu. Lunch, dinner. Bar. Children's menu. Casual attire. Outdoor seating. **$$**

213

HAWAII

★

★

★

☆

INDEX

★
★
★
★
★

B

217

INDEX

★
★
★
★
★

★
★
★
★

221

INDEX

★
★
★

223

INDEX

225

INDEX

★
★
★
★

★
★
★
★
★

227

INDEX

★
★
★

228

INDEX

229

INDEX

★

★

★

☆

☆

INDEX

★
★

★
★

★

Whale-Watching Trips (San Diego, CA), *118*

Whiskey Flat Days (Kernville, CA), *19*

Whispering Pines Lodge (Kernville, CA), *19*

Whist (Santa Monica, CA), *83*

White Jasmine Inn (Santa Barbara, CA), *154*

White Sands Beach County Park (Kailua-Kona, HI), *172*

Wild Animal Park (Escondido, CA), *118*

Wild Rivers Waterpark (Irvine, CA), *58*

Wild Water Adventures (Clovis, CA), *13*

Wildflower Season (Lancaster, CA), *20*

Will Rogers State Historic Park (Pacific Palisades, CA), *79*

William Heath Davis Home (San Diego, CA), *118*

Windansea Surfing (La Jolla, CA), *140*

Wine and Roses Charity Tasting Event (San Diego, CA), *140*

Wine Bistro (Studio City, CA), *85*

Wine Cask (Santa Barbara, CA), *156*

Wine Festival (Paso Robles, CA), *103*

Wine Valley Inn & Cottages (Solvang, CA), *157*

Winesellar and Brasserie (San Diego, CA), *130*

Winter Bird Festival (Morro Bay, CA), *91*

Wool Growers (Bakersfield, CA), *3*

World Invitational Hula Festival (Honolulu, HI), *203*

Wrigley Memorial and Botanical Garden (Avalon, CA), *41*

Wyndham Anaheim Park (Fullerton, CA), *39*

Wyndham Orange County Airport (Costa Mesa, CA), *51*

Wyndham Palm Springs Hotel (Palm Springs, CA), *101*

X

Xi'an (Beverly Hills, CA), *47*

Y

Yamabuki (Anaheim, CA), *39*

Yang Chow (Los Angeles, CA), *36*

Yen Ching (Orange, CA), *71*

Yiannis (Claremont, CA), *7*

Yongsusan (Los Angeles, CA), *36*

Yujean Kang's (Pasadena, CA), *74*

Z

Zabriskie Point (Death Valley National Park, CA), *11*

Zazou (Redondo Beach, CA), *75*

Zocalo Grill (San Diego, CA), *130*

Zosa Gardens Bed and Breakfast (Escondido, CA), *137*

Zucca (Los Angeles, CA), *36*

231

INDEX

NOTES

INDEX

★
★
★
★
★

NOTES

★
★
★
★
★

NOTES

NOTES

★
★
★
★
★

NOTES

★

★

★

★

★

NOTES

★
★
★
★
★

NOTES

★
★
★
★
★

NOTES

★
★
★
★
★

NOTES

240

INDEX

★
★
★
★
★

NOTES

★
★
★
★
★

NOTES

★

★

★

★

★

NOTES

★
★
★
★
★

NOTES

★
★
★
★
★

NOTES

★
★
★
★
★

NOTES

★

★

★

★

★

NOTES

★
★
★
★
★

NOTES

★

★

★

★

★

NOTES

★
★
★
★
★

NOTES

★
★
★
★
★

NOTES

★
★
★
★
★

NOTES

INDEX

★
★
★
★
★

NOTES

★
★
★
★
★

NOTES

★
★
★
★
★

NOTES

★
★
★
★
★

NOTES

★

★ ★

★ ★ ★

★ ★ ★ ★

★ ★ ★ ★ ★

NOTES

NOTES

★

★

★

★

★

NOTES

259

INDEX

NOTES

★
★
★
★
★

NOTES

★
★
★
★
★

NOTES

★
★
★
★
★

NOTES

NOTES

INDEX

★
★
★
★
★